SHAKESPEARE'S SISTERS

Feminist Essays on Women Poets

SHAKESPEARE'S SISTERS

FEMINIST ESSAYS ON WOMEN POETS

Edited, with an Introduction by
Sandra M. Gilbert
and
Susan Gubar

INDIANA UNIVERSITY PRESS

BLOOMINGTON & LONDON

Manufactured in the United States of America

Library of Congress Cataloging in Publication Data
Main entry under title:
Shakespeare's sisters.
1. American poetry—Women authors—History and criticism—Addresses,
essays, lectures. 2. English poetry—Women authors—History and criticism—
Addresses, essays, lectures. 3. Feminism and literature—Addresses,
essays, lectures. I. Gilbert, Sandra M. II. Gubar, Susan, 1944–
PS310.W64S5   821'.009   78–9510
ISBN 0–253–11258–3   2 3 4 5   83 82 81 80

For Luise David, Alice Dreyfuss, and Angela Mortola,
and in memory of Alexandra Mortola and Louise Mortola.

Contents

Acknowledgments ix

SANDRA M. GILBERT and SUSAN GUBAR, Introduction: Gender, Creativity, and the Woman Poet xv

I. "A Lonesome Glee"—Poets before 1800 1

1. CATHERINE F. SMITH, Jane Lead: Mysticism and the Woman Cloathed with the Sun 3

2. WENDY MARTIN, Anne Bradstreet's Poetry: A Study of Subversive Piety 19

3. KATHARINE ROGERS, Anne Finch, Countess of Winchilsea: An Augustan Woman Poet 32

II. "Titanic Opera"—Nineteenth-Century Poets 47

4. NINA AUERBACH, This Changeful Life: Emily Brontë's Anti-Romance 49

5. HELEN COOPER, Working into Light: Elizabeth Barrett Browning 65

6. DOLORES ROSENBLUM, Christina Rossetti: The Inward Pose 82

7. ADRIENNE RICH, Vesuvius at Home: The Power of Emily Dickinson 99

8. ALBERT GELPI, Emily Dickinson and the Deerslayer: The Dilemma of the Woman Poet in America 122

9. TERENCE DIGGORY, Armored Women, Naked Men: Dickinson, Whitman, and Their Successors 135

viii CONTENTS

III. "The Silver Reticence"—Modernists 151

    10. JEANNE KAMMER, The Art of Silence and the Forms of
Women's Poetry 153

    11. GLORIA T. HULL, Afro-American Women Poets: A Bio-Critical
Survey 165

    12. JANE STANBROUGH, Edna St. Vincent Millay and the Language
of Vulnerability 183

    13. SUSAN GUBAR, The Echoing Spell of H.D.'s *Trilogy* 200

IV. "The Difference—Made Me Bold"—Contemporary Poets 219

    14. ALICIA OSTRIKER, May Swenson and the Shapes of Speculation 221

    15. HORTENSE J. SPILLERS, Gwendolyn the Terrible: Propositions
on Eleven Poems 233

    16. SANDRA M. GILBERT, A Fine, White Flying Myth: The
Life/Work of Sylvia Plath 245

    17. SUZANNE JUHASZ, Seeking the Exit or the Home: Poetry
and Salvation in the Career of Anne Sexton 261

    18. BARBARA CHARLESWORTH GELPI, A Common Language: The
American Woman Poet 269

    19. RACHEL BLAU DUPLESSIS, The Critique of Consciousness and
Myth in Levertov, Rich, and Rukeyser 280

Selected Bibliography 301
Notes 315
About the Authors 335

Acknowledgments

The following essays were previously published. We are grateful to their publishers for permission to reprint.

Rachel Blau DuPlessis, "The Critique of Consciousness and Myth in Levertov, Rich, and Rukeyser," *Feminist Studies*, III½ (Fall 1975).

Albert Gelpi, "Emily Dickinson and the Deerslayer: The Dilemma of the Woman Poet in America," *San José Studies*, III, 2 (May 1977).

Barbara Charlesworth Gelpi, "From Colonial to Revolutionary: The Modern American Woman Poet," *San José Studies*, II, 3 (Nov. 1976).

Sandra M. Gilbert, "A Fine, White Flying Myth: Confessions of a Plath Addict," *Massachusetts Review*, XIX, 3 (Autumn 1978).

Susan Gubar, "The Echoing Spell of H.D.'s *Trilogy*," *Contemporary Literature*, 19 (Spring 1979).

Gloria T. Hull, "Black Women Poets from Wheatley to Walker," in *Black American Literature Forum* (Fall 1975).

Alicia Ostriker, "May Swenson and the Shapes of Speculation," *American Poetry Review*, VII, 2 (March 1978).

Adrienne Rich, "Vesuvius at Home: The Power of Emily Dickinson," *Parnassus,* 5, 1 (Fall-Winter 1976).

Parts of Catherine F. Smith's chapter, "Jane Lead: Mysticism and the Woman Cloathed with the Sun," have appeared in Dana V. Hiller and Robin Ann Sheets, eds. *Women and Men: The Consequences of Power* (University of Cincinnati: Office of Women's Studies, 1977).

Grateful acknowledgment is made for permission to include the following:

Lines from "King's Gambit," in *Lady of the Beasts*, by Robin Morgan. Copyright © Random House, Inc., 1976.

Lines from "'I Am in Danger—Sir—'" and "In the Woods," in *Adrienne Rich's Poetry*, ed. Barbara Charlesworth Gelpi and Albert Gelpi. Reprinted by permission of W. W. Norton & Co.

Lines from "Sun Gods Have Sun Spots," in *Dancing on the Grave of a Son of a Bitch*, by Diane Wakoski. Reprinted by permission of Black Sparrow Press.

Lines excerpted from *Homage to Mistress Bradstreet*, by John Berryman. Copyright © 1956 by John Berryman. Reprinted with the permission of Farrar, Straus & Giroux, Inc.

Lines from *The Poems of Anne, Countess of Winchilsea*, ed. Myra Reynolds. Copyright © 1903 by The University of Chicago Press. Used by permission of the publisher.

Lines from "My life had stood—a Loaded Gun—," "I'm ceded—I've stopped being Their's—," "I'm 'wife'—I've finished that—," and "Rearrange a Wife's affection!" by Emily Dickinson. Reprinted by permission of the publishers and the Trustees of Amherst College from *The Poems of Emily Dickinson*, edited by Thomas H. Johnson (Cambridge, Mass.: The Belknap Press of Harvard University Press), Copyright © 1951, 1955 by the President and Fellows of Harvard College.

Lines from poems #8, 45, 165, 273, 315, 353, 396, 410, 435, 488, 505, 508, 512, 539, 601, 642, 754, 786, 793, 822, 892, 919, 937, 974, 984, 997, 1059, 1062, 1335, 1412, and 1677 by Emily Dickinson. Reprinted by permission of the publishers and the Trustees of Amherst College from *The Poems of Emily Dickinson*, edited by Thomas H. Johnson (Cambridge, Mass.: The Belknap Press of Harvard University Press). Copyright © 1951, 1955 by the President and Fellows of Harvard College.

Lines from poems #341, 396, 410, 488, 539, 601, 754, 822, 974, 1353, and 1677 by Emily Dickinson, from *The Complete Poems of Emily Dickinson*, edited by Thomas H. Johnson. Copyright 1929 by Martha Dickinson Bianchi. Copyright © 1957 by Mary Leete Hampson. Reprinted by permission of Little, Brown and Company.

Lines from "Stopping by Woods" by Robert Frost, in *The Poetry of Robert Frost*, ed. Edward Connery Latham. Copyright 1923, 1934, © 1969 by Holt, Rinehart and Winston. Copyright 1951, © 1962 by Robert Frost. Reprinted by permission of Holt, Rinehart and Winston, Publishers; the Estate of Robert Frost; and Jonathan Cape, Ltd.

Lines from "Private Ground" and "In Plaster" by Sylvia Plath, in *Crossing the Water*. Copyright © 1971 by Ted Hughes. Used by permission of Harper & Row, Publishers, Inc. Published in London by Faber and Faber.

Lines from "Lady Lazarus" by Sylvia Plath, from *Ariel*. Copyright © 1965 by Ted Hughes. Used by permission of Harper & Row, Publishers, Inc. Published in London by Faber and Faber.

Lines from "The Mind Is an Enchanting Thing" by Marianne Moore, from *Collected Poems of Marianne Moore.* Copyright 1944, renewed 1972 by Marianne Moore. Published by permission of Macmillan Publishing Co., Inc.

The poem "Oread" by H.D., from *Selected Poems of H.D.* Used by permission of Grove Press and New Directions Publishing Corp.

Lines from Edna St. Vincent Millay, *Collected Poems,* ed. Norma Millay, 1956. Used by permission of Harper & Row, Publishers.

Lines from Edna St. Vincent Millay, *Letters of Edna St. Vincent Millay,* ed. Allan Ross Macdougall. Copyright 1952 by Norma Millay (Ellis). Used by permission.

Lines from *Trilogy* by H.D. Copyright 1944, 1945, 1946 by Oxford University Press. Copyright © 1973 by Norman Holmes Pearson. Reprinted by permission of New Directions Publishing Corp.

The poems "Bleeding," "Feel Me," "Fire Island," and "How Everything Happens" and lines from "The Beam," "The DNA Molecule," "Earth Will Not Let Go Our Foot," and "Welcome Aboard the Turbojet Electra" by May Swenson, from *Iconographs.* Copyright © 1970 by May Swenson. Used by permission of Scribner's and the author.

Lines from "The Forest," "Spring Uncovered," "Let Us Prepare," "Almanac," "Order of Diet," "Question," and "Organs" by May Swenson, in *To Mix With Time: New and Selected Poems.* Copyright © 1963 by May Swenson. Used by permission of Scribner's and the author.

The poems "We Real Cool," "Medgar Evers," "Malcolm X," "Strong Men Riding Horses" and lines from "Gay Chaps at the Bar," "The Anniad," "The Ballad of Chocolate Mabbie," "Stand Off, Daughter of the Dusk," "Still Do I Keep My Look, My Identity," and "The Old Marrieds" by Gwendolyn Brooks, from *The World of Gwendolyn Brooks.* Copyright © 1971 by Gwendolyn Brooks Blakely. Used by permission of the author and Harper & Row, Publishers, Inc.

Lines from "All the Dead Dears," and "The Disquieting Muses" by Sylvia Plath, in *The Colossus and Other Poems.* Copyright © by Alfred A. Knopf, Inc. 1962. Used by permission of the publisher.

Lines from "Purdah" by Sylvia Plath, in *Winter Trees.* Copyright 1971 by Ted Hughes. Used by permission of Faber and Faber (London) and Harper & Row.

Lines from "The White Bear" and "Mother and Child" by Susan Griffin, in *Like the Iris of an Eye.* Copyright © 1977 by Harper & Row. Used by permission of the publisher and the author.

Lines from *Tribute to Freud: Writing on the Wall: Advent* by H.D. Copyright © by Norman Holmes Pearson 1956, 1974. Reprinted by permission of David R. Godine, Publisher.

Lines from "The Mind Is an Enchanting Thing" (copyright 1944, renewed 1972 by Marianne Moore); "New York" and "Silence" (copyright 1935, renewed 1963 by Marianne Moore and T. S. Eliot), in *Collected Poems of Marianne Moore*. Used by permission of Macmillan Publishing Co., Inc.

Lines from "i am running into a new year" and "Turning" by Lucille Clifton, in *An Ordinary Woman*. Copyright © 1974 by Random House, Inc. Used by permission of the publisher.

Lines from "My Mama moved among the days" by Lucille Clifton, in *Good Times: Poems*. Copyright © 1969 by Random House, Inc. Used by permission of the publisher.

Excerpt from Introduction to *Adrienne Rich's Poetry*, ed. Barbara C. Gelpi and Albert Gelpi. Copyright © 1975 by W. W. Norton and Co. Used by permission of the publisher.

Excerpt from "The Ethnic Voice in American Poetry" by Arnold Rampersad. Copyright © 1976 by *San José Studies*. Used by permission.

Excerpt from *Survival: A Thematic Guide to Canadian Literature* by Margaret Atwood. Copyright © 1972 by House of Anansi Press, Ltd., Toronto. Used by permission of the publisher.

Lines from "Stepping Westward" by Denise Levertov, in *The Sorrow Dance*. Copyright © 1966 by Denise Levertov. Reprinted by permission of New Directions Publishing Corp.

Lines from "Hypocrite Women" by Denise Levertov, in *O Taste and See*. Copyright © 1964 by Denise Levertov Goodman. Reprinted by permission of New Directions Publishing Corp.

Lines from "Relearning the Alphabet" by Denise Levertov, in *Relearning the Alphabet*. Copyright © 1970 by Denise Levertov Goodman. Reprinted by permission of New Directions Publishing Corp.

Lines from "Snapshots of a Daughter-in-Law," "The Phenomenology of Anger," and "Diving into the Wreck" by Adrienne Rich, in *Poems, Selected and New, 1950–1974*. Copyright © 1975, 1973, 1971, 1969, 1966, by W. W. Norton and Co., Inc.

Lines from "Orpheus" by Muriel Rukeyser, in *Selected Poems*. Copyright 1951 by New Directions Publishing Corp. Used by permission of International Creative Management.

Lines from "The Children" and "Rowing" by Anne Sexton, in *The Awful Rowing Toward God*. Copyright © 1975 by Houghton Mifflin. Used by permission.

Lines from "Demon," "Talking to Sheep," "The Big Boots of Pain," and "Cigarettes and Whiskey and Wild, Wild Women" by Anne Sexton, in *45*

Mercy Street (Linda Gray Sexton and Lois Ames, eds.). Copyright © 1976 by Houghton Mifflin. Used by permission.

"To John, Who Begs Me Not to Enquire Further," by Anne Sexton, in *To Bedlam and Part Way Back*. Copyright © 1960 by Houghton Mifflin. Used by permission.

Lines from "For My People," "Dark Blood," "Lineage," "Molly Means," and "Kissie Lee" by Margaret Walker, in *For My People*. Copyright © 1942 by Yale University Press. Used by permission of Margaret Walker Alexander.

Lines from "On a Night of the Full Moon" by Audre Lorde, in *Coal*. Copyright © 1968, 1970, 1976 by Audre Lorde. Used by permission of W. W. Norton & Company, Inc.

Lines from "Hard Love Rock #II" by Audre Lorde, in *New York Head Shop and Museum*. Copyright © 1974 by Audre Lorde Rollins. Used by permission of Broadside/Crummell Press, Detroit, Mich.

"Personal Letter No. 2" by Sonia Sanchez, in *Home Coming*. Copyright © 1969 by Sonia Sanchez. Used by permission of Broadside/Crummell Press, Detroit, Mich.

Lines from "Liberation/Poem" by Sonia Sanchez, in *We A BaddDDD People*. Copyright © 1970 by Sonia Sanchez Knight. Used by permission of Broadside/Crummell Press, Detroit, Mich.

Lines from "Part Three; Present" by Sonia Sanchez, in *A Blues Book For Blue Black Magical Women*. Copyright © 1974 by Sonia Sanchez McRae. Used by permission of Broadside/Crummell Press, Detroit, Mich.

Introduction: Gender, Creativity, and the Woman Poet

Sandra M. Gilbert and Susan Gubar

> Alas! a woman that attempts the pen,
> Such an intruder on the rights of men,
> Such a presumptuous Creature, is esteem'd,
> The fault can by no vertue be redeem'd . . .
> How are we fal'n, fal'n by mistaken rules?
> And Education's, more than Nature's fools,
> Debarr'd from all improve-ments of the mind,
> And to be dull, expected and dessigned . . . .[1]

These lines were written by Anne Finch, the Countess of Winchilsea, in the late seventeenth century, and more than two centuries later even so successful an artist as Virginia Woolf was still speculating on their meaning. If Shakespeare had had a "wonderfully gifted sister," she mused in 1928, society would have sternly discouraged her literary aspirations. Judith Shakespeare might have run off to London to become a poet–playwright, for "the birds that sang in the hedge were not more musical than she." Yet she would have quickly found such a vocation impossible, "and so—who shall measure the heat and violence of the poet's heart when caught and tangled in a woman's body?—she killed herself one winter night and lies buried at some crossroads where the omnibuses now stop outside the Elephant and Castle."[2] Yet of course Shakespeare did—and does—have many sisters. Perhaps none have attained that equality of renown Anne Finch and Virginia Woolf envisioned, but neither are they all buried at an obscure crossroads. Some have lived and worked in other lands, other times— Shakespeare's foreign relatives or his older sisters, to pursue the metaphor. Others, akin in language as well as vocation to the poet himself, have struggled to perfect their art in England and America.

It is the purpose of this anthology to examine the achievement of representative members of this last group of poets, Shakespeare's English-speaking sisters, and to examine it specifically in relation to all those patriarchal social strictures, all those obstacles that discourage women from attempting the pen, which Anne Finch's lines describe and Virginia Woolf's parable defines. For women poets, from Finch herself to Sylvia Plath and Adrienne Rich, have known very well that they are *women* poets. Readers, critics, and sometimes even friends have reminded them that to attempt the pen has historically been a subversive act for a woman in a culture which assumes that, as Poet Laureate Robert Southey told Charlotte Brontë in 1837, "Literature cannot be the business of a woman's life, and it ought not to be."[3]

Significantly, Southey's remark was a response not to Brontë's fiction but to some poems she had sent him. While a number of fine feminist studies have recently explored the relationship between gender and creativity in the work of women novelists,[4] the problems as well as the triumphs of women poets in England and America still remain inexplicably obscure. Yet the obstructions such literary women confronted were even more formidable than those faced by female novelists. Though fiction writers like the Brontë sisters and George Eliot were often measured against an intellectual double standard that made them the targets of what Elaine Showalter wittily calls "*ad feminam* criticism,"[5] their literary efforts evidently seemed less problematical than those of women poets, even to misogynistic readers. Their art was not actively encouraged, but it was generally understood by the late eighteenth century and throughout the nineteenth century that under conditions of pressing need a woman might have to live by her pen. As a professional novelist, however, whether she was delighting her audience with fantasies of romance or instructing it with didactic moral tales, such a woman was not so different from her less gifted but equally needy sisters who went out into the world to earn their livings by "instructing" as governesses (if they were respectable) or "delighting" as actresses (if they were less respectable). As Woolf notes in *A Room of One's Own*, moreover, the realistic novel, with its appetite for physical and social detail, requires precisely the sort of reportorial skill women could develop even in their own drawing rooms, and since the discrimination of the passions was supposedly a special female talent, female novelists could use their socially sanctioned sensitivity to manners and morals in the delineation of characters or the construction of plots. Indeed, beginning with Aphra Behn and burgeoning with Fanny Burney, Anne Radcliffe, Maria Edgeworth, and Jane Austen, the English novel seems to have been in some sense a female invention.

Despite a proliferation of literary ancestresses, however, Elizabeth Barrett Browning commented mournfully in 1845 that "England has had many learned women . . . and yet where are the poetesses? . . . I look everywhere for grandmothers, and see none."[6] In 1862, moreover, Emily Dickinson, articulating in another way the same distinction between women's prose and women's verse, expressed similar bewilderment. Complaining that

> They shut me up in Prose—
> As when a little Girl
> They put me in the Closet—
> Because they liked me "still"—[7]

she implied a recognition that poetry by women was in some sense inappropriate, unladylike, immodest. And in 1928, as if commenting on both Barrett Browning's comment and Dickinson's complaint, Woolf invented a tragic history for her "Judith Shakespeare" because she so deeply believed that it is "the poetry that is still denied outlet."

Why did these three literary women consider poetry by women somehow forbidden or problematical? Woolf herself, after all, traced the careers of Anne Finch and Margaret Cavendish, admired the "wild poetry" of the Brontës, noted that Barrett Browning's verse-novel *Aurora Leigh* had poetic virtues no prose work could rival, and spoke almost with awe of Christina Rossetti's "complex song."[8] Why, then, did she feel that "Judith Shakespeare" was "caught and tangled," "denied," suffocated, self-buried, or not yet born? We can begin to find answers to these questions by briefly reviewing some of the ways in which representative male readers and critics have reacted to poetry by representative women like Barrett Browning and Dickinson.

Introducing *The Selected Poems of Emily Dickinson* in 1959, James Reeves quoted "a friend" as making a statement which expresses the predominant attitude of many male *literati* toward poetry by women even more succinctly than Woolf's story did: "A friend who is also a literary critic has suggested, not perhaps quite seriously, that 'woman poet' is a contradiction in terms."[9] In other words, from what Woolf would call the "masculinist" point of view, the very nature of lyric poetry is inherently incompatible with the nature or essence of femaleness. Remarks by other "masculinist" readers and critics elaborate on the point. In the midst of favorably reviewing the work of his friend Louise Bogan, for instance, Theodore Roethke detailed the various "charges most frequently levelled against poetry by women." Though his statement begins by pretending objectivity, it soon becomes clear that he himself is making such accusations.

> Two of the [most frequent] charges . . . are lack of range—in subject matter, in emotional tone—and lack of a sense of humor. And one could, in individual instances among writers of real talent, add other aesthetic and

moral shortcomings: the spinning out; the embroidering of trivial themes;
a concern with the mere surfaces of life—that special province of the femi-
nine talent in prose—hiding from the real agonies of the spirit; refusing to
face up to what existence is; lyric or religious posturing; running between
the boudoir and the altar; stamping a tiny foot against God or lapsing into
a sententiousness that implies the author has re-invented integrity; carrying
on excessively about Fate, about time; lamenting the lot of the woman;
caterwauling; writing the same poem about fifty times, and so on. . . .[10]

Even a cursory reading of this passage reveals its inconsistency: women are
taxed for both triviality and sententiousness, for both silly superficiality and
melodramatic "carrying on" about profound subjects. More significant, how-
ever, is the fact that Roethke attacks female poets for doing just what male
poets do—that is, for writing about God, fate, time, and integrity; for writ-
ing obsessively on the same themes or subjects, and so forth. But his lan-
guage suggests that it is precisely the sex of these literary women that
subverts their art. Shaking a Promethean male fist "against God" is one
perfectly reasonable aesthetic strategy, apparently, but stamping a "tiny"
feminine foot is quite another.

Along similar lines, John Crowe Ransom noted without disapproval in a
1956 essay about Emily Dickinson that "it is common belief among readers
(among men readers at least) that the woman poet as a type . . . makes
flights into nature rather too easily and upon errands which do not have
metaphysical importance enough to justify so radical a strategy."[11] Else-
where in the same essay, describing Dickinson as "a little home-keeping
person" he speculated that "hardly . . . more" than "one out of seventeen"
of her 1,775 poems are destined to become "public property," and observed
that her life "was a humdrum affair of little distinction," although "in her
Protestant community the gentle spinsters had their assured and useful
place in the family circle, they had what was virtually a vocation."[12] (But
how, he seemed to wonder, could someone with so humdrum a social
destiny have written great poetry?) Equally concerned with the problemati-
cal relationship between Dickinson's poetry and her femaleness—with, that
is, what seemed to be an irreconcilable conflict between her "gentle" spinster-
hood and her fierce art—R. P. Blackmur decided in 1937 that "she was
neither a professional poet nor an amateur; she was a private poet who
wrote indefatigably, as some women cook or knit. Her gift for words and
the cultural predicament of her time drove her to poetry instead of
antimacassars."[13]

Even in 1971, male readers of Dickinson brooded upon this apparent
dichotomy of poetry and femininity. John Cody's *After Great Pain* per-
ceptively analyzes the suffering that many of Dickinson's critics and biogra-

phers have refused to acknowledge. But his conclusion emphasizes what he too sees as the incompatibility between womanly fulfillment and passionate art.

> Had Mrs. Dickinson been warm and affectionate, more intelligent, effective, and admirable, Emily Dickinson early in life would probably have identified with her, become domestic, and adopted the conventional woman's role. She would then have become a church member, been active in community affairs, married, and had children. The creative potentiality would of course still have been there, but would she have discovered it? What motivation to write could have replaced the incentive given by suffering and loneliness? If in spite of her wifely and motherly duties, she had still felt the need to express herself in verse, what would her subject matter have been? Would art have sprung from fulfillment, gratification, and completeness as abundantly as it did from longing, frustration, and deprivation?[14]

Interestingly, these questions restate an apparently very different position taken by Ransom fifteen years earlier: "Most probably [Dickinson's] poems would not have amounted to much if the author had not finally had her own romance, enabling her to fulfill herself like any other woman." Though Ransom speaks of the presence and "fulfillment" of "romance," while Cody discusses its tormenting absence, neither imagines that poetry itself could possibly constitute a woman's fulfillment. On the contrary, both assume that the art of a woman poet must in some sense arise from "romantic" feelings (in the popular, sentimental sense), arise either in response to a real romance or as compensation for a missing one.

In view of this critical obsession with womanly "fulfillment"—clearly a nineteenth-century notion redefined by twentieth-century thinkers for their own purposes—it is not surprising to find out that when poetry by women *has* been praised it has usually been praised for being "feminine," just as it has been blamed for being deficient in "femininity." Elizabeth Barrett Browning, for instance, the most frequently analyzed, criticized, praised, and blamed woman poet of her day, was typically admired "because of her understanding of the depth, tenderness, and humility of the love which is given by women,"[15] and because "she was a poet in every fibre of her but adorably feminine. . . ."[16] As the "Shakespeare of her sex,"[17] moreover, she was especially respected for being "pure and lovely" in her "private life," since "the lives of women of genius have been so frequently sullied by sin . . . that their intellectual gifts are [usually] a curse rather than a blessing."[18] Significantly, however, when Barrett Browning attempted unromantic, "unfeminine" political verse in *Poems Before Congress*, her collection of 1860, at least one critic decided that she had been "seized with a . . . fit of insanity," explaining that "to bless and not to curse is a woman's function. . . ."[19]

As this capsule review of *ad feminam* criticism suggests, there is evidently something about lyric poetry by women that invites meditations on female fulfillment or, alternatively, on female insanity. In devising a story for "Judith Shakespeare," Woolf herself was after all driven to construct a violent plot that ends with her suicidal heroine's burial beneath a bus-stop near the Elephant and Castle. Symbolically speaking, Woolf suggests, modern London, with its technological fumes and its patriarchal roar, grows from the grim crossroads where this mythic woman poet lies dead. And as if to reinforce the morbid ferocity of such imagery, Woolf adds that whenever, reading history or listening to gossip, we hear of witches and magical wise women, "I think we are on the track of . . . a suppressed poet . . . who dashed her brains out on the moor or mopped and mowed about the highways crazed with the torture that her gift had put her to." For though "the original [literary] impulse was to poetry," and "the 'supreme head of song' was a poetess," literary women in England and America have almost universally elected to write novels rather than poems for fear of precisely the madness Woolf attributes to Judith Shakespeare. "Sure the poore woman is a little distracted," she quotes a contemporary of Margaret Cavendish's as remarking: "Shee could never be soe rediculous else as to venture at writeing books and in verse too, if I should not sleep this fortnight I should not come to that."[20] In other words, while the woman novelist, safely shut in prose, may fantasize about freedom with a certain impunity (since she constructs purely fictional alternatives to the difficult reality she inhabits), it appears that the woman poet must in some sense become her own heroine, and that in enacting the diabolical role of witch or wise woman she literally or figuratively risks a melodramatic death at the crossroads of tradition and genre, society and art.

Without pretending to exhaust a profoundly controversial subject, we should note here that there are a number of generic differences between novel-writing and verse-writing which do support the kinds of distinctions Woolf's story implies. For one thing, as we noted earlier, novel-writing is a useful (because lucrative) occupation, while poetry, except perhaps for the narrative poetry of Byron and Scott, has traditionally had little monetary value. That novel-writing was and is conceivably an occupation to live by has always, however, caused it to seem less intellectually or spiritually valuable than verse-writing, of all possible literary occupations the one to which European culture has traditionally assigned the highest status. Certainly when Walter Pater in 1868 defined the disinterested ecstasy of art for his contemporaries by noting that "art comes to you proposing frankly to give nothing but the highest quality to your moments as they pass, and simply for those moments' sake," he was speaking of what he earlier called "the poetic passion," alluding to works like the Odes of Keats rather than the novels of Thackeray or George Eliot. Verse-writing—the product of mysterious "inspiration," divine afflatus, bardic ritual—has historically been a holy vocation.[21] Before the nineteenth century the poet had a nearly priestly role, and "he" had a wholly priestly role after Romantic thinkers had appropriated the vocabulary of theology for the realm of aesthetics. But if in Western culture women cannot be priests, then how—since poets are priests—can they be poets? The question may sound sophistic, but there is a good deal of evidence that it was and has been consciously or unconsciously asked, by men and women alike, as often as women suffering from "the poetic passion" have appeared in the antechambers of literature.

As Woolf shows, though, novel-writing is not just a "lesser" and therefore more suitably female occupation because it is commercial rather than aesthetic, practical rather than priestly. Where novel-writing depends upon reportorial observation, verse-writing has traditionally required aristocratic education. "Learn . . . for ancient rules a just esteem;/To copy Nature is to copy them," Alexander Pope admonished aspiring critics and (by implication) poets in 1709, noting that "Nature and Homer" are "the same."[22] As if dutifully acquiescing, even the fiery iconoclast Percy Bysshe Shelley assiduously translated Aeschylus and other Greek "masters." As Western society defines "him," the lyric poet must have aesthetic models, must in a sense speak the esoteric language of literary forms. She or he cannot simply record or describe the phenomena of nature and society, for literary theorists have long believed that, in poetry, nature must be mediated through tradition—that is, through an education in "ancient rules." But of course, as so many women writers learned with dismay, the traditional classics of Greek and Latin—meaning the distilled Platonic essence of Western literature, history, philosophy—constituted what George Eliot called "spheres of masculine learning" inalterably closed to women except under the most extraordinary circumstances. Interestingly, only Barrett Browning, of all the major women poets, was enabled—by her invalid seclusion, her sacrifice of ordinary pleasures—seriously to study "the ancients." Like Shelley, she translated Aeschylus' *Prometheus Bound,* and she went even further, producing an unusually learned study of the little-known Greek Christian poets. What is most interesting about Barrett Browning's skill as a classicist, however, is the fact that it was barely noticed in her own day and has been almost completely forgotten in ours.

Suzanne Juhasz has recently and persuasively spoken of the "double bind" of the woman poet,[23] but it seems almost as if there is a sort of triple bind here. On the one hand, the woman poet who learns a "just esteem" for

Homer is ignored or even mocked—as, say, the eighteenth-century "Blue Stockings" were. On the other hand, the woman poet who does not (because she is not allowed to) study Homer is held in contempt. On the third hand, however, whatever alternative tradition the woman poet attempts to substitute for "ancient rules" is subtly devalued. Ransom, for instance, asserts that Dickinson's meters, learned from "her father's hymnbook," are all based upon "Folk Line, the popular form of verse and the oldest in our language," adding that "the great classics of this meter are the English ballads and Mother Goose." Our instinctive sense that this is a backhanded compliment is confirmed when he remarks that "Folk Line is disadvantageous . . . if it denies to the poet the use of English Pentameter," which is "the staple of what we may call the studied or 'university' poetry, and . . . is capable of containing and formalizing many kinds of substantive content which would be too complex for Folk Line. Emily Dickinson appears never to have tried it."[24] If we read "pentameter" here as a substitute for "ancient rules," then we can see that once again "woman" and "poet" are being defined as contradictory terms.

Finally, and perhaps most crucially, where the novel allows—even encourages—just the self-effacing withdrawal society has traditionally fostered in women, the lyric poem is in some sense the utterance of a strong and assertive "I." Artists from Shakespeare to Dickinson, Yeats, and T. S. Eliot have of course qualified this "I," emphasizing, as Eliot does, the "extinction of personality" involved in a poet's construction of an artful, masklike persona, or insisting, as Dickinson did, that the speaker of poems is a "supposed person."[25] But, nevertheless, the central self that speaks or sings a poem must be forcefully defined, whether "she"/"he" is real or imaginary. If the novelist, therefore, inevitably sees herself from the *outside*, as an object, a character, a small figure in a large pattern, the lyric poet must be continually aware of herself from the *inside*, as a subject, a speaker: she must be, that is, assertive, authoritative, radiant with powerful feelings while at the same time absorbed in her own consciousness—and hence, by definition, profoundly "unwomanly," even freakish. For the woman poet, in other words, the contradictions between her vocation and her gender might well become insupportable, impelling her to deny one or the other, even (as in the case of "Judith Shakespeare") driving her to suicide. For, as Woolf puts it, "who shall measure the heat and violence of the poet's heart when caught and tangled in a woman's body?"

In 1935 Louise Bogan wrote to John Hall Wheelock, her editor, to report that

Malcolm Cowley, a month or so ago asked me to edit an anthology of female verse, to be used in the pages of the New Republic. They have as you know, already published groups of Middle-Western verse, and what not. They are now about to divide mankind horizontally rather than vertically, sexually rather than geographically. As you might have expected, I turned this pretty job down; the thought of corresponding with a lot of female songbirds made me acutely ill. It is hard enough to bear with my own lyric side.[26]

Obviously, as Gloria Bowles has pointed out, Bogan had internalized just those patriarchal interdictions that have historically caused women poets from Finch to Plath anxiety and guilt about attempting the pen. In a sense, then, using Bogan's problem as a paradigm, we might say that at its most painful the history of women's poetry is a story of struggle against the sort of self-loathing her letter represents, while at its most victorious this literary history is a chronicle of the evolutionary processes through which "Judith Shakespeare" learned over and over again that, in Plath's words, "I / Have a self to recover, a queen."[27]

Until quite recently most criticism of poetry by women has failed to transcend the misogyny implicit both in Bogan's letter and in the sexist definitions her letter incorporates, just as it has failed to explore in any but the most superficial ways the crucial relationship between sexual identity and art. When not relegated to oblivion, women poets are often still sentimentally pictured as "disappointed in love," as the neurotic old maids or romantic schoolgirls of literature. That the themes, structures, and images of their art may have been at least in part necessitated either by the special constrictions of their sexual role or by their uncertain relationship to an overwhelmingly "masculinist" literary tradition is a matter that feminist critics have just begun to explore.

A number of feminist critics have, of course, studied the role of gender in literary history, and our work would be inconceivable without the pioneering achievements of Simone de Beauvoir's *The Second Sex*, Josephine Donovan's *Feminist Literary Criticism*, Mary Ellmann's *Thinking About Women*, Elizabeth Hardwick's *Seduction and Betrayal*, Kate Millett's *Sexual Politics*, and Ellen Moers's *Literary Women*, as well as seminal essays like Tillie Olsen's "Silences," or Adrienne Rich's "When We Dead Awaken: Writing as Re-Vision," and innumerable articles in such journals as *Signs*, *Feminist Studies*, and *Women's Studies*. For this reason we have included for each of the poets discussed here a selected bibliography which gives not only the volumes and available editions of their work, but also the criticism— especially the feminist criticism—that informs the insights of this volume. Yet, even as we pay tribute to these earlier thinkers, we need to remember that, with the exception of Suzanne Juhasz's *Naked and Fiery Forms: Modern American Poetry by Women, A New Tradition* and more recently Emily Stipes Watts's *The Poetry of American Women, 1650 to 1945*, the models of most feminist critics almost always derive from and pertain to prose writing and are not directly applicable to poetry. We have, therefore, emphasized practical criticism because we believe that a general theory can emerge only after a full comprehension of the range and richness of women's poetic voices, many of which have so far barely been heard.

All the essays in this anthology, then, seek to revise our inherited notions of literary history by recovering lost poets and lost poems, by finding the "grandmothers" Barrett Browning sought, and by thus tracing the outlines of a distinctively female poetic tradition. One book cannot, of course, compensate for generations of neglect and misunderstanding: although we have included essays on many major women poets, our table of contents does not represent a definitive canon. On the contrary, missing are such important writers as Margaret Cavendish, Katherine Phillips, Aphra Behn, Alice Meynell, Edith Sitwell, Amy Lowell, Gertrude Stein, and Louise Bogan, while significant and established poets like Marianne Moore, Margaret Walker, Adrienne Rich, and Muriel Rukeyser receive only passing attention in "omnibus" essays. Perhaps even more striking is the absence of essays on most of the contemporary women who have contributed to the recent renaissance in women's poetry: alta, Margaret Atwood, Diane Di Prima, Kathleen Fraser, Judy Grahn, June Jordan, Carolyn Kizer, Maxine Kumin, Marge Piercy, May Sarton, Ruth Stone, Diane Wakoski, Alice Walker, to name but a few. Their triumphant numbers, as well as the critical attention they have received (in part because of the recent gains of the women's movement), have inspired us to rediscover more obscure "grandmothers" in an attempt to redefine the literary history that we hope will eventually enrich our reading of current writing. Despite the limitations of space, however, we believe that the "presumptuous creatures" whose achievements this book examines offer us a vigorous and victorious matrilineal heritage.

Our exploration of this heritage begins with a section devoted to the poets who wrote before 1800, the writers whose art is least known and read today. Specifically, the first essay, by Catherine Smith, reminds us of those ages of silence when women did not publish poetry at all. Describing the mystical tradition in which Jane Lead worked, Smith shows us how women, "debarred from all improve-ments of the mind" and therefore excluded from poetry by their lack of education, channeled their poetic energies into apparently "lesser" genres. Excitingly, too, her reappraisal of Lead's spiritual autobiography demonstrates the striking continuity of women's literature from such obscurely self-defining beginnings to the contemporary "confessional" poetry of women like Rich, Plath, Morgan, and Wakoski. Along similar lines, Wendy Martin's essay on Anne Bradstreet and Katharine Rogers' study of Anne Finch explore in detail the difficulties women experienced when they did attempt "mainstream" forms, and the ways in which they characteristically subverted or revised genres originally created by and for men.

Moving from what Emily Dickinson spoke of as "a lonesome Glee"—the joy of creation that "sanctifies" even alienated or isolated artists—to a century when women poets read each other's work with sisterly enthusiasm, our second section shows how nineteenth-century women boldly used their own poems to dramatize and mythologize their own lives. These Victorian writers are the *grandes dames* of our matrilineal heritage, women whose energies and enactments constitute what Dickinson, speaking of Barrett Browning, called "Titanic Opera." Power is what characterizes their voices, as Nina Auerbach shows in her analysis of Emily Brontë's almost daemonic identification with mutability, and as Helen Cooper demonstrates in her history of Barrett Browning's extraordinary and consciously feminist self-evolution. At the same time, exploring Emily Dickinson's genius, three critics show how, artfully disguising her volcanic energy, Dickinson told the truth about her power but told it "slant." Albert Gelpi places Dickinson's poetry in the context of American frontier myths and thereby defines this New England artist's own female sense of her relationship to the new world. Adrienne Rich discusses the secret strength of this poet who chose seclusion not as an anxious retreat or a decorous withdrawal but as her only chance for artistic freedom. And Terence Diggory analyzes the need for "slant"— for camouflage, for protective costume—that distinguishes the powerful and theatrical poetry of Dickinson (and her contemporary heiresses, like Plath) from a male tradition of "nakedness" best exemplified by Whitman.

The title of our third section, "The Silver Reticence," refers to the linguistic compression that Jeanne Kammer considers a crucial characteristic of modernist poetry by women. Discussing this device and the ellipses and "diaphors" associated with it, Kammer explores the absences and silences in the poetry of such important foremothers as Dickinson, H.D., and Marianne Moore. All of the other essays in this part of the book also deal in one way or another with female reticence as a subject or a strategy. Gloria T. Hull, for example, traces the complex poetic tradition of black women in America, examining in particular the comparatively little-known work that women like Anne Spencer and Helene Johnson contributed to the Harlem Renaissance that preceded our own era's burst of black artistic energy. Her essay implies a crucial question: was the modesty of the women of the Harlem Renaissance intentionally chosen by them or ruthlessly inflicted on them? A related question is implied by Jane Stanbrough, who explores the covert sense of vulnerability that, despite Edna St. Vincent Millay's overt flamboyance, permeated the linguistic patterns of her verse. Finally, in "The Echoing Spell of H.D.'s *Trilogy*," Susan Gubar provides a close reading of a book-length narrative in which H.D. confronts the difficult necessity of revising the destructive signs of her times by returning to lost matriarchal myths and values.

Our last section, "The Difference—Made Me Bold," draws its title from a poem in which Dickinson celebrates her poetic gift: "It was given to me by the Gods— / When I was a little Girl—". With a sure sense of their right to intrude upon the rights of men, the contemporary poets to whom this section is devoted proclaim the verve and uniqueness of their art. Thus, Alicia Ostriker examines May Swenson's lucidity of observation, associating it with her brilliant exploitation of visual forms, while Hortense Spillers celebrates the stylistic versatility that Gwendolyn Brooks has brought to her poetic treatments of "Bronzeville" women. Similarly, Sandra Gilbert defines what she calls "the Plath myth" as a central paradigm of female experience, tracing Plath's movement from numb imprisonment to "flying" escape, and Suzanne Juhasz explores the risks and triumphs of Anne Sexton's consciously self-defining art. Finally, in two omnibus essays Barbara Charlesworth Gelpi and Rachel Blau DuPlessis offer distinctly different structures for understanding the present state of women's poetry in America. Using the model of colonial literature, Gelpi describes the stages through which a literary culture must evolve before it reaches authentic primacy, while DuPlessis explores the ways in which contemporary women poets engage in a radically feminist critique of our culture's mythology and ideology.

Although they represent only a beginning of the reassessment of women's poetry that must now be undertaken, all these essays suggest that at last the community has begun to form out of which a true feminist criticism can grow. For at last, so it seems, there are a number of talented and thoughtful critics who believe that, as Virginia Woolf wrote,

> If we live another century or so . . . if we have the habit of freedom and the courage to write exactly what we think; if we escape a little from the common sitting room . . . if we look past Milton's bogey . . . then the opportunity will come and the dead poet who was Shakespeare's sister will put on the body which she has so often laid down. Drawing her life from the lives of the unknown who were her forerunners, as her brother did before her, she will be born.[28]

In fact, we hope our anthology will definitively demonstrate that Shakespeare's sister has already been born, in many times and many places, and that we have only to look to our "grandmothers" to discover our grand, lost heritage of poetic presumption.

I

"A LONESOME GLEE"

Poets Before 1800

It is a lonesome Glee—
Yet sanctifies the Mind—
With fair association—
Afar upon the Wind

A Bird to overhear
Delight without a Cause—
Arrestless as invisible—
A matter of the Skies.

—Emily Dickinson, #774

1.

Jane Lead: Mysticism and the Woman Cloathed with the Sun

Catherine F. Smith

Jane Lead was an English Protestant mystic and spiritual autobiographer who lived from 1624 until 1704. In April 1670 she had a vision of "an over-shadowing bright Cloud and in the midst of it the Figure of a Woman." Three days later the luminous figure reappeared, saying "Behold me as thy Mother." Six days later the Woman promised "to transfigure my self in thy mind; and there open the Spring of Wisdom and Understanding."[1] After years of continuing visions—"I have learned to observe her Times and Seasons, I witness her opening as in the Twinkling of an Eye, a pure, bright, subtil, swift Spirit, a working motion, a Circling Fire, a penetrating Oil"—Jane Lead prophesied

> This is the great Wonder to come forth, a Woman Cloathed with the Sun . . . with the Globe of this world under her feet . . . with a Crown beset with stars, plainly declaring that to her is given the Command and Power . . . to create and generate spirits in her own express likeness. . . .[2]

This bright Woman is Lead's revision of Sophia, the Virgin Wisdom of God in esoteric theology and apocalyptic tradition. Recurrence of a similar ideal in poetry by women in the twentieth century—"I/am a pure acetylene/ Virgin"—"I am the woman/ . . . whose words are matches"—suggests a pattern of vocabulary shared across women's literary history.[3] It may point to a paradigm in women's imagination as well.

But we must know more history before we can see pattern and paradigm. Jane Lead's life is evidence that we know too little about one group of seventeenth-century writers, the millenarian, sectarian authors of spiritual autobiographies. Those earlier women might be said to have set turning for their time the wheel of self-revelation by women that we reinvent in our own.

Little is certain about Jane Lead's early life. Contemporary records are mainly retrospective appreciations of her visionary insight, written by herself or by sympathizers.[4] Those statements usually employ hagiographic conventions of recounting the lives of mystics or visionaries.[5] Nevertheless, a personality and a culture are apparent in them, individualizing her and connecting her life with persisting conditions for women writers.

She was born Jane Ward, probably in 1624, to an "honorable and esteemed" family, probably gentry, in the county of Norfolk. She received the limited education thought appropriate, either by private tutoring or in a parish petty school where girls were taught domestic skills along with reading, writing, and arithmetic. Early dissatisfaction with her life openly broke into a Christmas celebration when she was fifteen. Amid dancing and music, she was suddenly, deeply depressed and seemed to hear a voice whispering "Cease from this, I have another Dance to lead thee in; for this is Vanity."[6] She stopped dancing. During a crisis that lasted more than three years, she was obsessed with the biblical stricture that "Whosoever loveth and maketh a lie" must be left out of the New Jerusalem. At eighteen, relief came through ecstatic visualization of a pardon with a seal attached to it.[7]

Still intensely curious about her experiences, Ward persuaded her family to send her for a six-month visit to her brother, a merchant in London. There, she scoured public and private religious meetings in the political and religious turbulence of Cromwell's England, with its numerous sects such as the Ranters, the Diggers, and the Quakers. For eighteen-year-old Jane Ward, this brief, highly motivated education in ideas of the spirit served as the advanced schooling otherwise closed to her. When her parents rejected her choice of a marriage partner in London, she returned to Norfolk to refuse, in turn, several of their choices for her, saying that as a bride of Christ, she found earthly marriages repulsive.

Marriage being an economic necessity, however, she did marry a distant relative, William Lead(e), who met her standards for spiritual devotion. Four daughters were born during the twenty-seven-year union that was the most regular phase of Jane Lead's long life. The marriage ended in February 1670, when she was widowed at forty-six. Destitute, with two living daughters (the keeper of the family's money having proved dishonest), she resolved to commit herself to a "life of Spiritual Virginity," placing priority on exploration of her inner life. Writing later in her journal and transmuting her married experience into marriage metaphor, she quotes the Virgin Sophia's directive on setting aside material concerns to achieve conscious separateness.

. . . Being Dead wherein we were held fast, we should [be] . . . discharged from the law of the first Husband, to which we were married, after the Law of a Carnal Command . . . that first Husband who so long hindered my marriage with the Lamb.

(*Fountain of Gardens*, I, pp. 69–71)

Pragmatically, the change meant that she joined certain friends who admired her capacity for ecstatic knowledge and who had introduced her to the mystic thought of the German idealist philosopher and Protestant "Inner Light" theologian, Jacob Boehme (1575–1624). The group centered on Dr. John Pordage, the Anglican cleric who became one of the first commentators on Boehme's Reformation-bred thought when it entered religious life in England around 1644. Subject to trances himself, Pordage had a controversial record as a parish priest. He had married his first wife, Mary, "for ye Excellent Gift of God he found in her; wch Gift he also became in a high Degree Partaker of." Together they held ecstatic sessions in his village parish of Bradfield, in which Mary Pordage, "Cloathed all in White Lawne, from the crown of the Head to the Sole of the Foot, and a White rod in her hand," was hailed by dancing parishioners as a "Prophetess." These practices, and his reported acquaintance with Oxford hermeticists and with Ranter preachers such as Abiezzer Coppe, led to Pordage's loss of the Bradfield living. By 1663 he was the leader of a small, private, nonconformist congregation in London joined by Jane Lead, "whose Extraordinary Gift of Revelation y Dr gave great regard to & Attended upon."[8]

Conditions of existence for such small sectarian groups, difficult enough under Cromwell's uneven pressures, had become harshly repressive under the restored king, Charles II. The Conventicle Act of 1664, for example, forbade gatherings of more than five adults for practice of any religion other than allowed by Anglican liturgy, with penalties of three months imprisonment or five pounds for the first offense and up to deportation for seven years or a hundred pounds for the third. In spite of these threats, as well as the Great Plague that killed thousands in a week, and the 1666 London fire, Pordage's and Lead's group continued to meet.[9] After her vision of Sophia and her commitment to a new life, Jane Lead in 1674 moved into John Pordage's household.

Then was a new Charge for my self, and the Dr. that we should draw apart from all impertinent Fellowships; because called to act forth a Superiour part, as those who are designed to wait for the Triune Glory to fill our whole Temple Minds, who will in our Heavenly Conversation be, if no thing throngs in from this World.

(*Fountain of Gardens*, II, pp. 137–38)

Mary Pordage had died in 1668; very little is known about Pordage's second wife, Elizabeth. According to Jane Lead's journal from these years, she lived in the household as Pordage's partner in meditation and vision, in writing commentary on Boehme, and in the public work of forming the congregation, then numbering nearly a hundred. Pordage transcribed her revelations. As before, with marriage offers, Lead controlled the demands of external convention by asserting the authority of her inner life. When her brother "privately ordered" her to leave the Pordage household and accept his support or forfeit all future offers of assistance, she refused.

> It was said within me, thou art in a great strait, yet nevertheless stand by the Vow and Solemn Engagement . . . to go forward jointly with thy appointed Mate . . . to that work, which the present offer is much too low for to retard.
>
> (*Fountain of Gardens,* I, p. 328)

In 1681, her fifty-seventh year and the year of Pordage's death, she brought out her first book, a spiritual guide called *The Heavenly Cloud Now Breaking*. . . . Two years later she published her commentary on apocalypse, *The Revelation of Revelations* . . . , as well as Pordage's first work in print, *Theologica Mystica*, with her introduction.

Productiveness in the years with Pordage counterpoints the effort recorded in her journal to practice the contemplativeness she very much wanted to explore. The journal, which is her spiritual autobiography, takes its shape from tensions and growth in those years. Written from 1670 to 1686 in "loose Shreds of Paper, for the sake of her own Memory, and for Monitions and Encouragements to some few Particular Friends," the journal was eventually titled *A Fountain of Gardens* . . . and published in 1697–1701, in four volumes nearly two thousand pages long.[10] It includes set-piece visions followed by interpretation; dreams; conversations and argumentation with Sophia and with her heir and mate, Christ; symbolic narratives of spiritual progress; exuberant experiments with imagery and metaphor ("Every thought presents a Person, they are Magical Essences, subtle Spirits . . .") that pile up effect in an attempt to break beyond fixed form ("Vision and Prophecy were but as the Door-Post . . .") (*Fountain of Gardens*, III, p. 81; II, p. 522). The journal might be called a writer's diary, the working papers of an experimental stylist and theoretician of imagination, had Jane Lead thought of herself as an artist rather than a prophet. But she wrote when few women were considered artists, although a number, like her, imagined selves and ordered universes in their spiritual autobiographies.

After 1681 her hard-pressed congregation dwindled, and by 1692 Jane Lead was living alone in a house of charity in Stepney, on the outskirts of the city of London. Her writing went on, and she arranged its printing and sale. A common enough practice with sectarian writers before 1660, it was dangerous for both author and printer after the Restoration. In addition to the general suppression of unordained preachers that imprisoned John Bunyan, for example, virulent objections specifically to women preachers resulted in their special harassment and produced a large pamphlet literature of attack and defense, including many of the personal accounts by outspoken Quaker and other sectarian women such as Jane Lead. A note appended to her *Enochian Walks with God, Found Out by a Spiritual Traveller . . .* (1694) emphasizes her aggressive isolation in this period.

> This Book is to be Sold by the Author, Jane Lead, living at the Lady Mico's Colledge, right against Stepney Church; and at her Daughters Barbary Walton, at Mr. Mileman's in New-Street, at the end of Dean Street, right against the 3 Tuns.
> And if any one be dissatisfied in any Point handled in this Book, the Author is ready to give answer thereunto, while she is yet Living.

Another shift in Lead's life occurred around 1694, irrevocably making her a recognized figure in sectarian circles. One of her books having reached Germany, correspondence began with sympathizers there who published translations that stimulated continental interest in her work. In this way began her relationship with Dr. Francis Lee, who had found her work in The Netherlands and returned to England to meet her. An Orientalist of St. John's College, Oxford, Lee had become a non-Juror, forced to give up his university position for refusing to sign the oath of allegiance to the new king, William. He had then trained as a physician. Drawn to mysticism as a religious person, as a scholar particularly interested in the literature of the Apocrypha, and as a physician curious about trances and the causes of imagination, he was also out of money and a job when he decided to join Jane Lead, casting himself "upon God's most wise direction in all things."[11] About a year later Jane Lead became blind at seventy-one. At Lead's suggestion Lee, who was thirty-four, married her widowed daughter Barbara, and acted as Lead's secretary and editor until her death at eighty in 1704. Together they reorganized her congregation as the Philadelphian Society, advocating individual transformation as the means of bringing about the millennium, but rejecting the anarchism of the Ranters and the planned social reforms of the Diggers and the Quakers. Taking its name from the church of Philadelphia, or the remnant of believers at the beginning of Apocalypse, the new group was philosophically based in Jacob Boehme's ideas.[12]

In face of Reason's dominance in the developing Enlightenment, Boehme, a mystic, had resynthesized the long-respected but fading systems of gnosticism, Jewish and Christian mysticism, Neoplatonism, alchemy, and astrology in a hybrid called theosophy. Shoring up belief in a transcendant spirit and millennial harmony, his theosophy contributed importantly to Protestant theology of the individual "Inner Light" of God. His cosmology relies significantly on inherited expression, especially sexual metaphor for spiritual process. Sophia, female image for potential Being and for the soul, is an important example. Derived mainly from gnostic heresies, the Kabala, Wisdom literature, and apocalyptic language of Scripture, Sophia is the primary, unconditioned ground of Being out of which the self-actualizing, masculine will of deity creates.

> The Wisdom is the outflown word of the Divine Power . . . a Substance Wherein the Holy Ghost works, forms, and models . . . For the Wisdom is the Passive, and the Spirit of God is the Active . . . She is the true Divine Chaos, wherein all things lie . . . a Divine Imagination.[13]

In existence, this female potentiality continues in a dialectic with male power of manifestation, as the soul (a daughter-fragment of original mother Wisdom) coexists with separate, rational intellect and will. At apocalypse, the fiery female impulse rejoins conscious power of expression in an integrated, androgynous being imaged by Boehme as Sophia remarried to her son/mate, Christ. Mary, the mortal mother of Christ, is understood as a terrestrial "Type" of Sophia, as were Eve and other mothering figures in Christian history, a conception that influenced Jane Lead's identification with Sophia and her belief that "the pure in heart might come this Woman to be" (*Fountain of Gardens*, II, pp. 103–130, especially p. 125; I, p. 468).

Following the patriarchal outlines of his sources in nonrationalist philosophy, Boehme's androgyne is male, completed by nurturing female, who is generally assigned the values of the Other, as Simone de Beauvoir discusses that concept in *The Second Sex*.[14] And Behmenists John Pordage, Francis Lee, and Reverend Richard Roach, the sympathetic Anglican who served as historian for the Philadelphian Society, continue the metaphor unrevised in their writing about the soul as feminine and in their lives, as they literally ascribe special authority to the spiritual transformations of women. John Pordage depended first on his wife Mary's, then on Jane Lead's visions. Philadelphian Society historian Richard Roach asserts that Virgin Wisdom, "standing in the Female Denomination . . . will in an Extraordinary Manner Excite and Animate that sex whereby She is represented; and Endow them with her Peculiar Graces and Gifts, in such Degrees, that they shall Out-run and Exceed the Males themselves. . . ." Francis Lee attached himself to Jane

Lead until her death, considering her a "Pattern and Model in this and the Approaching Age."[15]

But what about the women, those token visionaries? Much in their experience might be familiar still. As Virginia Woolf and Adrienne Rich, among others, have observed, male patronage and wrongly-weighted, male-made tools for the urgently building female self have been continuous conditions for women writers.[16] But Behmenist ideas, their fantasies, and their social experiences as women *were* the tools for Jane Lead and others, who clearly used them. Philadelphian Society gatherings were so well attended by women, remarks Roach, "that it was thence call'd the Taffeta Meetings."[17] And, while Lead's imagination shows conflict between competing ideals— the apocalyptic mother/mate of Christ and the self-contained, primary female —she, like Woolf and Rich later, constructs a language of feeling, particularly female feeling, that speaks from the bound, radiant matrix of female experience. Working from her own actuality as a sentient human being uniting female soul with female intellect and will, she adapts received forms to accommodate her experience. To discover Sophia, for Jane Lead, is to recover self-sufficiency. "Now give me leave," she writes in her journal

> . . . to tell you the Beginning of my Way that the Spirit first led me into. In the first place, then, after some Years that I had lived in some good Degree of an Illuminated Knowledge, Setting under the Visible Teachings of Men, that could give no further light than they had arrived from others, through all of which I traced as a wandering Spirit that could find no Rest: but something still I found within my self that did open to draw in from a more pure Air, than I could meet without me: whereupon I introverted more into my own Inward Deep, where I did meet with that which I could not find elsewhere. . . .
>
> (*Fountain of Gardens*, I, p. 6)

With experience as guide, Lead urges

> Draw into thy Centre-deep . . . thy Heavens within . . . because the Virgin . . . there will first appear . . . Take present care of the Heavens of your Mind . . . Dive into your own Celestiality, and see with what manner of spirits you are endued: for in them the Powers do entirely lie for Transformation.
>
> (*Fountain of Gardens*, II, p. 137; 170)

The promise received in Lead's momentous April 1670 vision of Sophia is the power to give birth to a new self.

. . . Out of my womb thou shalt be brought forth after the Manner of a Spirit, conceived and born again; this shalt thou know by a new Motion of Life, stirring and giving a restlessness, till Wisdom be born within the inward parts of thy Soul . . . I will not fail to transfigure my self in Thy Mind. . . .

(Fountain of Gardens, I, pp. 18–21)

This bold break—"Thy mind must be cast in a new Mold of Imagination" —constitutes a new way of knowing. "None of her Offspring shall be brought up illiterate," remarks Lead, whose Society advocated female education, but who intended all acquired knowledge (the "Visible Teachings of Men") to illuminate inner capacity, "a creating Power, the Virgin's Omnipotency that will enable them to give a new Form, Virtue, and Purity to all things. . . ."[18]

One expression of this iconoclastic energy is literary form. Jane Lead freely chooses stylistic elements to represent the heightened, yet discursive, nature of her spiritual experience. Predominantly a mixture of exposition and symbolic narrative, her prose nevertheless relies on structural poetic effects of end-rhymed sentences, altered syntax, imagery, and extended metaphor. Especially in the earlier books, this poetic prose is also punctuated with formal poems, from short mottoes to several stanzas, that encapsulate theme and crystallize images from the prose. Overall, her oracular, epiphanic style suggests the mixed prose and poetry practiced by the Romantics, particularly William Blake in the varying experiments of *The Marriage of Heaven and Hell* and *A Vision of the Last Judgement*. Attempting, like Blake, to contain her idea of unified awareness in a compound style, she weaves her didactic statement imagistically and rhythmically to persuade rationality via affective, associative action, as Blake asks spectators to enter his *Last Judgement* by "The Fiery Chariot of . . . Contemplative Thought."

For purposes of initial inquiry and to describe her work most accurately, then, it is best not to classify Jane Lead exclusively as either poet or prose writer. Even more preliminarily, she should not be labeled solely as mystic, prophet, artist, model of the approaching age, fanatic, hysteric, or any other tag applied in her own day or more likely in ours. As the importance and historic range of women's imaginative writing is reexamined, new perceptions of women's ways of knowing and expressing necessarily follow. Generic categories of literature open up and standards of appreciation expand. The first task is to recognize, comprehensively, what in fact women have imagined, especially concerning selfhood, and then to devise adequately responsive criticism. Beginning at that open end, a critic of Jane Lead might initially describe her as a chronicler of subjectivity who employs the widely inclusive forms usually, though imprecisely, grouped as spiritual autobiography. In an age said to have had few women writers, she represents those women who saw themselves and were seen as visionaries rather than as artists; who wrote outside of literary mainstreams just as they had illuminations and formed congregations outside of institutionalized religion; and who made poetic form and tradition speak for them.

Although she worked largely in spiritual terms, the body of ideas Lead adapted is better known as poetic rather than as religious or philosophical tradition. Among the German idealist philosophers and radical Protestant theologians who contributed to English Romanticism, Jacob Boehme was enthusiastically admired by Blake, Coleridge, and the Yeats of *A Vision*.[19] Those poets' sexual metaphor for artistic process, with male creators and female materials and emanations, may well echo Boehme's cosmology. Long before the Romantics mined it for their poetry, Jane Lead discovered uses for the Behmenist ore.

The question of her own poetry is vexed, however. As noted, poems occur in her work. According to her son-in-law and editor, Francis Lee, she wrote those in her first book, *A Heavenly Cloud Now Breaking*. Internal evidence strongly suggests that she also wrote the poems in her second book, *The Revelation of Revelations*. Lee attributes others in her published journal to Richard Roach, who was poet as well as cleric. Still others in her other work, signed "by a friend of the author's," point to Roach more than Lead as author. Lee probably added them as editor. In turn, Lead's work appears extracted in Roach's polemic treatise, *The Imperial Standard of Messiah Triumphant . . .* (1727). Although sections of her *Heavenly Cloud* appear there, poems from that work are omitted; instead celebratory verses by Roach exhort her (then dead)

> Spy o' th' New Canaan, thither Millions lead;
> And our inferiour Souls at Distance due thy happy Foot-steps tread.
>
> (p. 244)

Though he courteously saw his soul as inferior, Roach apparently thought his poetic abilities superior to Lead's. In a poem from *Revelation of Revelations* that he includes in his *Imperial Standard* he makes unacknowledged changes of vocabulary and phrasing in nearly every line. Lead's "Heart of Deity/Whereout Spring secret pleasant things," for example, is changed to "Secret of the Deity/Whence Life immortal springs/All hidden Blessings, Pleasant Things" (*Revelation*, p. 24; *Imperial*, p. 237).

One conclusion is that Lead included her poetry in her work in the 1680s while she managed its editing and publication. After the editorial relationship with Lee began in the 1690s, he replaced her poems with ones by Roach, who went on to add "improved" versions of her poems in his own work. (Whether she continued to write poetry is not known. If she did not, the editorial relationship may have influenced her decision.) The framework of this interpretation is sexual politics of the spirit, or the sexual otherness of the inner life. Lee and Roach sincerely idealized Jane Lead as the image of their own souls and as indicative of the state of the primitive Christian church. They frequently defended women prophets in general and her in particular; they committed their spiritual lives largely to her guidance—and they helped to erase part of her experience. These university-trained men, one a scholar and critic of esoteric literature and the other a cleric-poet, perhaps felt ambivalence in their role as Boswells to little-educated women who wrote prolifically, sometimes even automatically. Evidence of such divided feeling appears in Lee's remarks on female imagination in another context, his *Dissertation Upon the Second Book of Esdras.* Citing ancient authorities on "diabolical conception" such as Eve's bearing the murderous Cain, Lee shows characteristic slippage between analogy of impregnation and its literal application to women, just as he concretizes the feminine soul.

> Indeed, the Key of the Matter is nothing but the Impregnation of the imaginative Power, in the superior Will, as descending into Materiality: To which some give the Name of the operative Idea; but others call it the magical Formation, or simply the *Magia.* In pregnant Women, the wonderful Effects of this operative Idea are so notorious, and the Impressions upon the Foetus, from the very Instant of its Conception, to the Birth, are so demonstrable, that I think it would be needless to say any thing on the Subject . . . It is most certain, that the Imagination of Eve was, whilst she bore Cain, most highly impregnated and exalted. And this Impregnation, and Exaltation of her Imagination, made her conceive, in her foolish Pride, among other Things, that she had gotten from the Lord, what she had really gotten from his Enemy the Wicked One, who had spirtually sown the evil Seed in the Faculties of her Mind. Whence, as a Woman transported out of herself, she could not but imagine that she was highly favoured of God herein.

(pp. 204–205)

This is standard, misogynist medical lore available to Lee as a physician, but contorted belief for the devoted secretary and advocate of a woman often transported out of herself and sure of her special gifts of mind.

Given the brief existence of Lead's actual poems, then, a sample from *A Heavenly Cloud Now Breaking* is here quoted in full.

The Ascension

What is this rushing sound which I now hear?
The fiery Chariots whirling through the Air,
For Souls to mount up to the Heavenly Station;
And there for to put on their Glorification.
Mount risen Souls, and not in Eden stay;
Life's Tree doth for you all its Fruits display.

Fear not, be bold, as Cherubs mount apace;
Ascend on high into your native place.
Love's Heart stands open; it is there alone,
You'l see God Face to Face in his bright Throne;
Where you shall Pleasures feel, Life, Joy, and Peace,
For you prepared that will never cease.

Mount then the Ladder, and to Heaven ascend;
There lies the Treasures, that shall never end;
Whose endless Riches so shall take your Eyes,
All temporal Wealth for it you shall despise.
The Income everlastingly shall flow;
And of the end of Wealth no one shall know.

In this Ascending State, all Spirits are
Free from all Thought, disburthen'd of all care:
For in this glorious, and this wealthy Land,
An endless Store, and Bank doth open stand;
Which still does multiply, increase, and grow,
As it does from the God-head Fountain flow.

(p. 33)

The poem is interesting, not so much for its technique, but for its historical value. That it exists at all is significant. That it exults in a state of expansive release signals one representative woman's awakening. That it is realized in traditional language shows her use of her culture on her own terms.

The rush of power that the poem describes, and that was associated with the bright Sun Woman, affected women other than Jane Lead, as the unpublished diaries of Philadelphian Society member Anne Bathurst show. She exclaims

I saw a pure white Light in me, like a bright beautiful Lamp, and in that light was my Angel . . . the Light being as a sun about her . . . And as I prayd I saw the Light and Her move in it, speaking every word which I prayd (it first arising from her) ... O Eternity has in it a large Subject to dip my pen & write from! And I see my angel of Spirit dip a pen ... Sure if my pen's liquor is to be from Eternity, it cannot be written dry.[20]

In both Lead's and Bathurst's accounts, formulaic elements of conversion experience and mystical vocabulary are apparent. That shared use of convention to stylize the self is part of what is being asserted in this discussion. Such accounts are neglected historical experiments by women constructing, from available forms and the authority of their experience, a language of self-presentation and self-affirmation. In the seventeenth century it was thought an impropriety for a woman to publish her activities, let alone her Inward Deep, as Jane Lead calls it, except within the sectarian audience.[21] There, the hunger for spiritual guidance made personal versions of apocalypse a type of popular literature. Along with a receptive audience, these women gained a genre, the revelation, in a confessional letter, journal, or essay. With it came a narrative voice, an artless speaker compelled by inner intensity. "It was in my purpose to have suspended any further manifestation of the Revelation that still followed me," Jane Lead wrote in 1683, "but Christ ... stood before me, and said, *Keep in Record the Journal of the new raised Life*, according to the Progression thou art going in ... Forbear not writing ..." (*Revelation of Revelations*, p. 1; italics in original). With traditional genre and speaker came individually sectarian conventions, in this case Boehme's symbolic structure of occult metaphysics, expressed in imagery of femaleness. For Jane Lead and others, revising the Behmenist Sophia gave access to their own apocalyptic identity—the image of their own fragmentation and potential unity. Lead exults "[Wisdom] would now be to me as Rebecca was to Jacob, to contrive and put me in a way how I should obtain the birthright-Blessing ... near at Hand, even in [my] own enclosed Ground" (*Fountain of Gardens*, I, pp. 25–26). The Blessing to be obtained, Lead affirms, is "one's own Native Country and original Virginity ..." (*Revelation of Revelations*, p. 47).

Having it out on her own premises, as Adrienne Rich puts it in a poem on Emily Dickinson.[22] Twentieth-century poetry is recovering that common ground, and the language of discovery strikingly resembles Jane Lead's.

In the morning after I was awaked from Sleep, upon a sudden I was insensible of any sensitivity as relating to a corporal Being, and found my self . . . being very sprightly and airy in a silent place . . . And I did suddainly see at a pritty distance . . . a rich splendrous thing come down all engraven, with Colours, the Ground whereof being all of Gold. It was in the form of a large Ship with Wings . . . it came down with the greatest swiftness imaginable . . . I saw myself, or something like my self, leaping and dancing and greatly rejoicing to meet it. But when I came up to it, then it did as suddainly go up agin, withdrawing out of all sight . . . After which I found my self in my Body of Sence, as knowing I had been ranging in my Spirit from it awhile. . . .

(*Fountain of Gardens*, III, pp. 66–67)

> My soul, my helicopter, whirred
> distantly, by habit, over
> the old pond with the half-drowned boat
>
> toward which it always veers
> for consolation: ego's Arcady:
> leaving the body stuck
> like a leaf against a screen. —
> . . .
>
> this time: my soul wheeled back
> and burst into my body
>
> Found! Ready or not.
> (Adrienne Rich, "In the Woods," 1963)

Flying ships, fiery chariots, wheeling souls leaving and returning to sensible bodies—the traditional aerial imagery of stages of transformation and enlightenment links these statements, although Rich's later one, showing the effects of added centuries of search, begins with deflated optimism and ends with surprise. The imagery is itself one surprise, since Rich writes in a context of political feminism that more adequately accommodates activity than passivity as a means of self-realization, but her poem explores contemplative self-awareness, nonetheless.

The whirling Wheel of my spirit finding no stay for itself, I resolve to make my Application, as not to be put off with anything less than the Kingdom and Reigning-Power of the Holy Ghost . . . and . . . to grasp in with love-violence, this my fair, wise, rich and noble Bride, well knowing . . . her Dowry was so great it would . . . set me free.

(*Fountain of Gardens*, I, p. 118)

> What they forget
> and what we must remember
> is that each queen can move, if she chooses,
> as far as she likes
> in any direction
> (Robin Morgan, "Kings' Gambit," 1976)

Recognitions of power for both Lead and Morgan here draw on familiar ecstatic language of riches, dowried brides, and queens. Combining these with other long-used images of effortless movement, fire, and light, and with appropriate dread in the search, Jane Lead and the poets seem to speak almost antiphonally across centuries.

> I am
> also a ruler of the sun,
> I am the woman
> whose hair lights up a dark room,
> whose words are matches
> (Diane Wakoski, "Sun Gods Have Sun Spots," 1973)

> . . . I
> am a pure acetylene
> Virgin
> (Sylvia Plath, "Fever 103°," 1961)

I did see my own Spirit as a Fire-flash, running up and down: sometimes descending into a Sea most deep, then ascending up to the Aetherial Clouds in a swift motion, taking up no rest, no where, but resolved to pass through all known and unknown Regions, to find out the Mystery of its own Original.

> (*Fountain of Gardens*, III, pp. 265–66)

> . . . but I
> Have a self to recover, a queen.
> Is she dead, is she sleeping?
> Where has she been,
> With her lion red body, her wings of glass?
>
> Now she is flying
> More terrible than she ever was. . . .
> (Sylvia Plath, "Stings," 1961)[23]

The most immediate literary background for these recent poets' female imagery might include Blakean or Yeatsian emanations, the elusive, glowing female forms of male creative struggle. But these women poets work with a Romanticism revised, with the female as both artist and emanation, with a female self irradiated.[24] Sandra M. Gilbert has pointed out the changes these and other poets are making in the self-defining, confessional mode traceable to English and American Romantics. Women, more ambivalently subjective than men in an androcentric universe, do not write confidently from a tradition of self-mythologizing, Gilbert suggests, but rather "in the hope of discovering or defining a self, a certainty, a tradition."[25] These poets alter the Blakean imagery of selfhood as they reshape the Wordsworthian narrator and genre, and in the process they do discover a double-strand tradition. Through the Romantic inheritance that includes Boehme, Blake, and aspects of Yeats, they reach ancient symbolism for transformation of the spirit. More important, by revising that inherited language, they extend the work of seventeenth-century sectarian women who reforged Behmenist language at an earlier stage to fit their actuality and to express a female ideal, the Woman Cloathed with the Sun, or, as Jane Lead sometimes calls her, "the Wonder Woman."

If, as evidence suggests, her awakening recurs from the Eleusinian mysteries of Demeter to the Protestant Reformation to present-day feminism, it is apparently a key metaphor for female selfhood. Generally we think of the act it represents as a response to history, a breaking out impelled by women's psychological reaction to oppression. But history, while it may account for the experience, only initially explains the structure of the metaphor. A developed explanation might include philosophy, biology, and anthropology, too.

The similarities of feminist theory and mystic philosophy are beginning to be noticed, but implications for literary study are still largely unexplored.[26] Yet, when Adrienne Rich describes feminist time—"We find ourselves at once in prehistory and in science fiction"—and critic Cynthia Secor maps feminist space—"I've been living on the edge so long it feels like the center to me"—the combined statements project a paradoxical world view of intensely subjective nonexistence that is as traditional to mysticism as it is familiar to feminists.[27] The intellectual history of feminist thought is usually traced to modern, rationally based, logical theories of equality and not to ancient analogues of transcendence.[28] Yet, the connections of ecstasy and feminism (as affirmation of the female) may be very old. Caroline Spurgeon remarks that our word "mysticism" was derived by the Neoplatonists from the Greek for the term originally applied to initiates in the worship of Demeter.[29] In feminist art, an art notably rooted in the personal that is also political and universal, the problems of subject and object demand consideration of backgrounds in idealist and nonrationalist philosophy.

Those roots of thought are helpful because they, more than empiric theories, try to comprehend unity or continuum of being among planes of existence. Sophia is an idea of expressing being, of giving identity to existence, on any plane. Following Jane Lead boldly into less-known regions to find out the mystery of origins (and turning inside-out Francis Lee's patriarchal theory of woman's body/mind), we must explore relationships between biological and imaginative expressivity. We have yet to sketch feminist cosmology in this sense, although it is a direction taken by groups currently interested in health and healing. Here, the red-bodied, flame-haired, disappearing and reappearing queen in recent poetry may well be projection of the menstrual cycle, transmuted to the capacity of renewing or giving birth to one's self. Ready or not, we must speculate that anatomy is part of epiphany. Our bodies, our visions is one of the aesthetic implications of feminist thought.[30]

The physical experience of a body converts into emotional attitudes and symbolism, according to Mary Douglas in her social anthropological study, *Natural Symbols: Explorations in Cosmology*. In systematic, symbolizing thought such as cosmology, we base our images in the system we "know" best, the body. But, Douglas suggests, there are really two bodies, the physical and the social. Body symbolism, especially as derived from body expression in blood, breath, and excrement, engages a social context in which the physical is perceived. For those who can identify themselves with authority and established institutions, with holding in, physical control and social control may become metaphors of each other. Women as a group, and others whose social experience is marginal, may value escape, abandonment, and release more than formal behavior. For Douglas, the high degree of women's membership in possession cults and ecstatic religions is more convincingly explained by societal position than by sexual repression, as psychoanalytic thought proposes.[31]

We need a comprehensive theory of women's imagination that draws, at the least, from these suggestions. Female imagination may work from biological patterning for emission of blood, babies, and milk, compounded with existence in a social context that ambivalently worships and fears precisely that expressivity and limits female range accordingly. If so, then it is not surprising that women's imaginative reality, including self-apotheosis, emerges from a fused core of felt capacity and restraint, of power and powerlessness, of peculiarly female wish and fear. Under receptive conditions of personal/cultural upheaval and accessible symbolic forms as they developed for Jane Lead in the seventeenth century and again for poets and other women in the twentieth, that core may well split to release the wish, the queen who can, if she chooses, move as far as she likes in any direction—be she prophet, poet, critic, or a new Mold of Imagination.

2.

Anne Bradstreet's Poetry:
A Study of Subversive Piety

Wendy Martin

Although Anne Bradstreet was careful to observe Puritan restrictions on the feminine role in her domestic life, her feminist predilections are clearly expressed in her poetry. In *The Tenth Muse Lately Sprung Up in America*, published in England in 1650, Bradstreet included an elegy "In Honor of the High and Mighty Princess, Queen Elizabeth, *Of Happy Memory*," in which she reminds her readers of a time when the prevailing patterns of power were reversed:

> Nay Masculines, you have thus taxt us long,
> But she, though dead, will vindicate our wrong.
> Let such as say our Sex is void of Reason,
> Know tis a Slander now, but once was Treason.[1]

By celebrating Elizabeth I's political power and personal magnetism, Bradstreet undermines the authority of the Puritan patriarchs:

> Full fraught with honour, riches and with dayes
> She set, she set, like *Titan* in his rayes.
> No more shall rise or set so glorious sun
> Untill the heavens great revolutions.
> If then new things their old forms shall retain,
> *Eliza* shall rule *Albion* once again.
>
> (361)

This poem is a tribute to female power that is not regulated and controlled by men; the Queen in her radiant splendor is depicted as inspiring her subjects rather than chastising or correcting her constituents as do the Puritan magistrates. Bradstreet's apotheosis of Queen Elizabeth is subversive in a culture in which history is providential, that is, viewed as a means for teaching and understanding the intricate design of God's plan for man. In order to understand just how daring Bradstreet was, it is necessary to examine the fabric of the Puritan society in which she lived.

When Anne Dudley Bradstreet (1612–1672) arrived in the new world with her father Thomas Dudley and her husband Simon Bradstreet, she admitted that her "heart rose" in rebellion against the Puritan mission. She was eighteen and unhappy about being forced to leave her comfortable life in the mansion of the Earl of Lincolnshire where her father was steward. The emigration of the Dudleys and the Bradstreets from England was the result of political and religious differences between the Puritans and King Charles I, but the grievances that spurred the formation of the Massachusetts Bay Colony and the vision that brought the *Arbella* to the American shore in 1630 were not hers but belonged to the two men she loved.[2] As John Berryman writes in his remarkable eulogy, "Homage to Mistress Bradstreet," "I come to stay with you, / and the governor, and Father, and Simon, and the huddled men."[3]

The conviction of divine destiny that spurred the Puritans to endure the hardships of the ocean crossing was later called by Samuel Danforth "the errand into the wilderness"; but this messianic mission was grounded in economic necessity as well as in spiritual consensus. The Massachusetts Bay joint stock company, of which Thomas Dudley was a founder and Simon Bradstreet a deputy secretary, specified the legal and financial requirements of the pilgrimage, just as the enumeration of the spiritual duties of covenant theology shaped the religious destiny of the Puritan tribe.[4]

Anne Bradstreet was dismayed by the conditions at Salem; in addition to sickness, housing was poor and food supplies uncertain. Whatever degree of pride she possessed caused her to deny her part in the tribal destiny:

> [I] came into this Country, where I found a new world and new manners, at which my heart rose. But after I was convinced it was the way of God, I submitted to it and joined the church at Boston.[5]

This was not *her* mission—her "heart rose"—but this was an assertion of self that had to be subdued and ultimately destroyed. Her submission, as she tells us, is to join the church at Boston; that is, by joining the congregation she reconciled herself to the Puritan mission and to her fate as a sinner and a pilgrim.

According to Puritan doctrine, "the prideful monster of independence" must give way to dependence on the Divine Will. Redemption required the surrender of individual autonomy to God: paradoxically, liberty is conferred through bondage. From the age of four or five, Puritan children were drilled in the lesson that the hopeless corruption of the human race could never be undone—"in Adam's Fall / We sinned All," they read in the *New England Primer*. Anne Bradstreet's poem "On Childhood" emphasizes this conviction of the indelibility of original sin, and the impossibility of ever again returning to a state of primal grace and innocence: "Stained from birth with Adam's *sinfull* fact, / Thence I began to sin as soon as act."[6]

Salvation was uncertain and could not be earned by good works; it was a gift from God, whose infinite grace and mercy was extended to the Elect. Because redemption was marked by faith not accomplishments, and salvation or election was uncertain, continual self-scrutiny and introspection were required in order to be ready for conversion: introspection was necessary in order to have a "heart prepared" to be called by God. This extraordinary uncertainty of spiritual destiny caused Puritans to scrutinize their lives for signs of salvation, for visible evidence for an invisible state. Experience was emblematic, history providential.

Ironically, suffering was a form of joy because the disaster that occasions it is a sign of God's love. In a domestic version of the fortunate fall, Anne Bradstreet writes to her children:

> Among all my experiences of God's gratious Dealings with me I have constantly observed this, that he never suffered me long to sit loose from him, but by one affliction or other hath made me look home, and search what was amiss—so usually it hath been with me that I have no sooner felt my heart out of order, but I have experienced correction for it, which most commonly hath been upon my own person, in sicknesse, weakeness, paines, sometimes on my soul, in doubts and feeres of God's displeasure, and my sincerity toward him.
>
> (5–6)

Anne Bradstreet accepted her illnesses as divine correction, and as a reminder of her moral frailty: "After some time I fell into a lingering sicknes like a consumption, together with a lamenesse, which correction I saw the Lord sent to humble and try me and doe mee good: and it was not altogether ineffectual" (5). Elizabeth Wade White speculates that Anne Bradstreet suffered recurrent illnesses due to a rheumatic heart;[7] it is significant that Anne Bradstreet's heartsickness was triggered whenever she was unable to sustain the tension, which was at times almost unbearable for her, between spirit and flesh, faith and doubt, renunciation and temptation, the regenerate and unregenerate, and the eternal and temporal that is the core of Puritanism.

As one of the most strenuous forms of Christianity, Puritanism is based on the central paradox that the death of the body brings the possibility of the eternal life of the spirit in union with God. The body pulls the Christian toward earth; "carnality" is Satan's lure. The body, then, becomes an arena for the battle between Satan and God. Anne Bradstreet conveys the intensity of this struggle in her poem "The Flesh and the Spirit," a dialogue between two sisters about the desires of the body and the aspirations of the soul:

> "Sister," quoth Flesh, "what liv'st thou on
> Nothing but Meditation?
> Doth Contemplation feed thee so
> Regardlessly to let earth go?
>
> (381–82)

Flesh proceeds to catalogue the pleasures of this world—honor, fame, accolades, riches: "Earth hath more silver, pearls, and gold / Than eyes can see or hands can hold." Spirit retorts:

> Be still, thou unregenerate part,
> Disturb no more my settled heart,
> For I have vowed, (and so will do)
> Thee as a foe, still to pursue,
> And combat with thee and must,
> Until I see thee laid in th' dust.
>
> (382–83)

Spirit berates Flesh for distracting her from God's glory with the "bait" of earthly treasures. Scorning secular honor, Spirit announces, "My greatest honor it shall be / When I am victor over thee" (383). The tension, even enmity of body and soul in the Christian *ethos* is resolved only with the destruction of the body, "the unregenerate part," which liberates the spirit from the body's cage so that it can wear royal robes, "More glorious than the glistr'ing sun" in a place where disease and death—the infirmities of the body—do not exist.

If physical suffering was a measure of piety, Anne Bradstreet's letters, occasional poems, and poetic aphorisms are a litany of the struggling spirit: "I had a sore fitt of fainting, which lasted 2 or 3 days," she writes on July 8, 1656. On September 30, 1657, she records, "It pleased God to visit me with my old Distemper," adding, "I can no more live without correction than without food" (23). For the Puritans, affliction is a sign of the intimate bond between God and His children, it is not an indication of cruelty. God is a stern—not a sadistic—father. On August 28, 1656, Anne Bradstreet wrote:

. . . God doth not afflict willingly, nor take delight in grieving the children of men: he hath no benefitt by my adversity, nor is he the better for my prosperity; but he doth it for my Advantage, and that I may be a Gainer by it. And if he knows that weakness and a frail body is best to make me a vessell fit for his use. Why should I not bare it, not only willingly but joyfully.

(20)

Anne Bradstreet's faith was often severely tested and her doubt was, at times, overwhelming: ". . . sometimes I have said, Is there any faith upon the earth? And I have not known what to think" (9–10). Sometimes Bradstreet's despair prevented her from sleeping:

> By night when others soundly slept,
>   And had at once both ease and Rest,
> My waking eyes were open kept,
>   And so to lie I found it best.

(11)

And she experienced more than one dark night of the soul:

I have often been perplexed that I have not found that constant Joy in my Pilgrimage and refreshing which I supposed most servants of God have. . . . Yet have I many times sinkings and droopings, and not enjoyed that felicity that sometimes I have done. But when I have been in darkness and seen no light, yet have I desired to stay myself upon the Lord.

(7)

It was expected that all pilgrims would have trials, and the afflictions that Anne Bradstreet records in her letters are part of the tradition of the testing of the soul to which both men and women were submitted. However, Cotton Mather's account of his soul's testing reveals significant differences. In his diary Mather recorded that once when he had doubts he lay prostrate on the floor lamenting his "Loathesomeness," overwhelmed "by a Flood of Tears, that ran down upon the floor . . . this Conversation with Heaven, left a sweet, a calm, a considerate, a sanctifying, an Heavenly Impression upon my Soul."[8] John Winthrop also reported that he underwent a process of humiliation and preparation before receiving confirmation of his faith; he wrote, "the good spirit breathed upon my soule, and said that I should live."[9] Although God's testing never ceased, permitting no rest for the Puritan conscience, Mather and Winthrop seem to have been comforted and sustained in their doubt, and they appear to have been much more certain of God's love than was Bradstreet. Her belief in God's grace was often the result of her willed resolution; her determination to resist temptation, and her self-discipline enabled her to welcome spiritual and physical affliction as God's "tender mercies."

Perhaps Anne Bradstreet's doubts about her worthiness were more intense than either Mather's or Winthrop's because she did not shape the world in which she lived. Both her father and husband were intensely involved in the governing of the church during frequent disputes about covenant theology and the fine points of church membership. Dudley was a church magistrate with Winthrop, and Bradstreet was governor of Massachusetts Bay; as pillars of the community, they were called upon to make decisions about the relationship of the church Elders—that is, the elected representatives of the church—to the congregation. Perhaps the social prominence and concrete responsibilities of these two men tended to mitigate their anxiety about salvation. Although the Puritans believed that God could be served in a variety of ways—that all callings were equal—domestic piety is less impressive than public service. Confinement to private life narrows the arena in which faith can be exercised and tested. The exhortation of Peter to "declare the wonderful deeds of him that called you out of the darkness into his marvelous light" (I Peter 2:9–10) is difficult to execute in the kitchen or nursery; it is more easily done from the pulpit or podium.

The field of service available to Anne Bradstreet was her home, her family, and her poetry. But even this internal, private landscape was treacherous, as the expulsion of Ann Hutchinson from Massachusetts Bay had demonstrated. Ann Hutchinson's efforts to participate in theological issues by holding meetings in her home proved the very real dangers of stepping beyond the boundaries of prescribed behavior. Her trial and subsequent exile demonstrated the dangers of listening too carefully to an inner voice which might be the voice of Satan and not God's at all. Both Hutchinson and Bradstreet were in a double bind: as part of the Puritan tribe, they were obliged to "go forth and make disciples of all nations" (Matthew 28:19), but the powerful intelligence of both women was not permitted public expression. It is not surprising that they found private solutions—Bradstreet in her poetry, Hutchinson in her meetings at home; however, religious politics proved to be more dangerous than writing poetry.[10]

Anne Bradstreet's isolation from the larger community was especially acute during her husband's frequent and sometimes long absences while he was on business for the church. Her poems to Simon Bradstreet make it clear that she loved him deeply:

> If ever two were one, then surely we.
> If ever man were lov'd by wife, then thee;

> If ever wife was happy in a man,
> Compare with me ye women if you can.
>   ("My Dear & Loving Husband," 394)

In another poem, titled "A Letter to Her Husband, Absent Upon Public Employment," she asks, "How stayest thou there, whilst I at Ipswich lye?" In still another, she laments:

> Commend me to the man more lov'd than life,
> Shew him the sorrows of his widdowed wife;
> My dumpish thoughts, my groans, my brakish tears
> My sobs, my longing hopes, my doubting fears,
> And if he love, how can he there abide?
>   (396)

She "bewail[s] my turtle true, who now is gone" and again expresses her longing for him:

> Together at one tree, oh let us brouze,
> And like two turtles roost within one house,
> And like the Mullets in one River glide,
> Let's still remain but one, till death divide.
>   (398)

As governor, Simon Bradstreet's duties to his constituents were time-consuming. It would have been selfish, therefore sinful, of Anne Bradstreet to claim more of his energy; to make further demands on him would mean that she was interfering with his calling by placing herself between her husband and God. Her role as wife and mother was carefully limited by Puritan custom, which defined marriage as a partnership for producing young Christians in which responsibilities were made explicit. While accepting the necessity of marriage, Puritans were concerned that conjugal love would tempt the married couple to lose sight of God, and they were warned against such idolatrous unions: "when we exceedingly delight ourselves in Husbands or Wives, or Children, [it] much benumbs and dims the light of the Spirit," warned John Cotton.[11] Anne Bradstreet's poems reveal that she struggled with the conflict between her love for her children and husband and her devotion to God; repeatedly, she reminds herself of her duty as wife and mother to assist her family in the service of God. To love them for their own sake would indicate a dangerous attachment to this world.

There was considerable emphasis placed on the family as the basic unit of the Puritan Commonwealth. Cotton Mather asserted that *"well-ordered* families naturally produce Good Order in other *Societies.* When Families

are under an *Ill Disciplined*, will feel the Error in *The First Concoction*."[12]
The relationship of husband and wife received considerable attention; her
duty was to "keep at home, educating her children, keeping and improving
what is got by the industry of the man."[13] She was to "guid the house and
not guid the husband."[14] Those husbands who failed to maintain a domi-
nant position were censured, as John Winthrop's excoriation of Ann Hutch-
inson's husband demonstrates: "A man of very mild temper and weak parts,
and wholly guided by his wife."[15]

Similarly, women who stepped beyond their domestic confines through
literature—by reading or writing—were considered dangerous to themselves
and society. John Winthrop's journal entry for April 13, 1645, reflects the
Puritan bias against intellectual women:

> [Anne Hopkins] has fallen into a sad infirmity, the loss of her understand-
> ing and reason, which had been growing upon her divers years, by occasion
> of her giving herself wholly to reading and writing, and had written many
> books.[16]

Puritans expressed considerable scorn for women who wrote or published.
In 1650 Thomas Parker wrote a public letter condemning his sister for pub-
lishing a book in London: "Your printing of a Book beyond the Custom
of your Sex, doth rankly smell."[17] This critical attitude toward women
writers was especially difficult for Anne Bradstreet to accept because child-
hood training prepared her to think of herself as an intelligent and articulate
person. Under her father's tutelage, she learned Greek, Latin, and Hebrew;
she read Sidney, Spenser, Shakespeare, Raleigh, and duBartas. She also
probably read Homer, Aristotle, Hesiod, Xenophon, and Pliny; and, of
course, she read the Geneva Bible.[18] In general, she was educated in the
Elizabethan tradition, which valued the educated and artistic woman.[19] It
must have been extremely difficult for Anne Bradstreet to sustain her faith
in her abilities as a poet in what she experienced as an alien environment.
But it was probably rebellion against her harsh, punitive environment that
energized her to write. Perhaps it was even a matter of writing or going
mad, as John Berryman suggests:

> Versing, I shroud among the dynasties;
> Quaternion on quaternion, tireless I phrase
> anything past, dead, far,
> sacred, for a barbarous place.[20]

It is true that there is a dogged quality in some of her longer works such as
"The Four Monarchies" which suggests a need to persist in the creation of
a large work that exceeded her desire for aesthetic expression. She wrote

her quaternions relentlessly, with considerable ferocity, possibly to subdue the considerable rage she must have felt as a thinking woman in a society which had no use for her abilities.[21]

Anne Bradstreet persisted in her poetry until she had enough material for *The Tenth Muse*, which was published in 1650 due to the efforts of her brother-in-law, Reverend John Woodbridge, who had taken her manuscript with him to London and had arranged for its publication there. The fact that Anne Bradstreet did not seek publication directly but did so by proxy has been interpreted as a sign of her modesty and piety, but this indirect approach was a practical way to circumvent the accusation of excessive ambition.

She was also careful to disclaim any interest in receiving the kind of attention given her male peers; however, more than one reader has perceived irony in these lines of her prologue: "Give Thyme or Parsley, I ask no bayes." In the preface to her volume, John Woodbridge proclaims it the

> Work of a Woman, honoured, and esteemed where she lives, for her gracious demeanor, her eminent parts, her pious conversation, her courteous disposition, her exact diligence in her place, and discreet managing of her Family occasions.
>
> (83–84)

Woodbridge makes it clear that no time was taken from her family obligations to write her book: "[it is] the fruit but of some few hours, curtailed from sleep and other refreshments" (84); and he insists that he has "presumed to bring to publick view, which she [Bradstreet] resolved in such manner should never see the sun" (84).

The Tenth Muse reveals Bradstreet's interest in a gynocentric universe. As we have seen, her elegy of Queen Elizabeth is a tribute to female power that is not regulated and controlled by men; the Queen eclipses the authority of the New England divines, and her regal self-assertion is a dramatic contrast to the fallen Christian woman whose only possibility for redemption lies in self-abnegation. Queen Elizabeth's royal edicts provide a healthy corrective for the passivity of the Puritan woman who was compelled to attend church meetings three times a week but forbidden to take part in the interpretation of Scripture.

In her poems "The Four Elements" and "Of the Four Humours in Mans Constitution," Anne Bradstreet stresses the unity of life rather than the dominance of one group over another; she creates a cosmology in which the Aristotelian hierarchy gives way to an elaborate allegorical scheme that depends on cooperation rather than competition. Bradstreet creates an essentially female cosmology that marks the shift from the stratified concept of the great Chain of Being in which disruption of the orderly sequence is perceived as chaos to a world in which balance is achieved by the mutual interaction of the elements.

The four elements—earth, air, fire, and water—and the four humors— blood, choler, phlegm, and melancholy—are depicted as antagonistic sisters whose quarrels threaten to disrupt the universe. In "The Four Elements" each sister was so intent on achieving dominance that the turbulence in the form of floods, fires, storms, and earthquakes resulting from their wrangling threatened to destroy the cosmos. In the hierarchical world-view such disruption is the harbinger of total chaos and therefore feared. But in Bradstreet's cosmology the sisters' struggle for dominance is resolved by their collective realization that each of them plays an essential part in the functioning of the cosmos, that the interaction of the elements creates balance. The feared chaos gives way to the birth of a new world-view in which process takes precedence over product, and dominance gives way to mutuality. This need for mutuality is also recognized by the sisters representing the four humors of the body:

> Unless we agree, all falls into confusion.
> Let Sanguine with her hot hand Choler hold,
> To take her moist my moisture will be bold:
> My cold, cold melancholys hand shall clasp;
> Her dry, dry Cholers other hand shall grasp.
> Two hot, two moist, two cold, two dry here be,
> A Golden Ring, the Posey unity.
>
> (145–46)

Unity based on cooperation, not order based on dominance, becomes the key to Bradstreet's view of the universe.

Unlike Cotton Mather in *Magnalia Christi Americani* or Edward Johnson in *Wonder-Working Providence of Scion's Saviour in New England*, Bradstreet did not focus her energy on providential history or on the exemplary lives of the saints. The communal destiny of the Puritan tribe did not engage her imagination; it was especially daring of her to ignore the acceptable subject of the Puritan Commonwealth because it was one of the few subjects deemed appropriate for literary efforts.

By determining her own priorities, Bradstreet risked being branded as a heretic. Ann Hutchinson had been exiled as an Antinomian for insisting on her intellectual autonomy, and Bradstreet, as a practicing poet, ran the risk of denunciation by the church elders. Bradstreet probably knew the details of Ann Hutchinson's trial and banishment. Both Simon Bradstreet, who was an assistant in the General Court, and her father, Thomas Dudley, who was deputy governor at the time of the trial, were on the board of public magistrates that convicted Hutchinson. Dudley was especially hostile to Hutchinson, accusing her of being a troublemaker from the moment she landed in Massachusetts Bay and blaming her for endangering the foundation of the church. He was, in short, one of her harshest critics. During the trial he badgered her with the subtlest distinctions in the points of theology, attempting to trick her at every turn with his legalistic definitions of difference between covenants of works and grace in order to get her to perjure herself.[22] Surely, her father's hostility to Ann Hutchinson was not lost on Anne Bradstreet.

Anne Bradstreet's father died in 1853, when she was forty-one, and his death marked a transition from the rigorous public codes of the old divines to a more relaxed and private approach to faith. Although the compromises regarding church membership intensified anxiety (by creating ambiguity), at least the inner life was less subject to the scrutiny of the church Elders. Perhaps as a response to the growing liberalism of the church, in the years following her father's death Anne Bradstreet wrote poems primarily about her domestic life and private religious meditations. In 1657, three years before her death, she wrote a long letter to her "dear children" in which she enumerated her sicknesses and afflictions, which she described as evidence of God's "abundant Love to my straying soul which in prosperity is too much in love with the world." One of her major poems of this period, "Contemplations," chronicled her struggle between her worldly inclinations and her longing for eternity. It is a poem of great power—lyrical, carefully crafted, sufficiently accomplished to cause some critics to speculate about its having been read by the Romantic poets.[23] While describing the vanity of this life and her yearning for eternity, she immerses herself in sensory experience celebrating the plenitude of nature and the generative power of the elements:

> Then higher on the glistering Sun I gaz'd,
> Whose beams was shaded by the leavie Tree,
> The more I look'd, the more I grew amaz'd,
> And softly said, what glory's like to thee?
> Soul of this world, this Universes Eye,
> No wonder, some made thee a Deity:
> Had I not better known, (alas) the same had I.
>
> (371)

Paradoxically, the more the poet longs to transcend the world, the more she feels drawn by nature's power. Her metaphor of sun as the earth's husband is suffused with eroticism:

Thus as a Bridegroom from my Chamber rushes,
And as a strong man, joyes to run a race,
The morn doth usher thee, with smiles & blushes,
The Earth reflects her glances in thy face.
Birds, insects, Animals with Vegative,
The heart from death and dulness doth revive:
And in the darksome womb of fruitful nature dive.

(371)

However, the poem concludes with an acceptance of mutability and death and underscores the vanity of earthly desires. In this poem Anne Bradstreet transcends this world by experiencing and even savoring its pleasures, and her final decision to reject earthly pleasures is achieved by immersing herself in them.

Bradstreet's "Meditations Divine and Moral," written for her son Simon in 1664, convey an entirely different mood of spare practicality. Based on the *Bay Psalm Book*, these aphoristic meditations correlate domestic observations with religious analogs. In terse form they are spiritual exercises which document a pilgrim's progress:

(VI) The finest bread hath the least bran;
the purest honey, the least wax; and the sincerest
Christian, the least self love. (49)

(XVI) The house which is not often swept,
makes the cleanly inhabitant soon loath it, and
the heart which is not continually purifying
itself, is no fit temple for the spirit of God
to dwell in. (51)

The spareness of language, the carefully worked-out metaphors demonstrate not only discipline but a concentration on spiritual concerns characteristic of her later years.

Perhaps Anne Bradstreet's most effective poem, certainly her most frequently anthologized, is "Verses Upon the Burning of Our House, July 10th, 1666." Like "Contemplations," this poem's power is the result of the very poignant tension between her worldly concerns as represented by her household furnishings and her spiritual aspirations:

Here stood that Trunk, and there that chest;
There lay that store I counted best:
My pleasant things in ashes lye,
And them behold no more shall I.
Under thy roof no guest shall sit,
Nor at thy Table eat a bit.

(41)

The poem leaves the reader with the painful impression of a woman in her mid-fifties who, having lost her domestic comforts, is left to struggle with despair at her loss, a loss which, however mitigated by faith in the greater rewards of Heaven, is very tragic: "Farewell my Pelf, farewell my Store. / The world no longer let me Love, / My hope and Treasure lyes Above" (42).

A poem written three years later on August 31, 1669, "Longing for Heaven," reveals a profound world-weariness: no longer is there a tension between earth and heaven, temporal and eternal concerns; instead there is a longing for release from physical frailty and hope for immortality.[24]

> As weary pilgrim, now at rest,
>   Hugs with delight his silent nest
> His wasted limbes, now lye full soft
>   That myrie steps, have troden oft
> Blesses himself, to think upon
>   His dangers past, and travailes done.
>   (42)

In the last months of her life Bradstreet was very sick; her son Simon Bradstreet wrote in his diary that she was "wasted to skin & bone . . . much troubled with rheum," and she had a badly ulcerated arm.[25] She died on September 16, 1672; she was sixty years old. For most of her life she was the dutiful and loving wife of Simon Bradstreet, the devoted mother of eight children, and the resolute child of God. Her poetry reflects the tensions and conflicts of a person struggling for selfhood in a culture that was outraged by individual autonomy and that valued poetry to the extent that it praised God. Anne Bradstreet's subversive piety made her vulnerable to both her earthly and heavenly fathers, but she dared to speak out and her voice can still be heard.

3.

Anne Finch, Countess of Winchilsea: An Augustan Woman Poet

Katharine Rogers

Anne Finch, Countess of Winchilsea (1661–1720), is important not only as a gifted poet but as a unique example—a poet who was both a woman and an Augustan. In many ways a typical Augustan, she wrote in all the traditional genres, from flippant songs to ponderous Pindaric odes. Yet because she was a woman, her poems are subtly different from those of her male contemporaries. She shows a distinctive sincerity in her love poetry, a distinctive standard in her satire, a distinctive simplicity in her response to nature, and a distinctive freedom from the Augustan writer's obligation to make public statements.

Generally speaking, this difference is not a matter of conscious outlook and aims. Winchilsea shared many characteristic Augustan attitudes, such as distrust for the mob and a sophisticated acceptance of human weaknesses coupled with suspicion of human grandiosity.[1] She consistently upheld reason—not only her satire on irrational deviations, but her devotion to her husband is rational, as well as her religion and her appreciation of nature. There is a reasonable basis for all her feelings, and none are expressed with sentimentality or "enthusiasm." Her love poems are restrained and her nature poems precise. She wrote in the usual Augustan verse forms, particularly heroic couplets, although she was less prone to smartly decisive antithesis than John Dryden or Alexander Pope.

As an Augustan writer who was also a woman, Winchilsea faced peculiar problems. Of course women authors have always written in a masculine tradition, but the Augustan period was especially male-oriented. For one thing, the poet saw himself as a public figure—celebrating national events, reprehending the vices of society, relating personal experience to universal moral principles. And women were confined, by their opportunities and experience and what was assumed to be their capacity, to private social life and the domestic sphere: they were not, supposedly, qualified to pronounce on the Use of Riches or the Reign of Dullness. For another, the poet was following in the footsteps of the Roman poets, who wrote from a conspicuously male point of view.

This is particularly evident in the genre of the love lyric. For the Roman erotic poets, love for a woman was a superficial feeling based on desire. It could be intensely pleasurable, though surprisingly often it was painful—but in any case it was classed with such sensual pleasures as drinking. Often love and drinking are balanced against the higher pleasure of friendship, which is always assumed to exist between men. Women appeared in this poetry only as more or less unworthy love objects, existing for the amusement of men.

Love poets of the Restoration and early eighteenth century followed this convention unquestioningly. Almost without exception, the love poems of John Wilmot, Earl of Rochester, Sir Charles Sedley, William Wycherley, and Matthew Prior (an almost exact contemporary of Winchilsea) are addressed to mistresses, not wives, and mistresses who are usually transient and never taken seriously. By definition they are beautiful (otherwise no one could love them); the only possible variations are that they may or may not be "kind" (that is, willing to sleep with the poet without marriage),[2] and they may or may not be constant (until he is ready to move on). The woman appears always as a generalized sex object, never individualized enough to be identifiable. Wycherley even argues that an ex-mistress has no right to reproach him for leaving her, for it is she who has changed, not he: he has remained "true to Love and Beauty" in leaving her for a younger woman.[3]

Because the Restoration poets wrote in reaction against the fatuous idealization of much Renaissance love poetry, their erotic verse is frequently hostile, showing the lover vilifying his mistress or relieving his frustrations by raping her.[4] The characteristic Restoration mood is total cynicism: honor and faithfulness are stupid, since women and men inevitably cheat each other. The fact that "The Imperfect Enjoyment" (resulting from impotence) was a favorite theme in this poetry shows both the total physicality of the love involved and its chronically unsatisfactory nature.[5] The poet Rochester constantly associates love with negative feelings. Not pleasure, but pain is its sure proof—"Kind jealous doubts, tormenting fears, / And anxious cares" provide the only reliable evidence. Even his relatively positive poems on love reveal a negative undertone. The love lyrics he exchanged with his wife led to the conclusion that she had better treat him with scorn and coldness lest she lose his love.[6]

Prior, writing some years later than the Restoration rakes, softened their attitude. But his affection for "Chloe," his long-term mistress, is superficial and patronizing. "On Beauty" would seem to flatter women by paying tribute to their power. However, this power is equated with beauty (as if that were a woman's only significance), and the triumph it produces is hardly complimentary: Chloe has shown her power by drawing him away from every important concern, from "Ambition, Business, Friendship, News, / My useful Books, and serious Muse." Her beauty has made him submit to sit with her and talk "Of Idle Tales, and foolish Riddles."[7]

Now how could a woman function in such a tradition? For one thing, unless she was prepared to cast off her reputation publicly like Aphra Behn, she was shut out by its licentiousness. Obviously, she could not write to her lovers as the men could write to their mistresses. Nor could she treat love as a trivial amusement, since it was not a pastime for her but a central focus of her life. The only man a respectable woman could write to was her husband, and in those days of mercenary arranged marriages she might well not find him a suitable inspiration. Winchilsea was fortunate in this respect—she and her husband loved each other deeply—so that she could write to him as passionately as the men did to their mistresses. More so, in fact, since the relationship she was celebrating was so much more significant.

In "To Mr. F. Now Earl of W." she cleverly makes use of the conventions to express her own deeper feelings. Her husband is away and has asked her to greet him on his return with a poem. In typical Augustan manner, she appeals to the Muses, who are ready to assist until they discover, to their amazement and shock, what she is asking them to do—to help her express love for her husband! No, they cannot lend their aid to such an outlandish enterprise. No beau in the coffee houses "That wore his Cloaths with common Sense" (notice how the sly equation of reason with dressing suggests the beau's superficiality) could excuse "mention of a *Spouse*."

The Muses all send excuses, but Urania, the muse of heavenly love, tells the poet in confidence that heartfelt love can be expressed without the Muses' inspiration. So Winchilsea relies on her own feelings, realizing that to express tenderness for one you truly love requires no aid of Muse or convention. However, considering how unfashionable such endearments are, she decides to reserve them until her husband comes home and she can confide them to him privately—when they too can enjoy "that Pleasure . . . Of stollen Secresy" which makes all the "fancy'd Happiness" of illicit lovers.

Winchilsea did express her love openly in another poem to her husband, in which she dispensed entirely with classical convention. She opens with passionate simplicity: "This to the Crown, and blessing of my life, / The much lov'd husband, of a happy wife." Notice, first of all, the mutuality of their feeling: she loves him, and he has made her happy. Their love is of paramount importance, and it gives, as love should, perfect happiness. She expresses her appreciation for his "constant passion," which conquered her initial resistance (perhaps she had resented the generally exploitative and superior attitude of contemporary men in love), and now flouts fashionable convention by combining the status of a husband with the attentive passion of a lover. For his sake she will even undertake "What I in women censure" —presumably, conforming to the accepted female role of frivolity and fashionable accomplishments. What emerges here is a real relationship, based on deep love, involving mutual concessions (his efforts to win her "stubborn, and ungratefull heart," her yielding to convention to please him), and irradiating both their lives equally.

Always preserving Augustan form and Augustan restraint in these poems to her husband, Winchilsea achieved an unusually personal, genuine tone simply by looking at their actual relationship directly. Her expression of uncomplicated wholehearted pleasure in the company of a loved spouse, free of pretentiousness in feeling or diction, is unique in her period. A good example is "An Invitation to Dafnis," in which she urges him to leave his study and take a walk in the fields with her. Light Augustan wit precludes any air of sentimentality. Dafnis, immersed in military history, must not:

> . . . plead that you're immur'd, and cannot yield,
> That mighty Bastions keep you from the feild,
> Think not tho' lodg'd in Mons, or in Namur,
> You're from my dangerous attacks secure.

He must come with her into a natural field, where:

> The Cristall springs, shall murmure as we passe,
> But not like Courtiers, sinking to disgrace;
>   . . . . .
> But all shall form a concert to delight,
> And all to peace, and all to love envite.[8]

Even when Winchilsea was writing on more modish themes, she introduced a refreshing feminine point of view. Considering men's constant complaints that marriage is a ball and chain, oppressive to the natural freedom of the male, it is nice to see a woman making exactly the same claim in "The Unequal Fetters." Accepting for the moment the Restoration attitude toward love, Winchilsea shows how unfair it is to women. To love would be worth our while, she opens—if we could stop time and preserve youth. But since we women must lose the beauty which has won your hearts, and since we know you will then seek it in new faces, to love is but to ruin ourselves—not through seduction, but through empty marriages. She, for her part, will remain as free as Nature made her, will not allow herself to be caught in matrimony, a male invention that restricts women far more than men:

> Mariage does but slightly tye Men
>   Whil'st close Pris'ners we remain
> They the larger Slaves of Hymen
>   Still are begging Love again
> At the full length of all their chain.

Happily, Winchilsea herself had escaped this dilemma by a marriage which, founded on a deeper feeling, did not turn into a galling yoke; but here she looked at marriage in general as it prevailed in her time. She claimed natural freedom as opposed to artificial institution just as the men did, but, considering contemporary marriage law, with much better reason. Like the typical Restoration wit, she saw how hypocritical and restrictive the institution was; unlike him, she saw and protested against its particular unfairness to women.

In her "Epilogue to the Tragedy of Jane Shore," Winchilsea was inspired by the whore's progress of Jane to contrast the lifetime courses of women and men. A beautiful young woman dwindles to fine and well-dressed, then to "well enough," and finally to merely good—which means she is no longer admired and has nothing to do but retire. A man, on the other hand, can pass from "pretty fellow" to witty freethinker to politician, and "Maintains some figure, while he keeps his breath." While she makes no comment on this disproportion—it would be out of place in the flippancy of a neoclassical epilogue—the unfairness of valuing a woman in terms of her beauty alone is implicit. Both these feminist protests are playful, but significant in that their subjects would never have occurred to a male writer.[9]

As a woman, Winchilsea could not treat love and marriage as flippantly as did men for whom they were a minor part of life; respectively, pastime or dull obligation. Because it was impossible for a woman to be comfortable in the convention, she could not follow it without question as they did. This inability proved to be fortunate, in view of its limitation and superficiality: the men's poems might be highly accomplished, but were rarely more. Generally the men were less interested in the women they claimed to love than in the cleverness with which they expressed their feelings. Almost never dealing with permanent or profound relationships, they had often to resort to obscenity or empty paradox in an attempt to give their songs liveliness and individuality. Isolated from this convention by her sex, Winchilsea was in a manner forced to be original. She looked directly at her feelings and described them sincerely, and thereby produced poems which were not only distinctively natural but refreshingly free of the superficiality and cynicism which tainted most love poetry in her time.

"Ardelia's Answer to Ephelia" likewise shows Winchilsea's personal adaptation of a popular Restoration form, derived ultimately from Horace (Book I, Satire ix) and more recently from Boileau (Third Satire). The poet meets a fool who aims at being socially pleasing, who takes possession of him or her for a long tedious time. A contrast with Rochester's "Timon" will bring out the distinctive characteristics of Winchilsea's satire. Rochester's Timon, like Winchilsea's Ardelia, is taken in tow by a pretender to wit and fashion, who drags him home to dinner. First the forcible host reads poor Timon an insipid libel and insists Timon wrote it, in spite of his protest that he "never rhymed but for my pintle's [penis's] sake." The company at dinner consists of bullies who pretend to wit and, even worse, the host's wife, a faded beauty who retains nothing of youth but affectation and shows her stupidity by insisting on an idealistic view of romantic love. They praise a string of bad plays, commending them for the very qualities which any person of taste would recognize as faults. At length the discussion degenerates into a fight, and Timon escapes.

In contrast to Rochester's consistent detraction—there is nothing positive in his poem—Winchilsea judges the follies she satirizes against clear moral and rational ideals. She rejects the Town because she finds it uncongenial to friendship as well as to intellectual fulfillment. And she explicitly disavows detraction, the staple of Rochester's poem. She will not fit into fashionable society, she says, because she cannot supplement her wit with the ill nature necessary "To passe a gen'rall censure on mankind," to sneer at unsophisticated young people as foolish and at moral people as dull, to cheapen the genuine heroism of a soldier or the genuine inspiration of a poet. In contrast, most Restoration writers agreed with Rochester's assumption that wit has to be linked with cynicism, slashing universal criticism, and obscenity: whenever Rochester needed a simile, a phallic image leapt to his mind.

Almeria takes Ardelia in tow as Timon's host did him, but there is a significant difference between the two objects of satire. While both are fools, Timon's host is a fool because he aims at but cannot achieve true fashion; Almeria, on the other hand, is a fool because she conforms perfectly to the model of a sophisticated Restoration lady. Timon judges the fools as an insider, one who has mastered and consummately practices society's standards of wit and breeding. Ardelia prides herself on being an outsider from a society whose rules she considers immoral and irrational.[10]

Almeria is an accomplished lady of fashion, much like a female Timon. She has the same talent for seeing faults: "she discerns all failings, but her own." Yet to one's face she is effusively complimentary: she embraces Ardelia, protests she has pined hourly for her company, and insists she come to dine, though in fact she considers her an old-fashioned prude. Almeria never stops slandering the absent, but when the subject is present, she maintains " 'tis want of witt, to discommend." After dinner they ramble about in Almeria's coach to see the fashionable sights—or, actually, "any thing, that might the time bestow." Ardelia stops to enter a church, thus forcing Almeria to be, as she puts it, "Porter to a Temple gate." But Almeria does not waste her time: she "Flys round the Coach" in order to display herself to the best advantage to any passing beau.

Almeria lists Ardelia's many faults to one of these fops, and thereby exposes herself, since she represents contemporary fashion in contrast to Ardelia's Right Reason. Ardelia not only "Dispises Courtly Vice," but insists "That sence and Nature shou'd be found in Plays," and therefore prefers the earlier Restoration masters, Dryden, Etherege, and Wycherley, to contemporary sentimental drama.[11] (Note that Winchilsea lists the good playwrights, while Rochester named only to pillory.) Moreover, Ardelia has no interest in Almeria's most absorbing concern—those trifles on which most women built their egos, as indeed convention encouraged them to. Almeria prides herself on judgment shown in such things as placing "a patch, in some peculiar way, / That may an unmark'd smile, to sight betray, / And the vast genius of the Sex, display." She is mortified that Ardelia drank tea without a single "complement upon the cup," even though Almeria had braved a storm at sea in order to get her first choice of the china on an incoming ship. Instead of gratefully attending when Almeria advised her about clothing shops, Ardelia cut her off with "I deal with one that does all these provide, / Having of other cares, enough beside."

They rush from the church to Hyde Park, lest they should "loose e're night, an hour of finding fault." There Almeria points out an "awk'ard creature," but when Ardelia looks for some monster she sees a lovely though undeveloped girl. Almeria proceeds to sneer at the gifted translator Piso (Lord Roscommon)—how can anyone consider him a wit when he makes no artful compliments on a lady's dress or new coach, never cries down a play for the fun of it, and refuses to praise every novelty? Almeria then greets her "best of friends" in a voice that carries across the park; Ardelia agrees that this woman has a mind as beautiful as her person. But instead of being gratified, Almeria is clearly put out by this praise of her dear friend; and she immediately confides that the woman is disgracefully in love. Finally Almeria sees the most ridiculous creature of all—a poetess ("They say she writes, and 'tis a common jest"). Ardelia asks whether the poet is conceited or spiteful. Otherwise, what is wrong with a woman's writing? At length Ardelia manages to escape, to return to the country the next day.

Like any Augustan poet, Winchilsea satirized deviations from reason. But her enforced detachment from the fashionable world—attributable mostly to her sex—sharpened her ability to see where accepted social norms diverged from reason. As an outsider, she was better qualified to evaluate the ideals of the dominant group. Moreover, isolation from Restoration fashionable circles kept her free of the withering cynicism that made Rochester's satires (as well as his love poems) so negative. She had no patience with vice or folly, and she could appreciate the slashing satire of Wycherley (whom Almeria detested for his exposure of hypocritical women)—but she had clear standards of positive morality which included charity and kindness.[12]

Winchilsea could satirize women very sharply, but her satire is always modified by the fact that it comes from a right-minded woman rather than a male censor of the sex. Thus, she avoided patronizing generalizations and expected women to meet a universal human standard rather than a specifically "feminine" one. She showed herself, as Ardelia in the "Answer" or the speaker in "On Myselfe," as one with sufficient rational morality to despise the frivolity charged to women, to value what is truly important, and, if necessary, to live on her own resources.[13] Moreover, she pointed out that society pressed women to be foolish: they are "Education's, more then Nature's fools" ("The Introduction"). Small-minded Almeria conforms to conventional standards; it is Ardelia who is the social misfit. Finally, Winchilsea saw follies primarily as a waste of women's time and resources, rather than as an annoyance to men. Ardelia scorns shopping not because it is expensive or takes her away from home and family, but because she is more interested in intellectual pursuits.

Winchilsea was keenly aware of the niggling details that clog women's lives—necessary details that are piled on them, and the expansion and overemphasis on these details made by those who wish to distract women from more significant occupation.[14] Her "Petition for an Absolute Retreat" is, like Andrew Marvell's "The Garden" and John Pomfret's "The Choice," a celebration of rational, virtuous retirement in nature, a common Augustan theme. But while Pomfret wants company, Winchilsea would exclude idle visitors, probably because women were obligated to entertain whoever came, while men could generally escape constant attendance (as Pomfret implies he would). Male authors of the period constantly twitted women for idle visiting; it took a woman to point out that it was a tiresome burden imposed by society's views of ladylike behavior. For the same reason, Winchilsea specifies that her table will not only be simply provided (as is usual in these poems), but "spread without my Care." Unlike male authors, women had to supervise their own housekeeping.

Pomfret would include female company in his ideal retreat—sometimes a man needs to relax in the sweet softness of women's conversation—but only in an incidental way. He specifies that he will not have a wife, but an obliging female neighbor who can provide occasional companionship without scandal. Winchilsea would have congenial friends of both sexes, primarily of course her husband:

> Give me there (since Heaven has shown
> It was not Good to be alone)
> A *Partner* suited to my Mind,
> Solitary, pleas'd and kind;
> Who, partially, may something see
> Preferr'd to all the World in me.

She proceeds to draw a blissful picture of a world in which a man and wife are all in all to each other.

This looks like a direct refutation of a passage in Marvell's "The Garden," the prototype for both "retreat" poems. Describing his idyllically peaceful garden and comparing it to Eden, Marvell rudely charged that in the original Eden "man . . . walked without a mate," until God made the mistake of adding a female help, as if a helpmate could be needed in a perfect place. That Marvell could put this piece of extreme and irrelevant misogyny into a pleasing philosophical poem, and that it could be accepted without question by generations of readers, dramatically demonstrates the need for a female voice in poetry.

Winchilsea's explicit feminism appears usually in connection with the plight of the woman poet. (The attitudes of her contemporaries are exemplified on the one hand by *Three Hours After Marriage*, by Pope, John Gay, and John Arbuthnot, in which a woman is pilloried for being a writer; and on the other by Prior's epilogue to a play of female authorship, in which he declares that a woman's writing must be praised because she belongs to the beautiful sex.[15]) More than any other eighteenth-century writer, Winchilsea adverted to the difficulties of the female author, from the petty details that distracted her to the widespread assumption that it was presumptuous for a woman to write poetry. She was unusually outspoken in maintaining that a creative woman has a right to express herself because it is wrong to force anyone to bury a talent. Far from apologizing for taking time to fulfill herself by writing, she roundly declared that the approved feminine occupations were unworthy of an intelligent person. Her description of the foolish pseudo-arts to which women were expected to devote themselves is withering: to

> . . . in fading Silks compose
> Faintly, th'inimitable *Rose*,
> Fill up an ill-drawn *Bird*, or paint on Glass
> The *Sov'reign's* blurr'd and undistinguish'd Face,
> The threatening *Angel*, and the speaking *Ass*.
>
> ("The Spleen")

Her "Introduction," written for a manuscript collection of her poems not published by her but wistfully left for publication, argues her right to be a poet. Starting with the common Augustan attack on various sorts of carping critics, she soon closes in on the charge all critics will find: her verses are "by a Woman writt." It is a general feeling that "a woman that attempts the pen" is "an intruder on the rights of men," that women should devote their minds to "Good breeding, fassion, dancing, dressing, play."

> To write, or read, or think, or to enquire
> Wou'd cloud our beauty, and exaust our time,
> And interrupt the Conquests of our prime;
> While the dull mannage, of a servile house
> Is held by some, our outmost art, and use.

In other words, men do not want women wasting their time and energy on anything that does not contribute to their usefulness to men, whether as sexual objects or household managers; nor do they want them to rise above trivia, lest they develop ideas of their own. She goes on to prove women's ability to write by some biblical examples, which may not appear very convincing today but seemed called for in an age when the Bible was constantly used to keep woman in her place. But Winchilsea's confidence falters when she considers the present state of women, and she comes to a depressing conclusion. Debarred from education, instead positively trained and expected to be dull, few women can rise above the mass. And if one is pressed by "warmer fancy, and ambition" to try, she cannot help wavering: "So strong, th'opposing faction still appears, / The hopes to thrive, can ne're outweigh the fears." She concludes that she had best keep her Muse's wing "contracted," keep her verses to herself and a few friends, not aspire to laurel groves but remain in her absolute retreat.

Such expressions of discouragement, and even more her occasional disparagement of her vocation as a feminine foible or disclaimers that her works would merit publication even if she were not a woman, show that Winchilsea was not completely at ease in her unconventional role.[16] Consistently, however, she insisted not only that she was a serious poet, but that poetry was the most important thing in her life. In "Ardelia to Melancholy," she lists the various remedies for depression that she has vainly tried: first, social mirth; second, friendship; last, writing poetry. When that failed, she knew further struggles were useless. She was chronically plagued by depression, to which her difficulties and ambivalence as a woman poet may have contributed. Certainly it affected her most painfully by undermining her confidence as a poet. When depressed, she feared that her poetry was degenerating, and even that those who decried her writing as "An useless Folly, or presumptuous Fault" might be right ("The Spleen").

Defending a woman poet against the unthinking sneers of Almeria, who follows fashion by viewing a female poet as a ridiculous object, Winchilsea asks: "Why shou'd we from that pleasing art be ty'd, / Or like State Pris'ners, Pen and Ink deny'd?" (*Poems*, p. 45). Thus, she makes a bold equation between the legal restrictions on a prisoner (who is either guilty or imprisoned by what all would agree was a violation of traditional English liberty) and the customary restrictions on a woman, imposed simply because of her sex. Winchilsea was particularly concerned with liberty—not the public liberty so constantly cited in British literature, freedom from autocracy and oppressive laws; but rather the domestic liberty which was harder to establish, especially for a woman, freedom from the petty restrictions of convention and trivial obligations. Declining Ephelia's invitation to London, she suggests that the country be "Our place of meeting, love, and liberty" (*Poems*, p. 39). They cannot express their thoughts and affection amid the fashionable conventions operating in London. In the "Absolute Retreat" she petitions that "the World may ne'er invade . . . My unshaken Liberty." Liberty was not a feature of Marvell's or Pomfret's similar retreats.

Considering the importance of liberty to Winchilsea, one is tempted to read her tale "The Bird and the Arras" as an allegory. A bird is caught in a room and mistakes the pictured scene on a tapestry for a real one, but, trying to alight on a tree, only beats herself against the flat surface. She rises to the pictured sky, seeing the pictured birds apparently flying there and glorying in her ability to rise above them. But then she strikes the ceiling and plummets to the ground. She flutters around "in endlesse cercles of dismay" until a kind person directs her out the window "to ample space the only Heav'n of Birds." The bird imprisoned in a man-made room suggests a woman imprisoned in man-made conventions; the bird which makes doomed efforts to rise through the ceiling, the poet who "wou'd Soar above the rest" of her sex, only to be "dispis'd, aiming to be admir'd" ("The Introduction").

Limitation seems to have had a special meaning for Winchilsea: it was not the Augustans' decorous acceptance of human limits, but the Romantics' painful awareness of the discrepancy between human beings' aspirations and achievement. Her poem "The Nightingale" anticipates Keats's "Ode" and Shelley's "To a Skylark" in its suggestion that the bird has a freedom and joy impossible to human self-consciousness. The poet aims to imitate the song of the nightingale, to compose a song as freely self-expressive as the bird's—for "Poets, wild as thee, were born, / Pleasing best when unconfin'd, / When to Please is least design'd." She aspires to unite the music of the bird with human awareness. But of course the attempt fails. The poem ends with a typical Augustan turn and moral, but the ideas of unfulfillable aims and of the loss when humans give up their natural freedom remain. It is the Romantic yearning to burst limits, perhaps occurring to Winchilsea because a woman was made particularly aware of the restrictions on human beings. An outsider by sex, as later pre-Romantics were outsiders by temperament, she anticipates the Romantic artist's yearning for something beyond the physical, social world in which she must live.

Winchilsea's "Nocturnal Reverie" has been seen as a pre-Romantic work ever since Wordsworth singled it out for praise.[17] But actually the poem is Augustan in attitude and technique. It opens with the classical references that naturally sprang into educated eighteenth-century minds and proceeds to a series of beautifully exact bits of description characteristic of Augustan appreciation of nature. She describes the thin clouds that flit across the moon, the alteration in colors under moonlight—the foxglove is still recognizably red, though its hue is blanched—the greater clarity of odors and sounds at night, the swelling haystacks visible only as masses, the large approaching shape which frightens her until the sound of forage being chewed reassures her that it is only a horse. Winchilsea achieves her effects through precise detailing, not through suggestive appeals to passion or imagination; and her use of metaphor is subdued to the point that it is barely visible. Intense as her appreciation is, she perceives physical creatures as such, making no attempt to inflate them into some higher significance. The focus is consistently on her conscious reflecting mind—from her classical allusions in the first lines, through her moral observation on the glowworms ("trivial Beauties watch their Hour to shine"), to the direct description of her own mental state which ends the poem. She is stirred not to ecstasy, but to generalizing from her sensory impressions.

Description of the animals' activity at night leads her to delicate sympathy: "Their shortliv'd Jubilee the Creatures keep, / Which but endures, whilst Tyrant-*Man* do's sleep." She is not deprecating obvious cruelty (as Pope did in "Windsor Forest"), nor even any specific oppression, but just the restrictions imposed on domestic and wild animals by man's dominion. The poet, too, enjoys an unaccustomed liberty in this peaceful solitary scene. In the subdued moonlight, she feels free from the distractions of day and able to respond to the spiritual influences which speak to her true nature; her "free Soul" can feel at home even "in th'inferiour World." The soul's affinity and longing for Heaven is of course a traditional religious idea, but one thinks also of the imprisoned bird finally escaping into "ample space."

What is most distinctive in Winchilsea's poem is its personal quality. When the Augustans related physical nature to human concerns, they typically thought in terms of large moral or national issues. Pope's "Windsor Forest" includes some lovingly precise nature description, but uses it as a springboard to celebrate the destiny of Great Britain. He starts his poem not with personal response but with an invocation followed by descriptive details neatly organized to support a generalization—"order in variety we see"—and usually reinforced with a stock simile. He appreciates English oaks not because they are impressive in themselves but because they will be used to build the mighty British navy.[18] His description of reflections in a river,

> The watery landskip of the pendant woods,
> And absent trees that tremble in the floods;
> In the clear azure gleam the flocks are seen,
> And floating forests paint the waves with green,

is beautiful in its way; but it does not equal Winchilsea's simple, honest attempt to convey what such reflections actually look like: "When in some River, overhung with Green, / The waving Moon and trembling Leaves are seen."

Pope as well as Winchilsea finds observation of nature conducive to religious thoughts, but he seems to be expressing the state of Man in general rather than that of a particular person. Happy the man who retires to these shades to study or practice benevolence, who

> Bids his free soul expatiate in the skies,
> Amid her kindred stars familiar roam,
> Survey the region, and confess her home!

The distinction is subtle, since of course Winchilsea assumed that her feelings were representative; but her closing lines are unmistakably more personal: they grow out of her own feelings as accumulated in the poem, and are free of pompous diction and grandiloquent generalization.

James Thomson is closer to Winchilsea in his direct observation of natural detail and his study of nature for its own sake. But here again the public tone predominates. Thomson is not communicating his personal response to the Seasons, but the sensations and thoughts they inspire in everyman. His exhaustive descriptions aim at scientific completeness and are elevated by inflated diction and moralizing set pieces. They contrast strongly with the plain details of Winchilsea, who aims simply to convey her response to a beautiful setting as accurately as she can, not to rise to some imagined occasion but to say exactly what she sees and feels.

This distinctively personal tone in Winchilsea's poetry results in large part, I believe, from her being a woman—one who could not see herself as a public spokesman. Women would not feel it appropriate to voice institutional attitudes, because they were excluded from organized intellectual activity. Winchilsea certainly resented this exclusion: indignantly, as she claimed that a woman had a right to be a poet; wistfully, as she envisioned the easy comradeship of men exchanging witty conversation and knowledgeable criticism at a London tavern:

> Happy You three! happy the Race of Men!
> Born to inform or to correct the Pen
> To proffitts pleasures freedom and command
> Whilst we beside you but as Cyphers stand
> T'increase your Numbers and to swell th'account
> Of your delights which from our charms amount.

Her regrets for what she is missing lead her to open protest against the assumption that women are a mere peripheral part of the human race; it is little consolation to be men's occasional love objects, if that is all they can be ("A Poem, Occasion'd by the Sight of the 4th Epistle Lib. Epist: 1. of Horace").

But it is unlikely that such restrictions significantly cramped the development of her particular talent. Of course she was exceptionally fortunate: she was of sufficiently high social station to be safe at least from crude ridicule and to be free of financial pressure and domestic drudgery; her leisure was increased by her childlessness and her enforced retirement from public life (when the Finches' patrons, King James and Queen Mary of Modena, were driven from the kingdom), which also gave her constant contact with nature, her primary source of inspiration. She had a loving and beloved husband, who not only permitted but encouraged her to write (and even publish), and she was surrounded by relatives and friends who did the same. Not only was she relatively free of inhibitions on her writing in general, but the circumstances of her life encouraged her to develop her particular gifts.

It is probable that the personal lyrics and nature descriptions she did write are far better than the satires and philosophical poetry she might have written.

Always working within Augustan forms, Winchilsea adapted them as necessary to fit her distinctive talent and point of view, and in doing so she added a much-needed feminine voice to a masculine tradition. On the most basic level, the fact that her poems make a woman's consciousness the center of awareness distinguishes them in a literature where women generally appear only as an incidental part of life, as they do in Pomfret's "The Choice" and most Augustan love poetry. In Winchilsea's love poems, woman appears not as an object to be idealized or fantasized about, but a human subject expressing her own feelings. In her poems on friendship, women are seen outside of sexual relationships, giving ardent affection or wise guidance to one another.[19] In her satire on women, the satirist is not a censor scolding or instructing an inferior class, but a right-minded person criticizing other human beings for degrading themselves below the standards which all should meet. Winchilsea's experience as a woman heightened her sensitivity to many things less evident to male contemporaries, especially the social restrictions upon human liberty. It is possible that she gained as much as she lost by her isolation from the masculine tradition, that this isolation, freeing her from conventional thought and feeling, helped her to develop her unique poetic voice.

II

"TITANIC OPERA"

Nineteenth-Century Poets

I think I was enchanted
When first a sombre Girl—
I read that Foreign Lady—
The Dark—felt beautiful—

And whether it was noon at night—
Or only Heaven—at Noon—
For very Lunacy of Light
I had not power to tell—

The Bees—became as Butterflies—
The Butterflies—as Swans—
Approached—and spurned the narrow Grass—
And just the meanest Tunes

That Nature murmured to herself
To keep herself in Cheer—
I took for Giants—practising
Titanic Opera . . . .

—Emily Dickinson, #593

4.

This Changeful Life:
Emily Brontë's Anti-Romance

Nina Auerbach

Gondal was the secret room in Emily Brontë's imagination. In transcribing poems she wanted no one but herself to see, she segregated the notebook headed "Gondal poems" from a second notebook which critics have optimistically labeled "personal poems." Despite the Victorian predilection for undiscovered countries, Brontë excised all references to Gondal from the poems she included in her sisters' ill-fated collection in 1846, changing what had begun as fluid dramatic utterances into grand general statements. Her ambition sprang from Gondal but could not include it.

Gondal is similarly sealed off from *Wuthering Heights*, Brontë's most direct attempt at literary success: the novel is embedded indelibly in Yorkshire. Moreover, it adheres to the fictional conventions of the day in that it is both a love story and a domestic drama, while Gondal is neither. Love in the novel assumes eternal status by the combined fiat of Catherine and Heathcliff, while its domestic rituals endure longer than do the humans who perform them. "Time will change it, I'm well aware": thus its heroine scornfully dismisses her love for Edgar Linton. But she is dismissing the hidden country of Gondal as well, whose imperious queen embodies time and feeds on change.

In her *Gondal's Queen: A Novel in Verse* (1955; rpt. Austin: University of Texas Press, 1977), Fannie E. Ratchford has reconstructed the world Emily Brontë set so carefully apart. In doing so, she has de-compartmentalized Gondal from Brontë's other poems, creating her own version of a golden notebook which is the unity of Brontë's imagination: "the majority, perhaps all of [the poems], pertain to . . . Gondal[.]"[1] Ratchford's "arrangement" of Brontë's "novel in verse" embraces the fluctuating world both

Wuthering Heights and Brontë's own poetic tradition struggled to transcend.

Brontë's poetry has been dismissed too easily as a late-blooming attempt at Victorian Romanticism, ignoring the "drear" integrity of its self-created world. Apparent echoes of Wordsworth, Byron, and Blake (though she is not known to have read Blake) often ask scathing, subtle questions which recast inherited material into a wry new shape.[2] Childhood in Gondal, for instance, is quietly but firmly demystified of its Romantic aura.

Typically, Romantic children are eternity's promise to time. Radiating pure Being, they deny the mutability in which they are trapped by their births. In *Songs of Innocence* (1789), the birth of Blake's "Infant Joy" is an act of glad and perpetual self-discovery. The "I" characteristically finds delight only in his own being as a radiantly eternal abstraction:

> I have no name
> I am but two days old.—
> What shall I call thee?
> I happy am
> Joy is my name,—
> Sweet joy befall thee![3]

Infant Joy clings exclusively to his own eternal essence amid the contingencies of life in time, while his counterpart in *Songs of Experience* (1793), "Infant Sorrow," has only his own rage to shield him against the "dangerous world" of his new prison:

> My mother groand! my father wept.
> Into the dangerous world I lept:
> Helpless, naked, piping loud;
> Like a fiend hid in a cloud.
>
> Struggling in my fathers hands:
> Striving against my swaddling bands:
> Bound and weary I thought best
> To sulk upon my mothers breast.
>
> (28)

In joy and sorrow, Blake's infants are particles wrenched out of eternity to violation by time. But in Wordsworth's vision, the peerless childhood self is a less reliable object of worship than its alluringly immutable source, "that imperial palace whence he came." The little girl in "We Are Seven" imbibes permanence from the security of her setting. Eternal life is located only "Twelve steps or more from my mother's door" (39), in the graveyard where time and loss are recovered. Eternity is available in acts of obsessive return:

> "My stockings there I often knit
> My kerchief there I hem;
> And there upon the ground I sit,
> And sing a song to them.
>
> "And often after sun-set, Sir,
> When it is light and fair,
> I take my little porringer,
> And eat my supper there."
>
> (41–49)

The Wordsworthian child clings to unity of setting as tenaciously as Blake's "Infant Joy" clings to unity of self. But Emily Brontë's Augusta Geraldine Almeda, who will grow up to rule all the Gondals, clings to nothing. A.G.A. joyfully begins her "changeful life" with a song that embraces fluctuation of scene, time, and being itself:

> Tell me, tell me, smiling child,
> What the past is like to thee?
> "An Autumn evening soft and mild
> With a wind that sighs mournfully."
>
> Tell me, what is the present hour?
> "A green and flowery spray
> Where a young bird sits gathering its power
> To mount and fly away."
>
> And what is the future, happy one?
> "A sea beneath a cloudless sun;
> A mighty, glorious, dazzling sea
> Stretching into infinity."
>
> (#3)

The lilting cadences of A.G.A.'s greeting to time and nature are less Blake-like than their joy and innocence suggest. For the young A.G.A., selfhood expresses itself not in insistent reiterations of "I" and "my," but in self-forgetfulness within a joyfully shifting landscape. Ironically, her temporal pageant lacks the culminating snowscape that will become the motif of her maturity and of the Gondal saga as a whole; but given its bare imminence, the little girl's "mighty, glorious, dazzling sea" has none of the celestial finality of "that immortal sea" whose sight crowns Wordsworth's majestic "Ode: Intimations of Immortality from Recollections of Early Childhood" (1802-1804). It provides as mortal and momentary a blessing as does the "cloudless sun" which gives it its glory.

Unlike the Wordsworthian child, who finds continual restoration through permanence of setting, the young A.G.A.'s vision of the mournful autumnal past expresses her early assurance that the past is lost, while the vernal present of the second stanza is ever about to vanish with its bird. Were Wordsworth her tender questioner, he would find it ominous that the little girl is so blithely at home in time: the cycle of past–present–future evokes for her a string of delicious idylls, in which temporality is not a "prison-house," but loss and gaiety in one. Though her culminating cloudless sea is "Stretching into infinity," the present participle suggests the tension of a process that is never consummated. Emily Brontë's child celebrates mutability as whole-heartedly as Blake and Wordsworth's children struggled against it. She seems to have no eternal home to miss, having popped, like the child in the nursery rhyme, "out of the nowhere into the here."

Under A.G.A.'s adult reign, children are less a Wordsworthian "eye among the blind" than inert objects to be dispatched: banishment or infanticide is the most common emotion they evoke in their raging parents, whose point of view we share. In sending the worshipful Amedeus, the "dark boy of sorrow," into exile, A.G.A. herself becomes the devouring time threatening the Romantic "holy child":

> And what shall change that angel brow
> And quench that spirit's glorious glow?
> Relentless laws that disallow
> True virtue and true joy below.
>   ("A.A.A.," #112, 15–18)

In dealing with her own child, A.G.A. identifies herself even less obliquely with time's "relentless laws." After the assassination of the great love of her life, the usurping emperor Julius Brenzaida, A.G.A. flees with their baby daughter to the snow-buried mountains, where she inexplicably abandons the child in a storm. This murder of the seal of her marriage to Julius, and perhaps of their empire as well, has no discernible motive in the text: infanticide seems as simple and compulsive an instinct to A.G.A. as it will be to George Eliot's Hetty Sorrel, replacing motherhood as the great overriding impulse that need ask no questions about itself. But to provide herself with philosophical justification, A.G.A. once again evokes the Romantic pieties her own childhood denied. She finds that the true home of the child is not earth, but the eternity in her eyes:

> "Methought the heaven, whence thou hast come,
> Was lingering there awhile;
> And Earth seemed such an alien home
> They did not dare to smile.

> "Methought, each moment something strange
> Within their circles shone,
> And yet, through every magic change,
> They were Brenzaida's own."
>
> ("Geraldine," #150, 29–36)

The child's existence as a remnant of eternity, both in itself and as the immortality of beloved Brenzaida, is twisted with Grand Guignol relish into the reason for its destruction. With dark wit, Emily Brontë takes Romantic child-worship as a motive for the annihilation of childhood itself:

> "Say, sin shall never blanch that cheek,
> Nor suffering charge [change?] that brow;
> Speak, in thy mercy, Maker, speak,
> And seal it safe from woe!

> "Why did I doubt? In God's control
> Our mutual fates remain;
> And pure as now my angel's soul
> *Must* go to Heaven again."
>
> (41–48)

No shades of the prison-house will darken little Princess Alexandrina. Romanticism has provided the epic with a motive for death, if not a guide to life. By Emily Brontë's sardonic use of its definitions, the child becomes most sacrosanct when the snow that is Gondal takes to itself her "frozen limbs and freezing breast" (#108, 32).

In her dance through time and her denial of the children that are eternity, A.G.A. is the anti-Wordsworthian spirit of Gondal, whose saga begins at birth and ends with assassination by her vengeful step-daughter. Her reigning murderousness may suggest the "swaddling bands" of Blake's Female Will, who in *Europe: A Prophecy* (1794) manacles a continent in the gloating form of "mother Enitharmon": but A.G.A. is "mother" only long enough to be killer. She enslaves the men and women who cluster about her, not by the murderous possessiveness Blake associated with "womans triumph," but by her commitment to mutability which repeatedly drives them away. She does not bind time, but sets it free.

Her unyielding self-assertion never collapses into the self-luxuriance of Byronism. Taking to herself the mantle of time's "relentless laws," A.G.A. never erects her ruined self against the process of love's erosion, as Childe Harold had done so frequently. *Don Juan*, an epic of potential endlessness, chooses to laugh at time's ocean in order not to weep at it. But Emily Brontë sails on it matter-of-factly, electing neither laughter, tears, nor Childe Harold's challenge. Love in Gondal is at one with parting, and its emotional essence lies in the laconic acceptance of "Song":

> Let us part, the time is over
> When I thought and felt like thee;
> I will be an Ocean rover,
> I will sail the desert sea
>   . . . . .
> Day by day some dreary token
> Will forsake my memory
> Till at last all old links broken
> I shall be a dream to thee.
>   (#118, 9–12; 21–24)

Unlike that of Blake's Female Will, or of Brontë's own Heathcliff, Gondal's love does not enforce eternity, but ruthlessly refuses it. The change A.G.A. embraces on her release from prison is the change she offers in return for love:

> But this is past, and why return
> O'er such a past to brood and mourn?
> Shake off the fetters, break the chain,
> And live and love and smile again.
>   (#15, 69–72)

A.G.A.'s sin against relationship, and her gift to it as well, lie in her precise inability to play the mothering, generating, and possessive role of Enitharmon. Like that of Blake's own Oothoon, A.G.A.'s longing to "break the chain" of possessive love is a cry for freedom from limiting nature.

For Gondal's queen is less a worshipper of nature than its furious victim. Her identification of herself with time seems at one with her denial of the Wordsworthian assurances of eternity through "nature and the language of the sense." Wordsworth's gateways become A.G.A.'s prison. Thus, in some of Brontë's most remarkable lines, A.G.A. wails against dawn's joyful awakening with an intensity of phallic and murderous imagery that makes Wordsworth's exhortation in "To My Sister" to "come forth and feel the sun" seem a bland invitation to execution:

> Blood-red he rose, and arrow-straight
> His fierce beams struck my brow:
> The soul of Nature sprang elate,
> But mine sank sad and low!
>   (#184, 21–24)

The rhythms of A.G.A.'s own soul are in total opposition to Nature's, as she defies its unified "soul" in favor of the calm multitudinousness of night's heavenly bodies presiding over the vicissitudes of her own consciousness:

> I was at peace, and drank your beams
> As they were life to me
> And revelled in my changeful dreams
> Like petrel on the sea.
>   (9–12)

A.G.A.'s life and her rule lie in fidelity to her "changeful dreams"; restorative Nature is her brand of Cain. Her antagonism to Nature, and to all the Romantic pieties that accompany it, is more comprehensible if we believe with Fannie Ratchford that the sun in this poem is the birth of "Julius as the sun of her life, paling into invisibility all other loves and loyalties" (*Gondal's Queen*, p. 87). Thus, A.G.A.'s revolt is at one with Catherine Earnshaw's cry in her dream against the consummation of Heaven and the unification of love: "I was only going to say that heaven did not seem to be my home; and I broke my heart with weeping to come back to earth; and the angels were so angry that they flung me out, into the middle of the heath on the top of Wuthering Heights; where I woke sobbing for joy.... I've no more business to marry Edgar Linton than I have to be in heaven; ... It would degrade me to marry Heathcliff now[.]"[4]

Here at least, Catherine equates Heathcliff as well as Edgar with the alien reductiveness of Heaven. Love and beatitude are threats to the living self and the integrity of its "changeful dreams." As Catherine asserts her dreams against love, marriage, and Heaven, the monumental pillars of novelistic bliss, so A.G.A. asserts hers against a standard moment of blessing in nineteenth-century poetry: the aubade that consecrates the imagination, as the rising dawn blesses Wordsworth's coming prophetic poems in book IV of *The Prelude*. But A.G.A.'s sexual and cosmic loyalty to the manifold and changing seems fruitless against the tyranny of unity and union:

> It would not do—the pillow glowed
> And glowed both roof and floor,
> And birds sang loudly in the wood,
> And fresh winds shook the door.
>   (33–36)

A.G.A.'s senses have no power against this choric dominion. Wordsworth's embrace of "all the mighty world of eye, and ear" is here a mighty betrayal. In Gondal, the senses collaborate with "the hostile light" of that coercive, vampiristic Nature "that does not warm, but burn—That drains the blood of suffering men" (44–45). A.G.A. accepts but inverts Wordsworth's contention that the senses are bulwarks against time and change. For her, they are thereby in league with the soul's enemy, instead of being potential organs of the soul as they are in Blake's *Marriage of Heaven and Hell*: "If the doors of perception were cleansed every thing would appear to man as it is, infinite" (p. 39).

Defining Brontë's quest for visionary freedom in terms of Blake's subordinates Brontë's uniqueness and her quietly biting wit. Standing alone, Blake's Nature reduces itself to the weary cycle of Generation grinding down the aspiring spirit, which our visionary capacity alone can surmount: properly "cleansed," our "vegetable" can meet our "visionary" eye. But in Gondal's spying, suspicious world, there is little hope that eyes and ears are our friends in our quest for liberty. Despite her supposed "Blakean" affinities, Brontë would only smile at the claim in *For the Sexes: The Gates of Paradise* that our mighty eye can determine the shape of the ravaging sun itself: "The Suns light when he unfolds it Depends on the Organ that beholds it" (p. 257). A.G.A.'s eye allows traitorous passage to the sun which violates the soul, while finally, in *A Vision of the Last Judgment*, Blake's eye simply becomes indistinguishable from soul and sun: " 'What,' it will be Question'd, 'When the Sun rises, do you not see a round Disk of fire somewhat like a Guinea?' O no, no, I see an Innumerable company of the Heavenly host crying, 'Holy, Holy, Holy is the Lord God Almighty' " (p. 555). This ultimate collusion of self, nature, and vision is eternally possible to the Blakean "I," but Brontë is comforted by no such crowning epithalamion. If there is an "Innumerable company" in her sun, it is in league with nature and the eye to insult the straining power of the bound-down self:

> Oh, dreadful is the check—intense the agony
> When the ear begins to hear and the eye begins to see;
> When the pulse begins to throb, the brain to think again,
> The soul to feel the flesh and the flesh to feel the chain!
> ("Julian M. and A. G. Rochelle," #190, 85–88)

These lines were not written for A.G.A., whom little checks or chains, but for a feebler victim of the Civil War between the Republicans and the Royalists. In the poem's dramatic context, the prisoner's recoil from her own senses is a symptom of her well-motivated death wish, which the robust A.G.A. scarcely shares. But queen and captive speak with the voice of a common rage against two great engines of eternity transmitted by Wordsworth and his acolytes: "nature and the language of the sense." Like his eternal "Child of Joy," these mighty gifts from the great patriarch of Rydal become in the hands of Emily Brontë's embattled women a poisoned fruit that strangles the soul it is supposed to feed, threatening with immutability the "changeful dreams" of the multitudinous self.

Equally blighting is the faculty which enriches and makes holy Wordsworth's trinity of child, nature, and sense: the baptismal visitation of memory. If A.G.A., daughter of time and anticipation, could become absolute monarch of her universe, she would decree a world without memory; but in the life she must inhabit, memory comes like blood-red dawn as a deadening invader. The Wordsworthian vocabulary of "awful," "roll," "flood," "sterner power" portends here the interfusion of an enemy:

> Listen, 'tis just the hour,
> The awful time for thee;
> Dost thou not feel upon thy soul
> A flood of strange sensations roll,
> Forerunners of a sterner power,
> Heralds of me?
>   (#37, 11–16)

In Gondal, memory is invariably the blighting conduit of guilt and sorrow, contaminating the joy it touches like the "spectre ring" A.G.A. finds in the sodden grass:

> A mute remembrancer of crime,
> Long lost, concealed, forgot for years,
> It comes at last to cancel time,
> And waken unavailing tears.
>   (#96, 5–8)

The "time" memory "cancel[s]" is the only saving power in Gondal's world. Neither love nor nature, memory nor sense, can provide the sustenance of the cycle of change, or of A.G.A.'s futile prayer to "Forget them—O forget them all" (#15, 76). Even the two famous elegies to Julius, "Cold in the Earth" and "Death, that struck when I was most confiding" (#182, #183), are paeans to forgetting and elegies to memory. The Julius evoked in "Cold in the Earth" is not the living, powerful man memory can reanimate—which is not surprising, as it was his coronation rather than his assassination that prostrated A.G.A. with brain fever. Instead of reanimating her lover, as Heathcliff does Catherine, she replaces the man with his grave, and the poem's sensuous excitement comes from the evocation of the changing face of that grave with time:

> Cold in the earth, and fifteen wild Decembers
> From those brown hills have melted into spring—
> Faithful indeed is the spirit that remembers
> After such years of change and suffering!
>   ("R. Alcona to J. Brenzaida," #182, 13–16)

Young love is not eternalized in memory, as was the bond of family in "We Are Seven," but embodied and hymned as mutable earth. A.G.A., here called Rosina, closes the poem with her tender promise to forget her dead husband: "Sweet love of youth, forgive if I forget thee While the World's tide is bearing me along:...And even yet, I dare not let it languish, Dare not indulge in Memory's rapturous pain" (13–14; 29–30). Memory here is not the source of growth, but a dark call like suicide, denying fullness of being and promise.

Similarly, in the lament which immediately follows Julius' death, A.G.A./ Rosina prays to die, not because she cannot live without her love, but because she knows she will forget to mourn him. Despairingly, she recalls her quick recovery from an earlier despair:

> Little mourned I for the parted Gladness,
> For the vacant nest and silent song;
> Hope was there and laughed me out of sadness,
> Whispering, "Winter will not linger long."
>   (#183, 17–20)

"Time for me must never blossom more!" (32), she cries loyally (and disingenuously) at the end, not because time compounds her loss, but because she knows time cannot fail to restore it. In the rhythm of her life, memory is the blight and time is the blossom. Adherence to memory alters Wordsworth's renewed and deepened life to flagrantly melodramatic self-destruction: there can be no connective principle unifying the self against its life in time.

Savage, cold, but endlessly receptive to the endless changes of her world, A.G.A. was the character with whom Emily Brontë spent the longest and most intense period of her creative life. Catherine and Heathcliff seem to have been mere bubbles on its surface, while the Gondal saga spanned her career; and their incessant clinging to a fixed childhood image of union may be subtly criticized by A.G.A.'s calm assurance that love and eternity are incompatible. The storm that presides portentously over her birth is as lurid in its fury as the storm that is the lovers' motif in the novel, but it bestows on her an adaptability they lack—that of a perpetual present tense:

> Shining and lowering and swelling and dying,
> Changing for ever from midnight to noon;

Roaring like thunder, like soft music sighing,
Shadows on shadows advancing and flying,
Lightning-bright flashes the deep gloom defying,
Coming as swiftly and fading as soon.
(#5, 13-18)

If this storm, like those of *Wuthering Heights*, portends the heroine's violent life and destiny, its repeated contrasts also endow her with the ambiguous gift of "changing for ever." Her ruling mutability bestows on her the royal ability both to kill and to let die. Born under the aegis of perpetual flashes of change, she fears most of all the traditional happy ending—the resolution into unity that banishes contrast:

"I well may mourn that only one
Can light my future sky
Even though by such a radiant sun
My moon of life must die."
("To A.G.A.," #110, 34-37)

As prelude to the great hymn of hate against the scorching, draining sun, this poem is a cosmic lament that the gentle, manifold signs of night and its "changeful dreams" must succumb to the monolithic tyranny of consciousness and day; while in the romance plot of Gondal, it is A.G.A.'s complaint that she cannot have two men at once, but must abandon her marriage to the gentle Lord Alfred to consummate her passion for imperial Julius Brenzaida. But above all, the first line of the quatrain—"I well may mourn that only one"—laments to the death Wordsworth's relieved discrimination among the richness of apparent chaos: "Fair as a star, when only one Is shining in the sky" ("She Dwelt Among the Untrodden ways," 7-8); "But there's a Tree, of many, one, A single Field which I have looked upon" ("Intimations Ode," 51-52).

The Wordsworthian choice "of many, one" is truly A.G.A.'s death knell. "The Death of A.G.A.," Gondal's longest narrative in which her assassination is starkly presented, locates her death in the disappearance of the change and contrast that were her identity:

You might have seen the dear, dear sign of life
In her uncovered eye,
And her cheek changing in the mortal strife
Betwixt the pain to live and agony to die.

But nothing mutable was there.
(#143, 270-75)

From birth to death, change confirms her cherished life in time. The mutability affirmed in this equivocal, epic queen, and in the empire that takes her shape, seems a unique virtue in the poetry of an age that yearned increasingly for fixity.

Gondal's land finds its being in its storm: changes—psychic, seasonal, and political—appear to rock its world forever. Such fluctuations fight against the unity Wordsworth sought in a nature where change threatened a betrayal so radical that his only defense was resolution into "of many, one." Despite the determined reaction of later, "High" Victorian poetry against many of its own perceptions of Romanticism, Wordsworth's will to draw the one out of the many grows into near-obsessive dominance. Tennyson's authoritative elegy, *In Memoriam A.H.H.* (1850), typically concludes its record of emotional and natural fluctuations with their resolution into "One God, one law, one element, And one far-off divine event, To which the whole creation moves" ("Epilogue," 142–44).

This insistently reiterated "one ... one ... one" was death rather than consolation to A.G.A., whose healing power sprang only from the interminable rhythms Tennyson's speaker mourns and fears:

> The hills are shadows, and they flow
> From form to form, and nothing stands;
> They melt like mist, the solid lands,
> Like clouds they shape themselves and go.
> *(In Mem.,* CXXIII, 5–8)

Though from Tennyson's own day to ours there has been little doubt that this woeful vision of mutability spoke for the cosmic anguish of "the Victorians," at least one contemporary poetic vision took from this same flow its own certainty that life remained.

For Robert Browning this vision of incessant change seems more vigorously compelling, but it too finally exists to be repudiated. In *Dramatic Romances*, published in 1845 when Emily was deep in Gondal, his "Englishman in Italy" eyes ambivalently the violent combat of a landscape about to be devastated by Scirocco:

> In the vat, halfway up on our house-side,
> Like blood the juice spins,
> While your brother all bare-legged is dancing
> Till breathless he grins
> Dead-beaten in effort on effort
> To keep the grapes under,

> Since still when he seems all but master,
>> In pours the fresh plunder
> From girls who keep coming and going
>> With basket on shoulder,
> And eyes shut against the rain's driving;
>> Your girls that are older,—
>
> (74–84)

"Dead-beaten" but grinning bravely in his dance to outface the omnivorous proliferation of "plunder," Browning's harvester seems to be fighting a losing battle against the perpetual motion that foments into the warning cry: "Scirocco is loose!" Unlike Gondal's, this storm does not define the poem's heroic virtues, but submerges them: "No refuge, but creep Back again to my side and my shoulder, And listen or sleep" (126–28). The threat to humanity underlying this sensuous dance may affect Browning's turn away from mutability and multitudinousness in the long poem he considered his great epic statement, *The Ring and the Book* (1868–69), whose introductory admonition states the theme and shape of the work to come:

> Rather learn and love
> Each facet-flash of the revolving year!—
> Red, green, and blue that whirl into a white,
> The variance now, the eventual unity,
> Which make the miracle.[5]

The heart of Browning's epic follows the Wordsworthian and Tennysonian resolutions: "of many, one"; "of variance, unity." Though this attempt to resolve diversity in unity, to make the dance of change "whirl into a white," is central to the nineteenth-century ideal of epic, the perpetual explorations of Gondal have no room for it. "The Gondals are discovering the interior of Gaaldine," Emily Brontë wrote provocatively in her notebook, eschewing both "have discovered" and "will discover." In this initiation to her world, as in that world itself, the present participle dominates as discovery perpetually takes place in a perpetual present. To "whirl" such a process "into a white" would destroy the very miracle these poems reveal.

To say that Emily Brontë alone wrote an epic about mutability in which mutability was not shunned is not to say that she embraced the anarchy that seems constantly seething up against the desperately grinning culture of Browning's grape-harvester. As Fannie Ratchford has taught us, the excesses of Gondal generate their own retribution.[6] Though "changing for ever" seems the insignia for A.G.A. and the world that expresses her, one thinks back to the Gondal epic as a checkerboard of dungeons. Ever-changing nature is most often a tantalizing flutter seen through the window of prison. In Gondal, dungeons are ruthlessly punitive, amenable to none of the Romantic transformations available in Wordsworth's "Nuns Fret Not at Their Convent's Narrow Room": "In truth the prison, into which we doom Ourselves, no prison is" (8–9). The cultural survey of Childe Harold's pilgrimage similarly observes that, at least in exotic Albania, enclosure becomes a hermitage of self-sufficient space for a loving woman:

> Here woman's voice is never heard: apart,
> And scarce permitted, guarded, veil'd, to move,
> She yields to one her person and her heart,
> Tamed to her cage, nor feels a wish to rove:
> For, not unhappy in her master's love,
> And joyful in a mother's gentlest cares,
> Blest cares! All other feelings far above!
> Herself more sweetly rears the babe she bears,
> Who never quits the breast, no meaner passion shares.
>
> (*CHP*, Canto II, st. LXI)

Female devotion reveals that the fixity of prison can become one with eternity. But in Gondal, both male and female prisoners are agonizingly possessed by the "wish to rove." Romantic transfiguration of a static protective spot is reduced to a sophistical denial of wholeness and joy:

> In dungeons dark I cannot sing,
> In sorrow's thrall 'tis hard to smile:
> What bird can soar with broken wing,
> What heart can bleed and joy the while?
>
> (#77)

For Emily Brontë prison is always prison, because like the fixity of eternity it locks its inhabitant away from change. Briefly incarcerated after the death of Elbë, A.G.A. grasps from her cell at mutability's very essence in "To a Wreath of Snow": "O transient voyager of heaven!" (#39, 1). In this transience is all the life the prisoner is denied. Although a wreath of snow will "melt like mist," as Tennyson was to write, denial of its properties is an excruciating denial of voyaging life itself.

But A.G.A. is not Brontë's only prisoner to yearn out of permanence for the shifting and changing. While Byron's Prisoner of Chillon involuntarily and tragically "grew friends" with the self-complete space of his dungeon, the captive in "Glenenden's Dream" is haunted only by a nature that is, like Browning's Italy, a country of verbs, a perpetual process:

Tell me, watcher, is it winter?
Say how long my sleep has been?
Have the woods I left so lovely
Lost their robes of tender green?

Is the morning slow in coming?
Is the night-time loath to go?
Tell me, are the dreary mountains
Drearier still with drifted snow?

(#63, 1–8)

Nature is time, change, the cycle of seasons, and imprisonment from it is no hermitage, but simply the end of life. Next to the daily reality of incarceration, Byron's cries in the "Sonnet on Chillon" seem grandiose slogans: "Brightest in dungeons, Liberty! thou art"; "Chillon, thy prison is a holy place" (2, 9). Ideally this heroism of the imagination should be possible for the Byronic "I," though Byron's prisoner himself manages to become a survivor only by shrinking into an inmate; but Gondal's characters can conceive no victory of consciousness in thriving away from time and space. When Julius betrays and imprisons Gerald Exina to lock all the islands under his empire, Gerald's incarceration embodies only the finality of immutability and death:

Set is his sun of liberty;
Fixed is his earthly destiny;
A few years of captivity,
And then a captive's tomb.

(#125, 21–24)

Transfiguration of enclosure dwindles into the fantasy with which a prisoner flatters himself. The epic's many dungeon poems assure us that if change is sustenance, fixity is not liberty but despair, and Gondal needs no other hell than the self-created heavens of many of its contemporaries. Cause of countless deaths, A.G.A. can be no more damned in any world than she is by her faithful servant's epitaph: "But nothing mutable was there" (#143, 274).

Yet Gondal's queen is not obliterated by eternity. If her body's ironic doom is immutability, the survival of her essence is assured; not because she is remembered, but because she is forgotten as in "Cold in the Earth" she pledged herself to forget. Only her servant mourns the lack of mourners that insure the survival of her vision: "How few, of all the hearts that loved, / Are grieving for thee now!" ("E.W. to A.G.A.," #171, 1–2).

In a century that enshrined memory and recovered the elegy, Emily Brontë alone fled the prison suggested by the words, "in memoriam." In releasing her queen from the dungeon of memory and permanence, she allows her to live, not as Wordsworth's Lucy did as an immortal thing among things— "No motion has she now, no force; She neither hears nor sees" ("A Slumber did my Spirit Seal," 5–6)—but as a consciousness of motion and a pledge to "changeful dreams":

> Blow west wind, by the lonely mound,
> And murmur, summer streams,
> There is no need of other sound
> To soothe my Lady's dreams.
> (#173, 25–28)

In death as in life, A.G.A. is queen of a perpetual present. In this continued empire of mutability and departure, Emily Brontë remains true to the vision of an epic that quietly relinquished her century's hope of transcendence and saw no reason to mourn its loss. Seen as a whole, Gondal shows us the power and the exhilaration of a world that refuses to end in a cosmic epithalamion. The saga of its queen and the silence of its creator suggest that this gaunt woman who wanted never to leave her father's Parsonage was a braver navigator into the straits of time and change than the sterner, more sonorous bards whose poetry constituted her age's official voice.[7]

5.

Working into Light:
Elizabeth Barrett Browning

Helen Cooper

A year after the publication of Elizabeth Barrett Browning's *Poems of 1844*, which established her as Britain's foremost woman poet, she was painfully aware of the absence of foremothers:[1]

> . . . England has had many learned women, not merely readers but writers of the learned languages, in Elizabeth's time and afterwards—women of deeper acquirements than are common now in the greater diffusion of letters; and yet where were the poetesses? The divine breath . . . why did it never pass, even in the lyrical form, over the lips of a woman? How strange! And can we deny that it was so? I look everywhere for grandmothers and see none. It is not in the filial spirit I am deficient, I do assure you—witness my reverent love of the grandfathers![2]

Chaucer, Spenser, Shakespeare, Milton, Pope, Wordsworth: British poetry embodied four hundred years of male practice of the art. Unlike Arthur Quiller-Couch, who describes how Britain nurtured the men who became its major poets—claiming a university education as a virtual prerequisite for "poetical genius"—Barrett Browning never formulated a penetrating political or social analysis of the factors contributing to the absence of great women poets.[3] However, in letters of 1845 she demonstrates some ambivalence over this issue. To Robert Browning she confesses:

> . . . let us say & do what we please & can . . there *is* a natural inferiority of mind in women—of the intellect . . not by any means, of the moral nature— & that the history of Art . . & of genius testifies to this fact openly. . . .

Seeming "to justify for a moment an opposite opinion," her admiration for George Sand undercuts this:

> Such a colossal nature in every way—with all that breadth & scope of faculty which women want—magnanimous, & loving the truth & loving the people—and with that "hate of hate" too. . . .[4]

In the same year she admits to a Miss Thompson, who had solicited some classical translations for an anthology:

> Perhaps I do not . . . partake quite your 'divine fury' for converting our sex into Greek scholarship. . . . You . . . know that the Greek language . . . swallows up year after year of studious life. Now I have a 'doxy' . . . that there is no exercise of the mind so little profitable to the mind as the study of languages. It is the nearest thing to a passive recipiency—is it not?—as a mental action, though it leaves one as weary as ennui itself. Women want to be made to *think actively*: their apprehension is quicker than that of men, but their defect lies for the most part in the logical faculty and in the higher mental activities.[5]

It is not women's "natural inferiority of mind" that hinders them, but their training into a "passive recipiency." Such a mental state is incompatible with the active thinking necessary for a poet.

Deprived of "grandmothers," Barrett Browning energetically explored what it meant to be a woman poet writing out of a male tradition, in which she was thoroughly self-educated. In 1857 she formulated a clear statement of the material appropriate to the woman poet when she challenged the critical reception to her discussion of prostitutes in *Aurora Leigh*:

> What has given most offence in the book . . . has been the reference to the condition of women in our cities, which a woman oughtn't to refer to . . . says the conventional tradition. Now I have thought deeply otherwise. If a woman ignores these wrongs, then may women as a sex continue to suffer them; there is no help for any of us—let us be dumb and die.[6]

The "conventional tradition" allowed to early nineteenth-century women poets is exemplified by the works of two of the most popular of them, Felicia Hemans (1793–1835) and Letitia Landon (1802–1838). In the preface to *The Venetian Bracelet* (1829), Landon justifies "Love as my source of song":

> I can only say, that for a woman, whose influence and whose sphere must be in the affections, what subject can be more fitting than one which it is her peculiar province to refine, spiritualise, and exalt? I have always sought to paint it self-denying, devoted, and making an almost religion of its truth. . . .[7]

Hemans's rage at the condition of women's lives is carefully controlled. Writing on "Evening Prayer at a Girls' School," she encourages the girls to enjoy the present, for

> Her lot is on you—silent tears to weep,
>   And patient smiles to wear through suffering's hour,
> And sumless riches, from affection's deep,
>   To pour on broken reeds—a wasted shower!
> And to make idols, and to find them clay,
> And to bewail that worship,—therefore pray!
>   . . . . .
> Meekly to bear with wrong, to cheer decay,
> And oh! to love through all things,—therefore pray!

Hemans's advice bristles with ambivalence. The contempt surfacing for "broken reeds" and "clay idols" that waste women's energy is undercut by the resignation of the last two lines. Landon and Hemans see self-denial and suffering, a woman's natural duty, as their subject matter. Barrett Browning grew to realize the abuse of women as her material, believing that the world may be made finer for women through their unflinching concern for one another. Refusing to be contained within boundaries prescribed as "woman's sphere," she interpreted the woman poet's special subject matter as being anything and everything which honestly illuminates her life.

Not only did Barrett Browning reject any limitation on the content of women's poetry, she also insisted on a rigorous assessment of women's work:

> The divineness of poetry is far more to me than either pride of sex or personal pride. . . . And though I in turn suffer for this myself—though I too . . . may be turned out of "Arcadia," and told that I am not a poet, still, I should be content, I hope, that the divineness of poetry be proved in my humanness, rather than lowered to my uses.[8]

This standard is revolutionary, for the "poetesses" had always been judged by very different criteria from their male counterparts. H. T. Tucker aptly demonstrates this:

> The spirit of Mrs. Hemans in all she has written is essentially feminine. . . . She has thrown over all her effusions, not so much the drapery of knowledge or the light of extensive observation, as the warm and shifting hues of the heart.[9]

Tucker exemplifies a criticism purporting to speak highly of women's work while in fact condemning it. To avoid recognizing her language as overly

sentimental and vague as he would that of a male poet, he praises the
"warm and shifting hues of the heart" and exonerates her from lacking
"the drapery of knowledge or the light of extensive observation."

To realize her aesthetic Barrett Browning took the idea of excellence from,
yet resisted the domination of, the male poetic tradition. Increasingly she
absorbed a woman's culture: her letters are peppered with references to
Hemans, Landon, and other women poets, to Jane Austen, Charlotte Brontë,
George Eliot, George Sand, Mrs. Gaskell, and Harriet Beecher Stowe, to
Harriet Martineau and Margaret Fuller, and to the young American sculptor
Harriet Hosmer. She probes their work, their assessment of themselves, their
strengths and weaknesses, creating for herself a network of support while
systematically breaking through the limiting proprieties ascribed to women
poets.

Informing this sense of community was the memory of the love between
herself and her mother, who died suddenly away from home in 1828 when
Barrett Browning was twenty-two. Three years later she records in her
diary:

> How I thought of those words "*You will never find another person who
> will love you as I love you*"—And how I felt that to hear again the sound
> of those beloved, those ever ever beloved lips, I wd barter all other sounds &
> sights—that I wd in joy & gratitude lay down before her my tastes &
> feelings each & all, in sacrifice for the love, the exceeding love which I
> never, in truth, can find again.[10]

The relationship between Barrett Browning and Edward Moulton Barrett,
her father, has become legend, but the love between the poet and Mary
Graham-Clarke, her mother, has been ignored by critics. Certainly her
father educated her from the full bookcases in his study and was intensely
a part of her adult life. However, the education the young poet received
from her mother about the nurturing power of love between women also
needs exploration and documentation, for it is this that resonates through
such poems as her sonnets to George Sand and *Aurora Leigh*.

By the age of twelve Barrett Browning had read Mary Wollstonecraft's
A Vindication of the Rights of Woman. Taplin, her biographer, records her
reading in 1828 in *The Literary Souvenir*:

> . . . a sentimental poem by Miss Landon called "The Forsaken," which repre-
> sented the lament of a country girl whose lover had left her to look for city
> pleasures. Elizabeth thought the verses were "beautiful and pathetic." She
> was also much affected by a poem by Mrs Hemans—it "goes to the heart," she
> wrote—describing the death of a mother and her baby in a shipwreck.[11]

Yet her second book, *An Essay on Mind*, privately published in the same year, bears the unmistakable imprint of Pope's style:

> Since Spirit first inspir'd, pervaded all,
> And Mind met Matter, at th' Eternal call—
> Since dust weigh'd Genius down, or Genius gave
> Th' immortal halo to the mortal's grave;

and so on for more than a thousand lines.

The Seraphim and Other Poems (1838) and *Poems of 1844* were Barrett Browning's first widely published volumes and the first in which a new sense of herself as a woman poet emerged. The latter especially brought good reviews:

> Mr. Chorley, in the "Athenaeum," described the volume as "extraordinary," adding that "between her poems and the slighter lyrics of the sisterhood, there is all the difference which exists between the putting-on of 'singing robes' for altar service, and the taking up lute or harp to enchant an indulgent circle of friends and kindred."[12]

"The Seraphim" (1838) and "The Drama of Exile" (1844) are both long dramatic poems, influenced by Milton's work. "A Vision of Poets" (1844) and "Lady Geraldine's Courtship" (1844), both about poets, seem traditional because the writers are male. In each case, however, the writer's vision is clarified through interaction with a strong and intelligent woman. In the former the woman specifically instructs the poet as to his true function. Although the poet is not yet identified as a woman, as she will be ten years later in *Aurora Leigh* (1856), this is a radical departure from male tradition, where the woman's function is not to know about poetry but to "inspire" the poet from afar through her beauty or to seduce him away from his work.

Barrett Browning was certain of her dedication to poetry:

> I cannot remember the time when I did not love it—with a lying-awake sort of passion at nine years old, and with a more powerful feeling since. . . . At this moment I love it more than ever—and am more bent than ever, if possible, to work into light . . not into popularity but into expression . . whatever faculty I have. This is the object of the intellectual part of me—and if I live it shall be done. . . . for poetry's own sake . . . for the sake of my love of it. Love is the safest and most unwearied moving principle in all things—it is an heroic worker.[13]

To this poet love is not self-denial and resignation, but a powerful energy
source for the transformation of vision into poetry. Sloughing off the male
mask in "The Soul's Expression" (1844), she describes forcefully her own
creative process:

> With stammering lips and insufficient sound
> I strive and struggle to deliver right
> That music of my nature, day and night
> With dream and thought and feeling interwound,
> And inly answering all the senses round
> With octaves of a mystic depth and height
> Which step out grandly to the infinite
> From the dark edges of the sensual ground.
> This song of soul I struggle to outbear
> Through portals of the sense, sublime and whole,
> And utter all myself into the air:
> But if I did it, —as the thunder-roll
> Breaks its own cloud, my flesh would perish there,
> Before that dread apocalypse of soul.

Her determination to "work into light" necessitates the "stammering lips
and insufficient sound" with which she struggles to "deliver right / That
music of my nature." Her vision comes through her senses, as she seeks
transcendence to "step out grandly to the infinite / From the dark edges of the
sensual ground." As a woman trained to a "passive recipiency," she experi-
ences the active energy of creativity as potentially destructive. Compelled to
deliver the "music of my nature," she fears to give herself totally to her
imagination "and utter all myself into the air," fears "my flesh would perish
there, / Before that dread apocalypse of soul." And yet it was through the
power of her imagination that she created her identity and her ability to deal
with her eight-year "captivity" as a Victorian female invalid, as "The
Prisoner" (1844) reveals:

> . . . Nature's lute
> Sounds on, behind this door so closely shut,
> A strange wild music to the prisoner's ears,
> Dilated by the distance, till the brain
> Grows dim with fancies which it feels too fine:

"Behind this door" she responded passionately to George Sand's novels,
and her sonnet "To George Sand: A Recognition" (1844) contains a clear
statement about the special nature of a woman's voice writing of women's
concerns:

> True genius, but true woman! dost deny
> The woman's nature with a manly scorn,
> And break away the gauds and armlets worn
> By weaker women in captivity?
> Ah, vain denial! that revolted cry
> Is sobbed in by a woman's voice forlorn,—
> Thy woman's hair, my sister, all unshorn
> Floats back dishevelled strength in agony,
> Disproving thy man's name: and while before
> The world thou burnest in a poet-fire,
> We see thy woman-heart beat evermore
> Through the large flame. Beat purer, heart, and higher,
> Till God unsex thee on the heavenly shore
> Where unincarnate spirits purely aspire!

The male mask can never hide the "revolted cry . . . sobbed in by a woman's voice forlorn." She implies no woman can "break away the gauds and armlets worn / By weaker women in captivity." Barrett Browning recognized that if women generally are exploited and oppressed, then all women as a class suffer, no matter any individual woman's apparent privilege. She identifies herself here as part of a community of women, "we," as opposed to "the world" of men.

In *Poems of 1844* there is a strongly evolving consciousness of herself as a woman poet and of her belief that the "sole work" of the poet "is to represent the age," as "The Cry of the Children"—about child factory-workers—shows.[14] But this new voice and subject matter were not supported by nor obvious to all of her old friends. In September 1843 she articulates to an early mentor, Hugh Boyd, her belief in this new poetry:

> Will you see the 'Cry of the (Children)' or not? It will not please you, probably. It wants melody. The versification is eccentric to the ear, and the subject (the factory miseries) is scarcely an agreeable one to the fancy. Perhaps altogether you had better not see it, because I know you think me to be deteriorating, and I don't want you to have farther hypothetical evidence of so false an opinion. Frankly, if not humbly, I believe myself to have gained power since . . . the 'Seraphim'. . . . I differ with you, the longer I live, on the ground of what you call the 'jumping lines' . . . and the tenacity of my judgement (arises) . . . from the deeper study of the old master-poets—English poets—those of the Elizabeth and James ages, before the corruption of French rhythms stole in with Waller and Denham, and was acclimated into a national inode ousness by Dryden and Pope.[15]

Barrett Browning asserts her "power," the "tenacity of her judgement," and her defiance of both her critics and the established poetic tradition. In the following year, August 1844, she explains to John Kenyon:

> I wish I could persuade you of the rightness of my view about 'Essays on Mind' and such things, and how the difference between them and my present poems is not merely the difference between two schools, . . . nor even the difference between immaturity and maturity; but that it is the difference between the dead and the living, between a copy and an individuality, between what is myself and what is not myself.[16]

She grew increasingly convinced that women writers should actively concern themselves with social conditions. In 1853 she exhorts the art critic and her life-long correspondent, Mrs. Jameson:

> Not read Mrs. Stowe's book! But you *must*. Her book is quite a sign of the times, and has otherwise and intrinsically considerable power. For myself, I rejoice in the success, both as a woman and a human being. Oh, and is it possible that you think a woman has no business with questions like the question of slavery? Then she had better use a pen no more. She had better subside into slavery and concubinage herself, I think, as in the times of old, shut herself up with the Penelopes in the 'women's apartment,' and take no rank among thinkers and speakers.[17]

"A Curse for a Nation" confirms Barrett Browning's refusal to "subside into slavery and concubinage." Written for the abolitionist movement in America and published in *Poems Before Congress* (1860), the poem incurred the wrath of critics disturbed by her interference in politics. Tough poetry results from her conviction that this is precisely her role:

> 'Therefore,' the voice said, 'shalt thou write
>   My curse to-night.
> Because thou hast strength to see and hate
> A foul thing done *within* thy gate.'
>
> 'Not so,' I answered once again.
>   'To curse, choose men.
> For I, a woman, have only known
> How the heart melts and tears run down.'
>
> 'Therefore,' the voice said, 'shalt thou write
>   My curse to-night.
> Some women weep and curse, I say
> (And no one marvels), night and day.

'And thou shalt take their part to-night,
        Weep and write.
A curse from the depths of womanhood
Is very salt, and bitter, and good.'

Barrett Browning specifically repudiates her assigned role as "lady" who knows only "How the heart melts and tears run down." She designates herself as spokesperson for those less-privileged women who "weep and curse, I say / (And no one marvels), night and day," thereby defying patriarchy's division of "ladies" from working-class women.

Her anger against critics who disavowed her right to step beyond the limits laid down for "lady poets" had been revealed some years earlier in a fascinating discussion of Florence Nightingale, whom she came to see as performing an age-old role, that of angel on the battlefield:

> I know Florence Nightingale slightly. . . . I honour her from my heart. . . .
> At the same time, I confess to be at a loss to see any new position for the sex, or the most imperfect solution of the 'woman's question,' in this step of hers. . . . Since the seige of Troy and earlier, we have had princesses binding wounds with their hands; it's strictly the woman's part, and men understand it so. . . . Every man is on his knees before ladies carrying lint, calling them 'angelic she's,' whereas, if they stir an inch as thinkers or artists from the beaten line (involving more good to general humanity than is involved in lint), the very same men would curse the impudence of the very same women and stop there. . . . For my own part (and apart from the exceptional miseries of the war), I acknowledge to you that I do not consider the best use to which we can put a gifted and accomplished woman is to *make her a hospital nurse*. If it is, why then woe to us all who are artists![18]

Barrett Browning wants to start healing the wounds of women by naming them. She writes of the Crimean War:

> War, war! It is terrible certainly. But there are worse plagues, deeper griefs, dreader wounds than the physical. What of the forty thousand wretched women in this city? The silent writhing of them is to me more appalling than the roar of the cannons.[19]

The "homely domestic ballad" which Chorley sees as being purified on "passing into female hands" is subverted by Barrett Browning to condemn men's seduction and exploitation of women.[20] "The Rhyme of the Duchess of May" (1844), a long ballad-poem set in the Middle Ages, tells of an orphaned girl betrothed by her guardian at twelve to his son. Grown into womanhood, she refuses this marriage, having chosen her own lover. The viewing of women as a commercial commodity is pointed up by her guardian's response to her decision:

> 'Good my niece, that hand withal looketh
>   somewhat soft and small
> For so large a will, in sooth.'

To which the niece astutely replies:

> 'Little hand clasps muckle gold, or it were
>   not worth the hold
> Of thy son, good uncle mine!'

The duchess secretly marries her lover. When her uncle's soldiers try to reclaim his "property," even her husband intends to kill himself on the assumption that his wife will be forgiven. She refuses to see herself as property and dies with her chosen husband to avoid life with a man she detests.

The finely honed ballad "Amy's Cruelty" (1862) hinges on the ironic observation that what seems to be a woman's cruelty to her lover is in fact her only defense against exploitation:

> Fair Amy of the terraced house,
>   Assist me to discover
> Why you who would not hurt a mouse
>   Can torture so your lover.
>   . . . . .
> But when *he* haunts your door . . . the town
>   Marks coming and marks going . . .
> You seem to have stitched your eyelids down
>   To that long piece of sewing!

Amy's life is circumscribed. She sits daily in the "terraced house" fulfilling her sewing duties. Yet she has the power to protect herself and the insight to know the dangers of love:

> He wants my world, my sun, my heaven,
>   Soul, body, whole existence.
>   . . . . .
> I only know my mother's love
>   Which gives all and asks nothing;
> And this new loving sets the groove
>   Too much the way of loathing.

> Unless he gives me all in change,
>   I forfeit all things by him:
> The risk is terrible and strange—
>   I tremble, doubt, . . . deny him.

The "risk is terrible": in "Void in Law" (1862) a court finds a marriage void because only one witness was competent. The husband can now marry another woman, approved by society, one whose:

> . . . throat has the antelope curve,
> And her cheek just the color and line
> Which fade not before him nor swerve.

The first wife and child are legally abandoned.

"Bianca Among the Nightingales" (1862), one of Barrett Browning's most technically exciting ballad-poems, opens with a frank celebration of sexuality. Bianca remembers embracing her lover in the Italian moonlight:

> And *we*, too! from such soul-height went
> Such leaps of blood, so blindly driven,
>   . . . . .
> The nightingales, the nightingales!
>
> We paled with love, we shook with love,
> We kissed so close we could not vow. . . .

The nightingales, whose singing "throbbed" in Italy with the passion of their love, haunt Bianca in "gloomy England," where she follows her lover who has abandoned her to pursue a woman of great beauty: "These nightingales will sing me mad." Bianca delineates the difference between his love for her and for the other woman:

> He says to her what moves her most.
>   He would not name his soul within
> Her hearing, —rather pays the cost
>   With praises to her lips and chin.

She is physically to be praised as ritualistically as any sonneteer's mistress. She has a "fine tongue" and "loose gold ringlets," but to Bianca she is "mere cold clay / As all false things are." The only person who will know this woman's soul is Bianca: "She lied and stole, / And spat into my love's pure pyx / The rank saliva of her soul." Barrett Browning explores the reality that a woman who truly wishes to be herself, to experience her sexuality and some kind of fruitful relationship with the male world will

be challenged by the more acceptable norm of the woman who has learned
to remain all beautiful surface, hidden both from herself and from the
men she must please. The refrain "The nightingales, the nightingales" moves
relentlessly from an affirmation of love to a taunting that drives Bianca to
madness. In the last stanza the extended refrain and repetition enact her
frenzy:

> —Oh, owl-like birds! They sing for spite,
>   They sing for hate, they sing for doom,
> They'll sing through death who sing through night,
>   They'll sing and stun me in the tomb—
> The nightingales, the nightingales!

Bianca knows she can never be like the other woman, but neither can she
bear the ostracism attendant on being different.

The woman who is not abandoned is just as easily prey to exploitation.
"Lord Walter's Wife" (1862) sets her husband's friend straight when he is
horror-stricken at her suggestion of an affair—the logical conclusion to his
flirtatious innuendoes:

> 'A moment, —I pray your attention!—I
>   have a poor word in my head
> I must utter, though womanly custom
>   would set it down better unsaid.
>   . . . . .
> 'You did me the honour, perhaps to be
>   moved at my side now and then
> In the senses—a vice, I have heard, which
>   is common to beasts and some men.
>   . . . . .
> 'And since, when all's said, you're too
>   noble to stoop to the frivolous cant
> About crimes irresistible, virtues that swin-
>   dle, betray, and supplant,
>
> 'I determined to prove to yourself that,
>   whate'er you might dream or avow
> By illusion, you wanted precisely no more
>   of me than you have now.'

This poem caused Thackeray much embarrassment when it was submitted
to him for publication in the *Cornhill Magazine* in 1861:

. . . one of the best wives, mothers, women in the world writes some verses which I feel certain would be objected to by many of our readers. . . . In your poem, you know, there is an account of unlawful passion, felt by a man for a woman, and though you write pure doctrine, and real modesty, and pure ethics, I am sure our readers would make an outcry, and so I have not published this poem.[21]

Barrett Browning replies in no uncertain terms:

I am not a 'fast woman.' I don't like coarse subjects, or the coarse treatment of any subject. But I am deeply convinced that the corruption of our society requires not shut doors and windows, but light and air: and that it is exactly because pure and prosperous women choose to *ignore* vice, that miserable women suffer wrong by it everywhere. Has paterfamilias, with his Oriental traditions and veiled female faces, very successfully dealt with a certain class of evil? What if materfamilias, with her quick sure instincts and honest innocent eyes, do more towards their expulsion by simply looking at them and calling them by their names?[22]

This strong conviction in the last year of her life that the responsibility of the woman poet was to confront and name the condition of women had manifested itself in her poetry from the *Seraphim* on, as she sought to delineate the complexity of female experience. She wrote powerfully about the institution of motherhood in patriarchy, and the experience of biological motherhood. "The Virgin Mary to the Child Jesus" (1838) is a meditation in Mary's voice. She begins poignantly, unsure what name she can call this child who is both of her flesh and also her Lord. She watches Jesus sleeping, imagines he dreams of God his father, whereas the best she can give him is a mother's kiss. Patriarchal Christian tradition exalts Mary as most honored; a woman writes of the pain Mary would experience mothering a child simultaneously hers and not hers:

> Then, I think aloud
> The words 'despised,'—'rejected,'—every word
> Recoiling into darkness as I view
>   The DARLING on my knee.
> Bright angels, —move not—lest ye stir the cloud
> Betwixt my soul and his futurity!
> I must not die, with mother's work to do,
>   And could not live—and see.

The implications of the poem point beyond the immediate meditation to a consideration of how patriarchy always destines its sons for a life beyond their mothers. Another early poem, "Victoria's Tears" (1838), explores how the young woman is jolted from her childhood into mothering her country as its queen (when women were not even enfranchised). Barrett Browning contrasts the grandiose coronation with her sense of what the young woman has lost:

> She saw no purples shine,
>   For tears had dimmed her eyes;
> She only knew her childhood's flowers
>   Were happier pageantries!
> And while her heralds played the part,
>   For million shouts to drown—
> 'God save the Queen' from hill to mart,—
> She heard through all her beating heart,
>   And turned and wept—
> She wept, to wear a crown!

Both poems pinpoint the isolation of the "token woman," whose position of supposed privilege is actually one of loneliness and confusion.

In "The Cry of the Children" (1844), she exposes how hopeless it is for the child factory workers to cry to mothers powerless to alleviate their suffering:

> Do ye hear the children weeping, O my brothers,
>   Ere the sorrow comes with years?
> They are leaning their young heads against their mothers,
>   And *that* cannot stop their tears.
>   . . . . .
> But the young, young children, O my brothers,
>   Do you ask them why they stand
> Weeping sore before the bosom of their mothers,
>   In our happy Fatherland?

The capitalization of "Fatherland" but not of "mothers" underlines the power structure: the natural flesh bond between the child and mother is helpless before the demands of patriarchy. The children mourn Alice, who died from the brutal working conditions: "Could we see her face, be sure we should not know her, / For the smile has time for growing in her eyes. . . ." That it is a girl who dies from such work in a society that draped its middle-class women with prudery, passivity and sentimentality should not go unnoticed. Repetition creates the delirium of these children's exhaustion, pulling us into their experience:

'For all day the wheels are droning, turning;
　　Their wind comes in our faces,
Till our hearts turn, our heads with pulses burning,
　　And the walls turn in their places:
Turns the sky in the high window, blank and reeling,
　　Turns the long light that drops adown the wall,
Turn the black flies that crawl along the ceiling:
　　All are turning, all the day, and we with all.
And all day the iron wheels are droning,
　　And sometimes we could pray,
"O ye wheels" (breaking out in a mad moaning),
　　"Stop! be silent for to-day!" '

Victimization is again exposed in "The Runaway Slave at Pilgrim's Point"
(1850), spoken in the voice of a young black woman slave being flogged to
death where the pilgrims landed. On the plantation she had loved a black
male slave. The white overseers, learning of this love, beat the man to
death and, seeing her grief, her owner rapes her. Her initial response to the
child born of this rape is love:

> Thus we went moaning, child and mother,
> One to another, one to another,

but

> . . . the babe who lay on my bosom so,
> 　Was far too white, too white for me;
> As white as the ladies who scorned to pray
> Beside me at church but yesterday.

Soon she cannot look at her son and strains a handkerchief over his face.
He struggles against this, wanting his freedom: "For the white child wanted
his liberty— / Ha, Ha! he wanted the master-right." The dichotomies her
son represents overwhelm her. She loves him but hates that, being male
and white, he will grow up with the right to violate a woman as her rapist,
his father, did. She loves him but:

> Why, in that single glance I had
> 　Of my child's face, . . . I tell you all,
> I saw a look that made me mad!
> 　The *master's* look, that used to fall
> On my soul like his lash . . . or worse!
> And so, to save it from my curse,
> 　I twisted it round in my shawl.

She strangles her son so she will neither have to repudiate him later, nor experience her rape reenacted every time she looks into his face. She runs from the plantation holding the child to her for many days before burying him. Her owner catches her and flogs her to death. Taplin's dismissal of the poem as "too blunt and shocking" only underscores the poem's explosive exposure of racism and sexism.[23]

Barrett Browning had four pregnancies in the four years after her marriage. Only the third ended with a birth, that of her son, Robert Wiedeman ("Penini") in 1849. The experience of childbirth and biological motherhood informs "Only a Curl" (1862), written on receiving a lock of hair from the parents of a dead child unknown to the poet. In language movingly reminiscent of "The Soul's Expression," written twenty years earlier about the creative process, Barrett Browning comforts by saying how once a mother has known her power in childbirth her child is always in some way part of the mother's experience:

> . . . I appeal
> To all who bear babes—in the hour
> When the veil of the body we feel
> Rent round us, —while torments reveal
> The motherhood's advent in power,
>
> And the babe cries!—has each of us known
> By apocalypse (God being there
> Full in nature) the child is our own,
> Life of life, love of love, moan of moan,
> Through all changes, all times, everywhere.

She records in her letters what a powerful and health-giving experience childbirth was. Even today, forty-three is considered "late" for giving birth to a first child. For Barrett Browning, almost given up as dead three years earlier, to have that much physical power was exhilarating.

One of her last poems, "Mother and Poet" (1862), confronts, like "The Virgin Mary to the Child Jesus," the conflict between a mother's relationship with her sons and their destiny within patriarchy. It is spoken in the voice of Laura Savio, an Italian poet and patriot dedicated, as was Barrett Browning, to the unification of Italy. Savio's two sons were killed fighting for "freedom." The poet reconsiders the meaning of both motherhood and patriotism after their deaths:

> To teach them . . . It stings there! I made them indeed
> Speak plain the word *country. I* taught them, no doubt,
> That a country's a thing men should die for at need.
> *I* prated of liberty, rights, and about
> The tyrant cast out.

She imagines the victory celebrations:

> Forgive me. Some women bear children in strength,
>   And bite back the cry of their pain in self-scorn;
> But the birth-pangs of nations will wring us at length
>   Into wail such as this—and we sit on forlorn
>   When the man-child is born.
>
> Dead! One of them shot by the sea in the east,
>   And one of them shot in the west by the sea.
> Both! both my boys! If in keeping the feast
>   You want a great song for your Italy free,
>   Let none look at *me*!

To Barrett Browning, whose son had grown up listening to her passionate political talk and at twelve spoke eagerly of his own desire to fight for freedom, this is an assessment of great integrity about her own complicity in patriarchy. She understands that the energetic womanhood manifest in the bearing of children is undermined by mothers, like herself, who incorporate patriarchal values into their own consciousness and become breeders of cannon fodder. Taplin brushes the poem off as "devoid of inspiration," quite missing the poet's sophisticated insight into women's contribution to their own oppression.[24]

"Mother and Poet" fuses three of Barrett Browning's preoccupations in her writing—art, politics, and motherhood—as a manifestation of powerful womanhood. "What art's for a woman?" she has Laura Savio ask. In her own career she was increasingly convinced that women as "artists and thinkers" must be concerned with social interaction, social conditions, and political events. Realizing that the "personal is the political," she used her physical and emotional experiences as a woman to illuminate the public sphere. In doing so she created a voice and vision for herself as a woman poet and became truly our "grandmother." Like many grandmothers, she has been unjustly ignored; like many grandmothers, she has healing wisdom to share. As early as 1845 she believed:

> . . . we should all be ready to say that if the secrets of
> our daily lives & inner souls may instruct other
> surviving souls, let them be open to men hereafter,
> even as they are to God now. Dust to dust, & soul-
> secrets to humanity—there are natural heirs to all
> things.[25]

6.

Christina Rossetti: The Inward Pose

Dolores Rosenblum

> It's a weary life, it is, she said:—
>   Doubly blank in a woman's lot:
> I wish and I wish I were a man:
>   Or, better than any being, were not:
>
> Were nothing at all in the world,
>   Not a body and not a soul:
> Not so much as a grain of dust
>   Or drop of water from pole to pole.[1]
> ("From the Antique," 28 June 1854)

So said Christina Rossetti, author of a large body of lyric and narrative verse that, like her elusive masterpiece "Goblin Market," is at once transparent and opaque. In these stanzas of "From the Antique," Rossetti contrives a disguise—the music-hall lilt, the sly attribution, "she said"—that allows her to reveal opinions she may have considered but could not, as a Victorian woman, have held.

This "doubleness," not duplicity, pervades her verse. Her themes are presence and absence, fulfillment and loss, joy and sorrow, time and eternity, life and death. There is no progression, no mediate condition, only radical shifts from one state to another in poem after poem. Thus, doubleness becomes a structural principle: her poetry is organized around distinctions so relentlessly absolute that the syntactic relation between opposed entities is as important as the semantic signification of the individual words. Doubleness as structure is also manifested in Rossetti's predilection for the colloquy form: the speaker exhorts herself and addresses a distant God who offers and withdraws, remonstrates and forgives. At its most extreme, doubleness is represented as sister-personae motivated by incompatible impulses. Its source is a self-division close to self-loathing. This is Rossetti lying awake, watching a spider and its shadow on a blank wall:

They jerked, zigzagged, advanced, retreated, he and his shadow, posturing in ungainly indissoluble harmony. He seemed exasperated, fascinated, desperately endeavouring and utterly hopeless.

What could it mean? One meaning and one only suggested itself. That spider saw without recognising his black double and was mad to disengage himself from the horrible pursuing inalienable presence.

To me this self-haunted spider . . . remains isolated irretrievably with his own horrible self.[2]

A striking instance of self-awareness, a personal revelation, as commentators on the passage have observed.[3] But the context, the devotional journal *Time Flies,* a chatty spiritual guide, suggests a rhetorical purpose: the passage is a cautionary tale to instruct others. As in the poems, Rossetti "hides" all the better to reveal.

Like most Victorian poets, Rossetti is sensitive to the disjunction between surface and depths, between appearances and the buried life. More than others, however, she is concerned with the point of juncture, literally the face that is looked at and the eyes that look out from it. Her poems are full of references to faces, masks, veils, shrouds, and, less frequently, bodies fixed in an attitude—all surfaces to be regarded. This preoccupation with being looked at is not surprising in a woman poet. As Simone de Beauvoir has pointed out, in a patriarchal culture woman inevitably experiences herself as object and other. The problem is especially acute during adolescence, when woman must make herself into or pretend to be an alluring object. Then "the very face itself becomes a mask."[4]

In order to appreciate Rossetti's variation on this broad theme we need to consider her special experience as an artist's model. From an early age she sat for sketches and portraits. This is not a unique situation in itself, except that the artist for whom she primarily sat was responsible for the period's most famous incarnations of woman as mysterious "other"—her brother, Dante Gabriel Rossetti. Further, she actually was a professional model, in that Dante Gabriel used her face and body (as well as his wife's and mistresses') for the subjects of his paintings. He painted not only Christina Rossetti, but also the Virgin Mary with Christina's features. Throughout her life, then, Rossetti was conscious of being carefully observed. Her presentation of self to the world was interdependent with the world's representations of her. This general and pervasive life situation generates the poetry more strongly than such accidents and calculated rearrangements of her life-plot as disappointment in love or broken engagements. Whatever its ultimate source, Rossetti's impulse toward self-scrutiny is reinforced by her persistent awareness of being scrutinized, transfixed with a look, killed into art.

A beautiful and wrathful little girl grows up into a reserved middle-aged woman with a melancholy, impassive face, a mask that effectively disguises all passion. In the years between, friends, physicians, and suitors see her as "interesting" rather than beautiful. To them her attractiveness consisted of an air of "mystery" and "sweetness," a convenient transformation of social liabilities into assets. Then, as now, conventional feminine beauty involved a certain studied animation which Rossetti either could not or cared not to master. Her devoted friend and biographer, Mackenzie Bell, wrote in 1898:

> When I first met her she had acquired much of the portliness of middle age, and her face in repose was sometimes rather heavy and even unemotional. But her smile was always delightful, and, when in animated conversation on some especially congenial theme, her face to the last was comely. It is this marked difference between the comparatively unattractive aspect of her features in repose, and the great change which came over their lineaments that makes her photographs taken later in life seem so unsatisfactory.[5]

What is remarkable about this account is Bell's discomfort, his need to apologize for something disquieting in Rossetti's appearance. Apparently he was relieved when Rossetti displayed a familiar and approved version of woman's mask—girlish animation. Once the woman is beyond girlhood, "mystery" and "sweetness" alone do not hold up; the face simply in repose is forbidding and unwomanly.

No doubt Rossetti's imperfect adaptation, the protective coloration that is subtly "off," was a problem shared by many Victorian women. But Rossetti knew from the beginning that she was expected to display herself in a special way. In fact, she had to learn how to pose: at the age of seven for the family friend and painter, Filippo Pistrucci, who executed a watercolor which, according to Bell, "fully justifies the opinion of most of her early friends that in youth Christina was beautiful";[6] at nineteen for an oil portrait by her first suitor, the faintest of the Pre-Raphaelite brothers, James Collinson; and always, of course, for her brother Dante Gabriel, who knew well how to capitalize on the mystery and sweetness for his ground-breaking paintings, "The Girlhood of Mary Virgin" and "Ecce Ancilla Domini." Thus haloed and etherialized, Rossetti must have soon realized that she could in no way compete with the languidly sensuous Pre-Raphaelite "stunners," Elizabeth Siddal, Jane Morris, Fanny Cornforth. What a misfortune, then, to contract a disease that was not only debilitating but also disfiguring—the exopthalmic bronchocele (Graves' disease), which at its worst produced bulging eyes and a darkening and roughening of her skin. Quite possibly the disease contributed to the masklike quality Bell found so disturbing.

Although Rossetti must have found being looked at painful, at times she must also have derived considerable pleasure from the attention. The model sits motionless, aware that her face is being scrutinized and transformed in ways beyond her control. As compensation she gets undivided attention and a kind of immortality. Yet being so exposed, especially in an age when faces were read as indices to character, Christina Rossetti could have feared revealing too much, perhaps an expression neither sweet nor humble.

As the word "model" signifies, Rossetti's posing suggests psychic constraints as well as physical immobility.[7] She models *for* her brother and his friends; she becomes a model of Christian—and female—forbearance and humility. In this exhortation from *Time Flies* she overtly expresses her sense of the need to maintain an appropriate mask: "Any one may be the observer; and equally any one may be the observed. Liable to such casualties, I advise *myself* to assume a modest and unobtrusive demeanour."[8] But the face which is rigidified by illness and depression, by holding a pose and maintaining decorum, becomes a powerful defense, even a mode of aggression, as this seemingly stoical declaration reveals: "Yea, therefore, as a flint I set my face."[9]

Being looked at calls to mind its active opposite, looking. Thus, Rossetti is able to retreat behind the icon of herself and see without being seen. Her mask—not only the impassivity but also the whole complex of her demeanor, including the girlishness and sweetness that she could often marshal to lighten her features—was an effective strategy for encapsulating the strong self that speaks out urgently through the poems. The mask stands between her and the active world in which she falls sick whenever the stresses are too great, as when she is presented with the options of becoming governess or wife. In this world, too, she loves mother best, attends high-church services regularly, ascribes lofty intellectual gifts to her plain and cheerful older sister, learns her main life and art lesson—*not to be first*. Never, never, a word of bitterness that *he*, the talented, sensual, extroverted brother, should be first.

The mask is not only a defense, however. The ability to observe without being noticed, to withdraw and mingle at the same time, is particularly useful to the artist. Rossetti's double-faced strategy is evident in an anecdote passed on by her chief modern biographer. Lona Mosk Packer relates that at Penkill Castle, William Bell Scott's residence in Scotland where Rossetti made several visits, she had a special turret apartment. Packer describes how "from the old-fashioned garden below, Christina was often seen standing in front of the little four-cornered window which, Arthur Hughes tells us, 'exactly framed her.' Her habitual position was to lean forward, 'elbows on the sill, hands supporting her face,' and she could be seen for hours 'meditating and composing.'" Packer adds, "But she could see as well as be seen," and goes on to sketch in the scene Rossetti must have observed.[10] This is

Rossetti moodily posing as artist/model, free to retreat behind her "mysterious" mask, free to retreat even further, to her lonely room, ostensibly feeling sorry for herself, but really free to do what she likes—write.

Rossetti reproduces this pose in the poem "Day-Dreams" (*Works*, p. 332), which describes "my soul's soul" as "Gazing through her chamber-window," sitting immobile and enigmatic "With her dreaming eyes." At her death the speaker will have this soul "carved in alabaster," in the identical attitude she assumed in life. Through the poem Rossetti becomes both artist and model, killing off the model in order to make art out of a life pose.

Just as much as Rossetti needs to hide behind her mask or pose in order to protect and develop her writer-self,[11] she longs to be *known* in all her conflicting aspects: rich/impoverished, humble/proud, fearless/fearful, independent/dependent. References to the concrete details of appearance are rare in Rossetti's poetry; the face is an icon with only a smile, golden or graying tresses, pallor or ruddiness, occasionally lines of "care." In a number of poems, however, Rossetti is explicit about the discrepancy between this iconic face and the "true" or "hidden" self that she wishes recognized. These include "Enrica, 1865," "In Progress," "A Soul," and "In an Artist's Studio."

"Enrica, 1865" describes the visit of a woman from Italy, Rossetti's "mother country." Here physical beauty is lightened and amplified by mobility, as opposed to the characteristic immobility that Rossetti's women cultivate:

> Our dimness brightened in her smile,
> Our tongue grew sweeter in her mouth.
>
> We chilled beside her liberal glow,
> She dwarfed us by her ampler scale.

While Enrica is "Warm-hearted and of cordial face," "We Englishwomen" are:

>   . . . trim, correct,
> All minted in the selfsame mould,
> Warm-hearted but of semblance cold,
> All courteous out of self-respect.
>
>   (*Works*, p. 377)

Whatever the constraints—inhibiting pride, unwillingness to take risks, social convention—they prevent the untrammeled expression of feeling. But the poem ends with a remarkable assertion of autonomy, the presentation of a self that needs to be known, and perhaps can only be recognized by another woman:

> But, if she found us like our sea,
>   Of aspect colourless and chill,
>   Rock-girt, —like it she found us still
> Deep at our deepest, strong and free.
> (*Works*, p. 378)

The trim and correct Englishwoman of "Enrica" has a counterpart in a poem written three years earlier. "In Progress" (*Works*, p. 352) presents a calm, patient, subdued woman, "Gravely monotonous like a passing bell."[12] The poem begins with the stark declaration, "Ten years ago it seemed impossible / That she should ever grow so calm as this"; it ends with a startling apotheosis: "Sometimes I fancy we may one day see / Her head shoot lightnings and her shoulders wings." So the subdued woman of the middle section, of time present, is in a developmental stage. She has emerged from her implied past turbulence but is still evolving toward an apocalyptic transformation. For the figure at the end is markedly aggressive, an avenging angel/Medusa dangerous to look upon.

The inner woman of "Enrica" is strong and free, endowed with a mobility that her outward restraint belies. The relatively immobile woman of "In Progress" seems to be biding her time, awaiting a dazzling apotheosis; the woman as soul in "A Soul" (1854) is totally immobilized, transfixed in a pose, and prepared to wait indefinitely, though she is at the end of her resources:

> She stands as pale as Parian statues stand;
>   Like Cleopatra when she turned at bay,
>
>   . . . . .
> She stands alone, a wonder deathly-white:
> She stands there patient nerved with inner might,
>   Indomitable in her feebleness,
> Her face and will athirst against the light.
> (*Works,* p. 311)

This is a soul's primary strength: to rigidify into a statuesque pose, to endure rather than act, her freedom reduced to choosing to make an asset of her "feebleness."

The soul as conquered Cleopatra may only appear weak—her strength is manifested in the tenacity with which she holds her pose. Perhaps we could see her strength if we could look into that face, a point of view reserved for God in the numerous devotional poems which present a face turned toward the light, or toward visions beyond ordinary sight. The Cleopatra-soul holds a pose that invites our gaze; she herself gazes at something beyond our vision.

The three poems discussed above are preoccupied with a kind of physical immobility that suggests striking a pose, whether artistic or social. They also hold out the possibility that the speaker and/or subject of the poem possesses an inner strength and freedom that is sometimes belied, sometimes engendered by the immobility, as in "A Soul." Again we see the doubleness of Rossetti's strategies—the surface appearance that both hides and reveals.

This configuration is given a particularly meaningful variation in "In an Artist's Studio." We know from William Michael's note, and from the internal evidence of the poem, that the figure referred to is Elizabeth Siddal, Dante Gabriel's wife and model. We know also that the Rossetti family, Christina especially, were rather hostile toward Siddal.[13] We may surmise that Rossetti felt considerable jealousy toward the beautiful young woman who had replaced her as *model*. Yet Rossetti's poem shows unusual compassion and insight:

> One face looks out from all his canvases,
>   One selfsame figure sits or walks or leans:
>   We found her hidden just behind those screens,
> That mirror gave back all her loveliness.
>
>   . . . . .
>   . . . every canvas means
> The same one meaning, neither more nor less.
> He feeds upon her face by day and night,
>   And she with true kind eyes looks back on him,
> Fair as the moon and joyful as the light:
>   Not wan with waiting, not with sorrow dim;
>   Not as she is, but was when hope shone bright;
>   Not as she is, but as she fills his dream.
>   (*Works*, p. 330)

Here Rossetti's repetitive formulations are a perfect realization of her theme: the various pictorial representations of a woman in different costumes and different poses all add up to one meaning. This meaning is not in any way transcendent; rather, it is frighteningly reductive. Whether she sits or walks or leans, this figure is immobile, the product of an *idée fixe*. The ambiguity of the pronoun in line three suggests that Rossetti intends a conflation of the living woman with the still picture; the verb "feed" in line nine reinforces this impression and also implies that the artist is a vampire who has drained life from the flesh-and-blood woman in order to gratify his dream. Elizabeth Siddal has clearly been killed into art—her monolithic "loveliness" disguising the woman as she *is*: drained by anxiety, or simply by the conversion of self into object. She is meant to be regarded, not treated with regard.

Behind the compassion lurks horror and rage. There is either nothing behind the portrait/mask, or something unspeakable. Rossetti wrote two poems, "The World" (*Works*, p. 182, dated 1854) and "Babylon the Great" (*Works*, p. 284, dated only "before 1893"), depicting the loathsome woman, the whorish Medusa.

The world-woman of the earlier poem is truly degenerate. She demonstrates the terrifying consequences of disintegration:

> By day she woos me, soft, exceeding fair:
>   But all night as the moon so changeth she;
>   Loathsome and foul with hideous leprosy,
> And subtle serpents gliding in her hair.

Although Rossetti is writing within a well-established tradition of biblical imagery, we can see how she again gives form to a personal and a cultural predicament. Trim, correct Englishwomen are really strong and free, but there is also the possibility that lies breed self-loathing and loathsomeness:

> By day she stands a lie: by night she stands
>   In all the naked horror of the truth,
> With pushing horns and clawed and clutching hands.

Unlike this lie/truth woman, Babylon stands undisguised: "Foul is she and ill-favoured, set askew." The loathsome woman in both cases has special powers, however. If the woman of "In an Artist's Studio" has been transfixed and dreamed out of existence, this woman has the power of transfixing the observer and filling his/her dream on her terms:

> Gaze not upon her till thou dream her fair,
>
>   . . . . .
>
>   . . . but filth is there
> Unutterable, with plagues hid out of view.

Nor is she immobile, but rather in frenzied motion: "Gaze not upon her, for her dancing whirl / Turns giddy the fixed gazer presently." Women who are not "posing," composed or in repose, are dangerous to themselves and others.

The repose of death is the ultimate opportunity to compose one's features before they decompose. Like other Victorian poets, Rossetti wrote "morbid" poems concerned with early death, variations on the moments before, the days and years after. Like them, too, she is obsessed with the corporeality of death: the earth lying heavily on the eyes, the body laid out on the bier, the face revealed or veiled but always an object of regard. The vulnerability and self-pity generating these poems are obvious: imagining herself dead, Rossetti can postulate two kinds of gratification. Then, at last, she will be the focus of all eyes, admired and pitied—no one will attempt a critical reading of her face. Also, as she reiterates in numerous religious poems, a lifetime of self-denial will be vindicated in a spectacular inversion: the last will become first, the meek sister now the star of the apocalypse.

These concerns with gratification underlie the "death" poems but do not account for their force or explain their structure. Similarly, it is clear that Rossetti frequently longed for release from the painfulness of living; death is rest from both striving and self-control: "Asleep from risk, asleep from pain" ("Life and Death," *Works*, p. 358). But again these regressive impulses do not vitiate or explain away some of her best poems: the famous lyric beginning "When I am dead, my dearest, / Sing no sad songs for me" (*Works*, p. 290) and the chilling "Dead before Death" (*Works*, p. 313).

What is really worth remarking about these poems is that out of her human, not neurotic, needs—to be admired and cared for, to be protected and yet encouraged toward autonomy (this latter need being the least likely to be fulfilled)—Rossetti made interesting poetry. Her tenacity and obsessiveness are her strengths. Poems that appear to be still another reworking of a dated convention, sentimental "graveyard" poetry—no hint yet of Hardy's irony—turn out to be ingenious variations on the subject of self-as-object, face-as-mask, and, ultimately, as death-mask. Further, through the death-mask Rossetti is able to explore the self's consciousness of self-as-object in a number of poems that represent the dead person as sense-deadened but intensely aware: "She doth not see but knows" ("Life Hidden," *Works*, p. 294). Imagined death is thus a way of being present while absent, seeing while being looked at but not really seen—a situation similar to that of the artist's model, or the "model" sister, daughter, pious church-goer, decorous lady of the drawing-room among Dante Gabriel's glamorous coterie.

In "After Death" (*Works*, p. 292), for instance, the dead woman is laid out for viewing but she is fully conscious, able to observe her mourner in an unguarded moment and hear what she has been wanting to hear: " 'Poor child, poor child,' " the pity that she must accept as a substitute for love. The mourner is caught off guard; the dead woman remains hidden, inscrutable, even though her corporeality is evoked in spite of—or perhaps because of —the negations:

> He did not touch the shroud, or raise the fold
>   That hid my face, or take my hand in his,
>   Or ruffle the smooth pillows for my head.

The speaker in "A Pause" (*Works*, p. 308) is also laid out in her death-chamber, her "love-bound" soul still loitering, watching and waiting for the one significant mourner. Unlike "After Death," this poem does not end with the stillness of the body, intensely present under the shroud, but with an apotheosis, a moment of bodily transfiguration and heightened consciousness:

> At length there came the step upon the stair,
>   Upon the lock the old familiar hand:
> Then first my spirit seemed to scent the air
>   Of Paradise; then first the tardy sand
> Of time ran golden; and I felt my hair
>   Put on a glory, and my soul expand.

A dazzling sight, not normally accessible to mortal vision. Like the angelic Medusa at the end of "In Progress," with her stars, wings, and lightnings, she might turn the gazer to stone.

The heavy earthbound body with its hidden face, the transfigured woman with a visage beyond earthly sight, the invisible woman who sees all—three variations on the pose of death. Rossetti's obsession extends to a number of poems that can be summed up by the title of one: "The Last Look" (*Works*, p. 316). What is it that the final pose hides? Sometimes nothing, nothing that can be *delineated*, that is. In "Life Hidden" Rossetti's voyeurism probes as always for the answer in the face:

> Roses and lilies grow above the place
>   Where she sleeps the long sleep that doth not dream.
> If we could look upon her hidden face,
>   Nor shadow would be there, nor garish gleam
> Of light; . . .
>
> <div align="right">(<i>Works</i>, p. 294)</div>

No shadow, no light—no portrait, in other words.

Whatever lies beneath the earth or behind the shroud—whether the martyr's composed smile ("A Martyr," *Works*, p. 186; "Song," *Works*, p. 300), or the virgin princess's lines of care "The Prince's Progress," or nothing that can be captured as form—the worst situation that Rossetti can imagine is to be caught in the fixed pose of death while still alive. Rossetti's cruelest poem, "Dead before Death," cancels out the sentimentalities that tinge the other after-death poems:

> Ah changed and cold, how changed and very cold,
>   With stiffened smiling lips and cold calm eyes!
>   · · · · ·
> Grown hard and stubborn in the ancient mould,
>   Grown rigid in the sham of life-long lies.
>
> <div align="right">(<i>Works</i>, pp. 313–14)</div>

William Rossetti was "unable to say what gave rise to this intense and denunciatory outpouring," but allows that it "may be regarded as an address to herself." Surely he is right, yet surely it cannot be as he says, that this is a portrait of Rossetti as she might become "if 'Amor Mundi' were to supersede the aspiration after divine grace" (*Works*, p. 479). More to the point is the echo of "mould" and "cold" in the later "Enrica," where the Englishwomen are "All minted in the self-same mould, / Warm-hearted but of semblance cold." If we are to read "Enrica" as in any way autobiographical, then the worst did not happen—Rossetti could always summon the self that was "strong and free." Also simply the power to give imaginative expression to the horror of "Dead before Death" may free the writer from the tyranny of "the sham of life-long lies."

It is doubtful that the "lies" mask a guilty love for William Bell Scott,[14] or the nonexistent lapses of an over-scrupulous sinner tempted by the sensuous pleasures of the world. Though she will admit it only indirectly, in poems that hide and reveal, Rossetti seems to have been aware that the face she presented to the world was itself the lie. It is far more difficult to say what she thought the "truth" was, but she expresses her disgust with the lying face compellingly in a number of poems. "The World," with its loathsome woman, bodies forth a destructive truth that must be confronted. " 'The Iniquity of the Fathers upon the Children' " (*Works*, p. 41) presents a wholesome truth and allows Rossetti, through a persona, to express considerable aggression and autonomy.

The speaker of " 'The Iniquity ...' " narrates a familiar story. The illegitimate offspring of a sixteen-year-old high-born mother, she was raised in secrecy by the mother's nurse and given an identifying gold ring on the nurse's death. Now the Lady of the Hall has taken the girl to live with her, never admitting that she is the true mother, although the girl soon catches on:

> I hate when people come:
> The women speak and stare
> And mean to be so civil.
>
> . . . . .
>
> I like the proud ones best
> Who sit as struck with blindness,
> As if I wasn't there.

Again the misery of being an object of regard, "With eyes glued on me for a gazing-stock," as the speaker of "A Martyr—the Vigil of the Feast" puts it. The girl resolves never to let her mother, the woman with an "untroubled" face, know that she holds "the tangled clue" her mother "huddles out of view" (*Works*, p. 257).

In one remarkable colloquy with herself she reveals the extent of her contempt for the life-long sham:

> Mother, in Paradise
> You'll see with clearer eyes;
> Perhaps in this world even
> When you are like to die
> And face to face with Heaven
> You'll drop for once the lie:
> But you must drop the mask, not I.

My Lady is determined to marry the speaker off, but this is one area where the speaker feels that she can offer resistance to the life-long lie. Her mind is made up "to accept [her] lot unmixed," to go to the grave as "nameless" as she came into the world—that is, completely her own person.

The Lady–mother, the authority figure who must maintain the mask of decorum even at the price of selling out her troublesome daughter, is one opponent in Rossetti's struggle to establish a self in spite of adaptive "lies." The long debate-poem "The Lowest Room" (*Works*, p. 16) presents a stronger confrontation than " 'The Iniquity . . . ,' " but ends with a profound capitulation to the enforcers of the mask. Impossible to challenge mother directly; one can, however, invent a sister stand-in. In "The Lowest Room" two sisters sit, possibly in a room that gives out on a garden, one idle, the other busily embroidering. One sister is pale and graying; the other has a "comely face" and "golden tresses." The speaker, the pale, graying sister, expresses openly her quarrel with the world, that " 'Some must be second and not first; / All cannot be first of all.' " An Arnoldian figure, she longs for the golden age when the structure of values was clearer, when purposeful action was possible. She longs in particular for "Old Homer's sting." Homer's world seemed to allow for the free expression of a range of emotions, from rage and hatred to "fuller love." Even the princess and her handmaidens had power in the world. We are not told what the golden sister is embroidering, but no doubt it is quite different from the ancient women's needlework: "Beneath their needles grew the field / With warriors armed to strike."

What the speaker wants is to be allowed to feel intensely and to articulate, even act on those feelings. The clear divisions between love and hate, and the ability to alternate between one state and the other, would possibly allow the speaker to feel less self-divided, less blurred and depressed. The mild sister is finally stirred to rebuke this troublesome, somewhat "childish" sister who wants all the wrong things. She claims that there is no reason why she and her sister should not attain "heroic strength" within their domestic sphere, and that the lesson to be learned from Homer is this: " 'Only Achilles in his rage / And sloth is less than man.' " Are these the qualities that Rossetti most feared in herself—anger followed by self-pitying withdrawal and depressed indolence?

At any rate, the appropriate model is not the bestially wrathful Achilles, but rather Christ. The speaker feels rebuked in her "secret self," where she nurses "silent envy" and "selfish, souring discontent." She goes on to resolve the problem by a reductive strategy that Rossetti often uses in her devotional poetry: all texts, whether world or word, have one meaning only—all is vanity, all shall pass. No need, then, to strive, to worry about who is first and who second. The golden sister walks out into the garden, leaving the speaker in what must have been a characteristic attitude of Rossetti's: sitting alone with a book, watching furtively while the more "natural" and well-integrated "sister" collects and arranges flowers "with instinctive taste." Suddenly the golden sister's beloved arrives, there is a break in the poem, and twenty years have passed. The golden sister has married, replicating herself with a daughter, and showing a face that has altered very little since the conversation in the garden. During these twenty years the speaker has remained fixed in one spot, much like a naughty child compelled to sit in the corner, free only to ruminate on her "lesson," and perhaps lead a secret inner life:

> . . . I sat alone and watched;
> My lot in life, to live alone
> In mine own world of interests,
> Much felt but little shown.

> Not to be first: how hard to learn
> That lifelong lesson of the past;
> Line graven on line and stroke on stroke,
> But, thank God, learned at last.

The lines and strokes suggest portraiture or sculpture rather than writing, and imply that she becomes a tableau of self-abnegation. But what exactly does Rossetti mean by "Not to be first"? What does it have to do with Homer's sting and Achilles' wrath? Not to be first in love? Not to be first in the life of the mind?[15]

All we can assume is that for a variety of converging reasons Rossetti felt compelled to adopt the persona of the lonely, unsatisfied watcher, through endurance and humility conjuring up a wholly blameless apotheosis: "not to be first" is transformed into the tag that ends "The Lowest Room," "And many last be first." Probably Rossetti also knew that she needed, for her psychic survival and her art, to hoard herself. In "The Lowest Room" she says dejectedly, "So now in patience I possess / My soul year after tedious year." In the later exotic dream-vision, "From House to Home" (*Works*, p. 20), she says more stoically, less self-pityingly, "Therefore in patience I possess my soul; / Yea therefore as a flint I set my face." Perhaps the persona of the lonely watcher was a necessary condition for the writing of poetry. Perhaps, rather, out of necessary conditions Rossetti invented the self that made poetry.

The polarized self-sisters of "The Lowest Room" reappear in "Goblin Market," written three years later. Much commented upon, this "unconscious" masterpiece has with a few exceptions eluded its commentators. Both Ellen Moers and Germaine Greer have made provocative suggestions about this enigmatic and "deeply perverse" poem, as Greer calls it.[16] Both are exactly right: "Goblin Market" springs from the rough-and-tumble sexuality of the nursery;[17] it fully explores the pleasure-pain of oral satiety, and it resists systematic allegorizing.[18] In a brief but insightful 1965 essay Winston Weathers discusses Rossetti's use of "sisters" to express parts of the divided self. The two sisters in "Goblin Market" are parts of a fragmented personality that becomes integrated when both of the sisters marry and thus take up "their appropriate tasks and operations within the larger integrity of sisterhood itself."[19]

"Goblin Market" has nothing to do with the presentation of self to observers, whether heavenly or worldly. Although the sisters are two, and different in temperament, the poem is not concerned wtih doubleness; there is no tension between a secret self and an apparent one. The poem really has less to do with temptation than with the consequences of indulgence. Once the fall has occurred, the sisters have a remarkably single purpose. Instead of the conflict between selves that motivates and structures "The Lowest Room," a drama takes place below the surface: a part of the self is "possessed" and has to be drawn out of a profound self-absorption.

Although "Goblin Market" deals with more than meets the eye, Rossetti's preoccupation with the act of looking and with the immobile watcher's stance does operate within the poem. The transfixed gaze at fascinating sights leads to the addiction of the other senses, while watching makes possible the cure. At the very beginning, Laura, the troublesome sister, says: "We must not look at goblin men," all the while looking. The appalled Lizzie warns: "Laura, Laura, / You should not peep at goblin men," and covers up her eyes "lest they should look" (*Works*, p. 1). Once Laura has looked—and listened—the fall is virtually accomplished. From the time she tastes the goblins' fruits Laura becomes an obsessed watcher, inactive but constantly on the lookout for the return of the goblin sellers. Lizzie, on the other hand, must actively seek out the goblin men ("And for the first time in her life /

Began to listen and look," *Works*, p. 5) and passively withstand their assaults on her senses—the evil men are simply worn out by her resistance. Immobility, sealed lips, and an impassive countenance are clearly advantages when one is in terrible danger. In her resistance to the goblins Lizzie shows the same strength as the statue-woman at the end of "A Soul," the woman "indomitable in her feebleness." Lizzie becomes a model of vigilance, the antidote for fascination, as she keeps watch both over herself and over the tormented Laura.

Whatever else can be said about the poem, Laura's "self-consuming care" is only a highly charged version of the torment that Rossetti probes at in poem after poem, in all the injunctions to the restive heart to be still. "Goblin Market" shows the consequences of succumbing to the inner fires—one does not break out, but rather turns deeper inward in a horrifying, obsessive way —and makes a good case for the necessity of the kind of vigilance and stoic endurance that are marshalled in so many of the poems. Vigilance and stoic endurance are not ends in themselves, but rather means to self-possession.

The meaning of "Goblin Market" depends on the oblique suggestiveness of fable. More characteristic of Rossetti's mode is the discursive and meditative structure of "The Lowest Room." The woman at the end of "The Lowest Room" is a composite of the speakers in Rossetti's poems: alone, immobile, watching, feeling but not showing, her gaze fixed on apocalyptic visions. The self that desires and that speaks out in wrath or in defense of wrath has been rebuked. Throughout Rossetti's work this self will need to be silenced time and time again: "O clamorous heart lie still" ("All heaven is blazing yet," *Works*, p. 134); "Lie still, my restive heart, lie still" (*Works*, p. 123). Helen Grey, who is rebuked for her wicked tongue as well as her vanity, must learn the hard lesson too: "Stoop from your cold height, Helen Grey, / Come down, and take a lowlier place" (*Works*, p. 355). And Lady Montrevor is praised for her "courage to be still" (*Works*, p. 290).

The rebuke to the restive, willful self is particularly rigorous in "An Old-World Thicket" (*Works*, p. 64). The speaker finds herself in an allegorical wood, discontent with her "blank" lot, all creation signifying only anguish. Her heart then arises "a rebel against light," "Ingathering wrath and gloom." Such revolt is "bitter" and "impotent," its punishment a terrible fixed staring:

> Mine eyes, that would not weep
> Or sleep, scaled height and depth and could not sleep;
>
> The eyes, I mean, of my rebellious soul.

What follows demonstrates a familiar pattern of anger converted into depression: "Rage to despair; and now despair had turned / Back to self-pity and mere weariness, / With yearnings like a smouldering fire that burned." The redemptive vision that ends the poem displays a "patriarchal" ram leading home a flock of sheep, "the sun / Full in their meek mild faces."

However mild the face, it is significant that Rossetti will not completely abjure the yearnings: they "might die out or wax to white excess" (*Works*, p. 67). Turbulence as well as piety fuels her devotional poems. In these the looking/looked at structure operates even more obsessively than in the secular poetry. The speaker is always in a fixed position, on the look-out, but now become a heavenly voyeur: she longs to *see*, not hear, the pipes and strings that produce the music of paradise (*Works*, p. 280). Her gaze is turned toward unearthly sights, and she becomes a model for a supernatural artist. As always, this situation is problematic—"O Lord on Whom we gaze and dare not gaze" (*Works*, p. 267)—and the earthly gazer may at times wish to hide from accusing or reproachful eyes—"Ah me that I should be / Exposed and open evermore to Thee!—" (*Works*, p. 219). Nevertheless, Rossetti seems to have struck a bargain with God. She watches and waits in order that she may be completely known, without any intervening mask: "I look to Thee while Thou dost look on me / Thou Face to face to me and Eye to eye" (*Works*, p. 267). From this perspective the "eyes of the rebellious soul" must be *over*looked, and Christ placated by complete passivity. In "A bruised Reed shall He not break" (*Works*, p. 150) Christ enjoins a poor soul that cannot will nor wish, "neither choose nor wish to choose," to "resign thyself, be still, / Till I infuse love, hatred, longing, will."

When the heavenly goal is in sight, then the watcher can afford to set the face "full against the light" (*Works*, p. 145). The face that from the earthly perspective seems heavy, rigidified, monotonously dour, can become an icon of admirable durability. Occasionally we get glimpses of what Rossetti might have considered a viable ideal to oppose both the faces of social and artistic convention and the faces of nightmare visions, the "Flesh-and-bloodless vapid masks," "Shades of bodies without souls" ("A Castle-Builder's World," *Works*, p. 132). The conventionally pretty little Eleanor of the poem of the same name has a cherry-red mouth and morning-blue eyes, but also a forehead "That spoke a noble mind" (*Works*, p. 105). And in a sonnet published only recently Rossetti reveals this much:

> Listen, and I will tell you of a face
> Not lovely, but made beautiful by mind;
> Lighted up with dark eyes in which you find
> All womanly affections have their place.[20]

But Rossetti, who believed that "Men work and think, but women feel" ("An 'Immurata' Sister," *Works*, p. 380), that "Woman was made for man's delight," and also that "Her strength with weakness is overlaid; / Meek compliances veil her might" ("A Helpmeet for Him," *Works*, p. 415), was bound to mask her strong will and her competitiveness. The woman with the face made beautiful by mind also has an even brow devoid of "trace of passion," and glossy golden hair that, like a "blind," "shadows her round cheeks blush full of grace."

Perhaps Rossetti shrank from all the implications of woman's mask; she certainly did not flinch from anatomizing her own passion, however, and she kept on protesting all her life. Hedged round by all kinds of prohibitions, struggling with "fightings without and fears within" ("The Offering of the New Law," *Works*, p. 134), she remained resolutely her own person. Nothing ever really changed for her. The situation of being looked at—as a woman who was either marriageable or not, as an artist's model, and finally as a rather odd celebrity: a swarthy, dour, dumpy Victorian-woman-poet—was simply a prevailing condition of her life. Out of it and against it she wrote poetry, moving from self-absorption to self-possession. Possessing her own soul comes down to lines like these:

> Thus am I mine own prison. Everything
> Around me free and sunny and at ease:
> Or if in shadow, in a shade of trees
>
> . . . . .
>
> Where sounds are music, and where silences
> Are music of an unlike fashioning.
>
> . . . . .
>
> I am not what I have nor what I do;
> But what I was I am, I am even I.
> ("The Thread of Life," *Works*, p. 262)

7.

Vesuvius at Home:
The Power of Emily Dickinson

Adrienne Rich

I am traveling at the speed of time, along the Massachusetts Turnpike. For months, for years, for most of my life, I have been hovering like an insect against the screens of an existence which inhabited Amherst, Massachusetts, between 1830 and 1886. The methods, the exclusions, of Emily Dickinson's existence could not have been my own; yet more and more, as a woman poet finding my own methods, I have come to understand her necessities, could have been witness in her defense.

"Home is not where the heart is," she wrote in a letter, "but the house and the adjacent buildings." A statement of New England realism, a directive to be followed. Probably no poet ever lived so much and so purposefully in one house; even, in one room. Her niece Martha told of visiting her in her corner bedroom on the second floor at 280 Main Street, Amherst, and of how Emily Dickinson made as if to lock the door with an imaginary key, turned and said: "Matty: here's freedom."

I am traveling at the speed of time, in the direction of the house and buildings.

Western Massachusetts: the Connecticut Valley: a countryside still full of reverberations: scene of Indian uprisings, religious revivals, spiritual confrontations, the blazing-up of the lunatic fringe of the Puritan coal. How peaceful and how threatened it looks from Route 91, hills gently curled above the plain, the tobacco-barns standing in fields sheltered with white gauze from the sun, and the sudden urban sprawl: ARCO, MacDonald's, shopping plazas. The country that broke the heart of Jonathan Edwards, that enclosed the genius of Emily Dickinson. It lies calmly in the light of May, cloudy skies breaking into warm sunshine, light-green spring softening the hills, dogwood and wild fruit-trees blossoming in the hollows.

From Northampton bypass there's a four-mile stretch of road to Amherst —Route 9—between fruit farms, steakhouses, supermarkets. The new University of Massachusetts rears its skyscrapers up from the plain against the Pelham Hills. There is new money here, real estate, motels. Amherst succeeds on Hadley almost without notice. Amherst is green, rich-looking, secure; we're suddenly in the center of town, the crossroads of the campus, old New England college buildings spread around two village greens, a scene I remember as almost exactly the same in the dim past of my undergraduate years when I used to come there for college weekends.

Left on Seelye Street, right on Main; driveway at the end of a yellow picket fence. I recognize the high hedge of cedars screening the house, because twenty-five years ago I walked there, even then drawn toward the spot, trying to peer over. I pull into the driveway behind a generous nineteenth-century brick mansion with wings and porches, old trees and green lawns. I ring at the back door—the door through which Dickinson's coffin was carried to the cemetery a block away.

For years I have been not so much envisioning Emily Dickinson as trying to visit, to enter her mind, through her poems and letters, and through my own intimations of what it could have meant to be one of the two mid-nineteenth-century American geniuses, and a woman, living in Amherst, Massachusetts. Of the other genius, Walt Whitman, Dickinson wrote that she had heard his poems were "disgraceful." She knew her own were unacceptable by her world's standards of poetic convention, and of what was appropriate, in particular, for a woman poet. Seven were published in her lifetime, all edited by other hands; more than a thousand were laid away in her bedroom chest, to be discovered after her death. When her sister discovered them, there were decades of struggle over the manuscripts, the manner of their presentation to the world, their suitability for publication, the poet's own final intentions. Narrowed down by her early editors and anthologists, reduced to quaintness or spinsterish oddity by many of her commentators, sentimentalized, fallen-in-love-with like some gnomic Garbo, still unread in the breadth and depth of her full range of work, she was, and is, a wonder to me when I try to imagine myself into that mind.

I have a notion that genius knows itself; that Dickinson chose her seclusion, knowing she was exceptional and knowing what she needed. It was, moreover, no hermetic retreat, but a seclusion which included a wide range of people, of reading and correspondence. Her sister Vinnie said, "Emily is always looking for the rewarding person." And she found, at various periods, both women and men: her sister-in-law, Susan Gilbert, Amherst visitors and family friends such as Benjamin Newton, Charles Wadsworth, Samuel Bowles, editor of the Springfield *Republican* and his wife; her friends Kate Anthon and Helen Hunt Jackson, the distant but significant figures of Elizabeth Barrett, the Brontës, George Eliot. But she carefully selected her society and controlled the disposal of her time. Not only the "gentlewomen in plush" of Amherst were excluded; Emerson visited next door but she did not go to meet him; she did not travel or receive routine visits; she avoided strangers. Given her vocation, she was neither eccentric nor quaint; she was determined to survive, to use her powers, to practice necessary economies.

Suppose Jonathan Edwards had been born a woman; suppose William James, for that matter, had been born a woman? (The invalid seclusion of his sister Alice is suggestive.) Even from men, New England took its psychic toll; many of its geniuses seemed peculiar in one way or another, particularly along the lines of social intercourse. Hawthorne, until he married, took his meals in his bedroom, apart from the family. Thoreau insisted on the values both of solitude and of geographical restriction, boasting that "I have travelled much in Concord." Emily Dickinson—viewed by her bemused contemporary Thomas Higginson as "partially cracked," by the twentieth century as fey or pathological—has increasingly struck me as a practical woman, exercising her gift as she had to, making choices. I have come to imagine her as somehow too strong for her environment, a figure of powerful will, not at all frail or breathless, someone whose personal dimensions would be felt in a household. She was her father's favorite daughter though she professed being afraid of him. Her sister dedicated herself to the everyday domestic labors which would free Dickinson to write. (Dickinson herself baked the bread, made jellies and gingerbread, nursed her mother through a long illness, was a skilled horticulturalist who grew pomegranates, calla lilies, and other exotica in her New England greenhouse.)

Upstairs at last: I stand in the room which for Emily Dickinson was "freedom." The best bedroom in the house, a corner room, sunny, overlooking the main street of Amherst in front, the way to her brother Austin's house on the side. Here, at a small table with one drawer, she wrote most of her poems. Here she read Elizabeth Barrett's "Aurora Leigh," a woman poet's narrative poem of a woman poet's life; also George Eliot; Emerson; Carlyle; Shakespeare; Charlotte and Emily Brontë. Here I become, again, an insect, vibrating at the frames of windows, clinging to panes of glass, trying to connect. The scent here is very powerful. Here in this white-curtained, high-ceilinged room, a redhaired woman with hazel eyes and a contralto voice wrote poems about volcanoes, deserts, eternity, suicide, physical passion, wild beasts, rape, power, madness, separation, the daemon, the grave. Here, with a darning-needle, she bound these poems—heavily emended and often in variant versions—into booklets, secured with darning-thread, to be found and read after her death. Here she knew "freedom," listening from above-stairs to a visitor's piano-playing, escaping from the pantry where she was mistress of the household bread and puddings, watching, you feel, watching ceaselessly, the life of sober Main Street below. From this room she glided downstairs, her hand on the polished banister, to meet the complacent maga-zine editor, Thomas Higginson, unnerve him while claiming she herself was unnerved. "Your scholar," she signed herself in letters to him. But she was an independent scholar, used his criticism selectively, saw him rarely and always on *her* premises. It was a life deliberately organized on her terms. The terms she had been handed by society—Calvinist Protestantism, Roman-ticism, the nineteenth-century corseting of women's bodies, choices, and sexuality—could spell insanity to a woman genius. What this one had to do was retranslate her own unorthodox, subversive, sometimes volcanic pro-pensities into a dialect called metaphor: her native language. "Tell all the Truth—but tell it Slant—." It is always what is under pressure in us, especially under pressure of concealment—that explodes in poetry.

The women and men in her life she equally converted into metaphor. The masculine pronoun in her poems can refer simultaneously to many aspects of the "masculine" in the patriarchal world—the god she engages in dialogue, again on *her* terms; her own creative powers, unsexing for a woman, the male power-figures in her immediate environment—the lawyer Edward Dickinson, her brother Austin, the preacher Wadsworth, the editor Bowles—it is far too limiting to trace that "He" to some specific lover, although that was the chief obsession of the legend-mongers for more than half a century. Obviously, Dickinson was attracted by and interested in men whose minds had something to offer her; she was, it is by now clear, equally attracted by and interested in women whose minds had something to offer her. There are many poems to and about women, and some which exist in two versions with alternate sets of pronouns. Her latest biographer, Richard Sewall, while rejecting an earlier Freudian biographer's theory that Dickinson was essen-tially a psycho-pathological case, the by-product of which happened to be poetry, does create a context in which the importance, and validity, of Dickinson's attachments to women may now, at last, be seen in full. She was always stirred by the existences of women like George Eliot or Elizabeth Barrett, who possessed strength of mind, articulateness, and energy. (She once characterized Elizabeth Fry and Florence Nightingale as "holy"—one suspects she merely meant, "great.")

But of course Dickinson's relationships with women were more than intellectual. They were deeply charged, and the sources both of passionate joy and pain. We are only beginning to be able to consider them in a social and historical context. The historian Carroll Smith-Rosenberg has shown that there was far less taboo on intense, even passionate and sensual, relationships between women in the American nineteenth-century "female world of love and ritual," as she terms it, than there was later in the twentieth century. Women expressed their attachments to other women both physically and verbally; a marriage did not dilute the strength of a female friendship, in which two women often shared the same bed during long visits, and wrote letters articulate with both physical and emotional longing. The nineteenth-century close woman friend, according to the many diaries and letters Smith-Rosenberg has studied, might be a far more important figure in a woman's life than the nineteenth-century husband. None of this was condemned as "lesbianism."[1] We will understand Emily Dickinson better, read her poetry more perceptively, when the Freudian imputation of scandal and aberrance in women's love for women has been supplanted by a more informed, less misogynistic attitude toward women's experiences with each other.

But who, if you read through the seventeen hundred and seventy-five poems—who—woman or man—could have passed through that imagination and not come out transmuted? Given the space created by her in that corner room, with its window-light, its potted plants and work-table, given that personality, capable of imposing its terms on a household, on a whole community, what single theory could hope to contain her, when she'd put it all together in that space?

"Matty: here's freedom," I hear her saying as I speed back to Boston along Route 91, as I slip the turnpike ticket into the toll-collector's hand. I am thinking of a confined space in which the genius of the nineteenth-century female mind in America moved, inventing a language more varied, more compressed, more dense with implications, more complex of syntax, than any American poetic language to date; in the trail of that genius my mind has been moving, and with its language and images my mind still has to reckon, as the mind of a woman poet in America today.

In 1971 a postage stamp was issued in honor of Dickinson; the portrait derives from the one existing daguerreotype of her, with straight, center-parted hair, eyes staring somewhere beyond the camera, hands poised around a nosegay of flowers, in correct nineteenth-century style. On the first-day-of-issue envelope sent me by a friend there is, besides the postage stamp, an engraving of the poet as popular fancy has preferred her, in a white lace ruff and with hair as bouffant as if she had just stepped from a Boston beauty parlor. The poem chosen to represent her work to the American public is engraved, alongside a dew-gemmed rose, below the portrait:

> If I can stop one heart from breaking
> I shall not live in vain
> If I can ease one life the aching
> Or cool one pain
> Or help one fainting robin
> Unto his nest again
> I shall not live in vain.

Now, this is extremely strange. It is a fact that in 1864 Emily Dickinson wrote this verse; and it is a verse which a hundred or more nineteenth-century versifiers could have written. In its undistinguished language, as in its conventional sentiment, it is remarkably untypical of the poet. Had she chosen to write many poems like this one we would have no "problem" of nonpublication, of editing, of estimating the poet at her true worth. Certainly the sentiment—a contented and unambiguous altruism—is one which even today might in some quarters be accepted as fitting from a female versifier—a kind of Girl Scout prayer. But we are talking about the woman who wrote:

> He fumbles at your Soul
> As Players at the Keys
> Before they drop full Music on—
> He stuns you by degrees—
> Prepares your brittle Nature
> For the Ethereal Blow
> By fainter Hammers—further heard—
> Then nearer—Then so slow
> Your breath has time to straighten—
> Your brain—to bubble Cool—
> Deals—One—Imperial—Thunderbolt—
> Then scalps your naked Soul—
>
> When winds take Forests in their Paws—
> The Universe—is still—
>
> (#315)

Much energy has been invested in trying to identify a concrete, flesh-and-blood male lover whom Dickinson is supposed to have renounced, and to the loss of whom can be traced the secret of her seclusion and the vein of much of her poetry. But the real question, given that the art of poetry is an art of transformation, is how this woman's mind and imagination may have used the masculine element in the world at large, or those elements personified as masculine—including the men she knew; how her relationship to this reveals itself in her images and language. In a patriarchal culture, specifically the Judeo-Christian, quasi-Puritan culture of nineteenth-century New England in which Dickinson grew up, still inflamed with religious revivals, and where the sermon was still an active, if perishing, literary form, the equation of divinity with maleness was so fundamental that it is hardly surprising to find Dickinson, like many an early mystic, blurring erotic with religious experience and imagery. The poem has intimations of both seduction and rape merged with the intense force of a religious experience. But are these metaphors for each other, or for something more intrinsic to Dickinson? Here is another:

> He put the Belt around my life—
> I heard the buckle snap—
> And turned away, imperial,
> My lifetime folding up—
> Deliberate, as a Duke would do
> A Kingdom's Title Deed
> Henceforth, a Dedicated sort—
> Member of the Cloud.
>
> Yet not too far to come at call—
> And do the little Toils
> That make the Circuit of the Rest—
> And deal occasional smiles
> To lives that stoop to notice mine—
> And kindly ask it in—
> Whose invitation, know you not
> For Whom I must decline?
>
> (#273)

These two poems are about possession, and they seem to me a poet's poems —that is, they are about the poet's relationship to her own power, which is exteriorized in masculine form, much as masculine poets have invoked the female Muse. In writing at all—particularly an unorthodox and original poetry like Dickinson's—women have often felt in danger of losing their status as women. And this status has always been defined in terms of relationship to men—as daughter, sister, bride, wife, mother, mistress, Muse. Since the most powerful figures in patriarchal culture have been men, it seems natural that Dickinson would assign a masculine gender to that in herself which did not fit in with the conventional ideology of womanliness.

To recognize and acknowledge our own interior power has always been a path mined with risks for women; to acknowledge that power and commit oneself to it as Emily Dickinson did was an immense decision.

Most of us, unfortunately, have been exposed in the schoolroom to Dickinson's "little-girl" poems, her kittenish tones, as in "I'm Nobody! Who Are You?" (a poem whose underlying anger translates itself into archness) or

> I hope the Father in the skies
> Will lift his little girl—
> Old fashioned—naughty—everything
> Over the stile of "Pearl."
>
> (#70)

or the poems about bees and robins. One critic—Richard Chase—has noted that in the nineteenth century "one of the careers open to women was perpetual childhood." A strain in Dickinson's letters and some—though by far a minority—of her poems was a self-diminutization, almost as if to offset and deny—or even disguise—her actual dimensions as she must have experienced them. And this emphasis on her own "littleness," along with the deliberate strangeness of her tactics of seclusion, have been, until recently, accepted as the prevailing character of the poet: the fragile poetess in white, sending flowers and poems by messenger to unseen friends, letting down baskets of gingerbread to the neighborhood children from her bedroom window; writing, but somehow naively. John Crowe Ransom, arguing for the editing and standardization of Dickinson's punctuation and typography, calls her "a little home-keeping person" who, "while she had a proper notion of the final destiny of her poems . . . was not one of those poets who had advanced to that later stage of operations where manuscripts are prepared for the printer, and the poet's diction has to make concessions to the publisher's style-book." (In short, Emily Dickinson did not wholly know her trade, and Ransom believes a "publisher's style-book" to have the last word on poetic diction.) He goes on to print several of her poems, altered by him "with all possible forbearance." What might, in a male writer—a Thoreau, let us say, or a Christopher Smart or William Blake—seem a legitimate strangeness, a unique intention, has been in one of our two major poets devalued into a kind of naiveté, girlish ignorance, feminine lack of professionalism, just as the poet herself has been made into a sentimental object. ("Most of us are half in love with this dead girl," confesses Archibald MacLeish. Dickinson was fifty-five when she died.)

It is true that more recent critics, including her most recent biographer, have gradually begun to approach the poet in terms of her greatness rather than her littleness, the decisiveness of her choices instead of the surface oddities of her life or the romantic crises of her legend. But unfortunately anthologists continue to plagiarize other anthologies, to reprint her in edited, even bowdlerized versions; the popular image of her and of her work lags behind the changing consciousness of scholars and specialists. There still does not exist a selection from her poems which depicts her in her fullest range. Dickinson's greatness cannot be measured in terms of twenty-five or fifty or even five hundred "perfect" lyrics; it has to be seen as the accumulation it is. Poets, even, are not always acquainted with the full dimensions of her work, or the sense one gets, reading in the one-volume complete edition (let alone the three-volume variorum edition) of a mind engaged in a lifetime's musing on essential problems of language, identity, separation, relationship, the integrity of the self; a mind capable of describing psychological states more accurately than any poet except Shakespeare. I have been surprised at how narrowly her work, still, is known by women who are writing poetry, how much her legend has gotten in the way of her being re-possessed, as a source and a foremother.

I know that for me, reading her poems as a child and then as a young girl already seriously writing poetry, she was a problematic figure. I first read her in the selection heavily edited by her niece which appeared in 1937; a later and fuller edition appeared in 1945 when I was sixteen, and the complete, unbowdlerized edition by Johnson did not appear until fifteen years later. The publication of each of these editions was crucial to me in successive decades of my life. More than any other poet, Emily Dickinson seemed to tell me that the intense inner event, the personal and psychological, was inseparable from the universal; that there was a range for psychological poetry beyond mere self-expression. Yet the legend of the life was troubling, because it seemed to whisper that a woman who undertook such explorations must pay with renunciation, isolation, and incorporeality. With the publication of the *Complete Poems,* the legend seemed to recede into unimportance beside the unquestionable power and importance of the mind revealed there. But taking possession of Emily Dickinson is still no simple matter.

The 1945 edition, entitled *Bolts of Melody*, took its title from a poem which struck me at the age of sixteen and which still, thirty years later, arrests my imagination:

> I would not paint—a picture—
> I'd rather be the One
> Its bright impossibility
> To dwell—delicious—on—
> And wonder how the fingers feel

Whose rare—celestial—stir
Evokes so sweet a Torment—
Such sumptuous—Despair—

I would not talk, like Cornets—
I'd rather be the One
Raised softly to the Ceilings—
And out, and easy on—
Through Villages of Ether
Myself endured Balloon
By but a lip of Metal
The pier to my Pontoon—

Nor would I be a Poet—
It's finer—own the Ear—
Enamored—impotent—content—
The License to revere,
A privilege so awful
What would the Dower be,
Had I the Art to stun myself
With Bolts of Melody!

(#505)

This poem is about choosing an orthodox "feminine" role: the receptive rather than the creative; viewer rather than painter; listener rather than musician; acted-upon rather than active. Yet even while ostensibly choosing this role she wonders "how the fingers feel / Whose rare—celestial—stir / Evokes so sweet a Torment—" and the "feminine" role is praised in a curious sequence of adjectives: "Enamored—*impotent*—content—." The strange paradox of this poem—its exquisite irony—is that it is about choosing not to be a poet, a poem which is gainsaid by no fewer than one thousand seven hundred and seventy-five poems made during the writer's life, including itself. Moreover, the images of the poem rise to a climax (like the Balloon she evokes) but the climax happens as she describes, not what it is to be the receiver, but the maker and receiver at once: "A privilege so awful / What would the Dower be / Had I the Art to stun myself / With Bolts of Melody!" —a climax which recalls the poem: "He fumbles at your soul / As Players at the Keys / Before they drop full Music on—." And of course, in writing those lines she possesses herself of that privilege and that "dower." I have said that this is a poem of exquisite ironies. It is, indeed, though in a very different mode, related to Dickinson's "little-girl" strategy. The woman who feels herself to be Vesuvius at home has need of a mask, at least, of innocuousness and of containment.

On my volcano grows the Grass
A meditative spot—
An acre for a Bird to choose
Would be the General thought—

How red the Fire rocks below—
How insecure the sod
Did I disclose
Would populate with awe my solitude.
                                    (#1677)

Power, even masked, can still be perceived as destructive.

A still—Volcano—Life—
That flickered in the night—
When it was dark enough to do
Without erasing sight—

A quiet—Earthquake style—
Too subtle to suspect
By natures this side Naples—
The North cannot detect

The Solemn—Torrid—Symbol—
The lips that never lie—
Whose hissing Corals part—and shut—
And Cities—ooze away—
                                    (#601)

Dickinson's biographer and editor Thomas Johnson has said that she often felt herself possessed by a demonic force, particularly in the years 1861 and 1862 when she was writing at the height of her drive. There are many poems besides "He put the Belt around my Life" which could be read as poems of possession by the daemon—poems which can also be, and have been, read, as poems of possession by the deity, or by a human lover. I suggest that a woman's poetry about her relationship to her daemon—her own active, creative power—has in patriarchal culture used the language of heterosexual love or patriarchal theology. Ted Hughes tells us that

the eruption of (Dickinson's) imagination and poetry followed when she shifted her passion, with the energy of desperation, from (the) lost man onto his only possible substitute, —the Universe in its Divine aspect... Thereafter, the marriage that had been denied in the real world, went forward in the spiritual ... just as the Universe in its Divine aspect became the mirror-image of her "husband," so the whole religious dilemma of New

England, at that most critical moment in its history, became the mirror-image
of her relationship to him, of her "marriage" in fact.[2]

This seems to me to miss the point on a grand scale. There are facts we
need to look at. First, Emily Dickinson did not marry. And her non-marry-
ing was neither a pathological retreat as John Cody sees it, nor probably even
a conscious decision; it was a fact in her life as in her contemporary Christina
Rossetti's; both women had more primary needs. Second: unlike Rossetti,
Dickinson did not become a religiously dedicated woman; she was heretical,
heterodox, in her religious opinions, and stayed away from church and dog-
ma. What, in fact, *did* she allow to "put the Belt around her Life"—what *did*
wholly occupy her mature years and possess her? For "Whom" did she
decline the invitations of other lives? The writing of poetry. Nearly two
thousand poems. Three hundred and sixty-five poems in the year of her fullest
power. What was it like to be writing poetry you knew (and I am sure she
did know) was of a class by itself—to be fueled by the energy it took first to
confront, then to condense that range of psychic experience into that lan-
guage; then to copy out the poems and lay them in a trunk, or send a few
here and there to friends or relatives as occasional verse or as gestures of
confidence? I am sure she knew who she was, as she indicates in this poem:

> Myself was formed—a carpenter—
> An unpretending time
> My Plane—and I, together wrought
> Before a Builder came—
>
> To measure our attainments
> Had we the Art of Boards
> Sufficiently developed—He'd hire us
> At Halves—
>
> My Tools took Human—Faces—
> The Bench, where we had toiled—
> Against the Man—persuaded—
> We—Temples Build—I said—
>
> (#488)

This is a poem of the great year 1862, the year in which she first sent a few
poems to Thomas Higginson for criticism. Whether it antedates or postdates
that occasion is unimportant; it is a poem of knowing one's measure, regard-
less of the judgments of others.

There are many poems which carry the weight of this knowledge. Here is
another one:

I'm ceded—I've stopped being Theirs—
The name They dropped upon my face
With water, in the country church
Is finished using, now,
And They can put it with my dolls,
My childhood, and the string of spools,
I've finished threading—too—

Baptized before, without the choice,
But this time, consciously, of Grace—
Unto supremest name—
Called to my Fill—the Crescent dropped—
Existence's whole Arc, filled up
With one small Diadem.

My second Rank—too small the first—
Crowned—Crowing—on my Father's breast—
A half unconscious Queen—
But this time—Adequate—Erect—
With Will to choose—or to reject—
And I choose—just a Crown—

(#508)

Now, this poem partakes of the imagery of being "twice-born" or, in Christian liturgy, "confirmed"—and if this poem had been written by Christina Rossetti I would be inclined to give more weight to a theological reading. But it was written by Emily Dickinson, who used the Christian metaphor far more than she let it use her. This is a poem of great pride—not pridefulness, but *self*-confirmation—and it is curious how little Dickinson's critics, perhaps misled by her diminutives, have recognized the will and pride in her poetry. It is a poem of movement from childhood to womanhood, of transcending the patriarchal condition of bearing her father's name and "Crowing—on my Father's breast—." She is now a conscious Queen, "Adequate—Erect / With Will to choose—or to reject—."

There is one poem which is the real "onlie begetter" of my thoughts here about Dickinson; a poem I have mused over, repeated to myself, taken into myself over many years. I think it is a poem about possession by the daemon, about the dangers and risks of such possession if you are a woman, about the knowledge that power in a woman can seem destructive, and that you cannot live without the daemon once it has possessed you. The archetype of the daemon as masculine is beginning to change, but it has been real for women up until now. But this woman poet also perceives herself as a lethal weapon:

My life had stood—a Loaded Gun—
In Corners—till a Day
The Owner passed—identified—
And carried me away—

And now We roam in Sovereign Woods—
And now We hunt the Doe—
And every time I speak for Him—
The Mountains straight reply—

And do I smile, such cordial light
Upon the Valley glow—
It is as a Vesuvian face
Had let its pleasure through—

And when at Night—our good Day done—
I guard My Master's Head—
'Tis better than the Eider-Duck's
Deep Pillow—to have shared—

To foe of His—I'm deadly foe—
None stir the second time—
On whom I lay a Yellow Eye—
Or an emphatic Thumb—

Though I than he—may longer live
He longer must—than I—
For I have but the power to kill,
Without—the power to die—

(#754)

Here the poet sees herself as split, not between anything so simple as "masculine" and "feminine" identity but between the hunter, admittedly masculine, but also a human person, an active, willing being, and the gun—an object, condemned to remain inactive until the hunter—the *owner*—takes possession of it. The gun contains an energy capable of rousing echoes in the mountains and lighting up the valleys; it is also deadly, "Vesuvian"; it is also its owner's defender against the "foe." It is the gun, furthermore, who *speaks for him*. If there is a female consciousness in this poem it is buried deeper than the images: it exists in the ambivalence toward power, which is extreme. Active willing and creation in women are forms of aggression, and aggression is both "the power to kill" and punishable by death. The union of gun with hunter embodies the danger of identifying and taking hold of her forces, not least that in so doing she risks defining herself—and being defined

—as aggressive, as unwomanly ("and now we hunt the Doe"), and as potentially lethal. That which she experiences in herself as energy and potency can also be experienced as pure destruction. The final stanza, with its precarious balance of phrasing, seems a desperate attempt to resolve the ambivalence; but, I think, it is no resolution, only a further extension of ambivalence.

> Though I than he—may longer live
> He longer must—than I—
> For I have but the power to kill,
> Without—the power to die—

The poet experiences herself as loaded gun, imperious energy; yet without the Owner, the possessor, she is merely lethal. Should that possession abandon her—but the thought is unthinkable: "He longer *must* than I." The pronoun is masculine; the antecedent is what Keats called "The Genius of Poetry."

I do not pretend to have—I don't even wish to have—explained this poem, accounted for its every image; it will reverberate with new tones long after my words about it have ceased to matter. But I think that for us, at this time, it is a central poem in understanding Emily Dickinson, and ourselves, and the condition of the woman artist, particularly in the nineteenth century. It seems likely that the nineteenth-century woman poet, especially, felt the medium of poetry as dangerous, in ways that the woman novelist did not feel the medium of fiction to be. In writing even such a novel of elemental sexuality and anger as *Wuthering Heights*, Emily Brontë could at least theoretically separate herself from her characters; they were, after all, fictitious beings. Moreover, the novel is or can be a construct, planned and organized to deal with human experiences on one level at a time. Poetry is too much rooted in the unconscious; it presses too close against the barriers of repression; and the nineteenth-century woman had much to repress. It is interesting that Elizabeth Barrett tried to fuse poetry and fiction in writing "Aurora Leigh"—perhaps apprehending the need for fictional characters to carry the charge of her experience as a woman artist. But with the exception of "Aurora Leigh" and Christina Rossetti's "Goblin Market"*—that extraordinary and little-known poem drenched in oral eroticism—Emily Dickinson's is the only poetry in English by a woman of that century which pierces so far beyond the ideology of the "feminine" and the conventions of womanly feeling. To write it at all, she had to be willing to enter chambers of the self in which

> Ourself behind ourself, concealed—
> Should startle most—

---

* See Chapter 6. —*Eds.*

and to relinquish control there, to take those risks, she had to create a relationship to the outer world where she could feel in control.

It is an extremely painful and dangerous way to live—split between a publicly acceptable persona and a part of yourself that you perceive as the essential, the creative and powerful self, yet also as possibly unacceptable, perhaps even monstrous.

> Much Madness is divinest sense—
> To a discerning Eye—
> Much sense—the starkest Madness.
> 'Tis the Majority
> In this, as All, prevail—
> Assent—and you are sane—
> Demur—you're straightway dangerous—
> And handled with a chain—
>
> (#435)

For many women the stresses of this splitting have led, in a world so ready to assert our innate passivity and to deny our independence and creativity, to extreme consequences: the mental asylum, self-imposed silence, recurrent depression, suicide, and often severe loneliness.

Dickinson is *the* American poet whose work consisted in exploring states of psychic extremity. For a long time, as we have seen, this fact was obscured by the kinds of selections made from her work by timid if well-meaning editors. In fact, Dickinson was a great psychologist; and like every great psychologist, she began with the material she had at hand: herself. She had to possess the courage to enter, through language, states which most people deny or veil with silence.

> The first Day's Night had come—
> And grateful that a thing
> So terrible—had been endured—
> I told my soul to sing—
>
> She said her Strings were snapt—
> Her Bow—to Atoms blown—
> And so to mend her—gave me work
> Until another Morn—
>
> And then—a Day as huge
> As Yesterdays in pairs,
> Unrolled its horror in my face—
> Until it blocked my eyes—

My Brain—begun to laugh—
I mumbled—like a fool—
And tho' 'tis years ago—that Day—
My brain keeps giggling—still.

And Something's odd—within—
That person that I was—
And this One—do not feel the same—
Could it be Madness—this?

(#410)

Dickinson's letters acknowledge a period of peculiarly intense personal crisis; her biographers have variously ascribed it to the pangs of renunciation of an impossible love, or to psychic damage deriving from her mother's presumed depression and withdrawal after her birth. What concerns us here is the fact that she chose to probe the nature of this experience in language:

The Soul has Bandaged moments—
When too appalled to stir—
She feels some ghastly Fright come up
And stop to look at her—

Salute her—with long fingers—
Caress her freezing hair—
Sip, Goblin, from the very lips
The Lover—hovered—o'er—
Unworthy, that a thought so mean
Accost a Theme—so—fair—

The soul has moments of Escape—
When bursting all the doors—
She dances like a Bomb, abroad,
And swings upon the hours . . .

The Soul's retaken moments—
When, Felon led along,
With shackles on the plumed feet,
And staples, in the Song,

The Horror welcomes her, again,
These, are not brayed of Tongue—

(#512)

In this poem, the word "Bomb" is dropped, almost carelessly, as a correlative for the soul's active, liberated states—it occurs in a context of apparent euphoria, but its implications are more than euphoric—they are explosive, destructive. The "Horror" from which in such moments the soul escapes has a masculine, "goblin" form, and suggests the perverse and terrifying rape of a "bandaged" and powerless self. In at least one poem, Dickinson depicts the actual process of suicide:

> He scanned it—staggered—
> Dropped the Loop
> To Past or Period—
> Caught helpless at a sense as if
> His mind were going blind—
> Groped up—to see if God was there—
> Groped backward at Himself—
> Caressed a Trigger absently
> And wandered out of Life.
>
> (#1062)

The precision of knowledge in this brief poem is such that we must assume that Dickinson had, at least in fantasy, drifted close to that state in which the "Loop" that binds us to "Past or Period" is "dropped" and we grope randomly at what remains of abstract notions of sense, God, or self, before—almost absent-mindedly—reaching for a solution. But it's worth noting that this is a poem in which the suicidal experience has been distanced, refined, transformed through a devastating accuracy of language. It is not suicide that is studied here, but the dissociation of self and mind and world which precedes.

Dickinson was convinced that a life worth living could be found within the mind and against the grain of external circumstance: "Reverse cannot befall / That fine prosperity / Whose Sources are interior—" (#395). The horror, for her, was that which set "Staples in the Song"—the numbing and freezing of the interior, a state she describes over and over:

> There is a Languor of the Life
> More imminent than Pain—
> 'Tis Pain's Successor—When the Soul
> Has suffered all it can—
>
> A Drowsiness—diffuses—
> A Dimness like a Fog
> Envelopes Consciousness—
> As Mists—obliterate a Crag.

> The Surgeon—does not blanch—at pain
> His Habit—is severe—
> But tell him that it ceased to feel—
> That creature lying there—
>
> And he will tell you—skill is late—
> A Mightier than He—
> Has ministered before Him—
> There's no Vitality.
>
> (#396)

I think the equation surgeon–artist is a fair one here; the artist can work with the materials of pain; she cuts to probe and heal; but she is powerless at the point where

> After great pain, a formal feeling comes—
> The nerves sit ceremonious, like Tombs—
> The stiff Heart questions was it He, that bore,
> And Yesterday, or Centuries before?
>
> The Feet, mechanical, go round—
> Of Ground, or Air, or Ought—
> A Wooden way
> Regardless grown,
> A Quartz contentment, like a stone—
>
> This is the Hour of Lead
> Remembered, if outlived
> As Freezing persons, recollect the Snow—
> First—Chill—then Stupor—then the letting go—
>
> (#341)

For the poet, the terror is precisely in those periods of psychic death, when even the possibility of work is negated; her "occupation's gone." Yet she also describes the unavailing effort to numb emotion:

> Me from Myself—to banish—
> Had I Art—
> Impregnable my Fortress
> Unto All Heart—
>
> But since Myself—assault Me—
> How have I peace
> Except by subjugating
> Consciousness?

> And since We're mutual Monarch
> How this be
> Except by Abdication—
> Me—of Me?

(#642)

The possibility of abdicating oneself—of ceasing to be—remains.

> Severe Service of myself
> I—hastened to demand
> To fill the awful longitude
> Your life had left behind—
>
> I worried Nature with my Wheels
> When Hers had ceased to run—
> When she had put away her Work
> My own had just begun.
>
> I strove to weary Brain and Bone—
> To harass to fatigue
> The glittering Retinue of nerves—
> Vitality to clog
>
> To some dull comfort Those obtain
> Who put a Head away
> They knew the Hair to—
> And forget the color of the Day—
>
> Affliction would not be appeased—
> The Darkness braced as firm
> As all my strategem had been
> The Midnight to confirm—
>
> No drug for Consciousness—can be—
> Alternative to die
> Is Nature's only Pharmacy
> For Being's Malady—

(#786)

Yet consciousness—not simply the capacity to suffer, but the capacity to experience intensely at every instant—creates of death not a blotting-out but a final illumination:

This Consciousness that is aware
Of Neighbors and the Sun
Will be the one aware of Death
And that itself alone

Is traversing the interval
Experience between
And most profound experiment
Appointed unto Men—

How adequate unto itself
Its properties shall be
Itself unto itself and none
Shall make discovery.

Adventure most unto itself
The Soul condemned to be—
Attended by a single Hound
Its own identity.

(#822)

The poet's relationship to her poetry has, it seems to me—and I am not speaking only of Emily Dickinson—a twofold nature. Poetic language—the poem on paper—is a concretization of the poetry of the world at large, the self, and the forces within the self; and those forces are rescued from formlessness, lucidified, and integrated in the act of writing poems. But there is a more ancient concept of the poet, which is that she is endowed to speak for those who do not have the gift of language, or to see for those who—for whatever reasons—are less conscious of what they are living through. It is as though the risks of the poet's existence can be put to some use beyond her own survival.

The Province of the Saved
Should be the Art—To save—
Through Skill obtained in themselves—
The Science of the Grave

No Man can understand
But He that hath endured
The Dissolution—in Himself—
That man—be qualified

To qualify Despair
To Those who failing new—
Mistake Defeat for Death—Each time—
Till acclimated—to—

                              (#539)

The poetry of extreme states, the poetry of danger, can allow its readers to go further in our own awareness, take risks we might not have dared; it says, at least: "Someone has been here before."

The Soul's distinct Connection
With immortality
Is best disclosed by Danger
Or quick Calamity—

As Lightning on a Landscape
Exhibits Sheets of Place—
Not yet suspected—but for Flash—
And Click—and Suddenness.

                              (#974)

Crumbling is not an instant's Act
A fundamental pause
Dilapidation's processes
Are organized Decays.

'Tis first a cobweb on the Soul
A Cuticle of Dust
A Borer in the Axis
An Elemental Rust—

Ruin is formal—Devil's work
Consecutive and slow—
Fail in an instant—no man did
Slipping—is Crash's law.

                              (#997)

I felt a Cleaving in my Mind
As if my Brain had split—
I tried to match it—Seam by Seam—
But could not make them fit.

> The thought behind, I strove to join
> Unto the thought before—
> But Sequence ravelled out of Sound
> Like Balls—upon a Floor.
>
> 　　　　　(#937)

There are many more Emily Dickinsons than I have tried to call up here. Wherever you take hold of her, she proliferates. I wish I had time here to explore her complex sense of Truth; to follow the thread we unravel when we look at the numerous and passionate poems she wrote to or about women; to probe her ambivalent feelings about fame, a subject pursued by many male poets before her; simply to examine the poems in which she is directly apprehending the natural world. No one since the seventeenth century had reflected more variously or more probingly upon death and dying. What I have tried to do here is follow through some of the origins and consequences of her choice to be, not only a poet but a woman who explored her own mind, without any of the guidelines of orthodoxy. To say "yes" to her powers was not simply a major act of nonconformity in the nineteenth century; even in our own time it has been assumed that Emily Dickinson, not patriarchal society, was "the problem." The more we come to recognize the unwritten and written laws and taboos underpinning patriarchy, the less problematical, surely, will seem the methods she chose.

8.

Emily Dickinson and the Deerslayer:
The Dilemma of the Woman Poet in America

Albert Gelpi

In nineteenth-century America there were many women poets—or, I should better say, lady poets—who achieved popular success and quite lucrative publishing careers by filling newspaper columns, gift books, and volumes of verse with the conventional pieties concerning mortality and immortality; most especially they enshrined the domestic role of wife and mother in tending her mortal charges and conveying them to immortality. Mrs. Lydia Sigourney, known as "the Sweet Singer of Hartford," is the type, and Mark Twain's Emmeline Grangeford is the parodic, but barely parodic re-creation. Emily Dickinson was not a lady poet, but she was the only major American woman poet of the nineteenth century—in fact, a poet of such great consequence that any account of women's experience in America must see her as a boldly pioneering and prophetic figure.

In the Dickinson canon the poem which has caused commentators the most consternation over the years is "My Life had stood—a Loaded Gun—." It figures prominently and frequently in *After Great Pain*, John Cody's Freudian biography of Dickinson, and more recently Robert Weisbuch prefaces his explication in *Emily Dickinson's Poetry* with the remark that it is "the single most difficult poem Dickinson wrote," "a riddle to be solved." The poem requires our close attention and, if possible, our unriddling because it is a powerful symbolic enactment of the psychological dilemma facing the intelligent and aware woman, and particularly the woman artist, in patriarchal America. Here is the full text of the poem, number 754 in the Johnson variorum edition,[1] without, for the moment, the variants in the manuscript:

My Life had stood—a Loaded Gun—
In Corners—till a Day
The Owner passed—identified—
And carried Me away—

And now We roam in Sovreign Woods—
And now We hunt the Doe—
And every time I speak for Him—
The Mountains straight reply—

And do I smile, such cordial light
Upon the Valley glow—
It is as a Vesuvian face
Had let it's pleasure through—

And when at Night—Our good Day done—
I guard My Master's Head—
'Tis better than the Eider-Duck's
Deep Pillow—to have shared—

To foe of His—I'm deadly foe—
None stir the second time—
On whom I lay a Yellow Eye—
Or an emphatic Thumb—

Though I than He—may longer live
He longer must—than I—
For I have but the power to kill,
Without—the power to die—

Despite the narrative manner, it is no more peopled than the rest of Dickinson's poems, which almost never have more than two figures: the speaker and another, often an anonymous male figure suggestive of a lover or of God or of both. So here: I and "My Master," the "Owner" of my life. Biographers have tried to sift the evidence to identify the "man" in the central drama of the poetry. Three draft-"letters" from the late 1850s and early 1860s, confessing in overwrought language her passionate love for the "Master" and her pain at his rejection, might seem to corroborate the factual basis for the relationship examined in this poem, probably written in 1863. However, as I have argued elsewhere,[2] the fact that biographers have been led to different candidates, with the fragmentary evidence pointing in several directions inconclusively, has deepened my conviction that "he" is not a real human being whom Dickinson knew and loved and lost or renounced, but a psychological presence or factor in her inner life. Nor does the identification of "him" with Jesus or with God satisfactorily explain many of the poems, including the poem under discussion here. I have come, therefore, to see "him" as an image symbolic of certain aspects of her own personality, qualities and needs and potentialities which have been identified culturally and psychologically with the masculine, and which she consequently perceived and experienced as masculine.

Carl Jung called this "masculine" aspect of the woman's psyche her "animus," corresponding to the postulation of an "anima" as the "feminine" aspect of the man's psyche. The anima or animus, first felt as the disturbing presence of the "other" in one's self, thus holds the key to fulfillment and can enable the man or the woman to suffer through the initial crisis of alienation and conflict to assimilate the "other" into an integrated identity. In the struggle toward wholeness the animus and the anima come to mediate the whole range of experience for the woman and the man: her and his connection with nature and sexuality on the one hand and with spirit on the other. No wonder that the animus and the anima appear in dreams, myths, fantasies, and works of art as figures at once human and divine, as lover and god. Such a presence is Emily Dickinson's Master and Owner in the poem.

However, for women in a society like ours which enforces the subjection of women in certain assigned roles, the process of growth and integration becomes especially fraught with painful risks and traps and ambivalences. Nevertheless, here, as in many poems, Dickinson sees the chance for fulfillment in her relationship to the animus figure, indeed in her identification with him. Till he came, her life had known only inertia, standing neglected in tight places, caught at the right angles of walls: not just *a* corner, the first lines of the poem tell us, but corners, as though wherever she stood was thereby a constricted place. But all the time she knew that she was something other and more. Paradoxically, she attained her prerogatives through submission to the internalized masculine principle. In the words of the poem, the release of her power depended on her being "carried away"—rapt, "raped"—by her Owner and Master. Moreover, by further turns of the paradox, a surrender of womanhood transformed her into a phallic weapon, and in return his recognition and adoption "identified" her.

Now we can begin to see why the serious fantasy of this poem makes her animus a hunter and woodsman. With instinctive rightness Dickinson's imagination grasps her situation in terms of the major myth of the American experience. The pioneer on the frontier is the version of the universal hero myth indigenous to our specific historical circumstances, and it remains today, even in our industrial society, the mythic mainstay of American individualism. The pioneer claims his manhood by measuring himself against the unfathomed, unfathomable immensity of his elemental world, whose "otherness" he experiences at times as the inhuman, at times as the feminine, at times as the divine—most often as all three at once. His link with landscape, therefore, is a passage into the unknown in his own psyche, the mystery of his unconscious. For the man the anima is the essential point of connection with woman and with deity.

But all too easily, sometimes all too unwittingly, connection—which should move to union—can gradually fall into competition, then contention and conflict. The man who reaches out to Nature to engage his basic physical and spiritual needs finds himself reaching out with the hands of the predator to possess and subdue, to make Nature serve his own ends. From the point of view of Nature, then, or of woman or of the values of the feminine principle the pioneer myth can assume a devastating and tragic significance, as our history has repeatedly demonstrated. Forsaking the institutional structures of patriarchal culture, the woodsman goes out alone, or almost alone, to test whether his mind and will are capable of outwitting the lures and wiles of Nature, her dark children and wild creatures. If he can vanquish her— Mother Nature, Virgin Land—then he can assume or resume his place in society and as boon exact his share of the spoils of Nature and the service of those, including women and the dark-skinned peoples, beneath him in the established order.

In psychosexual terms, therefore, the pioneer's struggle against the wilderness can be seen, from the viewpoint, to enact the subjugation of the feminine principle, whose dark mysteries are essential to the realization of personal and social identity but for that reason threaten masculine prerogatives in a patriarchal ordering of individual and social life. The hero fights to establish his ego-identity and assure the linear transmission of the culture which sustains his ego-identity, and he does so by maintaining himself against the encroachment of the Great Mother. Her rhythm is the round of Nature, and her sovereignty is destructive to the independent individual because the continuity of the round requires that she devour her children and absorb their lives and consciousness back into her teeming womb, season after season, generation after generation. So the pioneer who may first have ventured into the woods to discover the otherness which is the clue to identity may in the end find himself maneuvering against the feminine powers, weapon in hand, with mind and will as his ultimate weapons for self-preservation. No longer seeker or lover, he advances as the aggressor, murderer, rapist.

As we have seen, in this poem Emily Dickinson accedes to the "rape," because she longs for the inversion of sexual roles which, from the male point of view, allows a hunter or a soldier to call his phallic weapon by a girl's name and speak of it, even to it, as a woman. Already by the second stanza "I" and "he" have become "We": "And now We roam in Sovreign Woods— / And now We hunt the Doe—," the rhythm and repetition underscoring the momentous change of identity. However, since roaming "in Sovreign Woods—," or, as the variant has it, roaming "the—Sovreign Woods —" is a contest of survival, it issues in bloodshed. "To foe of His—I'm deadly foe," she boasts later, and here their first venture involves hunting the doe. It is important that the female of the deer is specified, for Dickinson's identification of herself with the archetype of the hero in the figure of the woodsman seems to her to necessitate a sacrifice of her womanhood, explicitly the range of personality and experience as sexual and maternal woman. In just a few lines she has converted her "rape" by the man into a hunting-down of Mother Nature's creatures by manly comrades—Natty Bumppo and Chingachgook in *The Last of the Mohicans*, Natty Bumppo and Hurry Harry in *The Deerslayer*.

Nor are we imposing a psychosexual interpretation on the naive innocence of an earlier Romantic idyll; the implications of the myth are all there in Cooper. Here is the first appearance of Natty and Hurry Harry in Chapter 1 of *The Deerslayer*. They hack their way out of "the tangled labyrinth" of the Great Mother's maw or belly. The description acknowledges the awesome solemnity of the "eternal round" of the Great Mother's economy but acknowledges as well the threat to the individual snared in her dark and faceless recesses and unable to cut his way free. Initially there is no sign of human life; then from her timeless and undifferentiated "depths" emerge first two separate voices "calling to each other" and at last two men, "liberated" and "escaped" into lighted space where they can breathe. The passage reads:

> Whatever may be the changes produced by man, the eternal round of the seasons is unbroken. Summer and winter, seed-time and harvest, return in their stated order, with a sublime precision, affording to man one of the noblest of all the occasions he enjoys of proving the high powers of his far-reaching mind, in compassing the laws that control their exact uniformity, and in calculating their never-ending revolutions. Centuries of summer suns had warmed the tops of the same noble oaks and pines, sending their heats even to the tenacious roots, when voices were heard calling to each other in the depths of a forest, of which the leafy surface lay bathed in the brilliant light of a cloudless day in June, while the trunks of the trees rose in gloomy grandeur in the shades beneath. The calls were in different tones, evidently proceeding from two men who had lost their way, and were searching in different directions for their path. At length a shout proclaimed success, and

presently a man of gigantic mould broke out of the tangled labyrinth of a small swamp, emerging into an opening that appeared to have been formed partly by the ravages of the wind, and partly by those of fire. This little area, which afforded a good view of the sky, although it was pretty well filled with dead trees, lay on the side of one of the high hills, or few mountains, into which nearly the whole of the adjacent country was broken.

"Here is room to breathe in!" exclaimed the liberated forester, as soon as he found himself under a clear sky, shaking his huge frame like a mastiff that had just escaped from a snow-bank. "Hurray, Deerslayer, here is day-light at last, and yonder is the lake."

Man "proves" "the high powers of his far-reaching mind" by "compassing" and "calculating" (that is, by comprehending and thus holding within bounds in the mind) the cycle of generation. From an elevated perspective above the woods "the brilliant light of a cloudless day in June" may grace "the leafy surface," but "in the shades beneath," where the men "had lost their way," was the oppressive gloom of the tree-trunks and "the tenacious roots." The two "gigantic" men emerge into an area cleared by wind and fire, the lighter and more spiritual elements, from the "small swamp," compounded of mud and water, the heavier elements conventionally associated with the feminine matrix.

True to the archetypal meaning of the situation, the first conversation between Hurry Harry and Natty turns on the question of proving one's manhood. The immediate victim is the doe, slain by Natty's rifle, Killdeer, but soon the real contention becomes clear. As the moral and sensitive woodsman, Natty finds himself defending his brother Delawares, arguing with the coarse Hurry Harry that they are not "women," as Hurry charges, but "heroes," despite the fact that they are dark children of the Great Mother. The conversation begins as follows:

"Come, Deerslayer, fall to, and prove that you have a Delaware stomach, as you say you have had a Delaware edication," cried Hurry, setting the example by opening his mouth to receive a slice of cold venison steak that would have made an entire meal for a European peasant; "fall to, lad, and prove your manhood on this poor devil of a doe, with your teeth, as you've already done with your rifle."

"Nay, nay, Hurry, there's little manhood in killing a doe, and that too out of season; though there might be some in bringing down a painter or a catamount," returned the other, disposing himself to comply. "The Delawares have given me my name, not so much on account of a bold heart, as on account of a quick eye and an actyve foot. There may not be any cowardyce in overcoming a deer, but, sartin it is, there's no great valor."

"The Delawares themselves are no heroes," muttered Hurry through his teeth, the mouth being too full to permit it to be fairly opened, "or they never would have allowed them loping vagabonds, the Mingoes, to make them women."

"That matter is not rightly understood—has never been rightly explained," said Deerslayer, earnestly, for he was as zealous a friend as his companion was dangerous as an enemy; "the Mengwe fill the woods with their lies, and misconstruct words and treaties. I have now lived ten years with the Delawares, and know them to be as manful as any other nation, when the proper time to strike comes."

"Harkee, Master Deerslayer, since we are on the subject, we may as well open our minds to each other in a man-to-man way; answer me one question: you have had so much luck among the game as to have gotten a title, it would seem; but did you ever hit anything human or intelligible? Did you ever pull trigger on an inimy that was capable of pulling one upon you?"

Not yet; but the subtitle of the book is *The First War-Path*, and in the course of the action Natty spills human blood for the first time, all of it Indian. Natty may be a doeslayer with a difference, but even his unique combination of the best qualities of civilization and nature does not exempt him from the conflicts and contradictions of the pioneer myth. Though a man of the woods, roaming the realm of the Great Mother, he must remain unspotted from complicity with her dark and terrible aspect, just as his manhood has to be kept inviolate from the advances of Judith Hutter, the dark and sullied beauty in *The Deerslayer*, and from his own attraction to Mabel Dunham in *The Pathfinder*.

In the psychological context of this archetypal struggle Emily Dickinson joins in the killing of the doe without a murmur of pity or regret; she wants the independence of will and the power of mind which her allegiance with the woodsman makes possible. Specifically, engagement with the animus unlocks her artistic creativity; through his inspiration and mastery she becomes a poet. The variant for "power" in the last line is "art," and the irresistible force of the rifle's muzzle-flash and of the bullet are rendered metaphorically in terms of the artist's physiognomy: his blazing countenance ("Vesuvian face"), his vision ("Yellow Eye"), his shaping hand ("emphatic Thumb"), his responsive heart ("cordial light"). So it is that when the hunter fires the rifle, "I speak for Him—." Without his initiating pressure on the trigger, there would be no incandescence; but without her as seer and craftsman there would be no art. From their conjunction issues the poem's voice, reverberant enough to make silent nature echo with her words.

In Hebrew the word "prophet" means to "speak for." The prophet translates the wordless meanings of the god into human language. Whitman defined the prophetic function of the poet in precisely these terms: "it means one whose mind bubbles up and pours forth as a fountain from inner, divine spontaneities revealing God.... The great matter is to reveal and outpour the God-like suggestions pressing for birth in the soul."[3] Just as in the male poetic tradition such divine inspiration is characteristically experienced as mediated through the anima and imaged as the poet's muse, so in this poem the animus figure functions as Dickinson's masculine muse. Where Whitman experiences inspiration as the gushing flux of the Great Mother, Dickinson experiences it as the Olympian fire: the gun-blast and Vesuvius. In several poems Dickinson depicts herself as a smoldering volcano, the god's fire flaring in the bosom of the female landscape. In her first conversation with the critic Thomas Wentworth Higginson, Dickinson remarked: "If I feel physically as if the top of my head were taken off, I know *that* is poetry. . . . Is there any other way."[4]

But why is the creative faculty also destructive, Eros inseparable from Thanatos? To begin with, for a woman like Dickinson, choosing to be an artist could seem to require denying essential aspects of herself and relinquishing experience as lover, wife, and mother. From other poems we know Dickinson's painfully, sometimes excruciatingly divided attitude toward her womanhood, but here under the spell of the animus muse she does not waver in the sacrifice. Having spilled the doe's blood during the day's hunt, she stations herself for the night ("Our good Day done—") as stiff, soldierly guard at "My Master's Head," scorning to enter the Master's bed and sink softly into "the Eider-Duck's / Deep Pillow." Her rejection of the conventional sexual and domestic role expected of women is further underscored by the fact that the variant for "Deep" is "low" ("the Eider-Duck's / Low Pillow") and by the fact that the eider-duck is known not merely for the quality of her down but for lining her nest by plucking the feathers from her own breast. No such "female masochism" for this doeslayer; she is "foe" to "foe of His," the rhyme with "doe" effecting the grim inversion.

Moreover, compounding the woman's alternatives, which exact part of herself no matter how she chooses, stands the essential paradox of art: that the artist kills experience into art, for temporal experience can only escape death by dying into the "immortality" of artistic form. The fixity of "life" in art and the fluidity of "life" in nature are incompatible. So no matter what the sex of the deer, it must be remade in the artist's medium; the words of the poem preserve the doe and the buck in an image of their mortality. These ironies have always fascinated and chilled artists. Is the vital passion of the youthful lovers on Keats's "Grecian Urn" death or immortality? In Eudora Welty's "A Still Moment" Audubon shoots the exquisite white bird so that he can paint it. In John Crowe Ransom's "Painted Head" the artist betrays the young man he has painted by shrinking him into an image. It seems a death's head now, yet this painted head of a now-dead man radiates unaltered health and happiness. No wonder Audubon is willing to shoot the bird. No wonder a poet like Emily Dickinson will surrender to painful self-sacrifice. The loss of a certain range of experience might allow her to preserve what remained; that sacrifice might well be her apotheosis, the only salvation she might know.

Both the poet's relation to her muse and the living death of the artwork lead into the runic riddle of the last quatrain. It is actually a double riddle, each two lines long connected by the conjunction "for" and by the rhyme:

> Though I than He—may longer live
> He longer must—than I—
> For I have but the power to kill,
> Without—the power to die—

In the first rune, why is it that she *may* live longer than he but he *must* live longer than she? The poet lives on past the moment in which she is a vessel or instrument in the hands of the creative animus for two reasons—first, because her temporal life resumes when she is returned to one of life's corners, a waiting but loaded gun again, but also because on another level she surpasses momentary possession by the animus in the poem she has created under his inspiration. At the same time, he *must* transcend her temporal life and even its artifacts because, as the archetypal source of inspiration, the animus is, relative to the individual, transpersonal and so in a sense "immortal."

The second rune extends the paradox of the poet's mortality and survival. The lines begin to unravel and reveal themselves if we read the phrase "Without—the power to die—" not as "lacking the power to die" but rather as "except for the power to die," "unless I had the power to die." The lines would then read: unless she were mortal, if she did not have the power to die, she would have only the power to kill. And when we straighten out the grammatical construction of a condition-contrary-to-fact to conform with fact, we come closer to the meaning: with mortality, if she does have the power to die—as indeed she does—she would not have only the power to kill. What else or what more would she then have? There are two clues. First, the variant of "art" for "power" in the last line links "the power to die," mortality, all the more closely with "the power to kill," the artistic process. In addition, the causal conjunction "for" relates the capacity for death in the second rune back to the capacity for life in the first rune. Thus, for her the power to die is resolved in the artist's power to kill, whereby she dies into the hypostasized work of art. The animus muse enables her to fix the dying moment, but it is only her human capabilities, working in time with language, which are able to translate that fixed moment into the words on the page. The artistic act is, therefore, not just destructive but in the end self-creative. In a mysterious way the craftsmanship of the doomed artist rescues her exalted moments from oblivion and extends destiny beyond "dying" and "killing."

Now we can grasp the two runes together. The poet's living and dying permit her to be an artist; impelled by the animus, she is empowered to kill experience and slay herself into art. Having suffered mortality, she "dies into life," as Keats's phrase in *Hyperion* has it; virgin as the Grecian urn and the passionate figures on it, her poetic self outlasts temporal process and those climactic instants of animus possession, even though in the process of experience she knows him as a free spirit independent of her and transcendent of her poems. In different ways, therefore, each survives the other: she mortal in her person but timeless in her poems, he transpersonal as an archetype but dependent on her transitory experience of him to manifest himself. The interdependence through which she "speaks for" him as his human voice makes both for her dependence and limitations and also for her triumph over dependence and limitation.

Nevertheless, "My life had stood—a Loaded Gun—" leaves no doubt that a woman in a patriarchal society achieves that triumph through a blood sacrifice. The poem presents the alternatives unsparingly: be the hunter or the doe. She can refuse to be a victim by casting her lot with the hunter, but thereby she claims herself as victim. By the rules of the hunter's game, there seems no escape for the woman in the woods. Emily Dickinson's sense of conflict within herself and about herself could lead her to such a desperate and ghastly fantasy as the following lines from poem 1737:

> Rearrange a "Wife's" affection!
> When they dislocate my Brain!
> Amputate my freckled Bosom!
> Make me bearded like a man!

The violent, exclamatory self-mutilation indicates how far we have come from the pieties of Mrs. Sigourney and her sisters.

Fortunately for Dickinson the alternatives did not always seem so categorical. Some of her most energetic and ecstatic poems—those supreme moments which redeemed the travail and anguish—celebrate her experience of her womanhood. The vigor of these dense lyrics matches in depth and conviction Whitman's sprawling, public celebration of his manhood. At such times she saw her identity not as a denial of her feminine nature in the name of the animus but as an assimilation of the animus into an integrated self. In that way "he" is not a threat but a force—and a source. As part of herself, "he" initiates her into the mysteries of experience which would otherwise remain "other"; "his" mind and will summon her to consciousness—not the fullness of manhood but the completion of her womanhood. There, in the privacy of her psyche, withdrawn from the world of men and even of family, she would live out all the extremes of feeling and response, all the states of mind which fall under the usual rubrics of love, death, and immortality.

Poem 508, probably composed a year or so before "My life had stood—a Loaded Gun—," describes her psychological metamorphosis in terms of two baptisms which conferred name and identity: the first the sacramental baptism in the patriarchal church when she was an unknowing and helpless baby; the second a self-baptism into areas of personality conventionally associated with the masculine, an act of choice and will undertaken in full consciousness, or, perhaps more accurately, into full consciousness. Since Emily Dickinson was not a member of the church and had never been baptized as child or adult, the baptism is a metaphor for marking stages and transitions in self-awareness and identity. The poem is not a love poem or a religious poem, as its first editors thought in 1890, but a poem of sexual or psychological politics enacted in the convolutions of the psyche:

> I'm ceded—I've stopped being Their's—
> The name They dropped upon my face
> With water, in the country church
> Is finished using, now,
> And They can put it with my Dolls,
> My childhood, and the string of spools,
> I've finished threading—too—
>
> Baptized, before, without the choice,
> But this time, consciously, of Grace—
> Unto supremest name—
> Called to my Full—The Crescent dropped—
> Existence's whole Arc, filled up,
> With one small Diadem.
>
> My second Rank—too small the first—
> Crowned—Crowing—on my Father's breast—
> A half unconscious Queen—
> But this time—Adequate—Erect,
> With Will to choose, or to reject,
> And I choose, just a Crown—

Some of the manuscript variants emphasize the difference between the two states of being. The variants for "Crowing" in "Crowned—Crowing—on my Father's breast—" are "whimpering" and "dangling," as contrasted with "Adequate" and "Erect" later. The variants in the phrase "A half unconscious Queen—" are "too unconscious" and "insufficient." As the poet comes to consciousness in the second and third stanzas, she assumes, as in the previous poem, something of the phallicism and privileges of the masculine. "Power" is the variant for "Will" in the second-to-last line, but now the power of will is the Queen's. She has displaced the Father, the crown he conferred replaced by her round diadem; she calls herself by her "supremest name."

Dickinson wrote several "Wife" poems on the same theme. Poem 199, written a little earlier than the one above, probably in 1860, sums the situation up:

> I'm "wife"—I've finished that—
> That other state—
> I'm Czar—I'm "Woman" now—
> It's safer so—
>
> How odd the Girl's life looks
> Behind this soft Eclipse—
> I think that Earth feels so
> To folks in Heaven—now—
>
> This being comfort—then
> That other kind—was pain—
> But why compare?
> I'm "Wife"! Stop there!

The passage from virgin girlhood to "wife" and "Woman" is again accomplished through the powerful agency of the animus, in this poem the "Czar." The "wife" and "Czar" couple into the androgynous completion of her woman's Self. However, for Dickinson it is a womanhood reached at heavy cost, a wifehood consummated on peculiarly private terms withdrawn from the risks and dangers of contact with actual men in a man-dominated culture. Only alone and in secret could this royal pair wed and be joined in the hierogamy, or mystic marriage, of identity. As the poem warns us, "It's safer so—."

Until recently, women poets since Emily Dickinson have found themselves caught in the same quandary, and, in exchange for more public recognition, have chosen to repress the "feminine" or the "masculine" aspects of themselves. Some, such as Marianne Moore and Elizabeth Bishop, tended to obscure or deflect passion and sexuality in favor of fine discriminations of perceptions and ideas. Others, such as Edna St. Vincent Millay and Elinor Wylie, took as their woman's strain precisely the thrill of emotion and tremor of sensibility which rendered them susceptible to the threats of the masculine "other." In the isolation of her upstairs bedroom, Emily Dickinson refused finally to make that choice; but in the first half of the century perhaps only H.D., especially in the great poems and sequences of her old age, committed head and heart, sexuality and spirit to the exploration of her womanhood: a venture perhaps made possible only through an expatriation from American society more complete than Gertrude Stein's or Eliot's or Pound's. During the last decade or two, however, in the work of poets as different as Sylvia Plath and Denise Levertov, Muriel Rukeyser and Robin Morgan and Jean Valentine, and most importantly, I think, in the work of Adrienne Rich, women have begun exploring that mystery, their own mystery, with a new sense of calling and community. Sometimes ecstatically, sometimes angrily, sometimes in great agony of body and spirit, but always now with the sustaining knowledge that they are not living and working alone, that more and more women and a growing number of men are hearing what they say, listening to them and with them. Such a realization makes a transforming and clarifying difference in the contemporary scene. And it is an important aspect of Emily Dickinson's enormous achievement that she pursued the process of exploration so far and so long on her own.

9.

Armored Women, Naked Men:
Dickinson, Whitman, and Their Successors

Terence Diggory

In 1860 Walt Whitman published four lines of verse that eventually appeared as a separate poem under the title "Visor'd":

> A mask, a perpetual natural disguiser of herself,
> Concealing her face, concealing her form,
> Changes and transformations every hour, every moment,
> Falling upon her even when she sleeps.[1]

In the same year, as nearly as her editor has determined, Emily Dickinson wrote a poem that concludes with these four lines:

> Mirth is the Mail of Anguish—
> In which it Cautious Arm,
> Lest anybody spy the blood
> And "you're hurt" exclaim![2]

The two poems share the theme of concealment expressed, if Whitman's title is taken into account, through the image of armor, but the context of each poet's work suggests radically different attitudes toward the common material. Considered in an even broader context, the difference points to a distinction not only between Whitman and Dickinson but between male and female traditions in American poetry that have their roots in these two great contemporaries.

The image of armor helps to define the female poetic tradition partly because its place in that tradition is so anomalous. Armor belongs historically to England rather than America, customarily to men rather than women, so its appearance in the verse of American women must have some special meaning. It is not important in the male tradition except in the scattered attempts to revive the Arthurian legends. Whitman rarely uses the image, which is not surprising, for every symbolic association of armor is antithetical to the traits that Whitman prescribed for the American bard. "One of the roughs" cannot be chivalrous, the brother of all men cannot be distinguished by knighthood, and, most important, the naked Adam would find no clothing more cumbersome than a suit of mail. The prominence of nakedness as a virtue in Whitman's poetry inevitably condemns the self-concealing woman of "Visor'd." She is in conflict with the poet's own stance, as expressed in "Song of Myself": "I will go to the bank by the wood and become undisguised and naked" (*LG* 29). She is necessarily a woman because, for Whitman, nakedness and the robust honesty it symbolizes are distinctively male.

Dickinson welcomes the associations of armor that make it so alien to Whitman. She recognizes the role of ceremony as insulation against the shock of ecstasy:

> To meet it—nameless as it is—
> Without celestial Mail—
> Audacious as without a Knock
> To walk within the Veil.
>   (1353)

Distinction from others is another kind of protection. One of Dickinson's favorite creatures, the bee, is all the more special because "His Helmet, is of Gold" (916). But the function of armor as concealment, repugnant to Whitman, was perhaps the service that Dickinson valued most highly. It can conceal the self from the world, as in the first poem discussed here, or it can conceal the world from the self: "Our ignorance—our cuirass is" (1462). Instead of Whitman's honesty Dickinson preferred, not dishonesty, but an honesty of reticence rather than of revelation.

Armor is important in defining a female poetic tradition not only because it is anomalous but because it is extreme. The image occupies a position most distant from the nakedness of Whitman and his successors and at one end of a series of images of covering used by female poets. Because armor is the climax of the series, we know that the other images are valued principally not as expressions of modesty or a desire for ornament, but as means of protection. If we ask, "Protection from what?", the simplest answer is, "Nakedness." Even when she stresses the joy of nakedness, Dickinson balances the joy with a pain to which Whitman would concede little reality.

In poem 315, for instance, Dickinson describes an experience that first suggests a comparison with music, that is characterized by the adjectives "ethereal" and "imperial," but that finally "scalps your naked Soul." The experience can only be ecstasy, but the scalping hurts, all the more so because it leaves the soul more naked than before. Dickinson frequently draws on religious tradition to portray the nakedness of souls after death. On the one hand, that condition represents a joyous return to innocence. On the other hand, innocence is regained only after the soul is exposed before "that Naked Bar— / Jehovah's Countenance," to pass from which is a "Severer Triumph" (455). The souls of the dead might prefer to forgo nakedness in favor of spiritual garments, such as those provided in poem 984,

> When Cerements let go
> And Creatures clad in Miracle
> Go up by Two and Two.

Miracle, however, is a fabric too thin to prevent the souls from recognizing in each other loved ones who have been the source of pain. For Dickinson this resurrection is "Anguish grander than Delight."

These last examples go some way toward answering the further question, "Why desire protection against nakedness?" To answer we need to know the situations in which nakedness is experienced. The first is the intrusion of God. He is the source of scalping ecstasy and searing judgment, both of which were part of the experience of the first woman in the Garden of Eden:

> Not when we know, the Power accosts—
> The Garment of Surprise
> Was all our timid Mother wore
> At Home—in Paradise.

> (1335)

The first line makes clear that Eve is not prepared for the experience. Her garment is inadequate protection because it does not conceal her, and concealment is what "our timid Mother" wants. "In all the circumference of Expression," Dickinson once observed, "those guileless words of Adam and Eve never were surpassed, 'I was afraid and hid Myself.' "[3] Armor is the proper garment for confronting God. In poem 263 Dickinson wishes for "One more new-mailed Nerve" to help her prevent "the Gods" (the plural offers additional protection) from removing her lover through death.

Nakedness is also experienced in death, as we have seen, and against death even armor may prove inadequate: "No Casque so brave / It spurn the Grave" (616). Elsewhere Dickinson demonstrates the inadequacy of all defenses against death by employing a debased version of the image of armor, that of metal plating. When death has cut off the beloved from the lover as if by an adz, the most successful response is to have "Plated the residue of Adz / With Monotony" (1344). But a reconcilement to monotony is not an unqualified success. Moreover, if the plating is recognized as such, and not taken for genuine metal, the wound that lies beneath the plating must still be remembered. Plating is armor that is donned after the blow has been struck, but that must be worn because the wound is too horrible to look at.

Such a wound may be exposed either to oneself or to others, and each case represents a further instance of the pain of nakedness. The first case has just been examined. The second is expressed equally well through the image of plating:

> this one, wears its merriment
> So patient—like a pain—
> Fresh gilded—to elude the eyes
> Unqualified, to scan—.
>
> (353)

The concealment involved here has many layers. Joy is being concealed in such a way as pain might be concealed. Both emotions deserve to be hidden, each by its opposite. Though the speaker is aware of each emotion beneath its plating, awareness of any sort is denied to the "unqualified" others. Indeed, the gilding, like the bee's gold helmet, provides not only a defense through concealment but a badge of superiority. It is an ornament which functions, like the coveted diadem of other poems (for example, 232, 466), to distinguish the self from others.

A brief survey of Dickinson's several poems that deal with the threat of prying eyes helps to establish the range of images of concealment used in response to that threat. In addition to plating and armor, worn in poem 165 "Lest anybody spy the blood," Dickinson could make more conventional coverings suit her purpose, as in poem 1412:

> Shame is the shawl of Pink
> In which we wrap the Soul
> To keep it from infesting Eyes—
> The elemental Veil
> Which helpless Nature drops
> When pushed upon a scene
> Repugnant to her probity—
> Shame is the tint divine.

This is Dickinson at an extreme of stereotypical femininity. The two articles of clothing, the shawl and the veil, are exclusively feminine, as is, supposedly, the emotion of shame which the clothing represents. One of the reasons that male poets like Whitman can rejoice in nakedness is that they are presumed to be shameless. The "proper" reaction of a woman to the mere thought of nakedness is to blush, whereupon her cheeks assume that "shawl of Pink" which, even in its color, is traditionally feminine. The one quality of this poem that is not a feminine cliché is its refusal to concede helplessness, despite the affectation of a "helpless Nature." The shawl and veil succeed in protecting the soul against "infesting Eyes." Dickinson redefines traditional images of feminine vulnerability and endows them with all the strength of armor.

Not all of Dickinson's images of concealment cover the body alone. Some have a wider compass that expands the implications of concealment in the poet's work. Another poem which deals with the concealment of grief opens with a common image in Dickinson's poetry, that of the house:

> Grief is a Mouse—
> And chooses Wainscot in the Breast
> For His Shy House—
> And baffles quest—.
>
> (793)

The poetic image of withdrawal into a house reflects Dickinson's real-life withdrawal into her parents' house at Amherst. As with the images of shawl and veil, the poet has at least partially revised a movement that traditionally betokens weakness or even entrapment. She is expressing the insight of a woman who, confined to her "proper place," discovers not a prison but a valuable defense, as the house in the poem functions for its inhabitant. It is not she but her pursuers who are baffled. They are baffled again at the end of the poem when they attempt to make Grief talk but discover that "Best Grief is Tongueless." For Dickinson silence is the ultimate technique of concealment.[4]

Like the image of armor, those of the house and of silence are used by Whitman as well as Dickinson, but once again consideration of each poet's work as a whole reveals important differences. Generally, enclosure for Whitman is an embrace, a means of uniting with others, preferably all others. In "The Sleepers," the soul "comes from its embower'd garden and looks pleasantly on itself and encloses the world" (*LG* 432). Since a house is too small to enclose the world, those who inhabit a house are lonely. Typically, for Whitman, they are women. In a famous passage from "Song of Myself," twenty-eight young men bathe out-of-doors, unaware that a young woman watches them from her house: "She hides handsome and richly drest aft the blinds of the window" (*LG* 38). The young men, the passage implies, are not dressed at all.

Whitman's young woman has enough imagination to remain in the house and yet still be "the twenty-ninth bather." Dickinson had that power, but her imagination also enabled her to discover advantages in being inside the house. She welcomes enclosure as exclusion, as a means of defending the self against others: "The Soul selects her own Society— / Then— shuts the Door" (303). The door is the most important feature of the house in the work of both poets, though Dickinson makes greater use of its various possibilities. Whitman finds unequivocal value in open doors, even when, as in "The Last Invocation," the opening means death: "From the clasp of the knitted locks, from the keep of the well-closed doors, / Let me be wafted" (*LG* 454). Although she also uses this traditional image of death as release (277), Dickinson places far greater emphasis on death as enclosure. The tomb is a house. In the room where a corpse lies, the house image joins the image of silence:

> There's something quieter than sleep
> Within this inner room!
> It wears a sprig upon its breast—
> And will not tell its name.
>
> (45)

As the corpse is concealed by the house, the identity of the corpse is concealed by silence.

At least two different motivations for Dickinson's respect for silence are revealed through her poetry. The first is a recognition of the expressive power of silence. The fact that the volcano on Teneriffe is "Clad in . . . Mail of ices" (666), an image that equates silence with armor, makes the mountain even more awesome than if it were actually erupting (cf. 1146). Second, silence defends against the destructive power of words in a way that armor cannot:

> There is a word
> Which bears a sword
> Can pierce an armed man—
>
> (8)

in "Flight to New York" from *The Dolphin*: "After fifty so much joy has come, / I hardly want to hide my nakedness."

Of more interest than such clear-cut examples are those which represent an apparent crossing over from one tradition to the other, thus challenging the validity of the distinction. In the previous section I suggested that confessional poetry was characteristic of men and anticonfessional poetry was characteristic of women, yet it is popularly accepted that the verse of some men is at least nonconfessional, while several women have become famous for their work in the confessional mode. If such cases are approached from the perspective of the author's sex, the distinction between the two traditions not only holds up but in fact proves to be a useful stimulus for more precise observation of the poetry. It is not necessary to maintain that confessional verse by a woman is somehow masculine, or that a man's verse becomes feminine when he avoids being confessional. To see the impulse in either case as headed *toward* something ignores the likelihood that the impulse originated as a departure *from* the tradition characteristic of that sex. On closer examination it usually appears that the departure has not been complete. Confessional verse by women appears more reticent, more closed, while nonconfessional verse by men appears more open, more naked, than in either case was previously thought.

Although a line of his is quoted above as an example of heroic nakedness in male poetry, no male poet seems more deliberately anticonfessional than Robert Frost. He conceals his identity either by speaking as the rural sage or by speaking about other people who are usually more intent on covering up than on stripping. The exception of "The Trial by Existence" may be explained not only by the fact that it is a relatively early poem, but also by the fact that it deals with the afterlife, where, as we saw in Dickinson, nakedness seems somewhat more appropriate. Frost did not often commit himself to such definite views on the nature of anything so inherently unknowable as the afterlife. More characteristically, he comes up to the edge of the dark woods but refuses to enter, as in "Come In" or "Stopping by Woods on a Snowy Evening." Like Dickinson, Frost dons the cuirass of ignorance in order to be excused from telling what the woods contain, but his silence is maintained under different circumstances that are partly a function of a difference in sex. That difference emerges in a comparison of Frost's "Stopping by Woods" with Dickinson's version of the same subject.

Frost begins his poem with a question about the owner of the woods. The answer to the question establishes the distance between the woods and humanity:

> Whose woods these are I think I know.
> His house is in the village, though;
> He will not see me stopping here
> To watch his woods fill up with snow.
>
> My little horse must think it queer
> To stop without a farmhouse near
> Between the woods and frozen lake
> The darkest evening of the year.[6]

Mention of the horse suggests that the woods are alien not only to humanity but to any life connected with humanity. A dog, or rather the absence of one, provides this suggestion in Dickinson's poem, which begins with a question similar to Frost's:

> Who occupies this House?
> A Stranger I must judge
> Since No one knows His Circumstance—
> 'Tis well the name and age
>
> Are writ upon the Door
> Or I should fear to pause
> Where not so much as Honest Dog
> Approach encourages.
>
> (892)

In both poems the ultimate object of contemplation is death, for Frost's refusal of the woods is a refusal to sleep, and the "house" which Dickinson approaches proves to be a grave. What distinguishes the poems is the different position from which each poet observes the object. Dickinson is in the village, in a domestic setting, though that setting is a symbol for a graveyard, while Frost is miles from the village or any house, alone at night, in a setting into which no woman, especially of Dickinson's time, would be allowed to venture unaccompanied. Though each poet finally refuses to speak about the unknown, Frost is permitted to travel much farther before that refusal becomes necessary.

Necessity rather than desire for enclosure determines Frost's use of the house image, which proves more helpful than the image of clothing in differentiating Frost and Dickinson. In his chapter on the house in *Robert Frost: Modern Poetics and the Landscapes of Self*, Frank Lentricchia notes that a number of Frost's house poems, including "A Servant to Servants," "Home Burial," "The Witch of Coös," "The Hill Wife," and "The Fear," focus on women. Lentricchia curiously reverses the implications of this association in his claim that Frost's women are threatened by madness because they cannot close themselves off from reality, while the men find refuge inside "the haven of everyday banality."[7] The more obvious interpretation is that the women's confinement in houses represents a spiritual confinement. They lack the sane contact which the men, who are more open, are able to establish with the everyday world, whether banal or not. This interpretation seems in closer accord with Lentricchia's own understanding of the woman in "A Servant to Servants," whose "inner dialogue tends to be paralytic and abates only when, for brief moments, the self is opened up to the landscape so that there is an energizing symbolic flow from the outside, from nature into the self."[8] The outside is not always so benign for Frost's women, as Lentricchia recognizes, and in such cases the house may offer a defense. But in contrast to Dickinson, Frost's emotional emphasis is usually placed not on the comfort within but on "The Fear" without. The outside, for Frost, cannot be securely closed off.

Lentricchia finds that the house image has more comforting associations in Frost's lyrics as opposed to his narratives. He does not stress the important fact that the poems he cites, "The Runaway," "Good Hours," and "Acquainted with the Night," all deal with houses from the outside. Moreover, in the last two poems at least, the lyric voice, being more closely associated with the poet's own voice than in the narratives, is distinctively male. In both cases the speakers, as in "Stopping by Woods on a Snowy Evening," have ventured into that no-woman's land beyond the lights of any house. Jean McClure Mudge has proposed a similar contrast, that the men are outside their houses and the women inside, in attempting to distinguish Dickinson's use of the house image from that of her male contemporaries.[9]

Another group of Frost's poems that negate the house image proves how strong are Frost's affinities with the tradition of male openness. The house in question may be abandoned, as in "The Black Cottage" or "The Census Taker," or it may be destroyed, as in "Directive" or "The Need of Being Versed in Country Things." In the last poem the chimney stands alone, "Like a pistil after the petals go," or like a man who has taken off his clothes. Such poems usually involve the theme that the tradition associates with nakedness, that of honesty, in this case the attempt to see no more than the desolation that is actually there. Amid the desolation we encounter a crossing of traditions from the other direction in the case of Sylvia Plath, who, though a woman, is famous for a type of confessional poetry that I have characterized as male. Like Frost, Plath also writes of abandoned houses, as in "Point Shirley," or of ruined houses, as in "Aftermath," both from *The Colossus*.[10] The difference is that, as a woman, Plath must participate in the rejection or destruction of the house, not merely observe the

"Aftermath." In that poem the house has been destroyed by a woman, Medea. In "Point Shirley" the poet submits to the sea that her grandmother's house defied. Both poems reject the meanings that a house has traditionally held for women.

Even if a female poet chooses the same direction as a male, the fact that she has an opposing heritage to reject would make her poetry different. The difference appears with unusual complexity in Plath's poem "Private Ground." She is a visitor at what I take to be the Yaddo artists' colony, where she feels at once protected and shut off: "I need hardly go out at all. / A superhighway seals me off."[11] A man's response to such a claustrophobic situation would be a gesture of openness or nakedness, a rejection of protective covering. But in the same poem Plath reminds us that nakedness has a different meaning for a woman. The grounds of the estate are adorned with statues of female nudes, and their nakedness is of a kind that needs protection against the oncoming winter: "Soon each white lady will be boarded up / Against the cracking climate." The image of being boarded up, which links the situation of the statues to the confinement of the speaker, is coffin-like, yet the danger of exposure is given equally fearful weight. The climate, after all, is cracking. In such a world, nakedness, however much desired, is simply not an option.

Women poets have had to redefine the meaning of nakedness before it could function for them as it did for men. The results of that redefinition can be seen in another poem by Plath, "In Plaster." Once again a statue is involved, this time represented by the body cast in which the speaker is confined:

> I shall never get out of this! There are two of me now:
> This new absolutely white person and the old yellow one,
> And the white person is certainly the superior one.[12]

Here the relationship between speaker and statue, the "white person," is intensified because it is the statue itself that seals off the speaker. The coffin image becomes explicit—"Living with her was like living with my own coffin"— and the ambiguity of the situation is correspondingly reduced. Though the white person is admittedly superior, the speaker makes no secret of her desire to discard the cast. To do so would be to achieve a nakedness that, so far from being ideal, is acknowledged to be ugly.

Female confessional poets approach their male counterparts as far as acknowledging the necessity of nakedness, but they deny the male claim that nakedness is beautiful. This denial is probably less a result of any desire to maintain an identity apart from the men than it is an attempt by these women to distinguish themselves from an earlier female image. In the visual arts in the nineteenth century the nude as an expression of human physical perfection, represented by Plath's statues, became exclusively female.[13] It is possible that the importance of the male nude in literature grew as the image was displaced from other media. What is certain is that the dominance of the female nude in the visual arts prevented literary nudity from having the same meaning for women as it did for men. If a woman took off her clothes in a book she would become "a nude"; she would not become naked. If the book were pornographic, the woman would simply invite the associations of a different set of ideals. In no case would her nudity express the real, or symbolize that raw honesty that nakedness embodied for Whitman and his successors. In their attempt to break out of the prison of ideals that male idolatry had constructed for them, female poets abandoned even honesty as an ideal, and presented nakedness as truly raw, in fact as ugly. Thus the female emphasis on the darker aspects of the confessional project, begun when Emily Dickinson stressed the pain of confession, continues in the work of poets such as Plath.

Stripping seems an intentional emblem of the confessional impulse in Plath's *Ariel*, where the motif appears in the title poem and in "Getting There," "Fever 103°" and "Lady Lazarus." The last poem emphasizes the ugliness that stripping might reveal, and thereby casts doubt on the value of nakedness:

> Peel off the napkin
> O my enemy.
> Do I terrify?[14]

Further doubts arise with the appearance, elsewhere in the volume, of images of clothing or covering that are of ambiguous value themselves. The image of armor appears in the protective dress of the beekeepers, who are first introduced in "The Bee Meeting": "they are knights in visors, / Breastplates of cheesecloth knotted under the armpits." The transition from breast to armpit already serves to devalue this armor, and during the course of the poem the beekeepers' suits function as troubling "disguises" that prevent the initiate from recognizing daily acquaintances. On the other hand, the suits are valuable as protection against stings and as something more. Toward the opening of the poem the initiate complains, "I am nude as a chicken neck, does nobody love me?" When "the secretary of bees" helps her to cover up, it is taken as a gesture of love.

The series of bee poems in *Ariel* brings together the various strands, including the image of armor, that lead back from Plath to Dickinson.[15] Bees, as was mentioned in the previous section, were favorite creatures of Dickinson's. Queens were also, and Plath combines the two images by focusing on the queen bee in "Stings." Plath identifies the queen with herself, indeed with the very idea of selfhood: "I / Have a self to recover, a queen." Her status distinguishes her from those around her:

I stand in a column

Of winged, unmiraculous women,
Honey-drudgers.
I am no drudge.

Similarly, Dickinson in poem 348 stands out as "The Queen of Calvary" to whom all of nature, including the bees, pay "gentle deference."

The mark of the queen, characteristically for Dickinson, is her dress. Despite her confidence in poem 348 she is still worried that her "childish Plumes" may not be enough, and in another poem she determines not to let queenhood overtake her in her "old Gown" (#373). Dress is also a problem for Plath in "Stings," for she fears that the queen within her hive and within herself may be naked:

Her wings torn shawls, her long body
Rubbed of its plush—
Poor and bare and unqueenly and even shameful.

In such a state the common bees in the combs that she is transferring to her hive may not recognize her authority, and may punish her nakedness with their stings.

The attack never comes. The completion of the transfer gives Plath a sense of control which encourages her to resurrect her queenhood in the final image of the poem:

Now she is flying
More terrible than she ever was, red
Scar in the sky, red comet
Over the engine that killed her—
The mausoleum, the wax house.

In this image of the hive as a house, Plath has virtually turned Dickinson's house image inside-out. Protection depends on keeping the bees, the threatening others, inside the house, while the self remains outside. Breaking out of the house is a victory for the queen in "Stings," but the hive is not always shunned in this manner. In "The Bee Meeting," the hive is a symbol of the purity which is represented by whiteness elsewhere in the volume: "The white hive is snug as a virgin, / Sealing off her brood cells, her honey, and quietly humming." The woman is here identified with her house.

When the hive has darker associations, the noise inside grows more ominous. In "The Arrival of the Bee Box," Plath is struck by the weird contrast of death and life suggested by the contrasting exterior and interior of the box:

> I would say it was the coffin of a midget
> Or a square baby
> Were there not such a din in it.

Her immediate impulse is to find a means to free the life from the death which contains it:

> How can I let them out?
> It is the noise that appals me most of all,
> The unintelligible syllables.

Suddenly the bees inside the hive have become words inside the poet, clamoring to be articulated.

As the poem proceeds, the question, "How can I let them out?", at first a plea for a solution, becomes a cry of indignation at a solution that is unacceptable. If the bees are released, the poet hopefully conjectures,

> They might ignore me immediately
> In my moon suit and funeral veil.
> I am no source of honey
> So why should they turn on me?

But they might turn on her and they might be able to penetrate her protective armor. We may recall Dickinson's warning,

> There is a word
> Which bears a sword
> Can pierce an armed man—.
> (8)

Though Plath promises herself that she will free the bees tomorrow, the reader is convinced that that day will never arrive. The poem itself is evidence that Plath is too clearly aware of the cost of letting out those stinging words.

The gradual replacement of the confessional impulse by the anticonfessional impulse within "The Arrival of the Bee Box" reflects the larger reassessment of the whole of Plath's work which must be undertaken if her work is approached through Dickinson's. Other women have continued the tradition in different ways. The purpose of grouping them as a tradition is not to minimize their differences nor to divide them inseparably from the men, but to show that certain poets, because they were women, had something distinctive to contribute to American poetry as a whole. Because women have sought means to suggest what they did not want to say, they have discovered means to suggest what cannot be said, and thus fulfilled the poet's basic aim.

III

"THE SILVER RETICENCE"

Modernists

This that would greet—an hour ago—
Is quaintest Distance—now—
Had it a Guest from Paradise—
Nor glow, would it, nor bow—

Had it a notice from the Noon
Nor beam would it nor warm—
Match me the Silver Reticence—
Match me the Solid Calm—

—Emily Dickinson, #778

10.

The Art of Silence
and the Forms of Women's Poetry

Jeanne Kammer

If every work of art is a statement about the nature of reality, and if it is possible that women apprehend and interpret experience in some ways differently from men, then we may attempt to identify and explain those principles of form which recur in women's writing and shape its vision. The labels assigned to women's poetry by generations of critics have seldom accurately described its method because they have implicitly devalued its effect: "subtle," "fine," "graceful," "sharp," "gemlike," "cryptic," "tight"—however positive, the list seldom includes the words of power. Strength and truth are missing. Either the art itself is genuinely limited—a conclusion difficult to defend—or the terms and models used to assign value are inappropriate.

It is this last possibility I wish to explore in these pages, by examining the work[1] of three figures who established precedents for women's poetry in this century: Emily Dickinson, H.D., and Marianne Moore. They are important because, despite the artistic influences surrounding them, each developed her poetic tactics in relative isolation and independence, making choices stubbornly in response to a personal, private aesthetic. And out of that setting, each developed her poetry as an art of silence where it has historically been treated as an art of speech.

Syntactic Compression

Perhaps the most subtle use of silence in poetry, and at the same time the most familiar to us, comes through the devices of linguistic compression: ellipsis, inversion, syntactic substitution, the omission of connectives in favor of dramatic juxtapositions of word and image, and complicated processes of sentence embedding. "I despise connectives," declared Marianne Moore, and Dickinson, with her habit of "circumference," felt them to be "the places where poetry opens up and its life's blood may run out."[2] H.D., the Imagist model, was a ruthless pruner of her lines, cutting back to the minimum of language necessary for life. Hugh Kenner, one of the few able explicators of Marianne Moore's work, calls her a "poet of erasures," and comments that "to delete was for her a kind of creative act."[3] The principle extends to all three.

In Dickinson's work, which can serve here as illustration for the rest, the extremity of emotion is usually directly proportionate to the degree of compression employed. In one of her most powerful poems the feeling lies just beneath the surface of language which purports to deal with the absence of feeling; what is articulated aims steadily at evoking in us a response to what has not been said:

> After great pain, a formal feeling comes—
> The Nerves sit ceremonious, like Tombs—
> The stiff Heart questions was it He, that bore,
> And Yesterday, or Centuries before?

In the first stanza—thicker, more orderly than the ones which follow— there is nevertheless careful syntactic space created: explicitly in the *caesurae* and dashes, implicitly in the tense pairing of awkward sounds (great/pain, stiff/heart) and terms (formal/feeling). These latter have the effect of pauses and draw attention away from the forward movement of the sentence. The result is an expressive use of what I will term "minor" silences, where they operate in close counterpoint to the surface diction to increase the complexity and emotional force of the statement. At the same time they suggest the difficulty of articulating the experience at all—that there is more to it than language can convey.

A more difficult sort of compressive silence is found in the extreme devices of juxtaposition and ellipsis used in the first lines of stanza two:

> The Feet, mechanical, go round—
> Of Ground, or Air, or Ought—
> A Wooden way
> Regardless grown,
> A quartz contentment, like a stone—

Here the six main terms are set off from one another in an artificial parallelism emphasized by strong iambic rhythm; the result is more matrix than statement, the ambiguous "Of" suggesting a variety of connections. Placed as it is, "Of" can be read as "belonging to," "made of," or, literally, "on," and it introduces terms whose meaning in the poem depends on the choices made by the reader.

For example: if the feet belong to the ground, they are heavy, rooted; if to the air, they are disembodied, sense-less; if to "Ought" (which can be read as anything, or nothing, or an undefined feeling of duty), they are caught in the same kind of confusion that underlies the heart's question in stanza one. If the feet go round on the ground, we are in the realm of literal, physical reaction to pain; if they go round in air, a metaphorical level of mental pacing, spiritual aimlessness; if they go round in "Ought," a hazy and disturbing world outside of time and space, invested with an oppressive sense of duty—or no world at all.

Each possible combination of terms—there are more than these—provides an insight into the nature of the experience described, like faces on a prism held in different relationships of distance and angle to a single light source. Each reading leads inward, toward the singularity of the experience, rather than outward toward other possible frames of reference or abstractions of it; each reading leads, peculiarly, not toward the concrete and available image of pacing feet, but toward the seemingly casual and colorless "Ought" at the end of the second line. More than a vague "et cetera" to ground and air, the word is a carefully chosen vehicle for both the nagging necessity of conventional rituals (with their burden of guilt and duty) and the indescribable, anything-or-nothing, hazy, uncertain element in the condition which follows pain without replacing it.

In the third stanza still another tactic for compression is adopted—an embedding process which holds the fragments of experience firmly together even as the surface statement and shape of the stanza suggest an increasing loss of control:

> This is the Hour of Lead—
> Remembered, if outlived,
> As freezing persons, recollect the Snow—
> First—Chill—then Stupor—then the letting go—

If we were to portray the sentence in a different manner, it would look like this: "This<remembered [as freezing persons recollect the snow (first chill—then stupor—then the letting go—)] if outlived> is the hour of lead." This reconstruction takes us deeper in toward a "letting go" that occurs at the center as well as the end of the poem. "This" in line 10 incorporates the "formal feeling" of the first stanza, the "Ought" of the second, the "white helplessness"[4] of the third—and more: despite the trappings of ceremony and rock-like calm, it is *pain* which emerges from the awkward syntactic silences of the poem, twisting and gnawing and pressing at the restraints of words and lines.

The connections the reader must discover or create in "After Great Pain" are connotative, imaginative ones, independent of the expected resolutions of syntax. The same characteristics are demonstrably present in the spare constructions of H.D.'s early poems and in the strongest work of Moore, where, Kenner points out, images appear on the page "without benefit of the syntactic lubricants that slide us past a comparison."[5] This shared impulse to compressive speech may arise in part from habits of privacy, camouflage and indirection encouraged in the manner of the gently-bred female. Moreover, for the reclusive, emotionally vulnerable personality—and that is what we are dealing with in these three figures—the ambiguity of saying and not saying may be the only acceptable axis for communication. All three found pleasure and a kind of social protection in the role of eccentric, enigma—apparently unassuming but curiously compelling: touch me / touch me not.

Add to this the stubborn determination of Emily Dickinson and those who came after her to be "distinctive"—to achieve recognition in a literary and social world where the effusiveness of women was expected and regarded with paternal amusement—and there emerges a complex psychology of linguistic parsimony related to a professional identity. Haunted by the specter of the sweet-singing "poetess," the woman poet may have come to the "modern" style of the early decades of the twentieth century by a very different route than her male counterparts.

Still, in describing the craft of this sort of poetry (which she, too, practices) Denise Levertov insists upon "the necessity of great rifts between perception and perception—great gaps which must be leapt across if they are to be crossed at all."[6] Syntactic compression, with its subtle use of silences, does not seem adequately to illustrate her statement. The silences are deeper than words.

The Diaphoric Mode

Philip Wheelwright's distinction between two kinds of metaphor (*Metaphor and Reality*) restored terms to the critical vocabulary which are especially useful in elaborating the practices of the poets treated here.[7] Briefly, *epiphor* involves the familiar activity of defining something intangible, or abstract, or infinite, in terms of a more available and concrete image ("My luv is a red, red rose..."). Epiphor sets in motion a primarily linear process of concretion to abstraction; this movement is reflected in language which, for all its creative tensions, still fulfills syntactic expectations and leads to a generalization predicted in the terms of the metaphor. Epiphoric poetry can be expected to be more conventionally rhetorical and more generally discursive in nature.

Diaphor, on the other hand, produces new meaning by the juxtaposition alone of two (or more) images, each term concrete, their joining unexplained ("a red wheelbarrow / glazed with rain water / beside the white chickens"). Rooted in the associational properties of the subconscious mind, its movement is not necessarily linear and does not require syntactic support. Diaphoric poetry is better understood as configuration rather than statement, and it is persistently present in the work of the women considered here.

To illustrate with a relatively simple example, consider H.D.'s "Oread," one of those early poems which attracted Pound's interest and became the proximate cause of the Imagist tenets he proposed:

> Whirl up, sea—
> whirl your pointed pines,
> splash your great pines
> on our rocks,
> hurl your green over us,
> cover us with your pools of fir.

The criticisms of this poem, as well as the parodies which have trailed it down the years, must have arisen in part from the expectation of epiphor where diaphor is present. As in many of H.D.'s poems, voice, action, and objects here are treated as equal elements in a system, rather than as subordinate in syntactic or philosophical relation to one another. The oread, a nymph of the forest, demands of the sea an action which rises in crescendo from "whirl" to "splash" to "hurl," then settles into senescence with "cover." It is sexual, suicidal, and it connects the speaker to the sea in an intense, intimate manner.

The remaining images of the poem—the waves, the rocks, the pines— interact diaphorically with voice and action, superimposing one upon the other, creating ambiguity. The great pointed pines of the forest, for example, in a violent transference beyond simple juxtaposition, *become* the crashing waves of the sea; the "green . . . pools of fir" raise conflicting associations of warmth and coolness, safety and peril, life and death. "Our" and "us" are cloudy referents which both tighten and obscure relationships: the sea and the oread? The pines and the nymph? The speaker and some unnamed other? all of these? We read again, trying to feel our way through the poem, trying out combinations of terms—just as we must do with the work of Dickinson and Moore.

Diaphor depends on this last silence for its operation. The failure of language alone to connect the pieces (a function of syntactic compression), along with the conspicuous absence of a named feeling or quality or abstraction to make up for the lack of connectives, force us to search for other, less rational entries to the poem. Further, the process of unexplained juxtaposition causes the metaphoric activity to turn inward rather than outward: the reader is forced *through* the singular experience of the poem, approaching its name even as the name is refused. What we find instead is a silence that takes the place of linguistic connectives and that stands for the unnamed feeling or quality or perception which fuses the various parts.

As with the practice of highly compressed speech, the diaphoric impulse is at the root of modern poetry in general. What distinguishes the practice of women poets from men working in a similar fashion? The answer, again, may lie in the *source* of aesthetic choice. Certainly we understand the connection between the growing isolation and alienation of the artist in this century and the adoption of forms which are increasingly minimal, silent. The diaphoric leaps in the work of such figures as Pound, Eliot, Williams and Stevens can represent both a dramatization of and a withdrawal from a culture fragmented, disordered, and lacking in central values and vision.

But just as certainly there must be in her exacerbated cultural situation of powerlessness and enforced containment the roots of the creative woman's particular attraction to a tightly controlled art form which ironically expresses her condition even as it is denied. Furthermore, the diaphoric mode, for women, may reflect an internal division and fragmentation, a private experience opposed to the public one of men. The effect of "Sweeney Among the Nightingales" is of an accumulation of images and archetypal associations which together suggest a condition of the collective modern temper; the effect of "After Great Pain" is of a group of images and associations gathered in to a singular, interior nerve center.

The use of silence in male artists is often characterized as an acknowledgment of the void, a falling-back in the face of chaos, nothingness; for women, there appears more often a determination to enter that darkness, to use it, to illuminate it with the individual human presence. I return for a moment to the element of voice in the two poems mentioned so far and in the work of all three poets more generally. Were it not for the urgent presence of a speaker, we would not embark so determinedly on a search for meaning in poems that offer only minimal speech and unexplained gatherings of images. Voice has a complex and paradoxical role in this sort of poetry: it is the source both of speech and of silence; it is a part of the diaphoric activity, treated as an element in configuration with others—yet it violates the purity of that activity by suggesting the epiphoric (abstractable) dimension. More and more, the speaker becomes a focus of our interest in the poem—the only available guide through its ambiguities, and the source of its human appeal.

This is far from a traditional use of poetic voice. "Like prophecy since Isaiah, poetry since Homer has imitated a voice crying,"[8] says Kenner, and value has historically been assigned to the strength of that voice in literature —to the beauty, appropriateness, and richness of its aural impact. The bardic model offers the voice as vehicle for music; the singer becomes famous for the capacity of his voice to interpret the melody with pathetic force. Likewise, the oratorical model depends on the capacity of the voice, not only to invest the words with a persuasive *timbre*, but to sustain the performance over a long enough time to move the listener to the desired conclusions. The two models, traditionally imaged as masculine, combine in the evolution of Western poetry; with the invention of print they are adjusted to the visual measure, but they continue in force.

The situation is complicated for the woman poet by a cultural hierarchy of vocal strength: the male voice carries more "universal" authority than the female. In diaphoric poetry, where (as Kenner points out in Moore) the voice is not the universal "we" of bard or orator, but an individual quality as distinctly *other* as the objects of experience it describes, the sex of the sayer is unimportant: male and female speech has equal validity. Here is the "neutrality" of our early women poets which has caused them, sometimes, to appear sterile, emotionless, or evasive to male and female critics alike.

It may have been partly a political acumen in these women that dictated their choice of ground; but it was also an artistic necessity, given the sort of poetic they were developing. The diaphoric apprehension of experience in its particularity, by its very nature "impedes the facilities of the conclusion drawn, the thing said, the instance appropriated into a satisfactory [general] system."[9] Yet the pieces of diaphor are clearly gathered and held within a self-contained, private system by the centrifugal energy of the speaking voice, seeking to have its riddles understood. The paradox of saying and not saying created by syntactic compression and ambiguity here becomes the paradox of voice-centered poems that are not written for the voice. There is a final use of silence which distinguishes Dickinson, H.D., and Moore even more sharply from the broad class of modern poets: departing from the exclusively oral tradition of Western literature (where the female persona is a handicap), they anticipate McLuhan's theories by generations in exploiting the poem as visual art.

The Use of Space

"Eyesight is insight," says Rudolph Arnheim simply in *Art and Visual Perception: A Psychology of the Creative Eye*.[10] What strikes us before anything else about a poem is its shape upon the page, and it begins to mean as soon as we identify its basic structural features and give them value. What are the visual values of poetry?

"Speech creates visual weight at the place from which it issues."[11] Arnheim is talking about the dance, but his statement applies as well to the poem on the page. The weight assigned to speech in Western culture has a strong hold on the forms of its literature. The epiphoric poem, like its counterpart in representational painting, aims at filling space: typically, it finds itself in longer, self-completing lines; thicker, self-contained stanzas; a body of print which commands the page and moves toward a resolution at the bottom, satisfying the laws of gravity as well as rhetoric. The compensation for so much artistic weight is the abstracted theme or quality which gradually replaces it in the reader's (or viewer's) perception.

Diaphoric poetry, by contrast, opposes this downward, oral emphasis with the functional use of what painters and photographers call "negative space." "Any visual shape," says Arnheim, "will cast its influence beyond its own reach and, to some extent, will articulate the emptiness around it."[12] In traditional, epiphoric art, objects acquire weight by virtue of their larger size and greater regularity; vertically directed forms have more weight than oblique ones. In modern art, where the diaphoric impulse eventually comes to dominate, smaller objects can take on weight according to their placement and compactness; isolation adds significance; the vertical pull may be denied.

White space, for the epiphoric poem, is often merely background before which speech performs. The voice is the vehicle for the metaphors and the authority for their "universal" extension (strength and truth). White space for the diaphoric poem, on the other hand, can interact with speech in such a way that the foreground/background relationship becomes indistinct. Dickinson's "After Great Pain," for instance, derives some of its power from the featureless space surrounding it on the page and emerging between its lines and stanzas—the "Ought" of line six, and the silent snow of the final image. The life and voice of the speaker pull against the "letting go" which tempts so awfully; the poem is the strongest challenge to the silence of the dead space around it.

In the same way, H.D.'s "Oread," alone on the page, creates a new extension of diaphor in the juxtaposition of the tiny block of speech with the large unit of space—a visual value analogous to the relative dimensions in the poem of nymph and sea, and to their relative power. The "oread" momentarily controls the sea by defining it in her own terms; the poem's presence on the page defines and controls the space around it. Both positions are tenuous, the poem and the speaker on the verge of being overwhelmed, annihilated by a force larger than themselves—indeed asking annihilation—yet both assert a stubborn, seductive weight that for all its disproportion maintains an equilibrium.

These are, however, relatively simple uses of visual space in poetry. Marianne Moore's complex "visual aesthetic" (the term is Kenner's) illuminates further the nature of the art:

The Mind Is an Enchanting Thing

is an enchanted thing
    like the glaze on a
katydid-wing
        subdivided by sun
        till the nettings are legion.
Like Gieseking playing Scarlatti;

like the apteryx-awl
    as a beak, or the
kiwi's rain-shawl
        of haired feathers, the mind
        feeling its way as though blind,
walks along with its eyes on the ground.

It has memory's ear
    that can hear without
having to hear.
        Like the gyroscope's fall,
        truly unequivocal
because trued by regnant certainty,

it is a power of
    strong enchantment. It
is like the dove—
        neck animated by
        sun; it is memory's eye;
it's conscientious inconsistency.

It tears off the veil; tears
    the temptation, the
mist the heart wears,
        from its eyes—if the heart
        has a face; it takes apart
dejection. It's fire in the dove-neck's

iridescence; in the
    inconsistencies
of Scarlatti.
        Unconfusion submits
        its confusion to proof; it's
not a Herod's oath that cannot change.

What strikes us about this poem as the eye meets the page? As in a cantilevered building, the force of its vertical gravity is opposed by its insistent lateral movements away from the left margin; the eye is not convinced that it can stand. Other elements also counteract the downward stress: the unfastening of the first line and its elevation to title draws the opening stanza (and the poem) upward; regularity in the repetition of stanza form is constantly in tension with the irregularity of line length and the visual randomness of upper-case letters and punctuation, adding to the overall effect of weightlessness.

The same activity can be felt inside the stanzas, where the visual tension of the poem as a whole is reenacted. Each one is "grounded" by the longer, syllabically denser bottom line, which is nevertheless visually lifted by the activity above it—delicate images captured in minimal phrases which often end in articles made fragile by their placement ("like the glaze on a"; "as a beak, or the"; "it is a power of"). Usually the left-to-right, downward sweep of a stanza should insure its solidity; but as the title draws the poem upward, the small, terse first lines of stanzas appear to draw what follows toward them. The peculiar effect is achieved of a right-to-left, upward movement, even as we read in the opposite direction.

Going further inside the stanzas, we notice that the generally prosaic rhythm of statement—what Moore calls the "pull of the sentence"—is thwarted and counter-balanced by the sweeps and lulls of blank space. These spaces are entirely functional, both to our precise seeing of the images and to our search for meaning beneath their diaphoric arrangement. For example, in stanza four: "it is a power of [space stretching to right margin, emerging mysteriously from the left] strong enchantment. It [space for accumulating the images of the first three stanzas] is like the dove- [space for a range of connotations, narrowing from the left to the precision of] neck animated by [long white space reopening from the left to] sun; it is memory's eye; [here the punctuation is a connective, forcing us *not* to use the open space but to go immediately to the parallel statement:] it's conscientious inconsistency." The negative space helps to give positive value, the illusion of concreteness, to terms which are not (power, enchantment, memory, and so on).

The fusion, repetition, and linkage of images in the poem, disguised and emphasized alternately by the placement of lines, run on into the last stanza, which ends the poem in an irregular, visually unstable unit. The last lines of the poem repeat for the whole the performance of the parts: confusion is unconfusion, stability is change. Still, the total effect is organically satisfying. Think of the impression of delight we receive from Moore's poem; look at it again, drawing back from the page and taking it in only as it confronts the eye. The "enchantment" of the poem is strikingly visual—not only in its textual variations on the motif of seeing and in the precision of its images, but also in the white light—iridescence—that physically surrounds and filters through the veil of words on the page, "like the glaze on a / katydid-wing / subdivided by sun / till the nettings are legion."

"She made visual patterns with her typewriter," says Kenner, "the way girls of her mother's generation made cross-stitch samplers."[13] The visual impact of Moore's poetry—or H.D.'s or Dickinson's, for that matter, even in the latter's handwriting—is different from that of *The Waste Land* or *Paterson* or the *Cantos*, in which older principles of aural solidity still apply. The blank page, not the public ear, has been the lure for these women poets; their lines, indeed, often lack rhythmic beauty entirely, violating successfully still another ancient premise of Western poetry. For possible explanation we may consider the myriad domestic and social occupations culturally assigned to women that involve the visual ordering of random elements (Kenner mentions Moore's experience as librarian and typing teacher). More important, we may recollect the experience of the eye that accompanies the long and interior silences of solitude.

The Aesthetic of Silence

The poetic principle I have been describing in these pages has its parallel in the other media of artistic expression; the advent of the diaphoric mode in painting, music, sculpture, and architecture coincides with its appearance in modern literature. (Michelangelo is replaced by Picasso and Klee; sonatas by tone poems; Rodin's "Thinker" by Calder's "Crab"; Gothic castles by Fallingwater, and *Hamlet* by *Ulysses*.) Again, what has come to be called modern cannot be defined or defended as exclusively female in origin, and it is not my intention to do so. Nevertheless, the point at which diaphor takes hold in art is also the historical point at which female artists of major rank begin to emerge and to receive recognition. It is possible—even probable—that women artists in the early decades of the century found this new direction peculiarly well-suited to their experience and to their creative instincts, for all the reasons I have suggested earlier.

Rudolf Arnheim, however, comments on the modern transition with mixed feelings, accepting the validity of the impulse but complaining of some disturbing secondary effects—notably the appearance of "the freezing of feeling and passion accompanied by withdrawal from reality."[14] Some artists, he says, seem to be "compelled by a fear of surrender to force the exuberance of life into a straitjacket of geometry . . . then formalism may be the expression of tragic human limitation."[15] He is echoed by the male critics who over the years developed for the work of competent but "difficult" women poets an Aesthetic of the Minor (that elegant, clever, private, controlled, and objective poetry of the self . . .) and, ironically, by the new feminist critics who decry the old restraints. But what the truly great artists have achieved with their aesthetic of silence—particularly the early women poets of this century—belies the language of "withdrawal," "straitjacket," "fear of surrender," or "tragic human limitation." Schooled in the terminology and the models of the older tradition, even as critics women have not yet fully understood themselves.

Literary philosophers (interpreting Coleridge) have assumed that the activity of the fancy (which juxtaposes images and events without interpreting them) is merely a prelude to the activity of the imagination (which moves the objects of our perception from existence to meaning), and that the second is inevitably more serious and useful than the first. We have, however, narrowly interpreted the function of the literary imagination as epiphoric, perhaps because of the confusing medium of language, but also because the diaphoric work of that faculty resembles so closely the unimpeded play of the fancy, the minor order. Rather, the diaphoric imagination acts not so much as a comfortable "bridge" between the real and the intangible, as a disturbing presence that validates the real, forces us to apprehend "things in their thingness" (including the person of the artist), and by that means to approach what hiddenness lies behind them. It is genuinely "universal" in its presentation of the acts of individual perception and experience, indeed more immediate and available than the generalized abstraction. The diaphoric impulse is at least as valid and valuable as its epiphoric alternate—perhaps more so in the existential confrontation it demands.

For the woman poet perhaps, the model is oracle, not bard; the activity seeing, not singing. In the end, the aesthetic of silence as it began and as it has persisted and developed in the work of our major women poets— Plath, Bishop, Levertov, Sexton, Rich, to name a few—supports a vision, not a cause. It is disciplined and sophisticated in its craft, profound in its epistemological clarity, strong and true. We have not even begun to explore its inner space, and it is possible that we cannot afford to lose its power.

11.

Afro-American Women Poets: A Bio-Critical Survey*

Gloria T. Hull

Black women poets are not "Shakespeare's sisters." In fact, they seem to be siblings of no one but themselves. Although Virginia Woolf realized that genius was not allowed to flourish among white women and the working classes, she never thought to extend this consciousness to even the "very fine negress" whom she mentions in the same passage.[1] Nor did many others of her time—in either England or America.

Even after black women began creating poetry in the United States under the most inhospitable of conditions, very few writers of any stripe rushed to claim them as kin. Being black, they were ignored, discredited, dismissed, or patronized as novelties or secondary talents—by both white men and white women. Being women, they were subject to even further exclusion, sometimes by their own brothers who, like most males, did not feel that literature was women's legitimate province.

Furthermore, since black women poets are African people kidnapped to America, they did not simply fall heir to an Anglo-Saxon tradition but gave birth to an Anglo-African one which forced together African and English modes of thought and expression. Perhaps, then, this makes them Shakespeare's half-sisters (on the wayward side?). Yet, it remains indisputably true that for all of the foregoing reasons Afro-American women poets, by and large, have had to "go it alone" as only children or support and nurture each

---

*This is a substantially revised and expanded version of my article "Black Women Poets from Wheatley to Walker," which appeared in *Black American Literature Forum* (Fall 1975). I also make some of these same points, particularly about the Harlem Renaissance, in "Rewriting Afro-American Literature: A Case for Black Women Writers," *The Radical Teacher* (Fall 1977).

other in an underground sisterhood. Thus they have forged and developed their own unique tradition.

That these black women poets have not received the popular or critical attention which they deserve is a fact too well known to require elaboration. Neglect notwithstanding, black American literature begins with a female poet, and an imposing line of her successors stretches from that time forward. Knowing them as women, black women, and poets enlarges our understanding of all three and prevents anyone from taking a myopic view of what it means to be a woman poet.

Even before a formal literary history began, slave women were, no doubt, helping to produce the earliest black poetry—the spirituals and secular songs. One of the curious and distinguishing characteristics of this folk poetry is its lack of an identifying sexual framework—that is, a reader usually cannot tell if the voice behind the song is male or female. Yet the explicit black womanness in some of them—notably lullabies, some play songs, and later blues—proves that women are to be counted among the "black and unknown bards."

This beginning period, rich in oral literature, is correspondingly sparse in formal, written poetry. However, the eighteenth century brought the emergence of the first widely known black American poet, Phillis Wheatley, who is, in fact, one of the few black poets whom everybody has at least heard of. Everyone is familiar, if only in outline, with her genius and remarkable history: how she was stolen from the African coast of Senegal when she was five or six years old and brought to America, where, in the congenial atmosphere of the Wheatley household, she learned to speak and read English in sixteen months and to write creditable poems in six years. And they also know of her abstract elegies and occasional poems modeled after the English neoclassical poets. The Table of Contents of her 1773 *Poems on Various Subjects, Religious and Moral* illustrates this preoccupation and influence:[2] "Thoughts on the Works of Providence," "An Hymn to the Morning," "On Recollection," "On Imagination," and then, in a particularly calamitous time, these three poems: "To a Lady on her coming to North America with her Son, for the Recovery of her Health"; "To a Lady on her remarkable Preservation in a Hurricane in North Carolina"; and, finally, "To a Gentleman and Lady on the Death of the Lady's Brother and Sister, and a Child of the Name of Avis, aged one year"—very complete and descriptive titles, typical of their day.

Almost as well known is the common criticism of Wheatley for her lack of race consciousness—at least of a kind which would have led her to empathize with the average slave or protest against the institution of slavery in her writings. All of these bits and pieces form a prevailing idea of her which one critic has summed up in this way: "that Phillis Wheatley was a pathetic little Negro girl who had so completely identified herself with her eighteenth century Boston background that all she could write was coldly correct neo-classical verse on dead ministers and even deader abstractions."[3] There is truth in this common view, but there are also corrective observations which need to be made.

The first is that her poetry is not as imitative and moribund as most commentators make it sound. Some of her images and conceits display an originality which shows that many of her thoughts are fresh ideas of her own even if her rhythm is almost always Pope's—for example, these lines from the hurricane poem just mentioned:

> Aeolus in his rapid chariot drove
> In gloomy grandeur from the vault above:
> Furious he comes. His winged sons obey
> Their frantic sire, and madden all the sea.

Second, Phillis Wheatley *was* conscious of herself as a poet, a black poet, a black female poet—as the numerous references to herself in her poems attest, their stylization notwithstanding. One should also remember that she was a thorough New England Puritan, and it is partly her Christianity that compels her to look upon deliverance from her native land as the blessing which she describes it to be in one of her best-known poems, "On Being brought from Africa to America." Furthermore, her personality was naturally delicate and reticent.

After being feted on both sides of the Atlantic, Wheatley and an infant child died in the squalor of a cheap Boston boardinghouse—a circumstance which is of course another tragic writer's tale, but also a chilling commentary on the precariousness of her status as a black female poet. Her posthumous critical footing has been no less shaky. Quite possibly, if Phillis Wheatley had not been a woman, she would never have become the "poor little Phillis" most critics represent her to be. By now, someone may even have conducted an ingenious study of the ironic mode of her language, stance, and poetic diction and discovered that there was a black renegade behind the neoclassical mask—or at least a shrewd accommodationist under the Puritan petticoats.

The period from 1800 to 1865 was a time of antislavery agitation and utilitarian literature. All resources, including the pens of writers, were marshalled for the abolitionist cause. Understandably, the slave narrative, the speech, and the essay flourished to the relative neglect of more belletristic literary genres. However, the poetry which was written shows its political involvement.

The key female poet of this period is Frances Ellen Watkins Harper. In addition to her abolitionist themes, she develops subjects and moods which give her greater variety and also reveal her special qualities as a woman writer. The editors of *The Negro Caravan* call her "easily the most popular American Negro poet of her time."[4] This popularity stemmed from the fact that she took her poetry to the people—just as did the young black poets of the 1960s and 70s. As a widely traveling lecturer of the Anti-Slavery Society, she spoke to packed churches and meeting halls, giving dramatic readings of her poems which were so effective that she sold over 50,000 copies of her first two books—an unheard-of figure—mostly to people who had, in the words of abolitionist William Still, "listened to her eloquent lectures."[5] Essentially this poetry is message verse, dependent on an oratorical and histrionic platform delivery for its effect.

However, Harper's speaking and writing did not end with 1865. The fight against slavery was only one of many battles which engaged her during her lifetime. She was also deeply involved in religious, feminist, and temperance movements—with no apparent conflict or lack of energy. From her feminism comes "A Double Standard," a poem spoken by a seduced and abandoned young woman who addresses the reader or listener in these terms:

> Crime has no sex and yet today
> I wear the brand of shame;
> Whilst he amid the gay and proud
> Still bears an honored name.
>   . . . . .
> No golden weights can turn the scale
> Of justice in His sight;
> And what is wrong in woman's life
> In man's cannot be right.

She also wrote about Vashti, the Persian queen in the Bible who gave up her throne rather than shame her womanhood. In her forms, Harper relies mainly on the ballad stanza and rhymed tetrameters.

Her last volume of poems, *Sketches of Southern Life* (1872), features a black heroine, Aunt Chloe, who is very well drawn and is firmly set in the folklife milieu that would furnish the dialect poets with their materials. Its "Learning to Read" epitomizes Harper's manner and catches up most of her themes. Although the "Rebs" hated the schools established for ex-slaves— education of blacks was "agin' their rule"—Aunt Chloe is determined to learn to read:

So I got a pair of glasses,
    And straight to work I went,
And never stopped till I could read
    The hymns and Testament.

Then I got a little cabin,
    A place to call my own—
And I felt as independent
    As the queen upon her throne.

After Harper herself there were no more queens on the poetry throne for a long while—nor kings either, for that matter. The Reconstruction-backlash period from 1865 to 1915 was not congenial to black literary activity. But near the very end of the century, a crop of writers auguring the Renaissance began to spring up. Chief among them were Dunbar and the other dialect poets.

When she was a little girl writing verses, Gwendolyn Brooks's mother encouraged her by predicting that she would be "the *lady* Paul Laurence Dunbar."[6] In his own time, however, Dunbar had no such female counterpart. But even beyond that, not one of the dialect poets who are usually encountered is a woman. This is a significant—and, in certain ways, a gratifying—fact, but one is not altogether sure of what it means. There does not seem to be anything inherently masculine in either the content or the manner of this largely plantation- and minstrel tradition-based dialect verse. Conceivably, women could just as easily have imagined or reminisced about cooking, kissing, and raising children in the antebellum South as the men did about eating, courting, and coon-hunting. Or, a woman poet could have followed the lead of Harper in her Aunt Chloe poems and given realistic and human depictions of folklife as Dunbar does in the best of his dialect work. But none of them did.

One half-facetious explanation is that women were too astute and principled to participate in the kind of debased, convention-ridden tradition which dialect writing had become. A less-biased explanation is that they probably did not write dialect verse because it would have been considered unladylike and unseemly, subtly undermining women's role as guardian of culture and refinement and contradicting the popular female seminary education of the day. This reveals how black women writers too are bound by sexual stereotypes and constraints, and how forms developed by men are not always open or suited to them. What happens in this instance is that, if one treats the dialect poetry movement as an important one, women will automatically be excluded.

At any rate, there is no major female poet in this period—although Dunbar's wife, Alice Dunbar-Nelson, produced some poems, one of which, "Sonnet," is almost always anthologized. But the most striking poem she wrote is a three-stanza lyric called "I Sit and Sew," in which she protests against her apparently petty occupation when real work is needed for the world war. The poem could be read as a rebellion against the chafing confinement of a "woman's place" couched in ironically appropriate, female terms. She writes:

> But—I must sit and sew.
>
> The little useless seam, the idle patch;
>
> . . . . .
>
> It is no roseate dream
> That beckons me—this pretty futile seam,
> It stifles me—God, must I sit and sew?[7]

The picture presented by the Harlem Renaissance years—roughly from 1915 to 1930—is, of course, very different from that of the preceding period. Black literature flourished. And there were women poets, seven of whom deserve notice here—Angelina Grimké, Anne Spencer, Georgia Douglas Johnson, Jessie Fauset, Effie Lee Newsome, Gwendolyn Bennett, and Helene Johnson. But none of them is considered "major." In fact, the phrase "poets of the Harlem Renaissance" elicits the almost automatic response "McKay, Cullen, and Hughes." These constitute the Big Three enshrined on a black Parnassus, with the women poets serving as handmaidens to the throne. A closer study of these women poets' work and lives reveals something else.

The most prolific writer was Georgia Douglas Johnson. Between 1918 and 1938, she published three volumes of poems. (Four years before her death in 1966, she brought out a final book.) This was enough to make her the first black woman after Harper "to gain general recognition as a poet."[8] However, a modern reader does not usually find all of her efforts impressive—mainly because of the sameness of her themes and manner, and her conventional style. She writes either melancholy love lyrics or muted, attenuated poems of racial protest. Illustrative of the first type is her poem "Welt," a frequently anthologized lyric that gathers up the themes of youth, aging, time, love, and death that recur in these poems. It also reveals Johnson's use of distinctly womanly imagery and of a delicately conceited, romantic diction reminiscent of Elizabethan sonnets.

The personae and characters are usually women (such as the suffering outcast in "Octoroon"), and her poetry almost always has a definitely feminine voice. For example, in her first book, *The Heart of a Woman* (1918), she talks about a "woman with a burning flame" that was kept covered and hushed until death, and in the title poem she likens the heart of a woman to a bird that "goes forth with the dawn" but

> falls back with the night,
> And enters some alien cage in its plight,
> And tries to forget it has dreamed of the stars,
> While it breaks, breaks, breaks on the sheltering bars.

Representative of her handling of the race theme is "The Suppliant":

> Long have I beat with timid hands upon life's leaden door,
> Praying the patient, futile prayer my fathers prayed before,
> Yet I remain without the close, unheeded and unheard,
> And never to my listening ear is borne the waited word.
>
> Soft o'er the threshold of the years there comes this counsel cool:
> The strong demand, contend, prevail; the beggar is a fool!

A more arresting poet is Anne Spencer. When asked by Cullen to write her biographical notice for his 1927 anthology, *Caroling Dusk*, she responded with the following paragraph:

> Mother Nature, February, forty-five years ago forced me on the stage that I, in turn, might assume the role of lonely child, happy wife, perplexed mother—and, so far, a twice resentful grandmother. I have no academic honors, nor lodge regalia. I am a Christian by intention, a Methodist by inheritance, and a Baptist by marriage. I write about some of the things I love. But have no civilized articulation for the things I hate. I proudly love being a Negro woman—it's so involved and interesting. *We* are the PROBLEM—the great national game of TABOO.[9]

Her civilized articulation about things that she loved include poems as varied as their titles: "Before the Feast of Shushan," "At the Carnival," "The Wife-Woman," "Dunbar," "Letter to My Sister," "Lines to a Nasturtium," "Neighbors," "Questing," and "Creed." Her forms are an eccentric mixture of free verse and rhymed, iambic-based lines. The result works, but it defies precise categorization. She also exhibits something of a predilection for casting herself into roles—a dramatic distancing which is surprising during this time of intensely self-centered lyric poetry. For instance, "Shushan" is a monologue spoken by a King (the material is the same biblical story treated by Harper in "Vashti"). In trying to make love to Vashti, he calls her Sharon's Rose and then says:

> And I am hard to force the petals wide;
> And you are fast to suffer and be sad.
> Is any prophet come to teach a new thing
> Now in a more apt time?[10]

Spencer also has a sense of woman–self and a female identity that comes through in her poems, notably in "Letter to My Sister," which gives advice about how a woman must live:

> It is dangerous for a woman to defy the gods;
> To taunt them with the tongue's thin tip,
> Or strut in the weakness of mere humanity,
>
> . . . . .
>
> Oh, but worse still if you mince timidly—
> Dodge this way or that, or kneel or pray,
> Be kind, or sweat agony drops
> Or lay your quick body over your feeble young;

Even though Spencer's poetic instincts are not unerring, her work is attractive because of the originality of her material and approach, and because of her terse—almost elliptical—style, apt or unusual diction, vivid images and metaphors, and the occasionally modern lines which stop the reader with their precise wording and subtly pleasing sounds and rhythms.

Anne Spencer did not write racial protest poems. However, the same statement cannot be made about Helene Johnson. The youngest of the Harlem group, she took "the 'racial' bull by the horns" (as James Weldon Johnson put it),[11] and she also wrote poems in the new colloquial-folk-slang style popular during that time. Of all the women poets, her work most reflects the themes commonly designated as the characteristic ones of the Renaissance. Her "Sonnet to a Negro in Harlem" is pro-black and militant and calls to mind the work of Claude McKay. In "Poem," she gushes over the "Little brown boy / Slim, dark, big-eyed" who croons love songs to his banjo down at the Lafayette:

> Gee, brown boy, I loves you all over.
> I'm glad I'm a jig. I'm glad I can
> Understand your dancin' and your
> Singin', and feel all the happiness
> And joy and don't-care in you.[12]

"Bottled" presents her notion that a black man dancing on 7th Avenue in Harlem has been bottled just like some sand from the African Sahara sitting on the shelf of the 135th Street public library. Finally, she has a poem that expresses a pro-African primitivism which should be better known than it is because it is superior to some of the more frequently encountered works on this theme. Entitled "Magalu," it seems to be a fantasy about meeting Magalu "dark as a tree at night, / Eager-lipped, listening to a man with a white collar / And a small black book with a cross on it." She propels herself into the scene and ends the poem thus:

> Oh Magalu, come! Take my hand and I will read you poetry
> Chromatic words,
> Seraphic symphonies,
>
> . . . . .
>
> Do not let him lure you from your laughing waters,
>
> . . . . .
>
> Would you sell the colors of your sunset and the fragrance
> Of your flowers, and the passionate wonder of your forest
> For a creed that will not let you dance?

The bulk of Helene Johnson's poems are more traditional lyrics. In them she uses much descriptive imagery and frequently treats young love and youthful sensuality.

Now, briefly, a word about each of the four remaining poets. Angelina Grimké wrote conventional lyric poetry before the Renaissance, but first saw it published during the 1920s. Her strength lies in her notable use of color imagery. Her most often reprinted poem is "Tenebris," which envisions a huge black shadow hand plucking at the blood-red bricks of the white man's house. Jessie Fauset, though primarily a novelist, is usually represented in poetry anthologies by her love poems. Some of them are distinguished by the French titles she gave them and by her sometimes humorous and ironic cast of mind. Effie Newsome primarily wrote children's verse based on nature lore. And, finally, there is Gwendolyn Bennett, whose poetry is quite good. She was, by occupation, an artist and consequently in her work she envisions scenes, paints still-lifes, and expresses herself especially well in color.

Looking back over this group of female poets of the Harlem Renaissance and assessing their impact and collective worth, one begins to see why they are not better known or more highly rated. In the first place, they did not produce and publish enough: Grimké no book, Spencer no book, Fauset no book, Newsome no adult book, Bennett no book, Helene Johnson no book— which means that six of the seven did not collect a single volume of their work. Why?

The case of Spencer is suggestive. During the Renaissance period, she lived in Lynchburg, Virginia, working and raising her children. How much writing could she or any other poet produce under those circumstances?

Grimké also published only a few poems. Her papers at the Moorland-Spingarn Research Center contain many holograph poems—some love poems —which are obviously written to women. Of course, one could always explain this away by invoking a male persona. However, a search of the manuscripts unearthed a love letter to her friend Mamie Burrell. This information helps to provide a more accurate idea of the motivations behind her poems— and it also helps to explain why most of them never saw the light of day. There was no way that she would/could ever have published them. (Furthermore, her father, the well-known black leader Archibald Henry Grimké, was a true patriarch who kept her "close" until he died.)

Also related to their infrequent publication is the fact that these women *as women* were isolated and could not participate fully in what we know as the Harlem Renaissance. First, they lived away from New York City and Harlem (although some women like Jessie Fauset, Gwendolyn Bennett, and Helene Johnson were there for varying periods of time). Many were based in or around Washington, D.C., and formed a large part of the literary circle that gathered at Georgia Douglas Johnson's home. Second, unlike the men, they could not be a part of the social networks of the time that assured one attention, money, and publication. In *The Big Sea,* Langston Hughes describes young Alfred A. Knopf, Jr., James Weldon Johnson, and Carl Van Vechten's annual celebrations of their common birthday—fraternizing of a sort that obviously helped the men professionally.[13] Finally, the overall definition of the Harlem Renaissance automatically excludes or devalues the contribution of the women writers. The prevailing concept of the period is that it was a time of racial assertion and poetic freedom. As the discussion of their themes and methods revealed, the majority of the women wrote aracial or quietly racial works in traditional forms. Hence, they are never taken to represent the era. Their poetry is usually described as "personal," and this adjective, as applied, becomes a synonym for female/ feminine and thus connotes a devaluation or dismissal of the work.

Knowing such facts about the period changes one's perspective on it and forces the conclusion that in a very real way these women poets were not even climbing the same mountain as the Big Three and, because they were not, have been relegated to the realm of footnotes and appendixes.

After this glorious and busy period, the country and black literary activity went into a slump. What poetry exists is tinged with depression, socialism, and sometimes protest. Between 1930 and 1945 the major poet was Margaret Walker and the most important poetic event the appearance of her 1942 volume *For My People,* which was published as No. 41 of the Yale Series of Younger Poets, making her the first black to appear in that prestigious group. At the time Walker was a twenty-seven-year-old professor of English at

Livingstone College in Salisbury, North Carolina, her first teaching position after she had received a Master of Arts degree from the University of Iowa's School of Letters two years earlier.

For My People is divided into three sections. The first seeks to define the poet's relationship to "her people" and her native Southland, and it begins with the title poem, a well-known work which anticipates the material and the manner of the rest of this section:

> For my people everywhere singing their slave
>   songs repeatedly: their dirges and their
>   ditties and their blues and jubilees,
>   praying their prayers nightly to an un-
>   known god, bending their knees humbly
>   to an unseen power;[14]

The form of "For My People" is the most immediately striking thing about it. Drawing on free-verse techniques, on the Bible, and on the black sermon (her father was a preacher), Walker fairly overwhelms the reader with her rhetorical brilliance. She continues this same method and approach in the poems that follow—reciting her heritage of "Dark Blood," tracing black people's blind belief in gods from Africa to America, singing of her "roots deep in southern life," and in the simple poem "Lineage" decrying the fact that she is not as strong as her grandmothers were:

> My grandmothers are full of memories
> Smelling of soap and onions and wet clay
> With veins rolling roughly over quick hands
> They have many clean words to say.
> My grandmothers were strong.
> Why am I not as they?

Part II of *For My People* is made up of ballads about black folk heroes known and unknown, famous and infamous. Two of the best have heroines as their central figures—Molly Means, who was "a hag and a witch: / Chile of the devil, the dark, and sitch," and Kissie Lee, a tough, bad gal, whose account ends like this:

> She could shoot glass doors offa the hinges,
> She could take herself on the wildest binges.
> And she died with her boots on switching blades
> On Talladega Mountain in the likker raids.

In these tall-tale and ballad narratives, Walker adheres pretty closely to the traditional ballad stanza, varying it with four-beat couplets and spicing it up with dialect speech, which she is successful at orthographically representing.

The final section, composed of only six poems, is much shorter than the first two. These are freely handled sonnets in which Walker gazes back on her childhood, writes about experiences she has had since leaving the South (such as talking to an Iowa farmer), and expresses needs and struggles common to all human beings.

For My People was and remains significant for many reasons. First, its mood coincided with the depression and hard times of the 1930s, and also with the social consciousness and militant integrationism of that decade and the following. In style, it was different in a worthwhile way from what had been written during the Renaissance. Walker's attention to black heroes and heroines was also timely and helped to communicate the "negritude" of the volume and delving for roots which is one of its major themes.

After *For My People*, Gwendolyn Brooks published *A Street in Bronzeville* in 1945 and went on to win the Pulitzer Prize (the first black to do so) in 1950 for her 1949 volume, *Annie Allen*. From this point on, black women are well-represented in poetry. In the 1950s and early 60s, Margaret Danner, Naomi Madgett, and Gloria Oden are significant. In the 1960s, poetry exploded (as did black America), and women were not excluded from this second Renaissance. Walker, after a twenty-eight-year-poetic silence, published two more books of poems. Brooks, though of an earlier period, has gone through changes and has remained current, productive, and good (see Chapter 15). And important new names are Audre Lorde, Sonia Sanchez, Lucille Clifton, Nikki Giovanni, Mari Evans, June Jordan, and Alice Walker—to mention only a few. These writers show all of the characteristics of the poetry of the black sixties while revealing, at the same time, their wonderful woman/human selves. They are a large and exciting group and, as a group, demonstrate a higher degree of quality and achievement than the comparable group of black male poets.

Because they are so numerous, diverse, and productive, it is not realistic in this essay to cover them in the same detail as their earlier sisters. Whereas in the thirty years from 1915 to 1945 one could name only about fourteen known/published female poets, the number swells easily to fifty and more for the thirty years following—and it is constantly growing. Therefore, a more feasible approach is to focus on two not necessarily typical, but representative writers from this period—Sonia Sanchez and Audre Lorde. While Sanchez and Lorde are distinctly individual, a discussion of them still permits us some generalization about contemporary black women poets—their lives, preoccupations, themes, forms, directions, and circumstances.

Sonia Sanchez (born 1935 in Birmingham, Alabama) first came to public attention as one of Broadside Press's New Black Poets writing the militant, antiwhite oppression, rhetorical poetry which was then in vogue:

> blues ain't culture
> > they sounds of
> oppression
> > against the white man's
> shit /
> > game he's run on us all
> these blue / yrs.[15]

She wrote this poetry well, being extremely good at capturing black dialect and devising her own notation to convey it. Like almost all of the New Black Poets, she also gave frequent public readings of her work (especially on the lecture circuit during that time when colleges and universities were being rocked by black student demands). Here, too, she excelled, doing hums, shouts, moans, rhythms, songs, etc. so enchantingly that even those persons who later walked out (in protest of her "obscenities") were momentarily seduced. All of this characterizes and parallels the Black Movement in poetry of the late 1960s and early 1970s. Sanchez and other young black women poets were fully a part of that movement.

However, at the same time, most of her poetry derived from a black female core, an aspect of themselves which many of these young women did not slight in their work. She writes of relationships between black men and women, of the problems and possibilities that lie in black children, and, most poignantly, of personal/black female selfhood and pain. She movingly unites all of these themes in the last poem of her first book, *Home Coming*:

> personal letter no. 2
>
> i speak skimpily to
> you about apartments i
> no longer dwell in
> and children who
> chant their dis
> obedience in choruses.
> if i were young
> i wd stretch you
> with my wild words
> while our nights
> run soft with hands.

> but i am what i
> am. woman. alone
> amid all this noise.[16]

Much of this personal poetry is written in standard English, proving (if it needed to be proven) that she could also "poet" in the mainstream tradition and manner. Perhaps the most impressive poem of this kind is her elegy for Malcolm X.

After the flaming heyday of militant poetry, most young black poets began to eschew "offing whitey" themes and started to address black people from an even more separatist position of "black togethery-ness," as Gwendolyn Brooks has dubbed it.[17] They also turned to expressing more inwardly directed concerns. Sanchez had been developing along these lines throughout her career. For her, this direction culminated in her 1974 volume, *A Blues Book for Blue Black Magical Women*. These lines, from Part 3 of the work, could serve as a fitting epigraph for it:

> this honeycoatedalabamianwoman
> raining rhythms of blue / black / smiles
> . . . . .
> is telling you secrets
> gather up your odors and listen
> as she sings the mold from memory.[18]

The secrets she tells are autobiographically based ones about herself. However, they chronicle a history which she shares with black women of her time. Sanchez seems to reflect a realization of this fact in the way that she draws on epic and myth for the form and content of this, her most elaborately written and structured work. Part 2, especially, is pregnant with black female history. First, she invites the reader to "Come into Black geography," the geography of herself "born / musician to two / black braids." Then she invokes the earth mother to sing her history, to "tell me how i have become, became / this woman with razor blades between / her teeth." The succeeding sections follow this black girl from her birth, to childhood game playing, to aphasic trauma caused by her stepmother, to teenage grinding in New York City project basements, to love and young womanhood as "a proper painted/ european Black faced american," to a crisis in racial identity and breakdown, to civil rights activism, to finally a womanhood of blackness. Here Sanchez reveals personal and collective history.

What transpired in her life outside the poetry is equally relevant to understanding modern–contemporary black women (and black women poets), because it reveals the searching and contradiction that are so much a part of the pattern. In Sanchez's particular case, they took the form of marriage to black poet Etheridge Knight (a difficult one which was eventually dissolved), then conversion to the Nation of Islam and a second marriage (when she was Laila Mannon), then breaking from the Nation for ideological and praxis-related reasons (one conflict being her dissatisfaction with the Muslim schooling of her young twin sons and with orthodox religion in general), and then the present, a time of self-reliance (teaching at Temple University and raising the children alone). Speaking sardonically of this last period, she writes:

> i've been two men's fool, a coupla of black organization's
> fool. if ima gonna be anyone else's fool let me be my own
> fool for awhile;[19]

Sanchez is undoubtedly one of the most under-appreciated poets writing today. Her pristine lyricism combined with her strong voice and black female themes make her special.

Though she had been writing for many years, Audre Lorde also achieved wider public notice during the Black Liberation Movement. However, overtly black nationalistic subjects have never constituted the sole thrust of her poetry, though poems such as "Naturally" and "Summer Oracle" have been frequently reprinted to represent her.

Perhaps the single most noteworthy observation to be made about Lorde is that she embodies a conscious and deliberate confluence of black women poets and the women's/feminist movement. Even though she had always written black women and woman-identified poems, it was not until the rise of the second-wave feminist movement that she was able to publish much of this work or to receive any widespread support and recognition for exploring issues of female identity and sexuality, including frankly feminist and lesbian–feminist themes. A good example of the latter is her symbolically titled "On a Night of the Full Moon." The first stanza reads:

> Out of my flesh that hungers
> and my mouth that knows
> comes the shape I am seeking
> for reason.
> The curve of your waiting body
> fits my waiting hand
> your breasts warm as sunlight
> your lips quick as young birds
> between your thighs the sweet
> sharp taste of limes.[20]

When Lorde writes feminist poems, she more often than not does so from a black feminist perspective. For example, her incisive "Who Said It Was Simple" presents a black woman at a feminist demonstration realizing that she is "bound by my mirror / as well as my bed" and wondering "which me will survive / all these liberations."[21] More acidic in flavor is her "Hard Love Rock # II," with its conclusion that "Black is / not beautiful baby,"

> not
> being screwed twice
> at the same time
> from on top
> as well as
> from my side.[22]

However, Lorde's poetry mirrors as well her personal life and politics, and shows how truly rich and/or complex black women's (and black women poets') existences can be.[23] Reading at the 1976 National Organization for Women Convention in Philadelphia, she declared that she was woman, poet, black, lesbian, mother, fat, sassy. Later, at the Modern Language Association Convention in New York City in December 1976, she expanded these remarks. Saying first that poets write from their many self-images, she confessed that she wrote what she lived and spoke out of all the selves which she seeks to define.

Understandably, then, her subjects and moods are many. One of her books, *Between Our Selves*, is illustrative.[24] A hand-set, women-printed, limited-edition volume of only seven longish poems, it yet manages to cover 1) racially resonant topics ("Power," "School Note," and "Between Ourselves") that show Lorde rejecting an "easy blackness as salvation" for the hellish truth of history and its varicolored consequences, 2) personal, woman-related themes ("Solstice" and "Scar") that trace movement from enervation and barrenness to a triumphant rebirth, 3) communication with "the mothers sisters daughters / girls I have never been" ("Scar"), 4) the poet's relationship with her parents and her growing into her selves ("Outside"), and 5) a reluctant abortion ("A Woman/Dirge for Wasted Children").

Recently, it seems that Lorde's style is becoming less dense and inscrutably allegorical, and achieving a light and refreshing clarity. She has even begun to reveal more openly and easily the strain of whimsy and playfulness that women, and especially feminist women, often display with each other. One delightful such manifestation is her poem "The Trollop Maiden," which appeared in the Spring 1977 issue of *Sinister Wisdom*.

Lorde frequently assumes the role of prophetess, crying out for what she calls the most important human movement—"the right to love and to define each of us ourselves." Probably related to this is a newly expressed interest in theory and criticism found in her essay "Poems Are Not Luxuries."[25] In it, she distinguishes two approaches to life: 1) the "european mode," which views living "as a problem to be solved" and relies exclusively on ideas, and 2) the "ancient, black, non-european view of living as a situation to be experienced and interacted with," a view which teaches one "to cherish our feelings, to respect those hidden sources of our power from where true knowledge and therefore lasting action comes." She continues:

> I believe that women carry within ourselves the possibility for fusion of these two approaches as a keystone for survival, and we come closest to this combination in our poetry.... For women, then, poetry is not a luxury. It is a vital necessity of our existence.
>
> (p. 8)

Some comparable notion of poetry as a necessity must always have motivated black women poets. Studying them—from the slave women singing spirituals down to Sanchez and Lorde—one is constantly amazed that they managed to write poetry at all. Among the many unique race- and sex-fostered hindrances they transcended, at least one bears some comment—if for no other reason than to illustrate briefly their distinct lives and conditions. None of these black women had leisure to write or freedom to concentrate on developing themselves as poets. Compare, for instance, the life of Elizabeth Barrett Browning, whose "luxurious scholarly idleness" Ellen Moers describes thus:

> Her younger sisters and brothers, who all adored her, tiptoed by her door; while full of affection, so devoid of responsibility was she, that she confessed to confusion about their ages. And so protected was she from even the awareness of domestic responsibilities that her own room was cleaned only once a year—a ritual occasion, managed by others so that she need not observe servant industry. Whenever her large family moved house, she herself was transported separately, a precious burden, to the new residence made ready by others for her convenience. Elizabeth Barrett was not to be disturbed.[26]

Such class privilege is simply overwhelming. Moers's title for this chapter, "Literary Life: Some Representative Women," prompts the query, "Whose lives are represented here?" Certainly not the lives of black women in America—the majority of whom were picking cotton and frying chicken on Southern plantations. Of course, very few white women—writers or potential writers—have lived such an unreal life. But there are even fewer, if any, such black women. Afro-American women poets have always worked—and worked hard—from economic necessity and from their conviction that as black people they are obligated to battle racial prejudice and "uplift" their sisters and brothers.

Sonia Sanchez begins a recent essay in the *American Poetry Review* by saying, "these are not good times for a black / woman / poet."[27] No, they are not. But, then, they never have been. Only when the conditions under which we live and write are changed can black women poets truly become the sisters of us all.

12.

Edna St. Vincent Millay and the Language of Vulnerability

Jane Stanbrough

In 1917, when Edna St. Vincent Millay moved to Greenwich Village, her image as a woman of spirit and independence was already legendary. Previously, at Vassar, Millay had become a notorious public figure. She was a publishing poet, an impressive actress, and a dramatist of growing reputation. She had all along flaunted her independence impudently, smoking against the rules, cutting classes that were boring, earning a severe faculty reprimand which nearly deprived her of participation in her graduation ceremonies. This image of defiance was enhanced by her move to Greenwich Village, known as a hotbed of free-thinking radicals, and by her publication of five poems under the heading "Figs from Thistles" in *Poetry* in 1918, poems which vivified her inclination toward bohemianism and promiscuity. The famous first fig—"My candle burns at both ends; / It will not last the night; / But ah, my foes, and oh, my friends— / It gives a lovely light!"— immortalized her public image of daring and unconventional behavior. It came as no real shock, then, when in 1920 she published an entire volume of poetry (including the first five figs) entitled *A Few Figs from Thistles*, dominated by a narrative voice that irreverently mocked public opinion and public morality, that scorned imposed values and prescribed behavior.

This image of liberation and self-assurance is the public image Millay deliberately cultivated, the self-projection that stole the show, demanded applause and attention, suited a loud and raucous jazz-age temper. For half a century it has captivated readers and critics and minimized or veiled entirely a private anxiety-ridden image of profound self-doubt and personal anguish with which Millay contended all her life. The braggadocio of the public image is, in fact, contradictory to experience as Millay inwardly felt it and is belied by both the language and the form through which she reflected her deepest sense of that experience. Although the poetry in *Figs* solidified that public image of defiance and independence, it did so in language and structural patterns that divulge a private image of submission and constriction. The dominant tone of the body of her work—the tone of heart-rending anguish—is apparent when she works at flippancy. Millay is unquestionably a woman who suffers, and the greatest source of her suffering seems to lie in an overwhelming sense of personal vulnerability—and ultimately of woman's vulnerability—to victimization by uncontrollable conditions in her environment.

This sense of vulnerability provides one of the richest linguistic patterns in her poetry, for in spite of her efforts to repress and protect a part of her emotional life, Millay is exposed and betrayed through a language pattern which calls attention to the emotional conflicts and tensions, the psychic realities of her existence. This pattern of self-revelation appears consistently throughout her work, though sometimes disguised by attitudes associated with the public image. "Grown-up," for example (from *Figs*), seems to be merely a cute, little versified cliché about the disillusioning process of growing up.

> Was it for this I uttered prayers,
> And sobbed and cursed and kicked the stairs,
> That now, domestic as a plate,
> I should retire at half-past eight?[1]

Notice the violence in the verbs; aptly, they do evoke an image of an unruly child, but they also suggest the strength of the frustration of the narrator for something absent from her life. The contrasting image, domestic as a plate, is perfectly appropriate to imply the flatness and brittleness and coldness that condition her existence. Growing into adult domesticity for this woman has been a process of subduing the will and shrinking the soul. The last line carries the shrinking image to its ultimate conclusion: oblivion, implied by the verb "retire." The woman is painfully aware of the disparity between her childhood hopes and the realities of her adult experience, a theme Millay treats at length in "Sonnets from an Ungrafted Tree." Here, the emptiness of the woman's life is made explicit by the fact that she retires at half-past eight, when for many the evening's activities have barely begun. This poem is a strong statement of protest against the processes that mitigate fulfilling and satisfying experience. Certainly, the poem might be read simply as a statement of the inadequacy of experience to measure up to the imaginative conception of it. But it is more. It is a specific statement about woman's experience. "Domestic as a plate" is an image that fits woman into her conventional place at rest on a shelf and out of the way. The poem reflects Millay's fears of her own fate and aids our understanding of the poet's excessive urge to proclaim herself a free and unconfined spirit.

Other poems in the *Figs* volume seem just as adolescently superficial as "Grown-up" but under closer analysis corroborate this deep sense of confinement and frustration. Both "The Unexplorer" and "To the Not Impossible Him" employ a central metaphor of limited travel to suggest the nature of the oppression and restriction felt by the narrators. In "The Unexplorer," the child-narrator is inspired to "explore" the road beyond the house, but on the basis of information provided by her mother—"It brought you to the milk-man's door"—she has resigned herself to confinement. She rather wistfully explains, "That's why I have not travelled more." The implications of familial repression in the socialization process of the female are rather grim. In "To the Not Impossible Him," while the tone is light and the pose coyly provocative, the issue again is serious. The last stanza concludes:

> The fabric of my faithful love
> No power shall dim or ravel
> Whilst I stay here,—but oh, my dear,
> If I should ever travel!
>
> (130)

Confining the female, denying her experience, the narrator suggests, is the only sure way of forcing her into the social mold. Millay says a great deal more about this process in *Fatal Interview*, a collection of fifty-one sonnets published in 1931.

The structural simplicity and childlike narrative voice are techniques Millay used frequently in her early work. "Afternoon on a Hill," published in 1917, appears to be too simple a poem to give a serious reading. In imitation of childhood speech and thus childhood experience, its regular meter and rhymed quatrains, its childlike diction and sentence structure effectively convey the notion of woman as child. The stanzas, significantly without metrical variation, measure out their syllables as repetitiously as the child's days:

> I will be the gladdest thing
> Under the sun!
> I will touch a hundred flowers
> And not pick one.

> I will look at cliffs and clouds
>   With quiet eyes,
> Watch the wind bow down the grass,
>   And the grass rise.
>
> And when lights begin to show
>   Up from the town,
> I will mark which must be mine,
>   And then start down!
>
>   (33)

Though appearing to lack subtlety and complexity, the poem does create a tension through an ironic disparity between the directness in tone and structure and the implications of the experience. The speaker seems to symbolize childhood's innocence and freedom. But the freedom, in fact, is artificial, for the child is regulated and restrained. She reaches out; she withdraws. "I will touch a hundred flowers," she decides, but then promises obediently: "And not pick one." The passivity outlined in this poem—looking, watching, obeying—again ends with the narrator's total retreat. It is, on the surface, an innocent-looking action. But it is a form of surrender. Throughout the poem one hears the promises of the "good little girl." She will do what is expected of her; she will watch quietly and disturb nothing.

Psychological experiences merely hinted at in this poem are verified directly and harshly in later poems. In "Above These Cares" Millay's narrator nearly screams out her recognition of her state:

> Painfully, under the pressure that obtains
> At the sea's bottom, crushing my lungs and my brains
> (For the body makes shift to breathe and after a
>   fashion flourish
> Ten fathoms deep in care,
> Ten fathoms down in an element denser than air
> Wherein the soul must perish)
> I trap and harvest, stilling my stomach's needs;
> I crawl forever, hoping never to see
> Above my head the limbs of my spirit no longer free
> Kicking in frenzy, a swimmer enmeshed in weeds.
>
>   (307)

The woman's vulnerability is absolute because she is so helplessly ensnared. Her feelings of oppression and spiritual suffocation are excruciatingly described, and she craves a numbing of her consciousness to dull the pain of her awareness. The psychological disintegration resulting from thwarted experience shown in this poem is further displayed in "Scrub," where the disillusioned narrator reflects bitterly on the meaning of her oppression and recognizes its origins in childhood:

> If I grow bitterly,
> Like a gnarled and stunted tree,
> Bearing harshly of my youth
> Puckered fruit that sears the mouth;
> If I make of my drawn boughs
> An inhospitable house,
> Out of which I never pry
> Towards the water and the sky,
> Under which I stand and hide
> And hear the day go by outside;
> It is that a wind too strong
> Bent my back when I was young,
> It is that I fear the rain
> Lest it blister me again.
>
> (160)

Made vulnerable by its natural inclination to stretch and grow, the tree is thus subjected to attack and mutilation by forces in its environment; it is bent and blistered into submission. Terrorized and intimidated in the process, the woman—like the child who reaches to touch the flowers—makes a complete withdrawal inside "An inhospitable house, / Out of which I never pry / Towards the water and the sky, / Under which I stand and hide. . . ." Imagining herself like the tree to be deformed and grotesque, the mutilated narrator bemoans the psychological crippling of denied opportunities and punitive restrictions.

Millay found the child-narrator device very suggestive of woman's susceptibility to intimidation. In her vulnerability to victimization, the child in "Afternoon on a Hill" is psychologically parallel to the terrorized woman of "Assault," a poem first published in 1920 in *The New Republic*.

> I had forgotten how the frogs must sound
> After a year of silence, else I think
> I should not so have ventured forth alone
> At dusk upon this unfrequented road.
>
> I am waylaid by Beauty. Who will walk
> Between me and the crying of the frogs?
> Oh, savage Beauty, suffer me to pass,
> That am a timid woman, on her way
> From one house to another!
>
> (77)

Here, ostensibly, is the narrator's expression of her sensitivity to and appreciation for the beauties of nature. But the word choice and the ideas evoked call into question so superficial a reading. The speaker describes the experience as an ambush where she is assaulted, "waylaid," forced by a savage attacker into terrified submission, an image obviously suggestive of rape. The woman is confused as well as terrified, and her bewilderment is apparent in the ambiguity of her perceptions. She calls her assailant Beauty, suggesting a benign, even attractive attacker. Yet, she describes the attack as savage and further qualifies its nature by defining Beauty in the shape of frogs. She thinks she hears them crying, and in a spontaneous outburst of identification with their pain, she too cries, "Oh, savage Beauty, suffer me to pass." The choice of "suffer" is brilliantly placed to capsulize the poem's theme, which is a vivid description of the author's sense of vulnerability and the suffering that accompanies it. The speaker feels isolated, unprotected, intimidated. In this poem Millay has cleverly succeeded in defining woman's sense of her true condition by capitalizing on a common assumption about the excessive emotional nature of women. At the same time, she has implied that woman's oppressor is a deceptively disguised external force.

Millay's insistent use of verbs of assault and bombardment is an index to her concept of reality. She may title a poem "Spring," but she really sees the brains of men eaten by maggots; she may claim that she sorrows over the "Death of Autumn," but she portrays a malign force controlling the world, for the autumn rushes are "flattened"; the creek is "stripped"; beauty, "stiffened"; the narrator, crushed. All around her in the systematic operation of the elements Millay perceives the processes of barbaric intrusion and fatal attack. Millay's use of nature, which seems to depict typical romantic disillusionment with the transcience of beauty, is in fact loaded with psychological and social implications. In "Low-Tide," the tide's movements, like the conditions of her existence, are inexorable. There are beautiful surfaces, but treacherous realities: "No place to dream, but a place to die." Here, again, the figure of a child qualifies the state of vulnerability. The narrator lacks knowledge and experience. Trusting and unsuspicious, she is susceptible to betrayal. This childlike susceptibility is consciously rendered in "Being Young and Green":

> Being young and green, I said in love's despite:
> Never in the world will I to living wight
> Give over, air my mind
> To anyone,
> Hang out its ancient secrets in the strong wind
> To be shredded and faded....

> Oh, me, invaded
> And sacked by the wind and the sun!
>
> (222)

Millay's use of "ancient secrets" is highly suggestive of the private self she wishes to protect, but neither consciousness nor will is a strong enough defense against attack and exposure. The words "invaded and sacked," like "waylaid" in "Assault," indicate both the treacherousness of the assailant and the devastation of the attack. Fearing ridicule as well as exposure, the narrator tries to forearm herself, but she is helpless against the assaulting invisible powers, which she names here as wind and sun. The intrusion is forced and, in a social context, implies the act of rape. The intensity of Millay's sense of personal violation is felt in the imagery of "Moriturus":

> I shall bolt my door
>   With a bolt and cable;
> I shall block my door
>   With a bureau and a table;
>
> With all my might
>   My door shall be barred.
> I shall put up a fight,
>   I shall take it hard.
>
> With his hand on my mouth
>   He shall drag me forth,
> Shrieking to the south
>   And clutching at the north.
>
> (206–207)

The attacker in this poem is identified as death, but for Millay the horror of the experience is not in the idea of dying, but in the vision of the brutalizing attack by which she is forced to a complete surrender. Millay's narrator is vulnerable to attack and to exploitation because of some basic inferiority, and, as the rape image implies, it lies in her sexuality.

When Millay left Vassar in 1917 to do whatever she liked with the world, as President McCracken had assured her she could, she must soon have been stunned and distressed at the world's reception of her. She tells her family:

> Mrs. Thompson, a lovely woman who helped put me through college wants me to come & be her secretary for a while— ... but I just don' wanna!

...Of course, I feel like the underneath of a toad not to do what she wants me to do—but I can't make up my mind to address envelopes and make out card catalogues all fall...be called on to answer the telephone and make appointments & reject invites. I might have been governess to the Aults, except for a similar feeling about my independence.[2]

Professionally, at graduation, she wanted more than anything to be an actress. She hoped also to continue to write plays and poetry. She believed in her own genius, and "The Bean-Stalk," published in 1920 in *Poetry,* seems to reflect the *Figs'* public image of self-confidence:

> Ho, Giant! This is I!
> I have built me a bean-stalk into your sky!
> La,—but it's lovely, up so high!
>
> This is how I came,—I put
> Here my knee, there my foot,
> Up and up, from shoot to shoot—
>
> (71)

The possibilities are exhilarating:

> What a wind! What a morning!—

But imagery in a middle section of the poem counteracts that sense of exhilaration and faith with a description of the real effects of the climb and the wind upon the climber. Even the first line's intention to emphasize the speaker's identity is undercut by the notion of "giant." The climber becomes suddenly insecure and uncertain in her position; she realizes that she is open to the wind, vulnerable to attack. She may even doubt her talent:

> ...bean-stalks is my trade,
> I couldn't make a shelf,
> Don't know how they're made,
>
> (73)

The wind, first viewed as an exhilarating force, is soon felt as an assailant which nearly dislodges her, an assailant which she can neither see nor combat:

And the wind was like a whip
Cracking past my icy ears,
And my hair stood out behind,
And my eyes were full of tears,
Wide-open and cold,
More tears than they could hold,
The wind was blowing so,
And my teeth were in a row,
Dry and grinning,
And I felt my foot slip
And I scratched the wind and whined,
And I clutched the stalk and jabbered,
With my eyes shut blind,—
What a wind! What a wind!

(72)

The blowing, whipping, cracking force of the wind strips her to a skeleton. Though the experience is terrifying and the climber confounded by the violence of the attack and the wind's capriciousness, the climber holds her position, struggling to resist the devastating power of her adversary. It is a tentative position, however, for the wind is a treacherous force, invisible, deceptive—an excellent symbol for the undefined powers which seem to impede Millay's efforts and cause her such suffering, powers she ultimately associates with social oppression and political tyranny.

Millay did not become an actress. She wrote few plays. She spent her life struggling for survival as a poet. This may be difficult for readers to understand who know that Millay was a Pulitzer Prize winner, a popular lecturer, a well-known and sought-after personality whose poems were published, reviewed, and read. But we are not dealing with external data merely; we are examining the poetry for insights into the truth of Millay's inner sense of herself and her achievements. The language pattern of vulnerability suggests strongly that Millay saw herself as a misfit and a failure and that she believed that some external forces in her life impeded her development and inflicted permanent injury. An untitled poem in her posthumous collection, *Mine the Harvest*, conveys an understanding of the power and insidiousness of the enemy and a resignation to her fate. Again the verb pattern defines the sense of vulnerability and impending disaster felt by the narrator; the image of the overpowering force of the wave summarizes a lifetime of futile effort to transcend and resist a society which she feels has conspired to destroy her.

Establishment is shocked. Stir no adventure
Upon this splitted granite.

I will no longer connive
At my own destruction:—I will not again climb,
Breaking my finger nails, out of reach of the reaching wave,
To save
What I hope will still be me
When I have slid on slime and clutched at slippery
    rock-weed, and had my face towed under
In scrubbing pebbles, under the weight of the wave
    and its thunder.
I decline to scratch at this cliff. *If* is not a word.
I will connive no more
With that which hopes and plans that I shall not survive:
Let the tide keep its distance;
Or advance, and be split for a moment by a thing very
    small but all resistance;
Then do its own chore.

                                (503)

Here Millay identifies the malignant force assailing her as the establishment, and the causes for her deep sense of victimization are less opaque. She feels outside the establishment, in opposition to social tradition and authority. She had sensed as a young woman that the world was "no fit place for a child to play." She had discovered that for women, as for children, the beautiful things were out of reach. For Millay, the realities of her life were found in the rigidly structured patterns of social behavior: you must not smoke at Vassar; you must not be an actress if you want Lady Caroline's financial assistance; you must consider being a social secretary if you really seek employment; you must marry; you must have children; you must not offend conventional morality if you want recognition; you must be male if you want serious criticism of your poetry.[3]

Millay concedes in this untitled poem that society does not tolerate its individualists; especially does it not tolerate its independent women. To be a nonconformist is to be exposed and intimidated, like the woman in "Assault"; it is to feel like the lone traveler in "How Naked, How Without a Wall," chilled by the night air, struck by sharp sleet, buffeted by wind, vulnerable to the wolf's attack. The social ramifications are explicit in this poem. For this traveler, since he chooses to venture "forth alone / When other men are snug within," the world is a terrifying place of loneliness, alienation, inevitable catastrophe. Most people, Millay feels, are vulnerable to social pressures; some will compromise. Some will suffer self-betrayal rather than isolation, as another of Millay's travelers does in "On the Wide Heath," surrendering himself to a loud shrew, a poaching son, a daughter with a disdainful smile:

> Home to the worn reproach, the disagreeing,
>   The shelter, the stale air; content to be
> Pecked at, confined, encroached upon,—it being
>   Too lonely, to be free.
>
> (301)

The imagery of confinement and attack offer an unbearable alternative to the individual who is forced to acknowledge, as this narrator does in that haunting statement of vulnerability: "it being / Too lonely, to be free."

For Millay, reality is oppression and victimization, and she feels attacked by forces that tyrannize, whether she names them sun and wind, as she does in her early poetry, or hangmen and huntsmen, as she does later. The shift in focus is significant, for it marks a deliberate attempt by Millay to explain her sense of victimization in a larger context of social injustices. She sees that justice is denied in Massachusetts and that the huntsman gains on the quarry.

Victimization by totalitarian powers is subtly suggested in "The Buck in the Snow," where we see death, as in slow motion, "bringing to his knees, bringing to his antlers / The buck in the snow." Horrified, with the narrator, we witness the capitulation, the ultimate defeat of beauty and freedom and life. The buck, vulnerable, defenseless, goes down before an invisible, armed, socially sanctioned slaughterer. In "The Rabbit," the speaker, suffering excruciatingly for her greater awareness of reality than the rabbit has, screams a warning to the rabbit:

> 'O indiscreet!
> And the hawk and all my friends are out to kill!
> Get under cover!' But the rabbit never stirred;
>   she never will.
> And I shall see again and again the large eye blaze
> With death, and gently glaze;
> The leap into the air I shall see again and again,
>   and the kicking feet;
> And the sudden quiet everlasting, and the blade of
>   grass green in the strange mouth of the
>   interrupted grazer.
>
> (326–27)

The real significance of the whole range of verbs of assault is crystalized here in the verb "kill." Millay's victims are all alike: innocent, helpless, unsuspecting, unarmed, in every way vulnerable. And they are all embodiments of Millay, the anguished, writhing, defenseless, and finally defeated victim. Millay's profound suffering and her constant rendering of personal vulnerability become increasingly comprehensible in the context of her imagery of woman as victim.

Virginia Woolf understood the agonies and stresses of gifted women struggling against conditions of oppression. "For it needs little skill in psychology," she wrote in *A Room of One's Own*, "to be sure that a highly gifted girl who had tried to use her gift for poetry would have been so thwarted and hindered by other people, so tortured and pulled asunder by her own contrary instincts, that she must have lost her health to a certainty."[4] Millay's personal feelings of oppression and the realities of social restrictions imposed on her own professional ambitions and desires are poignantly stated in Section V of "Not So Far as the Forest," where the figure of the wounded and confined bird suggests an authentic self-projection:

> Poor passionate thing,
> Even with this clipped wing how well you flew!—though
>   not so far as the forest.
>
> (339)

The bird initially presents an appearance of freedom and capability, striking for the top branches in the distant forest. But the bird's weakness, his vulnerability to defeat, invisible at first in his attempted flight, is ultimately disclosed. It is his ambition, described in the poem as "the eye's bright trouble," that has made him vulnerable. He has been victimized by "the unequal wind," that seductive environmental force with its seeming beneficence but real destructive power; and he has been chained by a human hand:

> Rebellious bird, . . .
> Has no one told you?—Hopeless is your flight
> Toward the high branches. . . .
>
> Though Time refeather the wing,
> Ankle slip the ring,
> The once-confined thing
> Is never again free.
>
> (339)

Millay responded passionately and deeply to visions of suffering victims, from the starving man in Capri to the war victims of Lidice. These visions correspond closely to her view of herself as victim, and her use of language patterns of vulnerability take on greater significance as she develops her understanding of herself as a woman in a world where women's values and feelings are either predetermined or discarded. Millay's frequent use of the childlike narrator is increasingly understandable in the context of her vulnerability to the world's view and treatment of her as a woman. The nature of her existence, like the nature of her vulnerability, is thus qualified by the fact that she experiences the world as a woman.

"The Fitting" is well titled to suggest Millay's sense of woman's social conditioning to fit the narrow role prescribed for her. Through verbs that attempt to mask the degree of harm inflicted in the process, the narrator bitterly expresses her sense of personal violation. She submits to the fitting in a state of mannikin-like paralysis.

> The fitter said, '*Madame, vous avez maigri,*'
> And pinched together a handful of skirt at my hip.
> '*Tant mieux,*' I said, and looked away slowly, and
>   took my under-lip
> Softly between my teeth.
>
> Rip—rip!
> Out came the seam, and was pinned together in
>   another place.
> She knelt before me, a hardworking woman with a
>   familiar and unknown face,
> Dressed in linty black, very tight in the arm's-
>   eye and smelling of sweat.
> She rose, lifting my arm, and set her cold shears
>   against me,—snip-snip;
> Her knuckles gouged my breast. My drooped eyes
>   lifted to my guarded eyes in the glass, and
>   glanced away as from someone they had
>   never met.
>
> '*Ah, que madame a maigri!*' cried the *vendeuse,*
>   coming in with dresses over her arm.
> '*C'est la chaleur,*' I said, looking out into the sunny
>   tops of the horse-chestnuts—and indeed it
>   was very warm.
>
> I stood for a long time so, looking out into the after-
>   noon, thinking of the evening and you....

> While they murmured busily in the distance, turning
>   me, touching my secret body, doing what
>   they were paid to do.
>
>   (342–43)

The narrator suffers both indignity and depersonalization in the fitting process. For one moment only—in a single line in the poem—does Millay allow the imaginative escape to seem a possibility. This emphasis is quite different from that of "The Bean-Stalk," where fantasized possibility is the poem's overriding effect.

Two of Millay's best and longest sonnet sequences, *Fatal Interview* and "Sonnets from an Ungrafted Tree," dramatize further through metaphors of love and marriage the fatality of woman's vulnerability to social conditioning. *Fatal Interview* is an extended metaphorical illustration of the consequences to women of their limited range of experience and their susceptibility to emotional exploitation. "Women's ways are witless ways," Millay states in a *Figs* poem, and *Fatal Interview* dramatically narrates how woman is trained to react emotionally to her environment and how devastating the results of such training are. The title suggests the nature of the results. Sonnet xvii of the sequence portrays woman's naiveté and lack of preparation for such an "interview" as she encounters:

> Sweet love, sweet thorn, when lightly to my heart
> I took your thrust, whereby I since am slain,
> And lie disheveled in the grass apart,
> A sodden thing bedrenched by tears and rain,
>
>   . . . . .
>
> Had I bethought me then, sweet love, sweet thorn,
> How sharp an anguish even at the best,
> When all's requited and the future sworn,
> The happy hour can leave within the breast,
> I had not so come running at the call
> Of one who loves me little, if at all.
>
>   (646)

An innocent believer in the value of her feelings, the woman opens herself to her lover's thrust. The sexual implications of "thrust" give emphasis to the irony of the woman's willing surrender to rape and murder. Through the image of happy submission to her slayer, Millay sharply renders the utter pathos of woman's susceptibility. Too late she discovers the insignificance of her self, her life. The sequence dramatizes the spiritual disintegration that must occur through the social conditioning that explains woman's nature as essentially emotional and her greatest need as love. The entire sequence is relentless in its presentation of love's ravaging and immobilizing effects upon women whose lives are so isolated and confined. Sonnet lxxi epitomizes the victim's scarred state:

> This beast that rends me in the sight of all,
>   . . . . .
> Will glut, will sicken, will be gone by spring.
>   . . . . .
> I shall forget before the flickers mate
> Your look that is today my east and west.
> Unscathed, however, from a claw so deep
> Though I should love again I shall not go. . . .
>   (631)

Throughout the sonnets, the narrator exposes her emotional vulnerability to assault, humiliation, abuse, abandonment, annihilation.

> How drowned in love and weedily washed ashore,
> There to be fretted by the drag and shove
> At the tide's edge, I lie—. . .
>   . . . . .
> Small chance, however, in a storm so black,
> A man will leave his friendly fire and snug
> For a drowned woman's sake, and bring her back
> To drip and scatter shells upon the rug. . . .
>   (636)

Brutalization and victimization characterize woman's existence.

In "Sonnets from an Ungrafted Tree" the New England woman narrator poignantly and unforgettably reveals how she has been trapped by her illusions of romance and by her dreams of beauty into a relationship which strangles her emotionally and spiritually. One of Millay's most brilliant images of woman's spiritual suffocation is found in Sonnet xi of this sequence:

> It came into her mind, seeing how the snow
> Was gone, and the brown grass exposed again,
> And clothes-pins, and an apron—long ago,
> In some white storm that sifted through the pane
> And sent her forth reluctantly at last
> To gather in, before the line gave way,
> Garments, board-stiff, that galloped on the blast
> Clashing like angel armies in a fray,

An apron long ago in such a night
Blown down and buried in the deepening drift,
To lie till April thawed it back to sight,
Forgotten, quaint and novel as a gift—
It struck her, as she pulled and pried and tore,
That here was spring, and the whole year to be
    lived through once more.

(616)

Representing woman's condition, the apron, confined to the clothesline, is contrasted to the figure of clashing armies, suggestive of her imagined dreams of adventure and romance—dreams fulfilled only in a masculine world. The apron, obviously an article of domestic servitude, is a symbol for the woman's relinquished self, "Board-stiff," "blown down and buried" years before. Even then, this woman had half perceived the futility of her dreams and had gone out reluctantly to pull and pry and tear at the apron to try to resurrect it. Ultimately, the woman surrenders

                    ... her mind's vision plain
The magic World, where cities stood on end ...
Remote from where she lay—and yet—between,
Save for something asleep beside her, only the
    window screen.

(617)

The restrictive realities of her life—something asleep beside her and the window screen—are stark contrasts to the waning dreams of her imagined self.

It is understandable why Millay's two extended narratives of woman's psychological disintegration are presented in sonnet sequences. Millay persistently resorts to the constraints of traditional verse forms. Given her time and place in the history of American poetry and given the external evidence of her unconventional childhood and youthful radicalism, one would expect to find her in the company of the avant-garde of American poetry. But Millay is no true Imagist. She eschews the freedoms of form which Ezra Pound had defined as essential to the new poetry. The sonnet, her best form, is a fit vehicle to convey her deepest feelings of woman's victimization. Through it, Millay imaginatively reenacts her constant struggle against boundaries. The wish for freedom is always qualified by the sense of restriction; couplets and quatrains suit her sensibility.

In Millay's poetry, women, in their quiet lives of fatal desires and futile gestures, are tragic and heroic. She identifies herself with suffering women, women whose dreams are denied, whose bodies are assaulted, whose minds and spirits are extinguished. She states her consciousness of the universality of women's vulnerability and anguish in "An Ancient Gesture," contrasting Penelope's tears with those of Ulysses:

> I thought, as I wiped my eyes on the corner of my apron:
> Penelope did this too.
> And more than once: you can't keep weaving all day
> And undoing it all through the night;
> Your arms get tired, and the back of your neck gets tight;
> And along towards morning, when you think it will never be light,
> And your husband has been gone, and you don't know where, for years,
> Suddenly you burst into tears;
> There is simply nothing else to do.
>
> And I thought, as I wiped my eyes on the corner of my apron:
> This is an ancient gesture, authentic, antique,
> In the very best tradition, classic, Greek;
> Ulysses did this too.
> But only as a gesture,—a gesture which implied
> To the assembled throng that he was much too moved to speak.
> He learned it from Penelope ...
> Penelope, who really cried.
>
> (501)

From the earliest volume, *Renascence*, where even her youthful awakening is accompanied by its grief-laden songs of shattering, through her posthumous harvest of mature experience, Millay records, unrelentingly, her life of pain and frustration. If she too loudly insisted on the public self's claims for freedom to love and think and feel and work as she pleased, she nevertheless quietly throughout her work continued to send out her linguistic distress signals. It is her profound insight into her self's inevitable capitulation that makes Millay ultimately so vulnerable and her poetry so meaningful.

13.

The Echoing Spell of
H. D.'s *Trilogy*

Susan Gubar

In a wonderful children's story called *The Hedgehog* (1936), appropriately written for her daughter, Perdita, H.D. tells the story of a little girl named Madge whose linguistic confusions can serve as a paradigm of a uniquely female quest for maturation that would concern H.D. in her own life and in her most ambitious poetic narratives. Called "Madd"[1] by the natives of Leytaux, Madge is as confused at the community's system of signs as they are by hers, and so she sets herself the task of discovering the meaning of a word she finds especially mysterious. Madge's situation as an expatriate resemble's H.D.'s early migration, first to London and then to Switzerland, and, like Madge, H.D. was persistently fascinated with the recalcitrant secrecy of words. From her early imagist poetry, which she published with the help of Ezra Pound before World War I, to her first novel, *Palimpsest* (1926), and her later translations of Greek literature, H.D. was clearly drawn to the elusive, foreign sounds and double meanings that tease Madge. Similarly, H.D.'s psychoanalysis with Freud in 1933 was at least partially based on their mutual interest in the hidden psychosexual associations of mythic and private vocabularies. And while her initials are most obviously a sigil for Hilda Doolittle, they also represent the *Hermetic Definitions* (1958) that would intrigue her until the very end of her writing career.

Madge learns the secret meaning of the word *hérisson* only after she finds an educated man, Dr. Blum, who owns and interprets for her a book on classical lore that explains how hedgehogs were used by the ancient Greeks. Her dependency on him recalls not only H.D.'s reliance on Dr. Freud, but also her earlier mystification as a child when she "could then scarcely distinguish the shape of a number from a letter, or know which was which" on the pages of writing she saw on her father's desk.[2] Certain, then, that her father possessed "sacred symbols,"[3] H.D. always remained conscious that mythic, scientific, and linguistic symbols are controlled and defined by men, so she repeatedly described her alienation from a puzzling system of inherited signs that do, nevertheless, finally reveal a special meaning to the female initiate. For Madge, the classical references and the successful completion of her quest lead to a joyously personal experience of her own powers which she articulates in her subsequent hymn to the moon, Artemis, who "loved little girls and big girls, and all girls who were wild and free in the mountains, and girls who ran races just like boys along the seashore" (pp. 75–76).

With its predictable emphasis on penis envy, what the standard Freudian interpretation of Madge's search for the bristly hedgehog[4] neglects is not only her attraction to the mysteries of the word *hérisson* but also this vision of Artemis which embodies Madge's distinctively female joy and her sense that, existing as she does in both the mythic past and the secular present, she contains multitudes. Far from seeking male forms of power, then, Madge manages to see and make of the enigmatic signs of her culture a new and sustaining story of female freedom. For all its blatant inadequacies, the Freudian interpretation of *The Hedgehog* is worth mentioning here because it reflects the critical reception accorded a poet who has been transformed into Pound's girlfriend, Freud's analysand, and the model for D. H. Lawrence's Isis in *The Man Who Died.*[5]

Significantly, it was at a time when she was divorcing herself from some of these male influences, in 1920 when her good friend and companion Bryher (Winifred Ellerman) rescued her from depression with a trip to Greece, that H.D. saw a vision on her hotel room wall of a tripod, the symbol of "prophetic utterance or occult or hidden knowledge; the Priestess or Pythoness of Delphi sat on the tripod while she pronounced her verse couplets, the famous Delphic utterances which it was said could be read two ways."[6] What Freud later considered her most dangerous symptom is, significantly, this vision of female divinity and prophecy that would inform the epic poems of her maturity. No wonder these female epics have been almost completely ignored by a critical establishment that reads her verse couplets only one way, from the monolithic perspective of the twentieth-century trinity of imagism, psychoanalysis, and modernism. While none of these contexts can be discounted, each is profoundly affected by H.D.'s sense of herself as a woman writing about female confinement, specifically the woman writer's entrapment within male literary conventions, as well as her search for images of female divinity and prophecy.

In one of her most coherent and ambitious poetic narratives, her book-length war *Trilogy*, H.D. explores the reasons for her lifelong fascination with the palimpsest. Like Madge, she presents herself as an outsider who must express her views from a consciously female perspective, telling the truth, as Dickinson would say, "slant." Inheriting uncomfortable, male-defined images of women and of history, H.D. responds with palimpsestic or encoded revisions of male myths. If her own reticence demanded that she write verses that retained their ambiguity because they could be read in at least two ways, she nevertheless uncovers behind the destructive signs of her times the same stories of female survival found by Madge. In the *Trilogy*, through recurrent references to secret languages, codes, indecipherable hieroglyphs, and foreign idioms, H.D. illustrates how patriarchal culture can be subverted by the woman who dares to "re-invoke, re-create" what has been "scattered in the shards / men tread upon":[7] in the first of the three sections, *The Walls Do Not Fall*, H.D. demonstrates the need for imagistic and lexical redefinition, an activity closely associated with the recovery of female myths, specifically the story of Isis; in *Tribute to the Angels* she actually begins transforming certain words, even as she revises Apocalyptic myth; finally H.D. translates the story of the New Testament in *The Flowering of the Rod*, feminizing a male mythology as she celebrates the female or "feminine" Word made flesh.

Written in three parts of forty-three poems each, primarily in unrhymed couplets, H.D.'s *Trilogy* was completed between 1944 and 1946, and it deals initially with the meaning of World War II. The title of the first volume, *The Walls Do Not Fall*, reveals the primacy of spatial imagery in H. D.'s analysis of a splintered world where "There are no doors" and "the fallen roof / leaves the sealed room open to the air" (*WDNF* 1). All of civilized history has failed to create forms that can protect or nurture the inhabitants of this wasteland, and the "Apocryphal fire" threatens even the skeleton which has incomprehensibly survived. The poet is especially vulnerable in a world that worships coercion, for the sword takes precedence over the word. Such so-called "nonutilitarian" efforts as poetry are deemed irrelevant as books are burned and the poet, who identifies herself as a member of a fellowship of "nameless initiates, / born of one mother" (*WDNF* 13), realizes that, with no possibility of altering this landscape of pain, only a shift in perspective can transform or redeem it: H. D. admits, then, that the fallen roofs, absent doors, and crumbling walls paradoxically transform the houses into shrines. Furthermore, because "gods always face two-ways" (*WDNF* 2), she considers the possibility of scratching out "indelible ink of the palimpsest" to get back to an earlier script on the still-standing walls. However, she knows that her search for "the true-rune, the right-spell" will be castigated as "retrogressive" (*WDNF* 2). In a world dominated by a God who demands *"Thou shall have none other gods but me"* (*WDNF* 37), the entire culture castigates the beauty of "Isis, Aset or Astarte" as the snare of "a harlot" (*WDNF* 2). But H. D. senses that the jealousy of this monotheistic god actually affirms the reality of those "old fleshpots" (*WDNF* 2).[8] Therefore, she seeks "to recover old values," although her attempt will be labeled heretical, and her rhythm will be identified with "the devil's hymn" (*WDNF* 2).

It is only in this context of her psychological and physical dispossession that H. D.'s famous poem about the spell of the seashell can be fully understood. In her first attempt to "recover the Sceptre, / the rod of power" associated with the healing powers of Caduceus (*WDNF* 3), H. D. portrays herself in the image of the "master-mason" or "craftsman" mollusk within the seashell (*WDNF* 4). No less an emblem of defensive survival in a hostile world than Madge's hedgehog, the mollusk opens its house/shell to the infinite sea "at stated intervals // Prompted by hunger." But, sensing its limits, it "snaps shut // at invasion of the limitless" so as to preserve its own existence. Managing to eat without being eaten, the mollusk serves as an object lesson when the poet advises herself and her readers to "be firm in your own small, static, limited // orbit" so that "living within, / you beget, self-out-of-self, // selfless, / that pearl-of-great-price." Self-sufficient, brave, efficient, productive, equipped to endure in a dangerous world, H. D.'s mollusk recalls Marianne Moore's snail whose "Contractility is a virtue / as modesty is a virtue," and Denise Levertov's "Snail" whose shell is both a burden and a grace.[9] Hidden and therefore safe, the mollusk is protected in precisely the way the poet craves asylum: neither fully alive nor fully dead, half in and half out, the mollusk in its shell becomes a tantalizing image for H. D. of the self or soul safely ensconced within the person or body, always and anywhere at home.

But the fascination goes much farther because the "flabby, amorphous" mollusk does not only protect itself with such impenetrable material as "bone, stone, marble," it also transforms living substance into formal object and thereby mysteriously creates the beautiful circularity of its house and also the perfectly spherical pearl. Shell and pearl are associated traditionally with art because the shell is a musical instrument, expressing the rhythm of the waves, and H. D. would know that it was Hermes who scooped out the shell of a tortoise, converting it into a lyre which he gave, under duress, to his brother Apollo. Hermes, who later becomes associated in the *Trilogy* with alchemy, reminds us of the transformative power that can make of nature an art and that caused the shell to become an important dream symbol for Wordsworth, who hears through it an ode foretelling destruction by deluge (*The Prelude*, v, 95–8). H. D.'s shell also forecasts apocalypse; however, she characteristically emphasizes not the onrushing baptism but the paradoxical powerlessness of the infinite waves which cannot break the closed-in "egg in egg-shell."

The self-enclosed, nonreferential completeness of pearl and shell recalls H. D.'s own earlier imagistic poems, but the limits of imagism are what emerge most emphatically since the mollusk can only combat the hostile powers of the sea by snapping shut "shell-jaws" in an action that malevolently evokes the threatening "shark-jaws" of the whale of circumstance. As Gaston Bachelard so brilliantly puts it, while "the animal in its box is sure of its secrets, it has become a monster of impenetrable physiognomy."[10] H. D. has spoken of the power of her verse to "snap-shut neatly,"[11] and the analogy implies that these tidy, enclosed poems may be unable to communicate or unwilling even to admit a content. True to the irony of its shell, imprisoned within what amounts to a beautiful but nevertheless inescapable tomb of form, the mollusk will not be cracked open or digested, but remains, instead, "small, static, limited," just as H. D.'s early imagistic poems refuse any rhetorical relationship with referential reality since they seem shaped by a poet rigidly and self-consciously in control of herself and her material. Far from representing the ultimate statement of her poetics, the seashell poem is a very limited statement that becomes altered and superseded by transformations of this image as the *Trilogy* progresses.[12]

While H. D. discusses her craft in terms of the crafts*man* mollusk, clearly she was drawn to the shell and pearl because of their feminine evocations. From the medieval poem *Pearl* to Boticelli's famous painting, whether associated with Virgin or Venus, the shell enclosing the pearl is a common image of the female genitals,[13] just as it may also represent pregnancy, because the pearl is a kind of seed in the womb of the shellfish. This implied hope of rebirth is supported by other associations, for instance the traditionally termed "resurrection shells," and by the mythic story that Hermes creates the lyre from the shell on the very day of his birth,[14] as well as by the identification of the shell with an eggshell. H. D. was careful to elaborate on these aspects of her initial self-portrait in succeeding images of female artistry. But, as the poet progresses in her identification with overtly feminine forms of creation, shells become identified with "beautiful yet static, empty // old thoughts, old conventions" (*WDNF* 17) when she draws her old self around her like a "dead shell" (*WDNF* 14). She wants not a shell into which she can withdraw but, on the contrary, an escape from entrapment: "My heart-shell // breaks open" (*WDNF* 25), she proclaims ecstatically when a grain, instead of a pearl, falls into the "urn" of her heart so that "the heart's alabaster / is broken" (*WDNF* 29). The locked-in image provided by male culture of female sexuality and creativity, complete with its emphasis on purity and impenetrability, is finally a "jar too circumscribed" (*WDNF* 31), and the poet renounces "fixed indigestible matter / such as shell, pearl, imagery // done to death" (*WDNF* 32) in her attempt to forge more liberating and nourishing images of survival.

In her next attempt to recover the scepter of power that is Caduceus, H.D. decides not to become the rod itself, which is transformed into an innocent blade of grass, but the snake–worm that travels up the rod in its circuitous spiral toward heaven. Small, parasitic, and persistent, the worm can literally eat its way out of every calamity and sustain life even in the overwhelmingly large world that is its home. Although people cry out in disgust at the worm, it is "unrepentant" as it spins its "shroud," sure in its knowledge of "how the Lord God / is about to manifest" (*WDNF* 6). The enclosed shroud of the worm is a shell that testifies to its divinity because it adumbrates regeneration: the winged headdress, we are told, is a sign in both the snake and the emerging butterfly of magical powers of transformation, specifically of the mystery of death and rebirth experienced by all those who have endured the worm cycle to be raised into a new, high-flying form. Wrapped in the "shroud" of her own self (*WDNF* 13), the poet feels herself to be a part of a poetic people who "know each other / by secret symbols" (*WDNF* 13) of their twice-born experience. Crawling up an "individual grass-blade / toward our individual star" (*WDNF* 14), these survivors are "the keepers of the secret, / the carriers, the spinners // of the rare intangible thread / that binds all humanity // to ancient wisdom, / to antiquity" (*WDNF* 15).

It is significant that Denise Levertov centers her discussion of H.D.'s poetry on this sequence of worm poems, expressing her appreciation for poetry that provides "doors, ways in, tunnels through." When Levertov explains that H.D. "showed us a way to penetrate mystery ... *to enter into* darkness, mystery, so that it is experienced," by darkness she means "not evil but the other side, the Hiddenness before which *man must shed his arrogance*" (italics mine).[15] In the innocuous form of the lowly worm both H.D. and Levertov recall the speaker of Psalm 22: after crying out, "I am a worm and no man; a reproach of men, and despised by the people," the petitioner in the Psalm asks that God, "who took me out of the womb," provide a loving substitute for that loss. Both H.D. and Levertov emphasize the ways in which the worm, like the woman, has been despised by a culture that cannot stop to appreciate an artistry based not on elucidation or appropriation but on homage and wonder at the hidden darkness, the mystery.[16] Both poets emphasize the worm's ability to provide another womb for its own death and resurrection. With visionary realism, both insist that the only paradise worth seeing exists not behind or beyond but within the dust. While "the keepers of the secret, / the carriers, the spinners" of such "Earth Psalms" are surely men as well as women, they are all associated with traditionally female arts of weaving, with uniquely female powers of reproducing life, and with a pre-Christian tradition that embraces gods (like Ra, Osiris, Amen) who are "not at all like Jehovah" (*WDNF* 16).

The "other side, the Hiddenness" which H. D. and Levertov seek to penetrate consists precisely of those experiences unique to women that have been denied a place in our publicly acknowledged culture, specifically the experiences of female sexuality and motherhood. Told that they embody mystery to men, even if they are indifferent to their bodies' miraculous ability to hide, foster, and emit another life, women may very well experience their own concealed sex organs as curiously mysterious, separate from their consciousness. Furthermore, the abrupt and total biological shifts that distinguish female growth from the more continuous development of men is surely one reason why the worm cycle and the Psyche myth have always fascinated women. With characteristic whimsy, in describing the fears of growing girls, Simone de Beauvoir quite simply says, "I have known little girls whom the sight of a chrysalis plunged into a frightened reverie."[17]

Less dramatically but just as significantly, women poets also confront positive images of women that are equally degrading because they trivialize or depersonalize. Redefining the traditional picture of the woman as social, pretty, flighty butterfly, an artist like Emily Dickinson experiences confinement as her "Cocoon tightens," realizing that "A dim capacity for Wings / Demeans the Dress" she wears.[18] We see the same conflict portrayed in Judy Chicago's recent portraits of creative women in which what she calls the "butterfly—vagina"[19] struggles in its desire for "easy Sweeps of Sky" against the enclosing geometrical boxes and scripts that attempt to contain it in the center of the canvas, and Dickinson seems to articulate the sense of contradiction depicted so brilliantly by Judy Chicago:

> So I must baffle at the Hint
> And cipher at the Sign
> And make much blunder, if at last
> I take the clue divine—
>
> (#1099)

This dilemma is not very different from the puzzlement experienced in *The Walls Do Not Fall* by a poet who feels ready "to begin a new spiral" (*WDNF* 21) but finds herself thrown back on outworn vocabularies and the terrible feeling that she has failed to achieve metamorphosis. Like Dickinson, who "must baffle at the Hint," H. D. blunders over an "indecipherable pal-

impsest" (*WDNF* 31) that she cannot read. Floundering, "lost in sea-depth
...where Fish / move two-ways" (*WDNF* 30), overwhelmed by confusion at
her own "pitiful reticence, // boasting, intrusion of strained / inappropriate
allusion" (*WDNF* 31), H. D. admits the failure of her own invocations.

Perhaps she has failed because she has tried to evoke Ra, Osiris, Amen,
Christ, God, All-Father, and the Holy Ghost, all the while knowing that she
is an "initiate of the secret wisdom, / bride of the kingdom" (*WDNF* 31).
The "illusion of lost-gods, daemons" has brought, instead of revelation, the
"reversion of old values" (*WDNF* 31) which inhibits, denying as it does the
validity of her female perspective. Specifically, she recalls now that the spin-
ners who keep the secret that threads humanity to the ancient wisdom are
aspects of the female goddess, Isis. She must remain true to her own perspec-
tive—"the angle of incidence / equals the angle of reflection" (*WDNF* 32)—
and to her own needs and hungers, so she now entreats a new energy: "Hest,
// Aset, Isis, the great enchantress, / in her attribute of Serget, // the original
great-mother, / who drove // harnessed scorpions / before her" (*WDNF* 34).

Seeking to become as wise *as scorpions, as serpents* (*WDNF* 35), H. D.
can now read her own personal psychic map to find the eternal realities.
Specifically, she can now reevaluate "our secret hoard" (*WDNF* 36). The
stars toward which the worm moves in its slow spiral toward the sky are
also "little jars . . . boxes, very precious to hold further // unguent, myrrh,
incense" (*WDNF* 24). Thus, they contain a promise of revelation not very
different from shells and cocoons, which can also disclose secret treasures.
Modern words, too, may reveal hidden meanings, thereby relinquishing their
alien impenetrability if the poet can somehow perceive their coded, palimp-
sestic status. Fairly early in the *Trilogy*, H. D. manages to take some small
comfort in the bitter joke wrapped in the pun *cartouche*: for her contempo-
raries it might mean a gun cartridge with a paper case, but she knows that
it also once signified the oblong figure in an Egyptian monument enclosing
a sovereign's name (*WDNF* 9). This kind of irony offers a potential consola-
tion when the poet realizes that it might still be possible to disentangle
ancient meanings from corrupt forms, for instance the "Christos-image . . .
from its art-craft junk-shop / paint-and-plaster medieval jumble // of pain
worship and death symbol" (*WDNF* 18). Finally, the poet knows and feels

the meaning that words hide;

they are anagrams, cryptograms,
little boxes, conditioned

to hatch butterflies . . . [italics mine].
                                (*WDNF* 39)

H. D. learns how to decipher what that other H. D.—Humpty Dumpty— called "portmanteaus," words which open up like a bag or a book into compartments.[20] By means of lexical reconstruction, she begins to see the possibility of purging language of its destructive associations and arbitrariness. Viewing each word as a puzzle ready to be solved and thereby freed of modernity, H. D. begins to hope that she can discover secret, coded messages which must be subversive to warrant their being so cunningly concealed by her culture.

Now *The Walls Do Not Fall* can end in a hymn to Osiris because the poet has managed to "recover the secret of Isis" (*WDNF* 40). Just as H. D. is now assured that the destructive signs surrounding her can be redefined for her own renewal, in the ancient myth Isis gathers together the scattered fragments of her lost brother/husband's body and reconstructs him in a happier ending than that to be enacted by the king's men for Humpty Dumpty. The resurrection of Osiris, the reconstruction of the magical power of the word, these testify to the healing, even the revivifying powers of the poet–Isis, who can now see the unity between "Osiris" and "Sirius." Since Sirius is the star representing Isis come to wake her brother from death, such an equation means that the poet glimpses the shared identity of the sibling lovers Osiris and Isis. Approaching this "serious" mystery, H. D. asks, "O, Sire, is" this union between the god and the goddess finally possible (*WDNF* 42)? She can even connect "Osiris" with the "zrr-hiss" of war-lightning.[21] The poet who uses words with reverence can release the coded messages contained or enfolded within them. Now, although the walls still do not fall, although they continue to testify to the divisions and barriers between people, between historical periods, within consciousness itself, they also preserve remnants of written messages — anagrams and cryptograms — which, by providing the thread from the present back to the past, allow H. D. to evade the destructive definitions of reality provided by those who utilize the word for modern mastery.

The poet's response to the shattered fragmentation of her world in the subsequent volumes of the *Trilogy* is stated in the first poem of *Tribute to the Angels:* dedicating herself to Hermes Trismegistus, patron of alchemists, H. D. undertakes not merely the archaeological reconstruction of a lost past, but also a magical transfiguration not unlike Christ's creation of the sustaining loaves and fishes, or the transubstantiation of bread and water into body and blood. Since alchemical art has traditionally been associated with fiery purification that resurrects what is decomposing in the grave into a divine and golden form, even the destructive lightning and bombs can now be associated with heat that could transform the contents of the dross in the alchemist's bowl into the philosopher's stone. The seashell of *The Walls Do Not Fall* itself becomes a testimony to such displacement, reappearing as a bowl that is cauldron, grave, and oven, yet another womb in which a new jewel can be created.

Now the poet sees the function of the poem–bowl as the transformative redefinition of language itself. Thus, she gives us the recipe by which she endows "a word most bitter, marah," and a word denigrated, "Venus," with more affirmative, nurturing meanings so that "marah" becomes "Mother" and "Venus" is translated from "venery" to "venerate" (*TA* 8, 12). Similarly, she seeks a way of evading names that definitely label the word-jewel in the bowl: "I do not want to name it," she explains, because "I want to minimize thought, // concentrate on it / till I shrink, // dematerialize / and am drawn into it" (*TA* 14). Seeking a noncoercive vocabulary, a new language that will consecrate what has been desecrated by her culture, H. D. is propelled by the unsatisfied duality between mother and father to reestablish the primacy to the "feminine" of what masculine culture has relegated as inessential.

Implicitly heretical and hermetic, Hermes' alchemy is associated with "candle and script and bell," with "what the new church spat upon" (*TA* 1), and H. D. does not evade the challenge her own alchemical art constitutes to the prevailing Christian conception of the Word. On the contrary, in *Tribute to the Angels*, she self-consciously sets her narrative in the context of the *Book of Revelations*, quoting directly from it in numerous poems in order to question John's version of redemption while offering her own revision. In many poems she appears to be arguing with John directly because his vision seems warped: H. D. quotes John's assertion of the finality of his own account, his admonition that *"if any man shall add // God shall add unto him the plagues,"* even while she determines to alter his story as she dedicates herself to making all things new (*TA* 3). She realizes that "he of the seventy-times-seven / passionate, bitter wrongs" is also "He of the seventy-times-seven / bitter, unending wars" (*TA* 3), and so she questions his severely vengeful version of the hidden future. While John sings the praises of seven angels whose seven golden bowls pour out the wrath of God upon the earth, H. D. calls on seven angels whose presence in war-torn London is a testament to the promise of rebirth that her bowl holds. While *"I John saw"* a series of monstrosities and disasters on the face of the earth, H. D. claims, "my eyes saw, / it was not a dream" (*TA* 23), and what she witnesses is a sign of resurrection: "a half-burnt-out apple tree / blossoming" (*TA* 23) is the fulfillment of her hope at the beginning of the *Trilogy* to recover the scepter, the lily-bud rod of Caduceus, which is now associated with the Tree of Life that links heaven and earth, the Cosmic Tree which represents the mysterious but perpetual regeneration of the natural world, the tree that miraculously lodges the coffin of the dead Osiris or the tree on which Christ was hanged to be reborn. Aaron's rod, which made the bitter (marah) waters sweet when it blossomed in the desert for the wandering children of Israel, is converted from a sign of Moses' control to an emblem of a Lady's presence.

Most significantly, H. D. contrasts the final vision of the holy Jerusalem, a city with no need of the sun or the moon to shine because lit by the glory of God, a city which John imagines as the bride and the Lamb's wife, with her own final revelation of redemption. Ironically beginning with an allusion, "of the *no need / of the moon to shine in it,*" H. D. first describes the appearance of a Lady in a bedroom lit up by the "luminous disc" of the clock by her bedhead (*TA* 25). But this appearance by the "luminous light" of "the phosphorescent face" of the clock (*TA* 26) is only a dream adumbration of the vision of this same Lady, who appears when H. D. is "thinking of Gabriel / of the moon-cycle, of the moon-shell, // of the moon-crescent / and the moon at full" (*TA* 28). Far from seeking a place with no need of moonshine, H. D. celebrates a Lady who is actually the representative of lunar time and consciousness. Furthermore, the poet is careful to remind us through a whole series of negatives that this Lady whom we have seen in all the various portraits of the female as she has been worshipped by various cultures is none of her previous representatives or incarnations, "none of these suggest her" as the poet sees her (*TA* 31). Not only isn't H. D.'s vision of the Lady hieratic or frozen, "she is no symbolic figure": while she has "the dove's symbolic purity," and "veils / like the Lamb's Bride," H. D. is insistent that "The Lamb was not with her, / either as Bridegroom or Child"; not He, but "*we* are her bridegroom and lamb" (italics mine, *TA* 39).

The miraculous transformation in the alchemical bowl and the equally mysterious flowering of the rod find their culmination in this revelation of the muse who is not only the veiled Goddess, Persephone, the *Sanctus Spiritus, Santa Sophia*, Venus, Isis and Mary, but most importantly the female spirit liberated from precisely these mystifications:

> but she is not shut up in a cave
> like a Sibyl; she is not
>
> imprisoned in leaden bars
> in a coloured window;
>
> she is Psyche, *the butterfly,*
> *out of the cocoon* [italics mine].
>   (*TA* 38)

Unnamed and elusive, the Lady's flight recalls the hatched and winged words of H. D. herself. Unlike John's whore of Babylon who carries abominations, this visionary Lady carries a book that "is our book" (*TA* 39). Whether this "tome of the ancient wisdom" whose pages "are the blank pages / of the unwritten volume of the new" (*TA* 38) is "a tribute to the Angels" (*TA* 41) or "a tale of a jar or jars" (*TA* 39) that will constitute the next volume of the *Trilogy*, H. D. closely identifies this new Eve who has come to retrieve what was lost at the apple tree with her own liberating "Book of Life" (*TA* 36).

As she evokes and thereby reinterprets the inherited signs of her culture which are said to contain the secret wisdom necessary for the attainment of Paradise, H. D. implies that "the letter killeth but the spirit giveth life" (2 Corinthians 3:6). And it is life that she sees finally created in the crucible, "when the jewel / melts," and what we find is "a cluster of garden-pinks / or a face like a Christmas-rose" (*TA* 43). In the final book of the *Trilogy*, the escaping fragrance of such flowering within the pristine glass of a jar represents the poet's success in finding a form that can contain without confining. No longer surrounded by splintered shards, H. D. makes of her jars a symbol of aesthetic shape not unlike those of Wallace Stevens or Hart Crane, beautiful and complete objects but also transparencies through which a healing content is made manifest. Purified of their opacity, shell, bowl, and box are now ready to reveal their previously secret and therefore inaccessible hoard. This promise of release is realized fully in *The Flowering of the Rod*: dedicated to the Lady who has escaped conventionally defined categories, the poet readies herself for flight as she asks us to "leave the smoldering cities below" (*FR* 1), the place of deathly skulls, to follow the quest of Christ who was "the first to wing / from that sad Tree" (*FR* 11) and whose journey is similar to that of the snow-geese circling the Arctic or the mythical migratory flocks seeking Paradise.

Not only does H. D. move even farther back in time, but her initial focus on seemingly insignificant animals and her subsequent naming of angelic powers seem to have made it possible for her finally to create human characters, as she retells the story of the birth and death of Christ from the unexpected perspective of two participants in the gospel—Kaspar the Magian and Mary Magdala. Furthermore, after two sequences of poems progressing by allusive associations, complex networks of imagery, and repetitive, almost liturgical, invocations, the final book of the *Trilogy* embodies the emergence of the poet's sustained voice in a story—if not of her own making—of her own perspective. She takes an unusual vantage on the ancient story to distinguish her vision: she claims to see "what men say is-not," to remember what men have forgot (*FR* 6), and so she sets out to testify to an event known by everyone but as yet unrecorded (*FR* 12).

Like Christ, who was himself "an outcast and a vagabond" (*FR* 11), and like the poet who is identified with the thief crucified by his side, both Kaspar and Mary are aliens in their society. The inheritor of ancient alchemical tradition, Kaspar owns the jars that hold "priceless, unobtainable-elsewhere myrrh" (*FR* 13), a "distillation" which some said "lasted literally forever," the product of "sacred processes . . . never written, not even in symbols" (*FR* 14). As a heathen, he represents pre-biblical lore that acknowledges the power of "daemons," termed "devils" by the modern Christian world. However, his education is a patrimony in an exclusively male tradition that assumes "no secret was safe with a woman" (*FR* 14). Kaspar is shown to be a bit of a prig, something of a misogynist, so it is highly incongruous that Mary Magdala comes to this Arab in his "little booth of a house" (*FR* 13). Unmaidenly and unpredictable, she is as much of an outcast as Kaspar, if only because of her ability "to detach herself," a strength responsible for her persistence in spite of Kaspar's insistence that the myrrh is not for sale: "planted" before him (*FR* 15), Mary identifies herself as "Mary, a great tower," and then she explains that, though she is "mara, bitter," through her own power she will be "mary-myrrh" (*FR* 16). Clearly, the coming together of Kaspar and Mary recalls the sibling lovers Isis and Osiris and implies the healing of the poet's own sense of fragmentation. Before the jar actually changes hands, however, H. D. dramatizes the discomfort of Simon, who views Mary at the Last Supper as a destructive siren. This "woman from the city" who seems "devil-ridden" to the Christian is recognized by Kaspar as a living embodiment of the indwelling daemons of "Isis, Astarte, Cyprus / and the other four; // he might re-name them, / Ge-meter, De-meter, earth-mother // or Venus / in a star" (*FR* 25).

Only after we recognize the seemingly antithetical wise man and whore as common representatives of reverence for the ancient principles of female fertility and creativity does H. D. return to the scene in the booth behind the market to describe fully the vision granted to Kaspar through the intervention of Mary. Here, at the climax of the *Trilogy*, Kaspar recalls the poet's experience with the Lady when he sees the light "on her hair / like moonlight on a lost river" (*FR* 27). In a fleck or a flaw of a jewel on the head of one of three crowned ladies, Kaspar discovers "the whole secret of the mystery" (*FR* 30). He sees the circles of islands and the lost center-island, Atlantis; he sees earth before Adam, Paradise before Eve. Finally he hears a spell in an unknown language which seems to come down from prehistorical times as it translates itself to him:

> *Lilith born before Eve*
> *and one born before Lilith,*
> *and Eve; we three are forgiven,*
> *we are three of the seven*
> *daemons cast out of her.*
>
> (*FR* 33)

This is an extremely enigmatic message, but it does seem to imply that a matriarchal genealogy has been erased from recorded history when this ancient female trinity was exorcised as evil, cast out of human consciousness by those who would begin with a secondary Eve who brings death into the garden. Because Lilith is a woman who dared pronounce the Ineffable Name and who was unabashed at articulating her sexual preferences, her presence among the crowned or crucified queens seems to promise a prelapsarian vision quite different from that of Genesis: created not out of Adam, but out of the dust, Lilith and the unnamed daemon actually predate the Bible, and so they establish a link back to Kaspar's pagan daemons; together they promise a submerged but now recoverable time of female strength, female speech, and female sexuality, all of which have mysteriously managed to survive, although in radically subdued ways, incarnate in the body of Mary Magdala. As a healer, a shaman of sorts,[22] Kaspar has in a sense recaptured Mary's stolen soul, her lost ancestors; he has established the matriarchal genealogy that confers divinity on her.

Reading Mary like a palimpsest, Kaspar has fully penetrated the secret of the mystery. H. D. then reverses the chronology of his life, moving backward from his confrontation with this Mary over the jars of myrrh to his delivery of the gift of myrrh to Mary in the manger. When Kaspar thinks in the ox-stall that "there were always two jars" (*FR* 41) and that *"someday [he] will bring the other"* (*FR* 42), we know that his prophecy *has been or will be* fulfilled: as he gives the myrrh to Mary mother, we know that he is destined to give the other jar to Mary Magdala, thereby authenticating his vision of the female trinity, his knowledge that the whore is the mother and that Isis, who has been labeled a retrogressive harlot, is actually the regenerative goddess of life. Through the two Marys, Kaspar recovers the aspects of Isis retained by Christianity—the lady of sorrows weeping for the dead Osiris and the divine mother nursing her son, Horus.[23] When Marah is shown to be Mother, the translation is complete, and the poem can end with a new word, as the gift is miraculously appreciated by a Mary, who might know that the blossoming, flowering fragrance is the mingling of the magical contents of the jar, the myrrh in her arms, and perhaps even the baby in her lap.

Dramatically ending at the beginning, moving from Apocalypse to Genesis, from death to birth, from history to mystery, H. D. illustrates the cyclical renewal she personally seeks of dying into life. Calling our attention to her own narrative principles, H. D. proclaims: "I have gone forward, / I have gone backward" (*FR* 8). And as we have seen, her point is precisely the need of going backward in time to recover what has been lost in the past, for this justifies her own progress backward in chronological time throughout the *Trilogy*: proceeding from the modern times of London in *The Walls Do Not Fall*, to the medieval cities of *Tribute to the Angels*, back to the ancient deserts of Israel in *The Flowering of the Rod*, she dedicates herself to finding the half-erased traces of a time "When in the company of the gods / I loved and was loved" (*WDNF* 5). Such a discovery, as we have seen, involves not a learning but a remembering. However, instead of progressing backward in a linear, sequential manner, she chooses three time-bands that seem to be relatively self-contained, like ever-narrowing circles enclosing some still point of origin. Furthermore, she calls our attention to just the disconnectedness of her three time spheres by isolating each within a book of the *Trilogy*. Concentric but never touching, these three distinct periods in time, when taken in themselves, are senseless and directionless, each repeating the others:

> you think, even before it is half-over,
> that your cycle is at an end,
>
> but you repeat your foolish circling—again, again, again;
> again, the steel sharpened on the stone;
>
> again, the pyramid of skulls.
>
> (*FR* 6)

The senseless wheeling within each of these foolish circles, caused by the lack of vision that cannot see "then" as an aspect of "now," is fittingly experienced as a tornado (*WDNF* 32). It can produce only war.

On the other hand, at least potentially, each of the moments of time in each of these historical cycles is related to a prehistoric origin, just as all points on the circumference of a circle are related to its center. The poet who understands the palimpsestic symbols of the past in today's imagery can interpret the "mysterious enigma" that merges "the distant future / with most distant antiquity" (*WDNF* 20). Similarly, seeing down the "deep, deep-well // of the so-far unknown / depth of pre-history," Kaspar realizes "a *point* in time— // he called it a fleck or flaw in a gem" on a circlet of gems on lady's head (*FR* 40). Since historical time is envisioned as a series of circles, enclosing a prehistoric center, H. D. can describe how Kaspar heard "an echo of an echo in a shell" (*FR* 28), a language he had never heard spoken, which seems translated "as it transmuted its message // through spiral upon spiral of the shell / of memory that yet connect us // with the drowned cities of pre-history" (*FR* 33).

That Kaspar hears "an echo of an echo in a shell" recalls not only the importance of the seashell earlier in the *Trilogy*, but also the fascination of Madge in *The Hedgehog* with Echo, who always answers her caller, "Echo":

> Or sometimes just O, O, O, just the same O, getting thin and far and far and thin like the sound of water. Echo melts into the hill, into the water. Now she is a real person . . . Echo is the answer of our own hearts, like the singing in a seashell (p. 44).

What tantalizes Madge about Echo's response, just as it informed her curiosity about *hérisson*, is the recalcitrance of the word, its refusal to yield up meaning, its emptiness of signification, as well as its ambiguous status as silent sound, the voice of nature, a living remnant of ancient Greece, an aspect of her own voice returned from a far distance, a female utterance of completion and circularity. In *Tribute to Freud*, H. D. returns to the image of the echoing shell when she describes how her unspoken expressions of gratitude go on singing,

> like an echo of an echo in a shell—very far away yet very near—the very shell substance of my outer ear and the curled involuted or convoluted shell skull, and inside the skull, the curled, intricate, hermit-like mollusk, the brain-matter itself.[24]

Clearly the spiraling echoes of the shell are a way of recognizing the intimate yet convoluted relationship between a central origin and its distant reaches. Hearing "the echoed syllables of this spell" (*FR* 33), Kaspar remains unsure about the status of his revelation: is it "a sort of spiritual-optical illusion" (*FR* 40), the answer of his own heart? Or could the echoing shell also contain the secret revealed in *Hermetic Definition*—a sound like that of water, "*Grand Mer*" or" "*Mère*"?[25]

Echo, we should remember, was punished for her only "failing," her fondness of talk, by being *deprived of the power of speaking first*. In this respect she serves as a paradigm of the secondary status of women who have traditionally been reduced to supporting, assuaging, serving, and thereby echoing the work, wishes, and words of men. Specifically, she serves as a model for H. D.'s sense of her own belatedness as she repeats the words she experiences as prior authorities over her own spiritual and psychic experiences. Like Echo, then, H. D. felt cursed because denied control over her own speech, destined to repeat the language of another's making and therefore hidden, if not obliterated, from her own creation. But, just as Echo manages to express her desires, even mocking the speech of those she mimics, H.D. gets her secrets sung. At the same time, however, the echoing shell is also an attractive image for H.D. because it serves as an escape from the danger of meaning into protective obscurity. As a "mere" echo, H.D. presents her voice as derivative and thereby assures herself a defense against being defined and confined within the prisonhouse of language. Like her visionary Pythoness of Delphi whose utterances could be read two ways, H.D. hides her private meaning behind public words, so her story is always "different yet the same as before" (*TA* 39) and therefore "only" a repetition. Herein lies both the courage and the anxiety of her art, as well as the reason why the echo is yet another infinitely decipherable (and therefore indecipherable) palimpsest.

Whether derivative or transmuted sound, however, the spiraling echo of the shell makes all of the enclosures of the first two poems comprehensible as metamorphoses of the circle. The shell with its spherical pearl, the bowl containing the gold, the boxes hatching butterflies, even the jars are circles surrounding a magical potent center. In an evocation of the spiraling turns of the worm approaching its star, the migratory geese of *The Flowering of the Rod* seek Paradise by circling "till they drop from the highest point of the spiral / or fall from the innermost center of the ever-narrowing circle" (*FR* 5). Their drowning would be a welcome end for the poet, who feels now that "only love is holy and love's ecstasy // that turns and turns and turns about one centre, / reckless, regardless, blind to reality" (*FR* 6). So the islands encircled by water become a fitting symbol of the time of prehistoric eternity before the fall into patriarchal history, especially the lost center-island of Atlantis. The poet seeks this center because it can serve as an escape from the repetitions of history and because it is an entrance to creative stasis. Such a center is neither temporally nor spatially bound: its potential for unfolding gains it extension in space as it detemporalizes the present into an emblem of both the past and the future.[26]

Finally we see the circumference as a flower which, contained in the grain or seed,

> opened petal by petal, a circle,
> and each petal was separate
>
> yet still held, as it were,
> by some force of attraction

to its dynamic centre;
and the circle went on widening

and would go on opening
. . . to infinity.

(*FR* 31)

Participating in a mystical literary tradition that extends from Dante to Roethke, H. D. evokes the unbroken, unfolding circle to satisfy her insatiable longing to "equilibrate" (*FR* 5) the antagonisms between desert and Arctic, spring and winter, or sound and silence, to heal the struggle between father and mother, thereby establishing a harmony dramatized by the recognition of commonality between Kaspar and Mary Magdala and by the image of the androgynous center of the flower. Seeking to be drawn into the center, H.D. sees resurrection as "a sense of direction" that takes her "straight to the horde and plunder, / the treasure, the store-room, // the honeycomb" to "food, shelter, fragrance" (*FR* 7). While she never denies the place of men in such an origin, H. D. does end the *Trilogy* with an emphasis on the feminine that extends Kaspar's consciousness that prelapsarian time is a time of woman-worship: she celebrates the baby or myrrh cradled in the arms of a woman whose very sex is represented as a circle on a stem   —the sacred *ankh*, which is the symbol of life in Egypt.[27] The medieval definition of God as the sphere whose center is everywhere and whose circumference is nowhere has been radically feminized. Here, again H. D. serves as a paradigm for contemporary women writers like Marge Piercy, whose sequence of poems "The Spring Offensive of the Snail" celebrates encircling, blossoming lovers, and Monique Wittig, who makes the circle an emblem of her Amazon utopia, and Margaret Atwood, who focuses on circularity in her revision of the myth of Circe's island, and Adrienne Rich, who circles around the wreck with a book of outworn myths.[28]

H. D. would not and does not deprive the center of its inaccessible mystery or the circumference of its distance from origin. On the contrary, as one of Jung's precursors, she testifies to the continued need for approaching the center, for retelling and rewriting and adding to a palimpsest even as she realizes that such an approach is a regression, and that—as the word "re-cover" implies—she hides what she seeks to reveal. Denise Levertov celebrates just this reverence for the unknowable in H. D.'s poetry when she explains that H. D. went "further out of the circle of known light, further in toward an unknown center."[29] If in some ways Kaspar the Magian was right that "no secret was safe with a woman" (*FR* 14), on the other hand, he failed to realize that the woman who models her speech on that of Echo or Sibyl or (less hopefully) Cassandra or Philomel would be telling a secret that retains the power of its hidden mystery. Singing a spell that conforms to none of the words she had ever heard spoken, H. D. reveals the ways in which one woman mythologizes herself and her gender, asserting herself as the center of the universe in a radical reversal and revision of the inherited images she so brilliantly echoes.

IV

"THE DIFFERENCE–
MADE ME BOLD"

Contemporary Poets

It was given to me by the Gods—
When I was a little Girl—
They give us Presents most—you know—
When we are new—and small.
I kept it in my Hand—
I never put it down—
I did not dare to eat—or sleep—
For fear it would be gone—
I heard such words as "Rich"—
When hurrying to school—
From lips at Corners of the Streets—
And wrestled with a smile.
Rich! 'Twas Myself—was rich—
To take the name of Gold—
And Gold to own—in solid Bars—
The Difference—made me bold—

—Emily Dickinson, #454

14.

May Swenson
and the Shapes of Speculation

Alicia Ostriker

Most humanists show very little curiosity about the physical world outside
the self, and usually a positive antipathy to the mental processes we call
scientific. This was not always the case. Although Western literature has
only one *De Rerum Naturam*, persons of letters were once expected to take
all knowledge as their province, and to interpret scientific understanding as
part of a unified vision of the world. Despite the expanding post-Renaissance
hostility between science and art, even as late as the nineteenth century
Blake was defining the implications of Newtonian mechanics for the human
imagination, and apparently anticipating aspects of post-Newtonian physics,
as he anticipated so much else. Shelley was thrilled by discoveries in elec-
tricity and magnetism. Tennyson registered the seismic shock of *The Origin
of Species*. When William Carlos Williams in *Paterson* makes Madame
Curie's discovery of radium a major metaphor for all artistic discovery, he
bridges the supposed "two cultures" completely. Science will not go away
because poets ignore it, and in fact we ignore any great human enterprise
at our peril. Yet few poets presently venture beyond dread or annoyance
toward the works and ways of physics, chemistry, biology, and fewer bring
back more than a gimcrack souvenir or two. The Bomb and a fuzzy idea of
Relativity were popular a while ago. Moon-landings and Ecology have re-
cently cornered the market.

May Swenson, born in Utah in 1919, New Yorker by adoption since
1949, has written six well-received books of poems, beginning with *Another
Animal* in 1954. She is known as a nature poet, "one of the few good poets
who write good poems about nature . . . not just comparing it to states of

mind or society," as Elizabeth Bishop has remarked.[1] You can cull a bestiary from her work that would include geese, turtles, an owl and its prey, a bee and a rose, frogs, fireflies, cats and caterpillars, at least one lion, and many horses. She writes of sun, moon, clouds, landscapes and cityscapes, and always with a wondering, curious eye, an intense concern about the structure and texture of her subject, an extraordinary tactility. "The pines, aggressive as erect tails of cats," begins a poem called "Forest."[2] Another called "Spring Uncovered" begins, "Gone the scab of ice that kept it snug, / The lake is naked," and ends where "a grackle, fat as burgundy,/ gurgles on a limb" with "bottle-glossy feathers."[3]

But beyond the naturalist's patient observation lies something else. What critics have called Swenson's "calculated naiveté"[4] or her ability to become "a child, but a highly sophisticated child,"[5] is actually that childlike ability to envision something freshly, to ask incessant questions and always be prepared for unexpected answers, required of the creative scientist. "How things really are we should like to know,"[6] she murmurs, and what else is the motive of the speculative intellect? Swenson's poetry asks as many questions as a four-year-old, and she wants to know not only how things are made and what they resemble, but where they are going and how we fit in. The opening poem of *To Mix With Time* unblushingly titles itself "The Universe." *Iconographs* includes poems on, for example, the response of a snail to tide, the rotation of a mobile, electronic sound, anti-matter, a telephoto of Earth taken from Orbiter 5, the history of astronomy, man as mammal and (maybe) anima, and the declaration that "THE DNA MOLECULE / is The Nude Descending a Staircase / a circular one."[7] In "Let Us Prepare," the poet seriously considers the possibility of evolution "beyond the organic,"[8] although in a poem about flight—from the thistle seed to flying mammals to Lindbergh to John Glenn—she begins and concludes that "earth will not let go our foot";[9] thus demonstrating that she can, as a good scientist should, speculate on both sides of a given hypothesis. "Almanac" takes note that between the rising and setting of a "moon"—a bruise on her fingernail:

> an unmanned airship
> dived 200 miles to the hem of space, and
> vanished. At the place of Pharaoh Cheops'
> tomb (my full moon floating yellow)
> a boat for ferrying souls to the sun
> was disclosed in a room sealed 5000 years.

> Reaching whiteness, this moon-speck waned
> while an April rained. Across the street
> a vine crept over brick up 14 feet. And
> Einstein (who said there is no hitching
> post in the universe) at 77 turned ghost.[10]

Process and connection concern her in the deepest ways:

> The stone is milked to feed the tree;
> the log is killed when the flame is hungry.
> To arise in the other's body?[11]

But curiosity is a habit of mind at all times. In "Welcome Aboard the Turbojet Electra":

> Why do they say 31,000 feet? Why
> not yards or miles? Why four
> cigarettes and no match?[12]

If this is not typical woman's poetry, Swenson is not a typical woman. All poetry by women just now is potentially interesting for the same reasons that all black poetry is potentially interesting: it may guide us where we've never been. As Carolyn Kizer has observed, women writers "are the custodians of the world's best-kept secret; / Merely the private lives of one-half of humanity." While Swenson does not write on feminist themes most of the time, she does so occasionally, with electrifying results. (I will look at one of those poems, "Bleeding," below.) Most often she blends, she balances. Science, technology, the mental life of observation, speculation: she has invaded these traditionally "masculine" territories. Yet her consistent intimacy with her world, which contains no trace of the archetypal "masculine" will to conquer or control it, seems archetypally "feminine." So does the way she lets herself be precise yet tentative and vulnerable about her observations, where a comparable male poet, perhaps driven by the need to overcome alienation, might be pretentious (Snyder?), pedantic (Olsen?), nervous (Ammons? James Wright?) or agonized (Kinnell?); and her affinity for the small-scale object, like Emily Dickinson's, also reads like a feminine characteristic.

Readers of contemporary American women's poetry will have noticed the extraordinary richness with which it dwells on the flesh, the body, to a degree unduplicated in most men's poetry. (Check your nearest anthology if you doubt this.) To Swenson, everything in the world speaks body-language: a tree has a toenail, spring grass grows "out of each pore . . . itching," a snowplow sucks "celestial clods into its turning neck." The same poet asks, "Body my house / my horse my hound / what will I do / when you are fallen,"[13] and concludes a poem on the senses, "in the legs' lair, / carnivora of Touch."[14] If anatomy is destiny, Swenson is at home (and humorous) with that, knowing we share that fate, finding no discrepancy whatever between what some would call a woman's body and a man's mind.

But poetic originality shows itself most obviously through an original form, some shape of a poem that we have not seen, some refreshing play of syntax, a new way words have been thrown in the air and fallen together, been lain one next to the other. Exploratory poetry invites—demands—exploratory forms. When entering new territory, form can become quite palpably "an extension of content," a ship's prow, an arm reaching, a dog's nose sniffing the air.

Swenson has always had an individual style, though bearing traces here and there of Cummings, Marianne Moore, and especially Emily Dickinson. She has always been committed to formal experimentation, and she has often played with the shapes of poems. I would like to dwell here on one book, *Iconographs*, in which the composition of shaped poems has become systematic.

Iconographs consists of forty-six poems, each of which plays a typographical game. Each has been given a unique shape or frame. Verticals, angles and curves, quirky spacings and capitalizations have all been used. The intention, Swenson suggests in a note, has been "to cause an instant object-to-eye encounter with each poem even before it is read word-for-word. To have simultaneity as well as sequence. To make an existence in space, as well as time, for the poem." The title, she further remarks, can imply:

> *icon* "a symbol hardly distinguished from the object symbolized"
> *icono-* from the Greek *eikonos,* meaning "image" or "likeness"
> *graph* "diagram" or "system of connections or interrelations"
> *-graph* from the Greek *graphe,* meaning "carve" . . . "indicating the
> instrument as well as the written product of the instrument."[15]

But such descriptions scarcely prepare us for the power of the opening poem, "Bleeding":

Stop bleeding   said the knife.
I would if I   could said the cut.
Stop bleeding   you make me messy with this blood.
I'm sorry   said the cut.
Stop or   I will sink in farther said the knife.
Don't   said the cut.
The   knife did not say it couldn't help it but
it   sank in farther.
If   only you didn't bleed said the knife I wouldn't
have   to do this.
I know   said the cut I bleed too easily I hate
that I   can't help it I wish I were a knife like
you and   didn't have to bleed.
Well   meanwhile stop bleeding will you said the knife.
Yes you   are a mess and sinking in deeper said the cut I
will have   to stop.
Have you   stopped by now said the knife.
I've almost   stopped I think.
Why must you   bleed in the first place said the knife.
For the same   reason maybe that you must do what you
must do said   the cut.
I can't stand   bleeding said the knife and sank in farther.
I hate it too said   the cut I know it isn't you it's
me you're lucky to be   a knife you ought to be glad about that.
Too many cuts around   said the knife they're
messy I don't know how   they stand themselves.
They don't said the cut.
You're bleeding again.
No I've stopped said the cut   see you are coming out now the
blood is drying it will rub   off you'll be shiny again and clean.
If only cuts wouldn't bleed   so much said the knife coming
out a little.
But then knives might become   dull said the cut.
Aren't you still bleeding a   little said the knife.
I hope not said the cut.
I feel you are just a little.
Maybe just a little but I can   stop now.
I feel a little wetness still   said the knife sinking in a
little but then coming out a   little.
Just a little maybe just enough   said the cut.
That's enough now stop now do   you   feel better now said the knife.
I feel I have to bleed to   feel I   think said the cut.
I don't I don't have to   feel said   the knife drying now
becoming shiny.[16]

It would be difficult, among feminist documents, to find a stronger state-
ment about the connection between *bleeding* and *feeling*, which in our cul-
ture are both believed to be natural to women, and a bit disgusting, and cer-
tainly threatening, while a dry superiority to feeling is a major sign of
desirable masculinity. And Swenson's methods are purely poetic: the low-key
"said" throughout the dialogue indicating a habitual everyday encounter; the
obsessively locked-in repeating of the key terms "bleeding," "bleed," "cut,"
and "blood"; the sound pattern intensifying "bleed," "easily," "meanwhile";
the sound effect of "messy" and "wetness" opposed to the hard sounds of
"knife," "drying," "shiny." What the cut "feels," of course, is self-loathing.
It agrees with the knife, accepts the values implicit in the terms "messy"
versus "shiny." It hates its own messiness, wishes it were a knife. And of
course it feels empathy for the knife, which the knife of course does not
reciprocate. Yet beyond the language, the most frightening thing in the
poem is that visible slash down the page, that speaks, that takes the breath
away.

Why, when the knife complains of messiness, cannot the cut cry out,
"I am bleeding and messy because you are cutting me, you bastard," instead
of saying "I'm sorry"? Must we ourselves identify feeling with bleeding? Is
the knife unable to feel, or merely unwilling? The poem does not tell.
We notice only that at its conclusion, after the back-and-forth, after the
pauses, the ragged streak which lacerates the text has begun to branch out.

By its sharply enclosed form, "Bleeding" epitomizes vast quantities of
writing by and about women, from the masochist thrills of *The Story of O*
and its ilk, to the sexual-political anguish of Marge Piercy or Robin Morgan,
as well as the large and dreary intermediate terrain of poems and novels
about crude and boorish male lovers. Yet—a most important further value—
it makes no explicit mention of sex or of sexual roles. It does not exclude
the possibility that men may be "cuts" (indeed, it recalls Shylock's moving
"If you cut me, do I not bleed" and his cringing masochistic role through-
out *The Merchant of Venice*) and that women may be "knives." Not persons
or personalities, but a universal form of sickness has been explored here, has
been stated as pattern, as coolly rendered as if the subject were the relation
between a microbe and its host.

At an opposite extreme from this sort of pattern-finding, a poem called
"Feel Me" takes a single induplicable event in the poet's life and focuses
on its most unique or "accidental" element. The mystery is the meaning of
a father's deathbed words:

"Feel   me to do right," our father said
on his   death bed. We did not quite
know—   in fact, not at all—what he meant.
  His last   whisper was spent as through a slot in a wall.
He left us   a key, but how did it
  fit? "Feel   me
            to do   right." Did it mean

that, though he   died, he would be felt
    through some   aperture, or by some unseen instrument
our dad just then   had come
        to know? So,   to do right always, we need but feel his
            spirit? Or   was it merely
        his apology for   dying? "Feel that I
        do right in not   trying, as you insist, to stay

            on your   side. There is the wide
        gateway and the   splendid tower,
    and you implore me to wait   here, with the worms!"
            Had he defined his   terms, and could we discriminate
            among his motives,   we might
        have found out how to "do   right" before *we* died— supposing
                he felt he   suddenly knew

            what dying   was.
            "You do wrong   because you do not feel
    as I do now" was maybe the sense.   "Feel me, and emulate
            my state, for I am   becoming less dense—
            I am feeling right, for   the first
        time." And then the vessel burst, and   we were kneeling
                around an   emptiness.

                We cannot   feel our
            father now. His power   courses through us, yes, but *he*—
                the chest and cheek,   the foot and palm,
                the mouth of oracle—   is calm. And we still seek
                    his meaning.   *"Feel* me," he said,
                and emphasized that   word.
                Should we have heard   it as a plea

for a caress—   A constant caress,
since flesh to flesh was all   that we could do right
if we would bless him? The   dying must feel
the pressure   of that
question— lying flat,   turning cold
from brow to heel—   the hot
cowards there   above

protesting their love,   and saying
"What can we do?   Are you all
right?" While   the wall opens
and the blue night pours   through. "What
can we do? We want to do what's   right."
"Lie down with me, and hold me, tight. Touch   me. Be
with me. Feel with me. *Feel* me,   to do right."[17]

Williams suggested, as a formula for the poetic process, "in the particular to discover the universal." This poem stands as a major enactment of that idea. It is particularly touching that the naturalist's habits of patient attention, and the scientific imperative of hypothesizing as many explanations as possible for any mystery, ready to accept each, yet fixing on none, have been applied so perfectly to the depths of the human condition.

Much of the power here, as well as the intelligence, derives from a cross-cut play of rhyming sounds and assonances, either reinforcing or counter-pointing meaning. The first stanza alone has "right" and "not quite," "said" and "bed," "all" and "wall," "key" and "me," and finally "how did it / fit?" Later come "dying" and "trying," "worms" and the deflating "terms," "sense" and "dense," "emulate" and "state," the pathos of "first" followed by "burst," "feeling" and "kneeling," "palm" and ironic "calm." In the penultimate stanza the poet repeats "caress," reinforces it with "flesh," "bless," "pressure," then creates the shocking contrast, in sound and sense, of "hot / cowards," and ends with the "all-wall" rhyme from the poem's opening, now fearsomely resonant, and the "do-blue-through" rhymes, and at last the "night," "tight," and final "right." These sound-links lace the poem into a tight unity even while its subject is the loss of unity. They also add a slight tone of levity to the dominant tone of intense attention and devotion—an intensifying device like the jokes in Ginsberg's *Howl*.

"Bleeding" and "Feel Me" have in common, technically, a white line cutting the text. This happens often in *Iconographs*, and I will not belabor the possibility that "inner space" may be available as actual substance to a woman poet. The point is that in both poems space *is* substantial. It stands in the verbal rhythm for hesitation, a gap the voice must leap in every line. It slows the tempo, enforces stillness, makes room for meditation. Visually it "means" separation, as if, between the knife and the cut, between the living and the dying, between experience and the ability to comprehend experience, falls this white shadow. Emotionally, the space expresses that sadness, appropriately wordless, which we feel in the face of all disunity we wish to heal but—so far, so ill—recognize we cannot.

In Swenson's more typical vein of natural observation and wonderment, but still intimately concerned with relationships and connections, here is a lovely piece about sky and sea, or about time and space:[18]

F
I
R
E
I S L A N D

The Milky Way
above, the milky
waves beside,
when the sand is night
the sea is galaxy.
The unseparate stars
mark a twining coast
with phosphorescent
surf
in the black sky's trough.
Perhaps we walk on black
star ash, and watch
the milks of light foam forward, swish and spill
while other watchers, out
walking in their white
great
swerve,
gather
our
low
spark,
our little Way
the dark
glitter
in
their
s
i
g
h
t

A trail of stars, a shoreline, the silhouette of a flying bird, the idea of reflection. Yet notice that the reflection, the symmetry, is not exact, as the poem thins out toward its close, just as a reflection in moving water can only sketchily duplicate its object, and just as our position in the galaxy makes it impossible for us to imagine "other watchers" as substantial as ourselves. The absoluteness of presence versus distance, which is in Einsteinian rather than Newtonian physics, has entered this poem's form. "Fire Island" also illustrates the fact that the shapes in *Iconographs* are commonly agreeable to look at, but never because of a mechanical symmetry. Order shapes these poems, but so do pinches of disorder and randomness. If one margin of a poem forms a straight line or a simple curve, another is ragged. If sentences are simple, line-breaks cut their syntax unexpectedly. Where rhyme occurs it does so irregularly, or if the rhyme and meter are regular, then the pattern imposed breaks up and disguises them. In other words, Swenson has taken care to make her poems by the same principles—mixing Law and Chance—which we believe nature itself employs to make all of its objects, from DNA molecules to clusters of galaxies.

The second half of *Iconographs*, located as the poet has become located on Long Island, contains eleven poems taking place around water, some describing scenes, some exploring the action of water on objects—a boat stave, a bottle, a stick. "How Everything Happens" states a rule for water, and more.[19] "To generalize is to be an idiot," says William Blake. To generalize about "everything" takes some temerity. Still, the sight of this extraordinary poem may persuade us first that it offers an authentic picture of the activity of waves, and then that this interdependence of impulses, "to happen" and "not to happen," with the quiescence and stasis between, defines organic as well as inorganic motion—defines the growth of plants, animals, humans, the flux of human creativity (Swenson has said this poem happened after a period of writer's block), the surges and withdrawals of anyone's emotional and intellectual life. Even the motions of history: revolution, counterrevolution, revolution.

Visually exciting where it depicts the strong positive and negative forces, visually dull (though the dynamic of the whole depends on that dull still-point) where it depicts stasis, the poem seems to flash our desires on its screen like an X-ray. Situated in a little historical trough, as we Americans at present are, perhaps melancholy about our incapacity to "stack up" to anything, we may find this a heartening and promising poem. For once, a credible upbeat ending!

HOW EVERYTHING HAPPENS (Based on a Study of the Wave)

                                     happen.

                              to

                          up

                    stacking

                is

            something

When nothing is happening

When it happens
          something

             pulls

                back

                  not

                    to

                      happen.

When   has happened.
    pulling back   stacking up
       happens

     has happened   stacks up.
When it   something   nothing
                pulls back while

Then nothing is happening.
                  happens.

              and

           forward

        pushes

      up

    stacks

  something

Then

Form in the history of poetry always comes back, more or less consciously, to an imitation of form in the natural world, prior to all art, which all art celebrates. One final point, then, about the method of *Iconographs*. If all poetry approaches metaphor insofar as it creates verbal equivalents for nonverbal experience, then consciously shaped poetry is a sort of P^2—poetry raised by one power. First the experience or perception, then the text necessary to state the experience and all its implications truly, then a visual shape related to both. Swenson distinguishes her method of composition from that of concrete poetry by insisting that the text of each poem comes first and can be considered complete and self-sufficient before the shapes are found. Shape then becomes a metaphor, enriching language as language enriches experience. But where concrete poems typically, and deliberately, have no interest separable from the visual, the technique in *Iconographs* maintains distinctions. Perhaps we should call it an art of simile rather than metaphor. Word and picture do not fuse, any more than the sensations experienced through our eye and ear can ever become one sensation, or any more than the external world we behold and the internal world which beholds it can ever become one. Connection exists instead of identity, tantalizing and delighting.

15.

Gwendolyn the Terrible:
Propositions on Eleven Poems

Hortense J. Spillers

For over three decades now, Gwendolyn Brooks has been writing poetry which reflects a particular historical order, often close to the heart of the public event, but the dialectic that is engendered between the event and her reception of it is, perhaps, one of the more subtle confrontations of criticism. We cannot always say with grace or ease that there is a direct correspondence between the issues of her poetry and her race and sex, nor does she make the assertion necessary at every step of our reading. Black and female are basic and inherent in her poetry. The critical question is *how* they are said. Here is what the poet has to say about her own work:

> My aim, in my next future, is to write poems that will somehow successfully "call" all black people: black people in taverns, black people in alleys, black people in gutters, schools, offices, factories, prisons, the consulate; I wish to reach black people in mines, on farms, on thrones; *not* always to "teach"—I shall wish often to entertain, to illumine [Emphasis Brooks]. My newish voice will not be an imitation of the contemporary young black voice, which I so admire, but an extending adaptation of today's G.B. voice.[1]

Today's G.B. voice is one of the most complex on the American scene precisely because Brooks refuses to make easy judgments. In fact, her disposition to preserve judgment is directly mirrored in a poetry of cunning, laconic surprise. Any descriptive catalog can be stretched and strained in her case: I have tried "uncluttered," "clean," "robust," "ingenious," "unorthodox," and in each case a handful of poems will fit. This method of grading and cataloguing, however, is essentially busywork, and we are still left with the main business: What in this poetry is stunning and evasive?

To begin with, one of Brooks's most faithfully anthologized poems, "We Real Cool," illustrates the wealth of implication that the poet can achieve in a very spare poem:

> We real cool. We
> Left school. We
> Lurk late. We
> Strike straight. We
> Sing sin. We
> Thin gin. We
> Jazz june. We
> Die soon.[2]

The simplicity of the poem is stark to the point of elaborateness. Less than lean, it is virtually coded. Made up entirely of monosyllables and end-stops, the poem is no non-sense at all. Gathered in eight units of three-beat lines, it does not necessarily invite inflection, but its persistent bump on "we" suggests waltz time to my ear. If the reader chooses to render the poem that way, she runs out of breath, or trips her tongue, but it seems that such "breathlessness" is exactly required of dudes hastening toward their death. Deliberately subverting the romance of sociological pathos, Brooks presents the pool players —"seven in the golden shovel"—in their own words and time. They make no excuse for themselves and apparently invite no one else to do so. The poem is their situation as *they* see it. In eight (could be nonstop) lines, here is their total destiny. Perhaps comic geniuses, they could well drink to this poem, making it a drinking/revelry song.[3]

Brooks's poetry, then, is not weighed down by egoistic debris, nor is her world one of private symbolisms alone, or even foremost; rather, she presents a range of temperaments and situations articulated by three narrative voices: a first-person voice, as in "Gay Chaps at the Bar."

> We knew how to order. Just the dash
> Necessary. The length of gaiety in good taste.
> Whether the raillery should be slightly iced
> And given green, or served up hot and lush.
> And we knew beautifully how to give to women
> The summer spread, the tropics of our love.
> When to persist, or hold a hunger off.
> Knew white speech. How to make a look an omen. . . .
>   (*WGB*, p. 48)

an omniscient narrator for the ballads:

> It was Mabbie without the grammar school gates
> And Mabbie was all of seven
> And Mabbie was cut from a chocolate bar
> And Mabbie thought life was heaven....
>
> (*WGB*, p. 14)

And then a concealed narrator, looking at the situation through a double focus. In other words, the narrator ironically translates her subject's ingenuousness. To this last group of poems belongs "The Anniad," perhaps one of the liveliest demonstrations of the uses to which irony can be put.

A pun on *The Aeneid* or *The Iliad*, the title of this piece prepares us for a mock heroic journey of a particular female soul as she attempts to gain self-knowledge against an unresponsive social backdrop. At the same time, the poem's ironic point of view is a weapon wielded by a concealed narrator who mocks the ritualistic attitudes of love's ceremony. The poem is initially interesting for its wit and ingenuity, but eventually G.B.'s dazzling acrobatics force a "shock of recognition." Annie, in her lofty naiveté, has been her own undoing, transforming mundane love into mystical love, insisting on knights when there are, truly, only men in this world. Annie obviously misses the point, and what we confront in her tale is a riot of humor—her dreams working against reality as it is. We protest in Annie's behalf. We want the dream to come true, but Brooks does not concede, and that she does not confirms the intent of the poem: a parodic portrayal of sexual pursuit and disaster.

Shaped by various elements of surprise, "The Anniad" is a funny poem, but its comedy proceeds from self-recognition. Brooks gives this explanation:

> Well, the girl's name was Annie, and it was my pompous pleasure to raise her to a height that she probably did not have. I thought of *The Iliad* and said: 'I'll call this "The Anniad."' At first, interestingly enough, I called her Hester Allen, and I wanted then to say "The Hesteriad," but I forgot why I changed it to Annie . . . I was fascinated by what words might do there in the poem. You can tell that it's labored, a poem that's very interested in the mysteries and magic of technique. . . .[4]

From the 1949 Pulitzer Prize winning volume, *Annie Allen*, "The Anniad" may be read as a workshop in G.B.'s poetry. Its strategies are echoed in certain shorter poems from *A Street in Bronzeville* and *The Bean-Eaters*, particularly the effective use of slurred rime and jarring locution in "Patent Leather" and "The Sundays of Satin-Legs Smith." In narrative scope and dramatic ambition, "The Anniad" anticipates *In the Mecca*, written some twenty years later.

Forty-three stanzas long, "The Anniad" is built on contradictions. Locating their "answer" or meaning constitutes the poem's puzzle and reward. Here are the two opening stanzas:

> Think of sweet and chocolate,
> Left to folly or to fate.
> Whom the higher gods forgot
> Whom the lower gods berate;
> Fancying on the featherbed
> What was never and is not.
>
> What is ever and is not.
> Pretty tatters blue and red,
> Buxom berries beyond rot,
> Western clouds and quarter stars,
> Fairy sweet of old guitars
> Littering the little head
> Light upon the featherbed. . . .
>
> (*WGB*, p. 83)

After saying all we can about the formal qualities of these stanzas, we are still not certain about the subject of the poem. By means of slurs and puzzles of language, the action is hustled on, and circumlocution—"tell all the truth, but tell it slant"—becames a decisive aspect of the work's style. This Song of Ann is a puzzle to be unraveled, and the catalog of physical and mental traits deployed in the first fifteen stanzas becomes a set of clues. Not unlike games or riddles played by children, the poem gathers its clues in stanzas, and just as the questioner in the child's game withholds the solution, the speaker here does the same thing, often to the reader's dismay. However, once we know the answer, the game becomes a ritual where feigned puzzlement is part of the ceremony. In a discussion of Emily Dickinson's poetry, Northrop Frye points out that the "riddle or oblique description of some object" is one of the oldest and most primitive forms of poetry.[5] In "The Anniad" the form gains a level of sophistication that is altogether stunning.

The dilemma of Annie is also that of "Chocolate Mabbie": the black-skinned female's rejection by black males. The lesson begins early for the black woman, as it does for young Mabbie. A too well-known theme of black life, this idea is the subject of several G.B. poems, but usually disguised to blunt its edge of madness and pain. With Mabbie's experience in mind, then, we are prepared for the opening lines of "The Anniad" and their peculiar mode of indirection.

The color theme is a crucial aspect of the poem's proposition and procedure, posing light skin and dark skin as antagonists. The question is not merely cosmetic, since hot combs and bleaching creams were once thought to be wonder workers, but it penetrates far and sharp into the psychic and spiritual reaches of the black woman's soul. I know of no modern poet before Brooks to address this subject, and as she does so, she offers the female a way out not only by awaking the phobia, but also by regarding it as yet another style of absurdity. The point is to bury inverted racism in ridicule and obscure reference, but not before contemplating its effects.

In "The Ballad of Chocolate Mabbie," the situation goes this way:

> Out came the saucily bold Willie Boone.
> It was woe for our Mabbie now.
> He wore like a jewel a lemon-hued lynx
> With sandwaves loving her brow.
>
> It was Mabbie alone by the grammar-school gates.
> Yet chocolate companions had she:
> Mabbie on Mabbie with hush in the heart.
> Mabbie on Mabbie to be.
>
> (*WGB*, p. 14)

An interesting contrast to Mabbie's ballad is "Stand Off, Daughter of the Dusk":

> And do not wince when bronzy lads
> Hurry to cream-yellow shining.
> It is plausible. The sun is a lode.
>
> True, there is silver under
> The veils of the darkness
> But few care to dig in the night
> For the possible treasure of stars.
>
> (*WGB*, p. 121)

If metaphor is a way to utter the unutterable, then "cream-yellow shining" and "veils of darkness" hint at It, but both are needlessly quaint, drawing attention away from the subject. Not one of her best or most interesting poems, it does articulate the notion of rejection without preaching a sermon about it. In "The Anniad," by contrast, the mood is sardonic and words are ablaze with a passion to kill, both the situation and one's tendency to be undone by it.

The male lover's ultimate choice to betray "sweet and chocolate" leads Annie's "tan man" to what he would consider the better stuff:

> . . . Gets a maple banshee. Gets
> A sleek-eyed gypsy moan.
> Oh those violent vinaigrettes!
> Oh bad honey that can hone
> Oilily the bluntest stone!
> Oh mad bacchanalian lass
> That his random passion has!
> (*WGB*, p. 88)

Clever synecdoche works here for the poet rather than against her, as it does in "Stand Off," and its comic distortions are reinforced by slant rhyme in the last two lines of the stanza. "Bad" honey is the best kind in colloquial parlance, "bad" having appropriated its antonym, and in the midst of "vinaigrettes" and "bacchanalian lasses," it is a sharp surprise.

"Tan man" himself gets similar treatment:

> . . . And a man of tan engages
> For the springtime of her pride,
> Eats the green by easy stages,
> Nibbles at the root beneath
> With intimidating teeth
> But no ravishment enrages.
> No dominion is defied.
>
> Narrow-master master calls;
> And the godhead glitters now
> Cavalierly on his brow.
> What a hot theopathy
> Roisters through her, gnaws her walls,
> And consumes her where she falls
> In her gilt humility.
>
> How he postures at his height;
> Unfamiliar, to be sure,
> With celestial furniture.
> Contemplating by cloud-light
> His bejewelled diadem;
> As for jewels, counting them,
> Trying if the pomp be pure. . . .
> (*WGB*, pp. 84–85)

Rodent, knight, god, by turn, "Tan man" is seen from a triple exposure: his own exaggerated sense of self-worth, the woman's complicity with it, and the poet's assessment, elaborated in the imaginative terms implied by the woman's behavior. Given the poem's logic, the woman and the man are deluded on opposing ends of the axis of self-delusion. As it turns out, he is not the hot lover "theopathy" would make him out to be, but Annie denies it, fearing that to say so would be to evoke an already imminent betrayal:

> . . . Doomer, though, crescendo-comes
> Prophesying hecatombs.
> Surrealist and cynical.
> Garrulous and guttural.
> Spits upon the silver leaves
> Denigrates the dainty eves
> Dear dexterity achieves . . .
>
> Vaunting hands are now devoid
> Hieroglyphics of her eyes
> Blink upon a paradise
> Paralyzed and paranoid.
> But idea and body too
> Clamor "Skirmishes can do.
> Then he will come back to you."
> (*WGB*, pp. 85–86)

This scene of "ruin," brought on by sexual impotence, gains a dimension of pathos because it anticipates the woman's ultimate loneliness, but this judgment is undercut by the caricature of the male.

In order to fully appreciate the very pronounced contrast between other G.B. poems and this one, we should note the quality of images in "The Anniad." The dominant function of imagery here is auditory rather than visual, because Brooks, as well as the reader, is so thoroughly fascinated with the sound of words: for example, "Doomer, though, crescendo-comes / Prophesying hecatombs." This heavy word-motion is sustained by the most unlikely combinations—"surrealist and cynical," "garrulous and guttural," etc. The combinations are designed to strike with such forceful contrariness that trying to visualize them would propel us toward astigmatism. We confront a situation where the simple image has been replaced by its terministic equivalent, or by words which describe other words in the poem.[6]

Brooks's intensely cultivated language in "The Anniad" appears to rely heavily on the cross-reference of dictionaries and thesauri. *Lexis* here is dazzling to the point of distraction, but it is probably a feature of the poem's moral ferocity. It is clear that the poet, like others, has her eye on the peculiar neurosis that often prevails in sexual relationships. Rather than dignify it, she mocks its vaunted importance, exaggerating its claims nearly beyond endurance. In effect, exaggeration destroys its force, desanctifying hyperbolean phallic status. At the same time, it appears that a secondary motivation shadows the primary one—the poet's desire to suggest a strategy for destroying motives of inferiority in the self. This psychological motif in Brooks's early poetry is disturbing. At times it appears to verge on self-hatred, but style conceals it. "Men of Careful Turns" (XV, *Annie Allen*; *WGB*, p. 123) offers an example, I think, by depicting an interracial love affair corrupted by racism and certain intervening class loyalties. To conceal her disappointment, the black female narrator claims moral superiority over the white male, but in this case, as in "The Anniad," the literal situation is carefully disguised.

In the hands of a lesser poet Brooks's pyrotechnics would likely be disastrous, but G.B. achieves her aim by calibrating the narrative situation of the poem to its counterpart in the "real" world. Grounded in solidly social and human content, the poem is saved from sliding off into mere strangeness. The mischievous, brilliantly ridiculous juxtapositions achieve a perspective, and we gain thereby a taste for, rather than a surfeit of, exaggeration toward a specific end: to expose the sadness and comedy of self-delusion in an equally deluded world.

By contrast, a poem whose principle of composition is based on continuity of diction is another of the sonnets, "Still Do I Keep My Look, My Identity." A model of precision, the poem reworks a single sentence to elaborate its message:

> Each body has its art, its precious prescribed
> Pose, that even in passion's droll contortions, waltzes,
> Or push of pain— is its, and nothing else's.
> Each body has its pose. No other stock
> That is irrevocable, perpetual
> And its to keep. In castle, or in shack.
> With rags or robes. Through good, nothing, or ill.
> And even in death, a body, like no other
> On any hill or plain or crawling cot
> Or gentle for the lilyless hasty pall
> (Having twisted, gagged, and then sweet-ceased to
>   bother),
> Shows the old personal art, the look. Shows what
> It showed at baseball. What it showed in school.
>
> <div align="right">(<i>WGB</i>, p. 49)</div>

This concentration on a single notion is essential to the working out of the poem, and the qualifying phrases, which establish momentum, create the effect of the poem's being made in front of us. The careful structuring of the body's lines, imitated in time and space, is inherently strategic.

In its directness of presentation, "Still Do I Keep My Look" (like "Gay Chaps at the Bar") may be relegated to the category of what might be called G.B.'s "pretty" poems: the sword has been blunted by a closer concession to the expected. An excerpt from "The Old Marrieds" provides another example:

> But in the crowding darkness not a word did they say
> Though the pretty-coated birds had piped so lightly all
>   the day.
> And he had seen the lovers in the little side streets.
> And she had heard the morning stories clogged with sweets. . . .
>
> (WGB, p. 3)

The opening poem of *A Street in Bronzeville*, "The Old Marrieds" belongs to G.B.'s early career. Its tender insistence is matched elsewhere: for instance, "In Honor of David Anderson Brooks, My Father" and "The Bean-Eaters," both from the volume *The Bean-Eaters*. An aspect of the poet's reality, this compassionate response to the lives of old people has its complement in her version of the heroic. Two poems from *After the Mecca*, "Medgar Evers" and "Malcolm X," are celebratory:

> The man whose height his fear improved he
> arranged to fear no further. The raw
> intoxicated time was time for better birth or
> a final death.
>
> Old styles, old tempos, all the engagement of
> the day— the sedate, the regulated fray—
> the antique light, the Moral Rose, old gusts,
> tight whistlings from the past, the mothballs
> in the love at last our man forswore.
>
> Medgar Evers annoyed confetti and assorted
> brands of businessmen's eyes.
>
> The shows came down: to maxims and surprise
> and palsy.
>
> Roaring no rapt arise-ye to the dead, he
> leaned across tomorrow. People said that
> he was holding clean globes in his hands.
>
> (WGB, p. 410)

A poem for the slain civil-rights leader of Mississippi, "Medgar Evers" reconciles celebration and surprise. G.B. has not exaggerated a feature of

reality—Evers' heroism—but has invested that reality with unique signif-
icance. A similar notion works for "Malcolm X," with a touch of the
whimsical added:

> Original
> Ragged-round.
> Rich-robust.
> He had the hawk-man's eyes.
> We gasped. We saw the maleness.
> The maleness raking out and making guttural the air
> And pushing us to walls.
>
> And in a soft and fundamental hour
> A sorcery devout and vertical
> beguiled the world.
>
> He opened us—
> who was a key,
>
> who was a man.
>
> (WGB, p. 411)

In these two poems, as well as others from the later volumes, Brooks ex-
plores various kinds of heroism by means of a shrewd opposition of under-
statement and exaggeration. From *The Bean-Eaters*, "Strong Men Riding
Horses" provides a final example:

> Strong men riding horses. In the West
> On a range five hundred miles. A thousand. Reaching
> From dawn to sunset.
> Rested blue to orange.
> From hope to crying. Except that strong men are
> Desert-eyed. Except that strong men are
> Pasted to cars already. Have their cars
> Beneath them. Rentless too. Too broad of chest
> To shrink when the Rough man hails
> Too flailing
> To redirect the challenger, when the Challenge
> Nicks; slams; buttonholes. Too saddled.
>
> I am not like that. I pay rent, am addled
> By illegible landlords, run, if robbers call.

What mannerisms I present, employ,
Are camouflage, and what my mouths remark
To word-wall off the broadness of the dark
Is pitiful.
I am not brave at all.

(*WGB*, p. 313)

This brilliant use of familiar symbols recalls the staccato message of movie advertisements. It conjures up heroes of the Western courtly love tradition from Charlemagne to Gawain to John Wayne and Superman. Counterpoised against this implied pantheon of superstars is a simple shrunken confessional, the only complete declaratives in the poem. That the speaker pits herself against the contrived heroes of a public imagination suggests that the comparison is not to be taken seriously. It is sham exactly because of the disparity between public idealism and the private condition, but the comic play-off between the poet's open, self-mocking language (a pose of humility) and the glittering, delirious "dig-me-brag" of the "strong men" is the demonstration, more precisely, of the opposing poles of reality—exaggeration and understatement. In the world of Gwendolyn Brooks, the sword is double-edged, constantly turning.

Only a fraction of the canon, the poems discussed in this essay represent the poet's range of strategies and demonstrate her linguistic vitality and her ability to allow language to penetrate to the core of neutral events. The titles of Brook's volumes, from *A Street in Bronzeville* to *In the Mecca*, suggest her commitment to life in its unextraordinary aspects. Reworking items of common life, Brooks reminds us that creative experience can be mined from this vast store of unshaped material. To see reality through the eyes of the clichéd or the expected, however, is not to revisit it but to hasten the advance of snobbery and exclusion. In her insistence that common life is not as common as we sometimes suspect, G.B. is probably the democratic poet of our time. That she neither condescends nor insists on preciousness is rewarding, but, above all, her detachment from poetry as cult and cant gives her access to lived experience, which always invigorates her lines. By displacing the familiar with the unfamiliar word, Brooks employs a vocabulary that redefines what we know already in a way we have not known it before. The heightened awareness that results brings to our consciousness an interpenetration of events which lends them a new significance.

Some of Brooks's poems speak directly to situations for which black women need names, but this specificity may be broadened to define situations that speak for other women as well. The magic of irony and humor can be brought to bear by any female in her most dangerous life-encounter—the sexual/emotional entanglement. Against that entanglement, her rage and disappointment are poised, but often impotently, unless channeled by positive force. For women writers, decorum, irony, and style itself are often mobilized against chaos. Thus, women don't cry in Brooks's poetry nor does she cry over them, but the poet is remarkably alive and questioning in the dialectical relationship she poses between feeling and thinking. Hers is a tough choice of weapons because it has little use for the traditional status of woman—connubial, man-obsessed. The style of Brooks's poetry, then, gives us by implication and example a model of power, control, and subtlety. No idealogue, Brooks does not have to be. Enough woman and poet, she merges both realities into a single achievement. Comedy and pathos, compassion and criticism are not estranged integers in this poetry, but a tangled skein of feeling, both vital and abstract, imposed on a particular historical order. With a taste for the city and an ear for change, Gwendolyn Brooks restores the tradition of citizen–poet.

16.

A Fine, White Flying Myth:
The Life/Work of Sylvia Plath

Sandra M. Gilbert

Though I never met Sylvia Plath, I can honestly say that I have known her most of my life. To begin with, when I was twelve or thirteen I read an extraordinary story of hers in the "By Our Readers" columns of *Seventeen*. It was called "Den of Lions," and though the plot was fairly conventional, something about the piece affected me in inexplicable, almost "mythic" ways —ways in which I wouldn't have thought I could be affected by a *Seventeen*-reader's story. For one thing, I was faintly sickened by the narrator's oddly intense vision of her experience, an evening spent at a bar with a suave young man and some of his friends. "Is that a real flower, Marcia?" asks one of the men in the story, "with [an] oily smile.... He had her cornered," thinks Marcia, the protagonist. "No matter what she thought to say, it would be meat for the sacrifice. 'Yes,' she said ... 'It's real, it's basic.' ... Basic. The word had been what they wanted. *Toss a slab of raw meat to the lions.* Let them nose it, paw it, gulp it down, and maybe you'll have a chance to climb a tree out of their reach in the meantime."[1]

Could the world really be like this, I wondered. *Was* it like this? How had selves of blood and meat been admitted into the glossily sanitized pages of *Seventeen*? How could anyone so close to my own age have imagined such selves? "Sylvia enjoys being seventeen—'it's the *best* age'" was an editorial comment I found next to another of her contributions. But did she?

Plath next surfaced, of course, as a guest editor of *Mademoiselle* and as winner of that magazine's College Fiction contest—the literary young wom-an's equivalent of being crowned Miss America. And when I myself became a guest editor, four years after she did, I found myself assigned to the same staff editor she had worked for. Now our likenesses, our common problems, as well as our divergences, began to clarify. What I had unconsciously responded to in "Den of Lions," what had made me uneasy about it, was probably that it was a story of female initiation, an account of how one girl learns to see herself as intelligent meat—victim and manipulator of men, costumes, drinks, cigarettes—flesh and artifice together. But what I much more consciously knew about the *Mademoiselle* experience was that for me, as for Sylvia and all the other guest editors, it was a kind of initiation ritual, a dramatic induction into that glittery Women's House of fashion and domesticity outside whose windows most of us had spent much of our lives, noses pressed to the glass, yearning to get in, like—to echo Yeats—Keats outside the candy shop of the world.

As *The Bell Jar* suggests, we guest editors were on the whole nice, ambitious young women from colleges all over the country. Some of us were interested in fashion, art, and design. But most had won the contest by writing stories or poems or think-pieces about our "Silent Generation," intellectual work that might in other circumstances produce a place on the Dean's List or a Phi Beta Kappa key—an entrance into the spacious male world of work. Instead, because all of us were ambivalent about ourselves, cashmere sweater collectors as well as collectors of good grades, we had entered the house of female work, a house, despite all our earlier peering through windows, astonishingly different from what we'd expected.

The magazine offices were pastel, intricately feminine, full of clicking spikey heels. One could almost believe that at midnight they mopped the floors with Chanel #5. And almost all the editors and secretaries and assistant editors were "career gals," who, as soon as we arrived, began giving us tokens of what we were and where we were, tokens quite unlike those we had become accustomed to at school. Instead of tests or books or grades, for instance, they gave us *clothes*. We sat around in a room that looked like a seminar room, and they wheeled in great racks of college-girl blouses and skirts. Into these we had to fit ourselves, like Cinderella squeezing into the glass slipper. Woe unto you if the blouse doesn't fit, was the message. If the skirt doesn't fit, wear it anyway—at least for the photographer. Later they gave us new hairdos; makeup cases, as in *The Bell Jar*; sheets and bedspreads; dances on starlit rooftops; and more, much more. On those long, hot June afternoons we sat around in our pastel, air-conditioned seminar room discussing these objects and events as if they were newly discovered Platonic dialogues.

For of course the whole experience of *Mademoiselle* was curiously metaphorical: events occurred, as in a witty fiction, that seemed always to have a meaning beyond themselves. The poisoning in Plath's year, for example, really happened. Yet that doesn't diminish its symbolic significance in *The Bell Jar*. The fashionable menus of Madison Avenue (*Mad* Ave for short) were figuratively as well as literally indigestible. And naturally such unexpected tokens of femininity took their toll among the guest editors. Some couldn't bear to go near the "official" residential hotel (which for good reason Plath calls the Amazon). Others became *hysterical*, portentous word, at work or after work. Esther Greenwood, perhaps like Plath herself, throws away her New York clothes, no doubt including all the free "collegiate" outfits.

To complicate things further, for me and for Plath, there was the woman Plath calls Jay Cee, the editor with whom we worked every day. Jay Cee was the only woman at the magazine who was not a stereotypical "career gal." Instead, she was a serious, unfashionable, professional woman. But in those ruffly, stylish corridors she seemed somehow desexed, disturbing, like a warning of what might happen to you if you threw away the clothes and entered the nunnery of art. And, like the bald "Disquieting Muses" in an early poem of Plath's, the "dismal-headed / Godmothers" who "stand their vigil in gowns of stone" (*The Colossus*, pp. 59–60), she constantly forced us to confront ourselves and, additionally, the abyss into which we seemed to be falling. "What are you going to do next?" she would ask. "What are your plans for the future? Have you attempted to publish? Have you thought about a career?" She was efficient; she was kind; she was perfect; yet she seemed, in some mysterious way, terrible.

The next I heard of Sylvia Plath was in the early sixties. She was publishing careful, elegantly crafted poems in places like *The Atlantic* and *The New Yorker*, poems that bore out Robert Lowell's later remarks about her "checks and courtesies," her "maddening docility."[2] Then one day a friend who worked at *The New Yorker* called to say "Imagine, Sylvia Plath is dead." And three days later "Poppies in July," "Edge," "Contusion," and "Kindness" appeared in *TLS*. Astonishingly undocile poems. Poems of despair and death. Poems with their heads in ovens (although the rumor was at first that Plath had died of the flu or pneumonia). Finally the violence seeped in, as if leaking from the poems into the life, or, rather, the death. She had been killed, had killed herself, had murdered her children, a modern Medea. And at last it was really told, the story everyone knows already, and the outlines of history began to thicken to myth. All of us who had read her traced our own journey in hers: from the flashy Women's House of *Mademoiselle* to the dull oven of Madame, from college to villanelles to babies to the scary skeletons of poems we began to study, now, as if they were sacred writ. The

Plath Myth, whatever it meant or means, had been launched like a queen bee on its dangerous flight through everybody's psyche.

The Plath Myth: is there anything legitimate about such a phrase? Is there really, in other words, an identifiable set of forces which nudge the lives and works of women like Plath into certain apparently mythical (or "archetypal") patterns? In answer, and in justification both of my imagery and of my use of personal material that might otherwise seem irrelevant, I want to suggest that the whole story I have told so far conforms in its outlines to a mythological way of structuring female experience that has been useful to many women writers since the nineteenth century. In Plath's case the shape of the myth is discernible both in her work and in the life that necessitated that work. In addition, the ways in which as woman and as writer she diverges from the common pattern are as interesting as those ways in which she conforms to it; perhaps, indeed, they will prove more valuable for women writers in the future.

The poet Robert Bly has recently been writing and speaking about the connection between the female psyche and what I am calling the mythological mode. He argues, for instance, that the fairy tale was distinctively a female form, a womanly way of coming to terms with reality, the old matriarchy's disguised but powerful resistance against the encroachments of the patriarchy. While I don't intend, here, to explore all the implications of this assertion, it is obviously related to what I am saying. Women writers, especially when they're writing *as women*, have tended to rely on plots and patterns that suggest the obsessive patterns of myths and fairy tales. For instance, what Ellen Moers has called "Female Gothic" is a characteristically mythological genre: it draws heavily upon unconscious imagery, apparently archetypal events, fairy-tale plots, and so forth.[3] And, to use Frank Kermode's distinction between myth and fiction, it implies not an "as if" way of seeing the world but a deep faith in its own structures, structures which, to refer briefly to Lévi-Strauss' theory of myth, offer psychic solutions to serious social, economic, and sexual-emotional problems. (Male writers, especially since the Romantic period, have also of course worked in this mode, but not with such evident single-mindedness. And male "confessional" poets, like Lowell and Berryman, seem quite able to organize their experience into serious metaphors without it.)

An important question then arises: *why* do so many women writers characteristically work the mythological vein? Some critics might account for the phenomenon—following Bachofen, Neumann, and others—with what I regard as a rather sentimental and certainly stereotypical explanation. The dark, intuitive, Molly Bloomish female unconscious, they would say, just naturally generates images of archetypal power and intensity.

But it seems to me that a simpler, more sensible explanation might also be possible. Women as a rule, even sophisticated women writers, haven't until quite recently been brought to think of themselves as conscious subjects in the world. Deprived of education, votes, jobs, and property rights, they have also, even more significantly, been deprived of their own selfhood. "What shall I do to gratify myself—to be admired—or to vary the tenor of my existence? are not the questions which a woman of right feelings asks on first awaking to the avocations of the day," Mrs. Sara Ellis admonished the Women of England in 1844.[4] Instead, that energetic duenna of Victorian girls, the Ann Landers of her age, formulated an ideal of ladylike unselfishness—or, better, *selflessness.* "Woman . . . is but a meager item in the catalogue of humanity," she reminded her readers, unless she forgets her "minute disquietudes, her weakness, her sensibility"—in short, unless she forgets her self.[5] So many important men (like Rousseau, Ruskin, and Freud) also expressed this idea that it is no wonder women haven't been able to admit the complex problem of their own subjectivity—either to themselves or others. Rather, they have disguised the stories of their own psychic growth, even from themselves, in a multitude of extravagant, apparently irrelevant forms and images.

For instance, when Charlotte Brontë undertook to write what is essentially a *Bildungsroman,* the story of one young woman's development to maturity, she couldn't write the serious, straightforward, neo-Miltonic account of the "growth of a poet's mind" that Wordsworth produced. A female version of such a narrative would be unprecedented. She couldn't really even use the kind of domestic symbolism Joyce and Lawrence employed, though attention to domestic detail was said by George Henry Lewes to be a special feminine talent.[6] Instead, she had to sublimate, disguise, mythologize her *rite de passage,* especially in *Jane Eyre* (though also to a lesser extent in *Villette*). This was partly, no doubt, for good commercial reasons. Female Gothic sells, sells now, still, as it sold then. But the main reason, neither inherent nor commercial, was psycho-social. Though Brontë, like many other women, could not think her own inner growth important enough to describe in naturalistic detail, the story itself is of course important: it is *her*story and forces its way out despite the "checks and courtesies" that have folded themselves around her mind, forces its way out in a more conventionally "interesting" and "acceptable" disguise. Thus, in Jane Austen's novels the *dramatis personae* of drawing-room comedy apparently replace the Wordsworthian egotistical sublime, while in the works of Mary Shelley and the Brontës the most intimate conflicts of the self with the self, consciously inadmissible, are objectified in exotic psychodramas—the self splitting, doubling, mythologizing itself until it hardly seems any longer to have an existence within itself. Finally, with Emily Dickinson, dressed in white, addressing unread riddles to the world; or Virginia Woolf, laden with stones, merging with the waters of that dull canal the river Ouse; or Sylvia Plath, head in a mythic oven, we see the woman writer herself enacting the psychodrama in life as she had in art, becoming—as Charles Newman says of Sylvia Plath—the "myth of herself."[7]

So, I would argue, the Plath Myth began with an initiation rite described in the pages of *Seventeen*, and continued with the induction into the fashionable world of *Mademoiselle* that is examined in *The Bell Jar*, and with the publication of doggedly symmetrical poems, and the marriage in a foreign country, and the births of two babies, to the final flight of *Ariel* and the dénouement in the oven and all the rest. And it was of compelling interest to Plath's female readers because, like the stories told by Charlotte Brontë and Mary Shelley, it was figuratively if not literally the same old story. Disguised, perhaps, but the same. And our own.

But what *was* the story exactly, what were its hidden lineaments, what was its message? I can best begin to answer this multiple question with references to a few good critics of Plath's work. Her husband, the poet Ted Hughes, commented shortly after her death that "the opposition of a prickly, fastidious defence and an imminent volcano is, one way or another, an element in all her early poems."[8] And the words "prickly" and "fastidious" recall Robert Lowell's remark about "the checks and courtesies" of her "laborious shyness," her "maddening docility." George Stade, in the best single essay I know about Plath's work, relates these statements about fastidiousness and docility versus volcanic intensity to the middle-period poem "In Plaster," a piece in which the speaker complains that she has been trapped in a tidy but murderous replica of herself, a plaster cast. "I shall never get out of this!" she exclaims. "There are two of me now: / This new absolutely white person and the old yellow one." "The persona speaking out of any given poem by Sylvia Plath, then," writes Stade

> may be either sulphurous old yellow, or the plaster saint, or a consciousness that sometimes contains these two and sometimes lies stretched between them. ...The outer shell of consciousness may be completely or dimly aware of the presence within: it may feel itself a puppet jerked by strings receding into an interior distance where a familiar demon sits in possession, or it may try to locate the menace outside of itself....[9]

Plaster, the outer shell, fastidious defense, checks and courtesies, docility: all these elements clearly fit together in some way. Yet the movement of "In

Plaster," as Stade notes, is *out* of the tidiness of plaster, away from the smug perfection of the carved saint, just as the movement of, say, *The Bell Jar* is out of the stale enclosure of the bell jar into a more spacious if dangerous life. And similarly the great poems of *Ariel* often catapult their protagonist or their speaker out of a stultifying enclosure into the violent freedom of the sky. "Now she is flying," Plath writes in "Stings," perhaps the best of the bee-keeping poems,

> More terrible than she ever was, red
> Scar in the sky, red comet
> Over the engine that killed her—
> The mausoleum, the wax house.
>   (*Ariel*, p. 63)

And in the title poem of the collection, the one that describes the poet's runaway ride on the horse Ariel, she insists that "I / Am the arrow, / The dew that flies / Suicidal, at one with the drive / Into the red eye, the cauldron of morning" (*Ariel*, p. 27). In *The Bell Jar* Plath informs us that Mrs. Willard, the mother of Esther Greenwood's repellent boyfriend, Buddy, believes that "What a man is is an arrow into the future and what a woman is is the place the arrow shoots off from." But, says Esther, "the last thing I wanted was . . . to be the place an arrow shoots off from. I wanted . . . to shoot off in all directions myself, like the colored arrows from a fourth of July rocket" (*The Bell Jar*, pp. 58, 68).

Being enclosed—in plaster, in a bell jar, a cellar, or a wax house—and then being liberated from an enclosure by a maddened or suicidal or "hairy and ugly" avatar of the self is, I would contend, at the heart of the myth that we piece together from Plath's poetry, fiction, and life, just as it is at the heart of much other important writing by nineteenth- and twentieth-century women. The story told is invariably a story of being trapped, by society or by the self as an agent of society, and then somehow escaping or trying to escape.

At the beginning of *Jane Eyre*, for instance, Jane is locked into a room—the Red Room, interestingly, where Mr. Reed, the only "father" she has ever had "breathed his last": in other words, a kind of patriarchal death chamber, for in this room Mrs. Reed still keeps "divers parchments, her jewel-casket, and a miniature of her dead husband" in a secret drawer in the wardrobe. Panicky, the child stares into a "great looking glass" where her own image looms toward her, alien and disturbing. "All looked colder and darker in that visionary hollow than in reality," the grownup narrator explains.[10] But a mirror, after all, is a sort of box, in which ideas or images of the self are also stored, like "divers parchments." Mirrors, says Sylvia

Plath in a poem called "The Courage of Shutting Up," "are terrible rooms /
In which a torture goes on one can only watch" (*Winter Trees*, p. 9). So
Jane is doubly enclosed, first in the Red Room, then in the mirror. Later,
of course, it is the first Mrs. Rochester, the raging madwoman, who is closely
locked in an attic room, while Jane is apparently free to roam Thornfield at
her pleasure. Yet both Jane and the madwoman, it becomes clear, have to
escape, whether from actual or metaphorical confinement, Jane by madly
fleeing Thornfield after learning of the madwoman's existence, and the mad-
woman by burning down her prison and killing herself in the process, just as
if, curiously, she were an agent not only of her own desires but of Jane's.

Similarly, when we first encounter Sylvia Plath in the macabre contem-
porary *Bildungsroman* we might as well call *Sylvia Plath*, she is figuratively
and later even literally locked into a patriarchal death chamber. "You do not
do," she writes at the beginning of "Daddy," in perhaps her most famous
lines, "you do not do / Any more, black shoe / In which I have lived like a
foot / For thirty years, poor and white, / Barely daring to breathe or achoo."
And then, significantly, "Daddy, I have had to kill you" (*Ariel*, p. 49).

The enclosure—the confinement—began early, we learn. Though her child-
hood was free and Edenic, with the vast expanse of ocean before her (as she
tells us in the essay "Ocean 1212-W") when she was nine, "my father died,
we moved inland"—moved away from space and playfulness and possibility,
moved (if she had not already done so) into the black shoe. "Whereupon,"
she concludes, "those first nine years of my life sealed themselves off like a
ship in a bottle—beautiful, inaccessible, obsolete, a fine, white flying myth."[11]
And this is an important but slightly misleading statement, for it was she
who was sealed into the bottle, and what she longed for was the lost dream
of her own wings. Because, having moved inland, she had moved also into a
plaster cast of herself, into a mirror image alien as the image that frightens
Jane in the Red Room or the stylish mirrors of the pages of *Mademoiselle*,
into the bell jar, into the cellar where she curled like a doped fetus, into
the mausoleum, the wax house.

In this state, she wrote, "the wingy myths won't tug at us anymore," in a
poem in *The Colossus* (p. 81). And then, in poem after poem, she tried to
puzzle out the cause of her confinement. "O what has come over us, my
sister . . . What keyhole have we slipped through, what door has shut?" she
asked in "The Babysitters," a piece addressed to a contemporary (*Crossing
the Water*, p. 15). "This mizzle fits me like a sad jacket. How did we make
it up to your attic . . . Lady, what am I doing / With a lung full of dust and
a tongue of wood . . . ?" she complained in "Leaving Early," a poem writ-
ten to another woman (*Crossing*, p. 19). "Soon each white lady will be
boarded up / Against the cracking climate . . ." she wrote in "Private

Ground" (*Crossing*, p. 21). And yet again, in a poem called "Dark House," she declared "This is a dark house, very big. / . . . It has so many cellars, / Such eelish delvings . . . / I must make more maps" (*Crossing*, p. 50). For her central problem had become, as it became Jane Eyre's (or Charlotte Brontë's), how to get out. How to reactivate the myth of a flight so white, so pure, as to be a rebirth into the imagined liberty of childhood?

Both Jane and Charlotte Brontë got out, as I suggested, through the mediating madness of the woman in the attic, Jane's enraged, crazed double, who burned down the imprisoning house and with it the confining structures of the past. Mary Shelley, costumed as Frankenstein, got out by creating a monster who conveniently burned down domestic cottages and killed friends, children, the whole complex of family relationships. Emily Dickinson, who saw her life as "shaven / And fitted to a frame," got out by persuading herself that "The soul has moments of Escape— / When bursting all the doors— / She dances like a Bomb, abroad."[12] Especially in *Ariel*, but also in other works, Plath gets out by 1) killing daddy (who is, after all, indistinguishable from the house or shoe in which she has lived) and 2) flying away disguised as a queen bee (in "Stings"), a bear (in the story "The Fifty-Ninth Bear"), superman (in the story "The Wishing Box"), a train (in "Getting There" and other poems), an acetylene virgin (in "Fever 103°"), a horse (in "Ariel" and other poems), a risen corpse (in "Lady Lazarus"), an arrow (in "Ariel," *The Bell Jar*, and "The Other"), or a baby (in too many poems to mention).

Of these liberating images or doubles for the self, almost all except the metaphor of the baby are as violent and threatening as Dickinson's bomb, Shelley's monster, or Brontë's madwoman. "I think I am going up. / I think I may rise— / The beads of hot metal fly, and I, love, I / Am a pure acetylene / Virgin," Plath declares in "Fever 103°," ascending "(My selves dissolving, old whore petticoats) / —to Paradise" (*Ariel*, pp. 54–55). But not a very pleasant paradise, for this ascent is "the upflight of the murderess into a heaven that loves her," to quote from "The Bee Meeting," and rage strengthens her wings, rips her from the plaster of her old whore life (*Ariel*, p. 57). As the bridegroom, the "Lord of the mirrors," approaches, the infuriated speaker of "Purdah," trapped at his side—"the agonized / Side of green Adam" from which she was born—threatens that "at his next step / I shall unloose . . . From the small jewelled / Doll he guards like a heart . . . / The lioness, / The shriek in the bath, / The cloak of holes" (*WT*, pp. 40–42). "Herr God, Herr Lucifer, / Beware / Beware," cries Lady Lazarus. "Out of the ash I rise with my red hair / And I eat men like air." "If I've killed one man, I've killed two—" Plath confesses in "Daddy." "The villagers never liked you. / They are dancing and stamping on you" (*Ariel*, pp.

9, 51). And in "The Fifty-Ninth Bear," a tale in which a couple traveling across the western United States on vacation have bet on the number of bears they'll encounter, a great hairy ugly bear lumbers out of the wilderness— and it is the fifty-ninth bear, the wife's bear, for she has chosen the number fifty-nine. First it mauls the woman's silly sunhat, symbol of her whorish domesticity; then it violently attacks the husband, who, "*as from a rapidly receding planet,*" (ital. mine) hears his wife's wild cry, "whether of terror or triumph he could not tell."[13] But we can tell. We know Sadie, the wife, is dancing like a bomb abroad, like Emily Dickinson or like Sylvia Plath herself. We know we are witnessing "the upflight of the murderess into a heaven that loves her."

Flying, journeying, "getting there," she shrieks her triumph: "The train is dragging itself, it is screaming— / An animal / Insane for the destination / . . . The carriages rock, they are cradles. / And I, stepping from this skin / Of old bandages, boredoms, old faces / Step to you from the black car of Lethe, / Pure as a baby" (*Ariel*, pp. 37–38). *Pure as a baby*! Skiing suicidally away from "numb, brown, inconsequential" Buddy, Esther Greenwood in *The Bell Jar* plummets down "through year after year of doubleness and smiles and compromise" toward "the pebble at the bottom of the well, the white sweet baby cradled in its mother's belly" (*The Bell Jar*, p. 79). *Sweet as a baby*!

How do we reconcile this tender new avatar with the hairy bear, the ferocious virgin, the violent and dangerous Lady Lazarus? That Sylvia Plath wanted to be reborn into the liberty of her own distant childhood—wanted once more to be "running along the hot white beaches" with her father—is certainly true (*The Bell Jar*, p. 60). Yet, at the same time her father represented the leathery house from which she wished to escape. And the baby images in her poems often seem to have more to do with her own babies than with her own babyhood. In fact, critics often puzzle over the great creative release childbirth and maternity apparently triggered for Plath. That she loved her children is indisputable, but does not seem any more immediately relevant to an understanding of the self-as-escaping baby than her longing for her own childhood. Yes, the baby is a blessing, a new beginning— "You're . . . Right, like a well-done sum," says Plath to her child in the poem "You're." Indeed, for the doting mother the baby is even (as in "Nick and the Candlestick") "the one/Solid the spaces lean on, envious . . . ," analogous to the redeeming Holy Child, "the baby in the barn" (*Ariel*, pp. 52, 34). But what have these blessings to do with the monster-mother's liberation? Doesn't the baby, on the contrary, anchor her more firmly into the attic, the dark house, the barn?

The answer to this last question is, I think, *no*, though with some qualifications. In fact, for Plath the baby is often a mediating and comparatively healthy image of freedom (which is just another important reason why the Plath Myth has been of such compelling interest to women), and this is because in her view the fertile mother is a queen bee, an analog for the fertile and liberated poet, the opposite of that dead drone in the wax house who was the sterile egotistical mistress of darkness and daddy.

We can best understand this polarity by looking first at some poems that deal specifically with sterility, nullity, *perfection*. "Perfection is terrible, it cannot have children," Plath wrote in "The Munich Mannequins." "Cold as snow breath, it tamps the womb / Where the yew trees blow like hydras, / ... Unloosing their moons, month after month, to no purpose. / The blood flood is the flood of love / The absolute sacrifice. / It means: no more idols but . . . me and you" (*Ariel*, p. 73). Snow, menstrual blood, egotism, childlessness, the moon, and, later in the poem, the (significantly) *bald* mannequins themselves, like "orange lollies on silver sticks"—all together these constitute a major cluster of images which appears and reappears throughout *Ariel* and the other books. Women like the frightening godmother Jay Cee seemed to be are what they equal for me, and I'm sure what they equaled for Plath. "My head ached," says Esther Greenwood at one point in *The Bell Jar*. "Why did I attract these weird old women? There was the famous poet and Philomena Guinea and Jay Cee . . . and they all wanted to adopt me in some way, and . . . have me resemble them" (p. 180). Bald, figuratively speaking, as "the disquieting muses" of Plath's poem and Chirico's painting, these emblems of renunciation were Plath's—and perhaps every academically talented girl's—earliest "traveling companions." They counseled "A"s, docility, working for *Mademoiselle*, surrendering sexuality for "perfection," using daddy's old red-leather thesaurus to write poems, and living courteously in daddy's shoe, not like a thumbtack, irascible and piercing, but like a poor white foot, barely daring to breathe or Achoo.

But "two girls there are," wrote Plath in "Two Sisters of Persephone"; "within the house/One sits; the other, without. / Daylong a duet of shade and light / Plays between these." The girl within the house, Jay Cee's girl, "in her dark wainscotted room . . . works problems on / A mathematical machine," and "at this barren enterprise / Rat-shrewd go her squint eyes." The other girl, however, "burns open to sun's blade . . . Freely becomes sun's bride . . . Grows quick with seed" and, "Grass-couched in her labor's pride, / She bears a king" (*Crossing*, pp. 46–47). Or, we might add, a queen.

The first girl, like the "childless woman" of another poem, sees her "landscape" as "a hand with no lines," her sexuality as "a tree with nowhere to go." The second girl, on the other hand, producing a golden child, produces flight from the folds of her own body, self-transcendence, the dangerous yet triumphant otherness of poetry. For, as Simone de Beauvoir acutely observes in *The Second Sex*, the pregnant woman has the extraordinary experience of being both subject and object at the same time. Even while she is absorbed in her own subjectivity and isolation, she is intensely aware of being an object—a house—for another subject, another being which has its own entirely independent life. Vitality lives in her *and* within her: an ultimate expression of the Shelley–Brontë–Dickinson metaphors of enclosure, doubleness, and escape. "Ordinarily," de Beauvoir remarks, "life is but a condition of existence; in gestation it appears as creative . . . [the pregnant woman] is no longer an object subservient to a subject [a man, a mother, daddy, Jay Cee]; she is no longer a subject afflicted with the anxiety that accompanies liberty; she is one with that equivocal reality: life. Her body is at last her own, since it exists for the child who belongs to her."[14]

That this liberating sense of oneness with life was precisely Plath's attitude toward childbirth and maternity is clear from "Three Women," a verse-play on the subject in which the voice of the First Woman, the healthily golden and achieving mother, is obviously the poet's own, or at least the voice for which the poet strives. Repudiating yet again the "horrors," the "slighted godmothers" (like the bald muses) "with their hearts that tick and tick, with their satchels of instruments," this speaker resolves to "be a wall and a roof, protecting . . . a sky and a hill of good." For, she exclaims, "a power is growing in me, an old tenacity. / I am breaking apart like the world . . . / I am used. I am drummed into use" (*WT*, pp. 53–54). Though this passage may sound as if it is about escaping or about writing poetry, it is really about having a baby. And when the child appears later on, he appears in flight—like the escaping virgin, the arrow, or the lioness—a "blue, furious boy, / Shiny and strange, as if he had hurtled from a star . . ." who flies "into the room, a shriek at his heel." And again Plath stresses the likeness of babies, poems, and miraculous escapes: "I see them," she says of babies, "showering like stars on to the world . . . These pure small images. . . . Their footsoles are untouched. They are walkers of air." Living babies, in other words, are escaping shrieks—as poems are; pure small images—as poems are; walkers of air—as poems are: all ways for the self to transcend itself.

Conversely, Plath speaks of dead poems, the poems of jeweled symmetry that would please the disquieting muses, as being like stillborn babies, an analogy which goes back to the male tradition that defines the offspring of "lady poets" as abortions, stillbirths, dead babies. "These poems do not live," she writes in "Stillborn." ". . . it's a sad diagnosis . . . they are dead and their mother near dead with distraction" (*Crossing*, p. 20). It becomes clear that certain nineteenth- and twentieth-century women, confronting *confinement* (in both senses of the word) simply translated the traditional baby-poem metaphor quite literally into their own experience of their lives and bodies. "I, the miserable and abandoned, am an *abortion*, to be spurned . . . ," said Mary Shelley's monster—and he was, for he escaped from confinement to no positive end.[15] I "step to you from the black car of Lethe/Pure as a baby," cried Plath—meaning, my poems, escaping from the morgue of my body, do that. And "I was in a boundary of wool and painted boards . . . ," wrote Anne Sexton. But "we swallow magic and we *deliver* Anne."[16] For the poet, finally, can be delivered from her own confining self through the metaphor of birth.

Can be, but need not necessarily be. And here we get to the qualifications I mentioned earlier. For while, as de Beauvoir pointed out, the processes of gestation link the pregnant woman with life even as they imply new ways of self-transcendence, they are also frightening, dangerous, and uncontrollable. The body works mysteriously, to its own ends, its product veiled like death in unknowable interior darkness. Just as the poet cannot always direct the flow of images but instead finds herself surprised by shocking connections made entirely without the help or approval of the ego, so the mother realizes, as de Beauvoir notes, that "it is beyond her power to influence what in the end will be the true nature of this being who is developing in her womb . . . she is [at times] in dread of giving birth to a defective or a monster."[17] (In other words, in Plath's case, to the ugly bear or the acetylene virgin that she both fears and desires to be.) Moreover, to the extent that pregnancy de-personalizes the woman, freeing her from her own ego and instead enslaving her to the species, it draws her backward into her own past (the germplasm she shelters belongs to her parents and ancestors as well as to her) and at the same time catapults her forward into her own future (the germplasm she shelters will belong to her children and their survivors as well as to her). "Caught up in the great cycle of the species, she affirms life in the teeth of time and death," says de Beauvoir. "In this she glimpses immortality; but in her flesh she feels the truth of Hegel's words: 'the birth of children is the death of parents.' "[18] To Plath, this network backwards and forwards was clearly of immense importance. For, if having babies (and writing poems) was a way of escaping from the dark house of daddy's shoe, it was also, paradoxically, a frightening re-encounter with daddy: daddy alive, and daddy dead.

Nowhere is that re-vision of daddy more strikingly expressed than in the bee-keeping sequence in *Ariel*. Otto Plath was a distinguished entomologist, author of many papers on insect life, including (significantly) one on "A

Muscid Larva of the San Francisco Bay Region Which Sucks the Blood of Nestling Birds." But his most important work was a book called *Bumblebees and Their Ways*, an extraordinarily genial account of the lives of bee colonies, which describes in passing the meadows, the nest-boxes, the abandoned cellars inhabited by bumblebees, and the "delicious honey" they make, but concentrates mostly on the sometimes sinister but always charismatic power and fertility of the queens.[19] The induction of the colony into the bee box, stings, wintering, "the upflight of the murderess into a heaven that loves her"—all these are described at length by Otto Plath, and his daughter must have read his descriptions with intense attention. Her father's red-leather thesaurus, we're told, was always with her. Why not also *Bumblebees and Their Ways*? Considering all this, and considering also the points made by De Beauvoir, it's almost too fictionally neat to be true that Plath told an interviewer after the birth of her son, Nicholas, that "our local midwife has taught me to keep bees."[20] Yet it is true.

Plath's bee-keeping, at least as it is represented in the *Ariel* sequence, appears to have been a way of coming to terms with her own female position in the cycle of the species. When the colony is put into the box by "the villagers," *she* is put into "a fashionable white straw Italian hat" (the sort of hat the fifty-ninth bear tears up, the sort of hat they would have given us at *Mademoiselle*) and led "to the shorn grove, the circle of hives." Here she can only imagine the "upflight" of the deadly queen—for she (both the queen and the poet), the poem implies, has been put into a box along with the rest of the colony. "Whose is that long white box in the grove, what have they accomplished, why am I cold," she asks. But the question is merely rhetorical, for the box is hers, hers and (we learn in the next poem) perhaps her baby's. "I would say it was the coffin of a midget," she decides there, "or a square baby / Were there not such a din in it." And the rest of the piece expresses the double, interrelated anxieties of poetry and pregnancy: "The box is locked, it is dangerous . . . I have to live with it . . . I can't keep away from it . . . I have simply ordered a box of maniacs . . . They can be sent back. / They can die, I need feed them nothing. I am the owner . . ." culminating in a hopeful resolution: "The box is only temporary."

But when the box is opened, in the third poem, the bees escape like furious wishes, attacking "the great scapegoat," the father whose "efforts" were "a rain / Tugging the world to fruit." And here, most hopefully, the poet, mother of bees and babies, tries to dissociate herself from the self-annihilating stings her box has produced. "*They* thought death was worth it, but I / Have a self to recover, a queen." And "Now she is flying / More terrible than she ever was, red / Scar in the sky, red comet / Over the engine that killed her— / The mausoleum, the waxhouse" (*Ariel*, pp. 56–63).

Alas, her flight is terrible because it is not only an escape, it is a death trip. Released from confinement, the fertile and queenly poet must nevertheless catapult back into her dead past, forward into her dead future, like Esther Greenwood, plummeting toward the "white sweet baby cradled in its mother's belly," which is, after all, likened to a dead inanimate thing, a still "pebble." "I / Am the arrow, / The dew that flies / Suicidal, at one with the drive / Into the red / Eye, the cauldron of morning," Plath had cried in the poem "Ariel." But just as the fertile poet's re-vision of daddy is killing, so the suicidal cauldron of morning is both an image of rebirth and a place where one is cooked; and the red solar eye, certainly in Freudian terms, is the eye of the father, the patriarchal superego which destroys and devours with a single glance.

A profound and inescapable irony of many literary women's works and lives is that in her flight from the coffin of herself the woman–writer or the character who is her surrogate is often consumed by the Heraclitean fires of change that propel her forward. Charlotte Brontë's madwoman burns up Rochester's house *and* herself; Mary Shelley's monster plans a funeral pyre to extinguish himself entirely, soul and all; Emily Dickinson's bomb of the spirit will surely explode any minute; and Sylvia Plath, dissolving into the cauldron of morning, "is lost," as she says in the poem "Witch-Burning," "lost in the robes of all this brightness" (*Crossing*, p. 53). One may be renewed like a baby in the warm womb of the mythic oven, but the oven is also Auschwitz, Dachau, a place where one is baked like a gingerbread body back into the plaster cast of oneself.

For this reason, it is the paradox of Plath's life (perhaps of any woman's life) and of the Plath Myth that even as she longs for the freedom of flight, she fears the risks of freedom—the simultaneous reactivation and disintegration of the past it implies. "What I love is / The piston in motion," Plath says in the poem "Years," then adds ambiguously "My soul *dies* before it." "And you, great Stasis," she continues, "What is so great in that!" Yet at the same time she is drawn to the sea, "that great abeyance"—to the pool of Stasis where the hair of the father spreads in tides like unraveled seaweed (*Ariel*, pp. 72, 20). "Father," she had complained in an early poem "this thick air is murderous . . . I would breathe water" (*Colossus*, p. 48). And elsewhere, "Stone, stone, ferry me down there," she begged (*Colossus*, p. 23): ferry me into the pit, the oven, the sea of stasis, the bottom of the pool where (as she says in "Words") "fixed stars govern a life" and (as she declares in "Edge") "the woman is *perfected*," her children—her independent adulthood—"folded back into her body," "the illusion of a Greek necessity" flowing in "the scrolls of her toga; her bare feet . . . saying, we have come so far, it is over" (*Ariel*, pp. 85, 84).

What is the way out of this dilemma? How does a woman reconcile the exigencies of the species—her desire for stasis, her sense of her ancestry, her devotion to the house in which she has lived—with the urgencies of her own self? I don't know the answer. For Sylvia Plath, as for many other women, there was apparently, in real life, no way out. But there was a way out in art. And, to honor Sylvia Plath, to honor the achievement of her poems as well as their place in my own life, I want to stress the positive significance of her art and its optimistically feminine redefinition of traditions that have so far been primarily masculine.

Women and Romantic poets are, after all, alike in certain interesting respects. "Not I, not I, but the wind that blows through me," cried D. H. Lawrence, echoing Wordsworth, Shelley, and a whole Norton Anthology full of others. "A fine wind is blowing the new direction of time."[21] So, to Plath, when she was working at her best it must have seemed that, as she tells us in *Ariel*, "some god got hold" of her; the processes of body and mind worked their own will, independent of the observing consciousness (which was itself by turns pleased, amused, disgusted, and terrified); cells of thought buzzed and multiplied like bees swarming, or wintering, quiescent; and the babies arrived, Ted Hughes tells us, easily, Frieda, the first, "at exactly sunrise, on the first day of April, the day [Sylvia] regularly marked as the first day of Spring."[22] And so also, and also at sunrise, in (Plath herself noted) "that still blue almost eternal hour before . . . the glassy music of the milkman,"[23] the "cool morning hours" when Otto Plath wrote that it was best to work and the bees were least "pugnacious," the poems began to arrive, with the strenuous ease of babies, as if the same musing double, the lion-red queen bee whom Robert Bly would call the "ecstatic mother," had liberated them and herself from some Pandora's box.[24] And like the babies, the poems had, now, a squalling imperfection. Where the lines of the earlier "stillborn" works had been stonily symmetrical, jeweled, chiseled, the lines of these later works are long and short, irregular as gasping breath, deliberately imperfect, not because of an impulse to self-indulgence or a failure of control, but because of a conscious decision that "perfection is terrible, it cannot have children."

"The poets I delight in are possessed by their poems as by the rhythms of their own breathing. Their finest poems seem born all of a piece, not put together by hands," Plath wrote toward the end of her life.[25] The description applies to her own late poems: possessed of the imperfections of breath, they are nevertheless "born all of a piece," alive, viable, self-sufficient. Out of the wax house of *Mademoiselle*, out of the mausoleum of the woman's body, out of the plaster of the past, these poems fly, pure and new as babies. Fly, redeemed—even if their mother was not—into the cauldron of morning.

17.

Seeking the Exit or the Home: Poetry and Salvation in the Career of Anne Sexton

Suzanne Juhasz

If you are brought up to be a proper little girl in Boston, a little wild and boycrazy, a little less of a student and more of a flirt, and you run away from home to elope and become a proper Boston bride, a little given to extravagance and a little less to casseroles, but a proper bride nonetheless who turns into a proper housewife and mother, and if all along you know that there lives inside you a rat, a "gnawing pestilential rat,"[1] what will happen to you when you grow up? If you are Anne Sexton, you will keep on paying too much attention to the rat, will try to kill it, and yourself, become hospitalized, be called crazy. You will keep struggling to forget the rat and be the proper Boston housewife and mother you were raised to be. And into this struggle will come, as an act of grace, poetry, to save your life by giving you a role, a mission, a craft: an act, poetry, that is you but is not you, outside yourself. Words, that you can work and shape and that will stay there, black and true, while you do this, turn them into a poem, that you can send away to the world, a testimony of yourself. Words that will change the lives of those who read them and your own life, too. So that you can know that you are not only the wife and mother, not only the rat, but that you are the poet, a person who matters, who has money and fame and prizes and students and admirers and a name, Anne Sexton.

But what about the mother and wife, and what about the rat, when Anne Sexton becomes a poet? This essay is about the end of Sexton's career and poetry, and it looks at the role that her poems played in her life and in ours. It is a tale for our times, because it is also about what poetry can do for women and what it cannot do for women. Something we need to know.

Since the recent publication of Sexton's letters, there is now no doubt how conscious she was of the craft of poetry, of the work that it is, and how devoted she was to doing that work. "You will make it if you learn to revise," she wrote to an aspiring poet in 1965:

> if you take your time, if you work your guts out on one poem for four months instead of just letting the miracle (as you must feel it) flow from the pen and then just leave it with the excuse that you are undisciplined.
> Hell! I'm undisciplined too, in everything but my work...and the discipline the reworking the forging into being is the stuff of poetry....[2]

In fact, for Sexton the poem existed as a measure of control, of discipline, for one whom she defined as "given to excess." "I have found that I can control it best in a poem," she says. "If the poem is good then it will have the excess under control . . . it is the core of the poem . . . there like stunted fruit, unseen but actual."[3]

Yet the poem had another function in her life, the one which gives rise to that label "confessional," which has always dogged her work and is not usually complimentary. Her poetry is highly personal. She is either the overt or the implicit subject of her poem, and the she as subject is the person who anguishes, who struggles, who seems mired in the primary soil of living: the love/hate conflict with mother and father, the trauma of sex, the guilt of motherhood. The person in the poem is not the proper lady and mother and wife who is always trying her best to tidy up messes and cover them with a coating of polish and wax. Rather, it is the rat, a creature of nature rather than culture, who is crude and rude, "with its bellyful of dirt / and its hair seven inches long"; with its "two eyes full of poison / and routine pointed teeth."[4] The rat person, with her "evil mouth" and "worried eyes,"[5] knows that living is something about which to worry: she sees and tells. In form her poem often follows a psychoanalytic model, as I have pointed out in an earlier essay,[6] beginning in a present of immediate experience and probing into a past of personal relationships in order to understand the growth (and the damaging) of personality. As such, the poem for Sexton is an important agent in her quest for salvation: for a way out of the madness that the rat's vision engenders, a way that is not suicide.

Very early in her career, in "To John, Who Begs Me Not to Enquire Further," she presents an aesthetics of personal poetry which is conscious that the poem, because it is an object that communicates and mediates between person and person, can offer "something special" for others as well as oneself.

> I tapped my own head;
> it was glass, an inverted bowl.
> It is a small thing
> to rage in your own bowl.
> At first it was private.
> Then it was more than myself;
> it was you, or your house
> or your kitchen.
> And if you turn away
> because there is no lesson here
> I will hold my awkward bowl,
> with all its cracked stars shining
> like a complicated lie,
> and fasten a new skin around it
> as if I were dressing an orange
> or a strange sun.
> Not that it was beautiful,
> but that I found some order there.
> There ought to be something special
> for someone
> in this kind of hope.[7]

In such poetry, she warns, there is no "lesson," no universal truth. What there is is the poem of herself, which, as she has made it, has achieved an order; that very order a kind of hope (a belief in salvation) that might be shared. The poem of herself is, however, not herself but a poem. The imagery of this poem attests to that fact, as it turns self into object, a bowl, an orange, a sun, while it turns the poem about self into a coating or covering that surrounds the self. The bowl is like a planet in a heaven of "cracked stars shining / like a complicated lie"; if he should turn from this poem, she promises to "fasten a new skin around" or "dress" her orange, that strange sun.

Of course Sexton was right when she said that there ought to be something special in that gesture her poems made toward others. People responded to her poetry because she had the courage to speak publicly of the most intimate of personal experiences, the ones so many share. She became a spokesperson for the secret domestic world and its pain. And her audience responded as strongly as it did, not only because of what she said but because of how she said it. She was often, although not always, a good poet, a skilled poet, whose words worked insight upon her subject matter and irradiated it with vision.

But what about herself, in the process? What did her poems do for her?

In a letter she speaks of the necessity for the writer to engage in a vulnerable way with experience.

> I think that writers ... must try *not* to avoid knowing what is happening. Everyone has somewhere the ability to mask the events of pain and sorrow, call it shock ... when someone dies for instance you have this shock that carries you over it, makes it bearable. But the creative person must not use this mechanism anymore than they have to in order to keep breathing. Other people may. But not you, not us. Writing is "life" in capsule and the writer must feel every bump edge scratch ouch in order to know the real furniture of his capsule . . . I, myself, alternate between hiding behind my own hands protecting myself anyway possible, and this other, this seeing ouching other. I guess I mean that creative people must not avoid the pain that they get dealt. I say to myself, sometimes repeatedly "I've got to get the hell out of this hurt" ... But no. Hurt must be examined like a plague.[8]

The result of this program, as she says in a letter to W. D. Snodgrass, is writing "real." "Because that is the one thing that will save (and I do mean save) other people."[9]

And yet the program is not only altruistic in intent. Personal salvation remains for her an equally urgent goal. As she writes in "The Children," from one of her last books, *The Awful Rowing Toward God* (1975):

> The place I live in
> is a kind of maze
> and I keep seeking
> the exit or the home.[10]

In describing this position of vulnerability necessary for poetry, she tells Snodgrass that a poet must remain "the alien." In her vocabulary for herself, that alien is of course the rat. But there is a serious problem here, because Anne Sexton the woman (who is nonetheless the poet, too) does not like the rat. The existence of the rat obstructs salvation. In "Rowing," the opening poem of *The Awful Rowing Toward God*, salvation is described as an island toward which she journeys. This island, her goal, is "not perfect," having "the flaws of life, / the absurdities of the dinner table, / but there will be a door":

> and I will open it
> and I will get rid of the rat inside me,
> the gnawing pestilential rat.
>
> (p. 2)

In the "Ninth Psalm" of her long poem, "O Ye Tongues," an extended description of the state of salvation includes this vision: "For the rat was blessed on that mountain. He was given a white bath."[11]

In other words, Sexton, recognizing at the age of twenty-eight her possession of a talent, turned her mad self to good work (and works): into a writer, an active rather than a passive agent. For she had defined madness as fundamentally passive and destructive in nature. "Madness is a waste of time. It creates nothing . . . nothing grows from it and you, meanwhile, only grow into it like a snail."[12] Yet the rat who is the mad lady is also the poet. To have become a poet was surely an act toward salvation for Sexton. It gave her something to do with the knowledge that the rat possessed. Left to her silence, the rat kept seeing too much and therefore kept seeking "the exit." Words brought with them power, power to reach others. They gave her as well a social role, "the poet," that was liberating. Being the poet, who could make money with her poetry, who could be somebody of consequence in the public world, was an act that helped to alleviate some of the frustration, the impotence, the self-hatred that Sexton the woman experienced so powerfully in her life. The poet was good: how good she was Sexton, as teacher and reader and mentor, made a point of demonstrating.

But the rat was not good; in yet another image of self-identification, Sexton called that hated, evil, inner self a demon.

> My demon,
> too often undressed,
> too often a crucifix I bring forth,
> too often a dead daisy I give water to
> too often the child I give birth to
> and then abort, nameless, nameless . . .
> earthless.
>
> Oh demon within,
> I am afraid and seldom put my hand up
> to my mouth and stitch it up
> covering you, smothering you
> from the public voyeury eyes
> of my typewriter keys.[13]

These lines are from "Demon," which appears in her posthumous volume, *45 Mercy Street*. The poem begins with an epigraph from D. H. Lawrence: "A young man is afraid of his demon and puts his hand over the demon's mouth sometimes." It goes on to show why the demon, though frightening, cannot be covered, smothered, or denied speech; because the demon, exposed, is at the center of her poetry. At the same time the poem, with its bitter repetition of "too often," reveals a hatred, not only of the demon, but of the act of uncovering and parading it. Of the act that is nonetheless essential to making the poem.

Finally, the poem's imagery points to a further aspect of the demon that is for Sexton perhaps the most terrible of all. The demon is crucifix, icon of salvation through death; is dead daisy for which the poem alone provides water; is child which, through the act of the poem, is both birthed and aborted. The demon may begin as something that lives within and is a part (albeit frightening and nasty) of herself; but the poem, in being written, turns the demon into an object separate and alien from herself. This disassociation, this conversion of self into other, is as distressing to Sexton as the self-hatred that she must experience each time she acknowledges the existence of the demon or the rat. Because, as "Demon" makes clear, the self as object, the self in the poem, is dead. To use the self in making poems is to lose the self, for the poem is never the experience that produces it. The poem is always an artifice, as she herself observes in another poem from *45 Mercy Street*, "Talking to Sheep":

> Now,
> in my middle age,
> I'm well aware
> I keep making statues
> of my acts, carving them with my sleep—
> (p. 7)

The poems can never offer personal salvation for their poet, and she has come to understand why. First, because she defines salvation as a life freed at last from the rat and her pain ("I would sell my life to avoid / the pain that begins in the crib / with its bars or perhaps / with your first breath"[14]), and yet she cannot kill the rat without killing the vision that is the source of her poetry. Second, because the poems themselves are a kind of suicide. She knows that poetry must be craft as well as vision; that the very act of crafting objectifies the poem's content. What has lived within her, externalized and formalized by art, becomes something other than herself; is form but not flesh.

She expresses this new knowledge in the only way she knows, by making poetry of it. In poems like those quoted, or in the following lines from "Cigarettes and Whiskey and Wild, Wild Women," the other side of "To John, Who Begs Me Not to Enquire Further" is revealed: the implications of this aesthetic of personal poetry for the poet herself.

Now that I have written many words,
and let out so many loves, for so many,
and been altogether what I always was—
a woman of excess, of zeal and greed,
I find the effort useless.
Do I not look in the mirror,
these days,
and see a drunken rat avert her eyes?
Do I not feel the hunger so acutely
that I would rather die than look
into its face?
I kneel once more,
in case mercy should come
in the nick of time.[15]

In an earlier essay on Sexton I maintained that poetry had saved her from suicide. It did, for the years in which she wrote and was the poet. But it is equally true that poetry could not prevent her death, "the exit," because it could not bring her to salvation, "the home."

For Sexton, salvation would have meant sanity: peace rather than perpetual conflict, integration rather than perpetual fragmentation. Sanity would have meant vanquishing at last her crazy bad evil gnawing self, the rat, the demon. Yet the rat was, at the same time, the source of her art. Its anxious visions needed to be nurtured so that she might be a poet. Sanity might bring peace to the woman, but it would destroy the poet. And it was not the woman, who made the peanut butter sandwiches and the marriage bed, whom Sexton liked. It was the poet. The discipline of her craft and the admiration, respect, and power that it brought allowed her to feel good about herself. That the woman and the poet were different "selves," and in conflict with each other, she was well aware. "I do not live a poet's life. I look and act like a housewife," she wrote. "I live the wrong life for the person I am."[16] Although this fragmentation of roles wrought conflict and confusion, it nonetheless made possible the kind of poetry that Sexton wrote. But more and more in her final years she seemed to have come to despise the balancing act itself, demanding all or, finally, nothing.

Perhaps the kind of salvation that Sexton sought was unattainable, because its very terms had become so contradictory. Certainly, her poetry could not offer it. In poetry she could make verbal and public what she knew about her private self; she could shape this knowledge, control it, give it a form that made it accessible to others. But she could not write what she did not know, so that while her poems document all the rat has seen, they never offer an alternative vision. They are always too "close" to herself for that. And they are at the same time too far from her. By creating through externalization and formalization yet another self with which to deal, her poetry increased her sense of self-fragmentation in the midst of her struggle toward wholeness.

Yet Sexton's poetry has offered salvation to others. Personal poetry of this kind, a genre that many women, in their search for self-understanding and that same elusive wholeness, have recently adopted, must be understood to have a different function for its readers and for its writers. Art as therapy appears less profitable for the artist, who gives the gift of herself, than for its recipients. I think that I can learn from Sexton's poems as she never could. They project a life that is like my own in important ways; I associate my feelings with hers, and the sense of a shared privacy is illuminating. At the same time, they are not my life; their distance from me permits a degree of objectivity, the ability to analyze as well as empathize. Possibly I can use the insights produced by such a process to further change in my own life. For the artist, however, because the distance between herself and the poem is at once much closer and much greater, it is more difficult, perhaps impossible, to use the poem in this way. Salvation for the artist must come, ultimately, from developing a life that operates out of tensions which are creative rather than destructive. Sexton's life, art, and death exemplify some of the difficulties faced by women artists in achieving this goal and also dramatically underline the necessity of overcoming them.

18.

A Common Language:
The American Woman Poet

Barbara Charlesworth Gelpi

Feminists since the time of Mary Wollstonecraft have noted the analogies between women's position in a male-dominated society and that of underprivileged ethnic groups, particularly blacks, in a society ruled by whites. For an almost equally long time economic theorists have recognized that women in an industrial society have, economically speaking, much the same function as colonies: they provide the underpaid work force and the completely unpaid domestic labor which serve as the system's working base, and they are the consumers of its finished products. It is not, then, upon reflection surprising, but it is very interesting that Margaret Atwood's schema for the description of Canadian literature and Arnold Rampersad's for an analysis of American ethnic poetry, though arrived at completely independently, should be so similar and that both should have such a clarifying applicability to a study of American women's poetry.[1] The parallels between the situations of colonials, of underprivileged ethnic groups, and of women create parallel consequences. The extent of social and economic victimization suffered by each group or by individuals within groups may vary, but the consciousness of all takes on qualities universal among victims.

In Atwood's theory there are four possible reactions to victimization; Rampersad sets up five, but his first two may be subsumed under the first of Atwood's, and the last three in each are closely parallel. The first reaction described by Atwood is denial of victimhood altogether and suppression into unconsciousness of the anger felt at victimization. Locked in with it unfortunately are also many of the potentially positive and creative aspects of the psyche. Often in a slightly better situation than that of fellow victims, those who follow this first strategy for coping with victimization are afraid to lose what advantages they have by exploring the true nature of their status and tend instead to identify with the victimizer. If they do feel anger, it tends to vent itself against fellow victims, particularly against those who attempt to bring them into fuller consciousness of victimization.

Rampersad's first category, analogously, is that of ethnic writers who seem to write either in ignorance or in complete unconsciousness of the historical and cultural pressures under which they live and work, an unconsciousness that Rampersad can only take to be in some obscure way *willed* by the "extreme self-doubt and . . . fear of self-investigation that attempts to suppress rather than to assimilate the lessons of history" ("The Ethnic Voice," p. 31). Regionalism, his second category, needs a place of its own in a discussion of ethnic poetry but simply as a reaction to victimization is another aspect of his first position. Like the first, its strategy is an identification with the victimizer so complete that the writer's own culture is seen as exotic or quaint.

The next attitude described by both Rampersad and Atwood acknowledges victimization as a fact but considers it the result, in Atwood's words, of "an act of Fate, the Will of God, the dictates of biology (in the case of women, for instance), the necessity decreed by History or Economics, or the Unconscious, or any other large general powerful idea" (*Survival*, p. 37). Her analysis of this position describes it as one filled with self-scorn and self-hatred as well as scorn for fellow-victims. Those in it have unconsciously internalized and thus share the victimizers' contemptuous attitudes toward them, yet they feel bitterly as well a sense of personal worth for which they can find no definition. Rampersad's definition of this state is "double consciousness," and using W. E. B. DuBois's phrasing he describes it as "this sense of always looking at oneself through the eyes of others, of measuring one's soul by the tape of a world that looks on in amused contempt and pity" ("The Ethnic Voice," p. 33).

Both Atwood and Rampersad see this reaction to victimization as one which can be broken down only by anger, a refusal to see oneself any longer as a *fated* victim or to seek victimization unnecessarily. It is, then, a creative anger, releasing the pent energies suppressed by refusal to admit victimization or by passive acceptance of it as inevitable. Although the writing coming out of this phase 3 may be excessive or violent, that "craziness," Rampersad points out, "is only the residue of its vigor" ("The Ethnic Voice," p. 35). Anger, nonetheless, cannot be a permanent source of creativity. It is the position of those demanding transcendence for themselves into a sense of full personhood. To remain angry without such transcendence is eventually to be so frustrated that one may fall back into position 2. But at its best and most creative, the anger of position 3 moves its possessor forward to a new vision of self and thus a new base for creativity.

The fourth position is that which Rampersad describes as "a reintegration of self" ("The Ethnic Voice," p. 35) and what Atwood calls the attitude of "a creative non-victim" (*Survival*, p. 38). Those in it do not identify with the oppressor as do those in position 1, nor do they, like those in position 2, find their identity in the role of victim, thereby shaping themselves and their sense of their own experience in terms given them by their oppressors. Nor again do they need, as do those in position 3, to expend their energy on repudiation of the victim role, for the role does not tempt them. The gift of insight into the meaning they wish to give to their own experience is the reward of this position's self-acceptance.[2]

With these categories as a grid or a hermeneutic, I would like to think about the background and present state of American poetry written by women. As hermeneutic, this system does not provide for literary judgments. A poem written from the first attitude may be exquisite, an expression of the fourth totally inadequate to the idea it attempts to describe. So as to obviate any misunderstanding, I have decided to mention only poems I think well written. But although these categories are not always useful for analysis of the purely aesthetic value of a work, they do help to define the state of consciousness expressed through a lyric poem. Their function is moral rather than purely literary, for as we analyze the attitudes to be found in a poem we learn constantly about our own attitudes as well. Besides this self-revelatory function, the schema has some historical use: although one may find different categories of poems in the work of any single writer, and although the work of a poet like Emily Dickinson, for instance, can throw out notions of a strict historical progression in women's poetry, there is none-theless a discernible movement in women's poetry through this century from a predominantly No. 1 position through 2 to what is now predominantly 3 with breakthroughs into 4. These breakthroughs occur even though women have not fought a revolution and the sources of victimization have not disappeared. Yet here again women's situation resembles that of Canadian writers and of ethnic poets: for them, too, revolution by combat is neither practicable nor desirable; rather they must change their condition through the longer and less obviously exciting process of thought and legislation, and the breakthroughs in such a process come gradually.

In describing the problems of Canadian literature E. K. Brown wrote:

A colony lacks the spiritual energy to rise above routine, and . . . it lacks this energy because it does not adequately believe in itself. It applies to what it has standards which are imported, and therefore artificial and distorting. It sets the great good place not in its present, nor in its past nor in its future, but somewhere outside its own borders, somewhere beyond its own possibilities. (Quoted in *Survival*, p. 183).

Women's poetry in the past has suffered from the sense that great poems were written "somewhere outside its own borders"—that is, by men, but now women poets have Adrienne Rich's sense of writing, as she says Emily Dickinson did, on their own premises.[3]

Marianne Moore is a fine example of a poet who wrote primarily from the first victim position. But how, one may well ask, am I distinguishing the first from the fourth? If a poem does not acknowledge victimization, will it not sound the same as a poem which has transcended it? No—because avoiding that acknowledgment means limiting one's subject matter in ways unnecessary and indeed undesirable to a person in position 4. Moore, for instance, shows her acceptance of limits by the way in which she turns her quick, intelligent gaze outward both to the world of living forms and shapes and to the formal shaping of her verse. Her animal poems are so elegant and rich in vocabulary and technique, so *curious* in both senses of that word, that a captive prince might have written them in prison to keep himself sane.

Although her poetry is often at the same time speculative and interior, its ruminations veer away from the area of purely personal emotion. In "The Mind is an Enchanted Thing," for instance, Moore says of mind that

> It tears off the veil, tears
>   the temptation, the
> mist the heart wears
>   from its eyes, —if the heart
>   has a face; it takes apart
> dejection.

The heart exposed by mind is not really exposed at all; it is dismissed with the line "if the heart has a face." Emotion, "the mist the heart wears," tempts one to explore it further by suffering it more and more deeply. Moore prefers to avoid it altogether by dissipating it through mind. In another poem, "New York," she draws back even more emphatically from exploration of interior darkness. She writes of

> the scholastic philosophy of the wilderness
> to combat which one must stand outside and laugh
> since to go in is to be lost.

Perhaps the best example of this escape through standing outside and laughing is the poem "Silence":

My father used to say
'Superior people never make long visits,
have to be shown Longfellow's grave
or the glass flowers at Harvard.
Self-reliant like a cat—
that takes its prey to privacy,
the mouse's limp tail hanging like a shoelace
   from its mouth—
they sometimes enjoy solitude
and can be robbed of speech
by speech which has delighted them.
The deepest feeling always shows itself in silence;
not in silence, but restraint.'
Nor was he insincere in saying, 'Make my house your inn.'
Inns are not residences.

As Moore's notes to the poem make clear, this is not autobiography. Much of it is based on a quotation she cites from Amy Homans, and the devastating line, "Make my house your inn," is taken from Sir James Prior's memoir on the life of Burke, where its effect is very different. It is there a genial and open invitation: " 'Throw yourself into a coach,' said he. 'Come down and make my house your inn.' "

The poem then is not personal revelation—that is part of its point—but it is a wonderful study of the internalization of values. The speaker recognizes the limitations of her father's point of view and is ironic about them, but her irony involves recognition that she has herself been patterned in a similar mold. So if in one sense father is the cat, she the mouse, and the poem the limp tail which shows that she knows what has been done to her, in another sense she also is the cat and her writing of the poem is the mouse enjoyed in privacy. These ironies bring "Silence" to the verge of position 2, but they are so understated that they do not move it there.

Adrienne Rich has a nicely succinct paragraph on the history of women poets in America which, while not using Atwood's categories, describes very clearly the position 1 state of consciousness:

> Vague sorrow, chaste ironic coolness, veiled whatever realities of sexual ambivalence, bitterness, frustration were experienced by such women as Louise Guiney, Sara Teasdale, Elinor Wylie and their lesser-known contemporaries. Edna Millay alone seems a precursor of what was to come, and only at times. Marianne Moore fled into a universe of forms; H.D. (Hilda Doolittle) to the more fertile region of myth.[4]

I would take it from these comments that Rich would consider H.D.'s poetry, like Marianne Moore's, to be expressive of the position 1 attitude.

Actually in the course of her writing life H.D., like Adrienne Rich herself, seems to have moved from position 1 through to position 4. A dream that H.D. relates in her prose memoir *A Tribute to Freud* shows that she was perfectly aware of the conflict in her situation as woman and poet in a world imaginatively dominated by men and that she was able to verbalize it. Her late poem *Helen in Egypt* studies the conflict between masculine and feminine in order to transcend it. But the dream came earlier and expresses a position 2 state of consciousness. In it she was going to a dance with a man:

> Now we go out together but I am in evening dress, that is, I wear clothes like his. (I had been looking at some new pictures of Marlene Dietrich, in one of the cafe picture-papers.) I am not quite comfortable, not quite myself, my trouser-band does not fit very well; I realize that I have on, underneath the trousers, my ordinary under-clothes, or rather I was wearing the long party-slip that apparently belonged to the ball-gown. The dream ends on a note of frustration and bewilderment. This dream seems to have some associations with Ezra; though he danced so badly, I did go to school-girl dances with him.[5]

Frustration and the bewilderment born of the conflict between believing what one is told about one's nature and destiny as a woman and desiring yet resenting the prerogatives assumed by men—these are the position 2 emotions, not usually as amusingly expressed as the witty unconscious managed to do in H.D.'s dream. The conflict is multiple: from the position 2 angle of vision men and women are hopelessly at odds, bound into an opposition which is the necessary and inescapable foundation of all social system; at the same time women in that system are all in competitive conflict with each other and are conflicted within themselves.

Man-hatred, mother-hatred, woman-hatred, body-hatred, self-hatred: this is the wheel of the position 2 consciousness. Among its most powerful and memorable expressions are many of the poems of Sylvia Plath. For although Plath opened to women writers of the last fifteen years many themes and images for works in position 3, she herself is for the most part bound by guilt into position 2. "Purdah," from *Winter Trees*, is a good example. The title refers to the Hindu custom of keeping women in strict seclusion. Its narcissist speaker describes herself as "so valuable"; rapt in self-contemplation she is nonetheless only seeing herself as her bridegroom, "Lord of the mirrors" sees her, a reflection of him:

> I am his.
> Even in his

> Absence, I
> Revolve in my
> Sheath of impossibles,
>
> Priceless and quiet.

The tension behind that quiet continues to build through the lines that follow until there comes this dénouement:

> Attendants!
>
> Attendants!
> And at his next step
> I shall unloose
>
> I shall unloose—
> From the small jeweled
> Doll he guards like a heart—
>
> The lioness,
> The shriek in the bath,
> The cloak of holes.

Clytemnestra's revenge on Agamemnon for the ritual killing of their daughter Iphigenia is the allusion bound into the last lines. Involved here is a woman's vengeance not for a daughter's slaying but for the death of the girl she herself had been. But Clytemnestra's is not, as we remember, a self-fulfilling vengeance. And although another play, *The Doll's House*, is also in the speaker's mind at the end of the poem, the conclusion stresses Clytemnestra's tragedy not Nora's possibilities.

Plath's imagination is haunted by a sense of inescapable Fates. Her quarrel may be with a man, but her doom is to be woman, both her condition and her conditioning swallowing her up. She is Clytemnestra in the poem I just quoted, but in others she is also a female Orestes pursued by the Furies, with no hope of salvation from a beneficent Minerva. These lines from "All the Dead Dears" contain a theme repeated in many different ways in her poetry. The speaker is looking in a mirror whose mercury-backed reflection becomes the god Mercury, the psychopomp who leads her to the underworld:

> From the mercury-backed glass
> Mother, grandmother, great grandmother
> Reach hag hands to haul me in.

There are three of these personal Erinyes, as there are three Fates in "The Disquieting Muses." The mother in the latter poem has strategies to frighten them away, but, like the stepmother and the witch in "Hansel and Gretel," she and the Fates are actually in malevolent alliance:

> Day now, night now, at head, side, feet,
> They stand their vigil in gowns of stone,
> Faces as blank as the day I was born,
>
> . . . . .
>
> And this is the kingdom you bore me to,
> Mother, mother. But no frown of mine
> Will betray the company I keep.

These poems which explore her ambivalence toward images of mother figures may actually be more central to an understanding of her work than are "Daddy" and "Lady Lazarus."

Susan Griffin too, who is deservedly well known for poems of anger, such as "I Like to Think of Harriet Tubman" and "Is the Air Political Today," writes at least as often out of a brooding sense of hopeless conflict between mothers and daughters. In an early poem, "White Bear," she describes her own daughter as "the innocent jailer" who locks them both into a meaningless domestic round; yet she as mother is guilty of perpetuating the round:

> I teach her
> to beware of
> electricity and
> fire.
> What else she learns,
> I am afraid to
> name.

In "Mother and Child," a poem whose theme and images bring Plath to mind, Griffin attempts to work out the bitterness toward her own mother that "Grenadine" also explores—to be sufficiently angry at her mother to exorcise her image while bringing to consciousness how much her body, her personality, the very integument of her sense of being are formed by her mother. To clear herself of that presence is to kill herself as well, to be reduced to bones in a glass casket:

> Now
> in my dreams
> the mother who never was
> finds the bones of her child
> and says,
> "How we both have suffered."

> Now the
> child opens the
> box which becomes
> a mirror. She stares at her
> bony self
> and does not
> look away.

The poem's conclusion is ambiguous, open to interpretation. Its white immobility, its narcissistic stare may be the return to position 2 and to repetition of an eternal conflict like that described in Blake's "The Mental Traveller," or the bones cleansed by the rage of perception may now be beginning to live.

Certainly the efficacy of rage, its psychically constructive importance for breaking the deadlock of position 2 is celebrated now by any number of women poets, Griffin among them. The destructive witches and Furies of Plath's poems are more likely in the poetry of the last few years to be co-conspirators and patronesses than avengers. It is exhilarating to join the Erinyes in their anger, not flee them in guilt; like the flame of pure acetylene in Adrienne Rich's "Phenomenology of Anger," the rage of the Furies can bring a new sense of oneself, a new innocent clarity. Yet, if the anger effects no real change, if the fight therefore comes to seem hopeless, then the fighter, guilt-ridden once more and defeated to boot, may sink back to position 2, her last state worse than her first.

Within the history of women's poetry in this century, we are at that moment of pause, of crisis virtually, between positions 3 and 4. The reasons for anger have not disappeared, but the poems needed for discovering and describing anger have been written. What now? What, after anger, is our subject?

In pondering that question it might be useful to consider the span of Lucille Clifton's poetry, for the drama going on beneath it humanizes and fleshes out the categories used by Atwood and Rampersad. Clifton's first book, *Good Times*, was dedicated to her mother, and one of its first poems describes her. Written with the attitudes and feelings of the third stage, its love is tinged with reproach for the mother's having remained in the ultimately passive state of the second:

> She got us almost through the high grass
> then seemed like she turned around and ran
> right back in
> right back on in

Other poems in her books, but particularly those in *An Ordinary Woman*, record Clifton's own struggle to obliterate the white values she has internalized, the poems noting her progress, "at last / turning out of the white cage, turning out of the lady cage," as she writes in "Turning." Another description of the struggle comes in "i am running into a new year":

> it will be hard to let go
> of what i said to myself
> about myself
> when i was sixteen and
> twentysix and thirtysix
> even thirtysix but
> i am running into a new year

The title poem of the volume is placed last, where its effect is especially powerful. The breathless rhythms of "Turning," the violence of "She Is Dreaming" in which "the whole world of women / seems a landscape of / red blood and things / that need healing" change to a meditative, almost wondering quiet. In that quiet the poet accepts identification with her mother, yet sees her mother as separate from the fantasies woven around her. Releasing her mother from them, the speaker herself steps out of narcissism but into a sudden loneliness. Her reference is to that loneliness as she continues:

> if it is western
> if it is the final
> Europe in my mind,
> if in the middle of my life
> i am turning the final turn
> into the shining dark
> let me come to it whole
> and holy
> not afraid
> not lonely
> out of my mother's life
> into my own.
> into my own.
>
> i had expected more than this.
> i had not expected to be
> an ordinary woman.

Perhaps it can be argued that the poem's acceptance of diminished expectations makes it an expression of phase 2, but I think not. The sense of being "an ordinary woman" results from gripping a reality unavailable at stage 2. Yet the vision is not culminating or final. It looks forward rather to a still unknown future, and although its willingness to embrace "the shining dark" is a long mental journey away from Marianne Moore's belief that "to go in is to be lost," the journey's end, even its continuation, is not visible.

But looking at women's poetry within this schema brings me to a certain hope: out of the shared experience of victimization and of the shared attitudes which that creates—be they dreamy, misguided, courageous, withdrawn, or divisive—women poets have found common themes and that "common language," in Adrienne Rich's phrase, which make it possible to transcend the divided victim's consciousness into that of a common experience as ordinary women.

19.

The Critique of Consciousness and Myth in Levertov, Rich, and Rukeyser

Rachel Blau DuPlessis

"There is no private life which is not determined by a wider public life."[1] From George Eliot, this is one of two epigraphs Adrienne Rich chose for her book *Diving into the Wreck*; it announces a complex of concerns that Rich shares with two other contemporary poets, Muriel Rukeyser and Denise Levertov. In the last decade and a half, these poets have posited the relations of self and society as a primary poetic situation and have explored these relations in several ways. It is not simply that they speak to public issues (such as the Vietnam War), but rather that within lyric poetry they enact a personal awakening to political and social life, and situate their consciousness and its formation at a specific historical moment.[2]

The summary statement epitomizing these poets' concern for the relationships of consciousness and society is joined, on that first page of Rich's book, by a citation from André Breton's *Nadja* about self-exploration and quest. "Perhaps my life is nothing but an image of this kind; perhaps I am doomed to retrace my steps under the illusion that I am exploring, doomed to try and learn what I should simply recognize, learning a mere fraction of what I have forgotten." Fluid, self-dramatizing, and self-questioning, Breton announces an exploration which doubles back on itself and which incorporates a critical posture into his mythic and formative journey. The citation indicates that the invention of reevaluative quest myths is crucial to Rich; this is also true of the other two poets.

In poems about women, politics and war, and myth the poets construct critiques of culture and ideology from a radical and often feminist point of view. The act of critique guides the central acts of perception in the poems.

Their poems analyze women's assumptions and patterns of action, revealing the cultural norms that uphold traditional consciousness of women. The poets discuss the role of the individual in history, especially in the creation of social change. Their myths have an unusual dimension, for critique becomes the heart of the myth. Their myths are critical of prior mythic thought; they are historically specific rather than eternal; they replace archetypes by prototypes.[3] The poets learned, from the critique of women's consciousness and from the discussion of the individual in history, to honor the experiences of individual and social change that belie cyclic interpretations of history and archetypal readings of their own lives.

The creation and re-creation of the self is one of Denise Levertov's fundamental themes. Her richest poems are epiphanies of self-discovery and moments of sacramental rededication to the self. Levertov has written that the Romantic themes of "soul-making," to borrow Keats's term—as Levertov herself does—are naturally integrated with

> what, woman,
>
> and who, myself,
> I am....[4]

Here, discovering womanhood and discovering personhood are one seamless quest. Yet the question of women does sometimes emerge as a specific problem for Levertov. Some of the conflicts she writes about can be analyzed as classic conflicts for women, which recur in women's writing because they reflect the conditions of women's lives and the demands of the culture. The conflict between the claims of the self and the claims of others is one thematic motif of women's writing.

Poems such as "An Embroidery (I)," "In Mind," and "About Marriage" show the conflicting pull between the nurturing of others and self-absorption, between marriage and pilgrimage. Levertov works from the tacit assumption that a resolution to these conflicts can be found. Yet that resolution is often unstable. Even for the woman who takes an interior journey, like Rose White in "An Embroidery," a bridegroom is expected, but he has not yet arrived, and his ambiguous status is reflected in two conflicting uses of the word "shall" at the end of the poem: indicating both simple, inevitable futurity and indefinite, conditional futurity.

The story of Psyche and Amor, in general so suggestive a myth in its quest motifs and a prime myth of soul-making, structures Levertov's attitudes to women, because in this myth marriage and pilgrimage are not, finally, in conflict. After her long trials and her journey, including a trip to the under-world, Psyche is reunited with her transformed bridegroom, whom, in part, she has altered in her search for knowledge, and yet who, conversely, with the power of a god elevates her as his bride in a sacrament of joy. Because a balance between striving and passivity in the female personality is achieved in this myth, it has been taken as a model of "the psychic development of the feminine."[5] Levertov, too, seeks this balance. The marriage will be strength-ened and enriched by her pilgrimage; the claims of the self and the claims of others will not be in conflict.

"Hypocrite Women," however, is a poem in which Levertov discusses the special burdens and pressures that make womanhood a barrier to the achieve-ment of personhood.[6] The poem inserts the "woman question" into the larger context of the soul's journey, asking what can prevent or inhibit one's choos-ing to make one's life a pilgrimage. In answering this question, Levertov studies self-repression in women.

In the poem, the "hypocrite women" repress whatever they feel—even their own self-doubt—to preserve a generous, unruffled surface, while they "mother man in his doubt," encouraging the nuances and moods necessary for his self-expression. They act unthinkingly a nurturing role in their rela-tions with men. The poet is outraged by the women's bland acquiescence in the pompous male attack on their integrity, and asks, in an archly bitter tone, why women continue unquestioningly to defer to men. She traces this defer-ence to a conflict between what the women really feel and what the culture suggests they should feel. To hide the apparent paradox that a woman should feel "unwomanly," they put on the mask the culture has long made available to them: flirtation used as self-repression.

The women mask their "coldness" with an excessive display of flirtatious-ness, thus also hiding the intensity of the conflict from themselves. Hence they are doubly hypocritical—with men and with themselves—and become liars by this self-censorship.

> Whorishly with the psychopomp
> we play and plead—

> (p. 70)

The term "psychopomp" alerts us to what is at stake. This "soul guide," waiting to lead the women forward to mystery or to transformation, is assailed by a teasing display of charm, which the women use as a deliberate strategy of refusal. They deny their own capacity for growth and turn against their deepest selves. Key phrases such as "to mother," "whorishly," and frivolously cutting off dreams "like ends of split hair" are allegories in metaphor criticizing the roles the women play. The poem closes with a sharply etched portrait of women who, concerned with pleasing men and easing their situations, ignore messages of myth and dream, always so vital in Levertov. By their self-censorship, women evade the challenge of soul-making.

The emphasis of "Hypocrite Women" falls on the women's strategies for self-denigration, not on the nuances of the acts of a man. The women have agreed with the man that they—that their cunts—are ugly. In this poem, the word "cunt" has been used boldly and carefully as a counter-strategy of affir-mation. The explicit naming of sexual organs and bodily functions in this and other recent poems by women is, I think, an attempt to reappropriate so-called "dirty" or "clinical" words, and by so doing, to construct a critique of the cultural values regarding women that have kept these words taboo and unspeakable. As "cunt" is a hidden word, so other words about women have been censored, and, the poem implies, women should begin to speak them. By the act of writing, women see themselves contributing to the under-mining of repressive cultural structures by reevaluating canons of proper lan-guage and canons of proper subject.

A recent poem by Muriel Rukeyser, "Despisals," likewise consciously and programmatically uses forbidden words, here in a poem exploring the social implications of self-denigration and self-hatred.[7]

> In the body's ghetto
> never to go despising the asshole
> nor the useful shit that is our clean clue
> to what we need.—— Never to despise
> the clitoris in her least speech.
>
> (p. 5)

Rukeyser suggests that first self-hatred and then the hatred of others come about through the repression of one's childhood anal and sexual interests in the name of cleanliness. The ghettos of the body precede and, in some way, have caused the ghettos of the city. Through the creation of individual con-sciousness, reproduced in the upbringing of every child, an intolerant, de-structive society is also created. The poem is a study in the continuity of repression from the individual psyche to the collective city.

And through the flat, bold words of "Despisals," Rukeyser has dramatized the power of the reader's assumptions, just as Levertov did. For at first the reader is likely to be startled at the forbidden words and shocked that the poet did not exclude them. But because the theme of the poem is the rejection of all forms of shame and contempt, readers are taught that their normative expectations for the poem's tone and diction are a version of the repressive "despisals" the poem criticizes.

In the deliberate use of uncensored words, and with the thematic purpose these words symbolize, the poems confirm Virginia Woolf's argument in "Professions for Women" that women writers and professionals have two major tasks.[8] First, they must "kill the angel in the house," that self-sacrificing, charming, flirtatious spirit of the womanly. Levertov's "Hypocrite Women" can be viewed as one more invitation to that murderous struggle in one's own defense. The death of the spirit of self-repression—in fact, the death of the old consciousness—will eliminate sex-linked taboos on women's self-exploration.

The second task of the woman writer will then be the aggressive act of truth-telling from a woman's experiences, which Woolf poignantly states she had not succeeded in doing. Talking about woman's sexuality, passion, and the body has been inhibited by literary conventions, long socialization in self-censorship, and fear of male disapproval. Although Woolf notes the exclusively sexual taboos, her argument could extend to all aspects of women's lives. And what inhibits this investigation? Precisely those configurations of consciousness that these poets confront: women's internalization of repressive patterns, women's self-hatred, women's womanly roles. The two parts of women's task now appear to be dialectically related. The real expression of a woman's feelings can be accomplished only by including and transcending the recurrent "murder" of the old consciousness of women. These women poets have therefore chosen to attack their own patterns of consciousness and the social and cultural structures that uphold them, all to achieve the truth about themselves.

Adrienne Rich's "Snapshots of a Daughter-in-Law," dated 1958-1960, is an outstanding poem of this critique of consciousness, analyzing the mental and cultural structures that have formed women and inspecting their strategies of response. As Rukeyser and Levertov have confronted canons of acceptable language in their concern for women, so Rich, beginning the poem, had to pit herself against canons of subject: "I had been taught that poetry should be 'universal,' which meant, of course, non-female."[9] In an act of self-defense she excluded the pronoun "I" from the work (although she ends with "we"), she used extensive allusions (which constitute one of the striking features of the poem), and she chose a title with a somewhat ironic reference to "feminine" sources of her authority in writing the poem: her marital status and her family relationships.

The poem alludes to many texts, references, and cultural figures, lifts them into view, examines them, and sets them in the new context formed by this "re-vision." A critique of assumptions about women's roles and behavior takes shape in three sections of three poems each; finally, a coda projects a new woman beginning to liberate herself from the cultural constraints the poem details.

The three poems of the first section discuss the intricate but limited patterns of behavior of actual women in Rich's own family. They have few options. The mother lives through memories of past elegance; yet because she does not think, but only feels, all her experience is "useless." Although the daughter-in-law almost churlishly tries to differentiate herself from the older woman, both are in fact disintegrating. The younger woman hears, and, with a deep self-denying perversity, represses unseen voices that call on her to rebel or to be selfish. The third poem of the first section exposes sisters without sisterhood who express the monstrous dimensions of their self-hatred through hostility to each other. Such a bleak sketch of the limited personal options available to women—frustration taking shape as vagueness, madness, and bitchiness—demands some causal explanation, which the poet gives by referring to and analyzing classic, often literary, texts that evoke the history of women's condition and the fate of their gifts.

When a woman as gifted as Emily Dickinson appears, as she does suddenly in the next poem, as an image of Rich herself, she is compelled, as a woman, to pursue her ideas and images in the interstices of domestic life, a life that exists in diffuse, interruptible contrast to Dickinson's explosive power. Alternately, endless tasks will themselves give shape to a woman's time; she will dust "everything on the whatnot every day of life."[10]

If domesticity is one social expectation that shapes a woman's personality, and to which her gifts must conform, the demands of beauty (set forth in the next poems) are another. The clear, grotesque lines

> she shaves her legs until they gleam
> like petrified mammoth-tusk
>
> (p. 49)

present the woman as idol, objectified by the necessity to preserve a sleek and beautiful surface. "Mammoth" also suggests the buried power of an extinct animal.

The poem that follows, with its oblique citation from Campion, argues that the customs of courtship, including the love lyrics of our literary tradition, immobilize women. The accomplished woman bending over a lute is not truly immersed in art for its sake or for hers. Art is one of the ornaments of her beauty; it enhances her as an image to be worshipped. Love, then, along with domesticity and beauty, is the third term, creating the traditional boundaries that mold and define women. Each woman takes shape as an individual drastically limited by social norms. And in each of the three poems, women's conditions create typical traits: a combination of repressed power and actual powerlessness; the bitterness of those prevented from full fruition; a "keenness" about Nature and human relationships that comes from women's utter dependence on love.

Having summed up three, centuries-old social expectations, and having shown how they create the individual, Rich turns to other touchstones of cultural attitudes to women, showing with condensation and subtlety the complex psychological paralysis and the kinds of failure that have been the lot of women who themselves internalize and are controlled by various opinions of their possibilities: the purely sexist, the moderately patronizing, or the "deliciously" exculpating. Diderot's loving praise of the flowering of women, for instance, when internalized, reappears as women's lush self-pity and narcissistic regrets. As Levertov exposes women's self-censorship, Rich here exposes their self-indulgence.

In the poem's most brilliant section, Rich caustically challenges both majority opinion about women and women's acceptance of it.

> Our blight has been our sinecure:
> mere talent was enough for us—
> glitter in fragments and rough drafts.
>
> Sigh no more, ladies.
>   Time is male
> and in his cups drinks to the fair.
> Bemused by gallantry, we hear
> our mediocrities over-praised,
> indolence read as abnegation,
> slattern thought styled intuition,
> every lapse forgiven, our crime
> only to cast too bold a shadow
> or smash the mould straight off.
>
> For that, solitary confinement,
> tear gas, attrition shelling.
> Few applicants for that honor.
>
>   (p. 50)

Here is the crux. Women are praised precisely when their work does not call male "superiority" and patriarchal analysis into question. Women are adored because of—not in spite of—their failure to grow and to persevere. Rich exposes the double face of the prevailing culture—its paternal protection of female mediocrity and its destructive attack on female boldness or innovation.

Given what the poem says, a woman must literally reinvent herself. To construct her new consciousness, she should at once move beyond the destructive ideologies of the past, while also transcending the presence of those ideologies in herself. So she must be like a "helicopter" in flight, cutting and brilliant, free to move like a "boy," open to ways of behaving and perceiving not limited by former notions of what a woman should be.[11] "Snapshots of a Daughter-in-Law" traces a critique of culture by reexamining key texts and justifications from the past, noting their assumptions, and showing the way a woman is molded within these cultural and social constraints. Rich's aim is "not to pass on a tradition but to break its hold over us" by analyzing the controlling paradigms of consciousness.[12]

All three poets have found some evidence of a double consciousness—whether in their own views of themselves, in women generally, or in society's views about women. One consciousness is traditional and corresponds in roles, attitudes, and language to Woolf's "angel in the house"; the other consciousness is critical, trying to evaluate—and change—what the traditional consciousness would unquestioningly accept. These poems by Levertov, Rich, and Rukeyser share a concern for individual mental structures and their cultural roots. The poems examine the consciousness of women and the sets of expectations in society and culture about women's feelings, acts, and possibilities. Finding that the contents of consciousness inhibit and narrow women's options, they mount critical attack on traditional patterns of perception and behavior.

The concerns that provoked their poems about women—to investigate, to criticize, to protest against the commonplaces of perception and behavior—also led the poets to examine political forces and power relations that inform individual consciousness. The Vietnam War (and, for Rukeyser, other twentieth-century wars) become focal issues because, in a historical sense, war is the concrete manifestation of political realities in which they feel implicated, and, in a symbolic sense, war epitomizes the destructive values and acts which the old consciousness produces and which society upholds.

As a group, the poems that comment on the Vietnam War and talk about political protests ask how the individual psyche is related to history. Or, to phrase the question somewhat differently, as the poets themselves do also, the poems ask how to extend the model of personal changes of consciousness to produce social change. In "Breaking Open" Rukeyser documents a series of linked conversions and communions which extend personal change outward to small groups. In "Staying Alive" Levertov is overcome by the pain and loss that can follow when one climactic collective action of the new spirit (the building of People's Park, quickly destroyed in a police attack) does not lead to another action. Rich asks how personal psyche is related to history and returns to a study of the difference between male and female consciousness. But in these political poems all three poets place greater emphasis on personal consciousness than they do on social change. Although no poem records the political and social revolution each desires, what remains a significant discovery is the degree to which a specific historical conjuncture has decisively changed the individual. A person and the historical moment interpenetrate in the poems, even if the role of the individual in triggering permanent social change is not so clear as the poets had hoped to make it.

"Käthe Kollwitz" is one of Rukeyser's series of "Lives" telling the stories of humanistic, secular saints, investigating the qualities, character, and acts of selected women and men.[13] In these poems Rukeyser documented the struggles and decisions of historical heroes, situating them on a human scale, at once accessible and inspiring to others. War is a living reality which Kollwitz must confront and transcend by an affirmation of life-giving values. Kollwitz's forging of her art is a model heroic act, since the "truth" of her art is transformative.

> the confession of great weakness, war,
> all streaming to one son killed, Peter;
> even the son left living; repeated,
> the father, the mother; the grandson
> another Peter killed in another war; firestorm;
> dark, light, as two hands,
> this pole and that pole as the gates.

> What would happen if one woman told the truth about her life?
> The world would split open
>
> (pp. 102–103)

As a woman learns to "tell the truth" about her own life, giving voice to her voiceless feelings and groping toward the elucidation of repressed desperation, her full consciousness, born in this effort, will be able to serve others. In "Käthe Kollwitz" Rukeyser affirms the continuity between individual changes of consciousness and changes in the world. The difficulty—as Woolf, Levertov, and Rich all discuss—lies in learning to "tell the truth"; the transformation of the world, Rukeyser states, is a necessary result.

But this affirmation of continuity between psyche and its effects on history is, in another sense, exactly the problem. If a person told the truth about her life and about the life around her, would the world break open? How is it possible to move from individual awareness and transformation to the social change so acutely desired? In "Breaking Open" Rukeyser proposes a communion so intense that it "breaks open" the self to others, providing a new basis for community.[14] Yet the affirmation at the end of this poem is mingled with a sense of failure. The difficulties may be attributable as much—or more —to the relative impasse of the left and the antiwar movement on this issue in the early 1970s as to a private lack of vision or perception on Rukeyser's part. This long poem is indeed a lyric document of its time.

The problem she sets in the poem is the "re-imagining" of a life sufficient to overcome the waste and destruction that is most acutely presented by the Vietnam War, so that her images and her acts will contribute to the realization of a new world and a new set of social relations. In prose meditations on the relationship between the outer and inner worlds, Rukeyser states that psyche and history are really versions of each other.

> The conviction that what is meant by the unconscious is the same as what is meant by history. The collective unconscious present in consciousness, waking or sleeping. The personal "unconscious" is the personal history.
>
> (p. 110)

In order to reach history and the capacity to act in history, one must reach buried parts of personal life (our personal unconscious) which we hold in common with others (the collective unconscious). This recalls Rukeyser's argument in "Despisals" that our repressions, although laid down individually, in fact constitute a collective stratum that has immense repercussions for the social structure.

So, "breaking open" must simultaneously incorporate knowledge of our historical and our personal moments and must lead to a transformation of both—history through psyche and psyche through history. The poem sequence "Searching / Not Searching," in the same volume, can be read in conjunction with this search for transformation in "Breaking Open," for it illuminates the concern for the relationships of individual psychology and history. The phrase "inner greet," which appears in both poems (pp. 31 and 113), describes those people with such self-knowledge and generosity of spirit that they create communion with others. In her argument, Rukeyser has put the emphasis on the level and sacramental quality of the "inner greet" which must be attained to bring about social transformation.

She tests for this human capacity in several episodes, through her experiences as a prisoner, with the jury, in jail. She discovers in jail that some of the prisoners have already forged a community into which they welcome the poet. "You'll find people share here," stated her prison guard. The poem implicitly asks what allows some people to move beyond apparent social and structural impasses, such as prison, and enter, as prophets or avatars, the more human community that the poem foresees.

Rukeyser identifies the reasons in a section that begins "I do and I do," suggesting that the movement "to make the world"—a creative act, an act of affirmation and even of marriage—is the motivation for social change. But then, killing, torture, and repression are equally things people "do," and they may even feel satisfaction and righteousness in these acts. To this problem she suggests that by being in touch with the underlife of dream, desire, fantasy, and nonrational feeling, one can avoid becoming the "rational man" whose genocides and tortures she has catalogued in an earlier section.[15] Postulating that the fullness of one's own inner life will prevent political horrors puts tremendous stress on the transformation of individuals.

> That I looked at them with my living eyes.
> That they looked at me with their living eyes.
> That we embraced.
> That we began to learn each other's language.
>
> (p. 133)

The diction suggests that the experience is solid and verifiable, yet also absolute and unanalyzable. Hence the tone of the statement necessitates the "inner greet" of the reader, for others enter this affirmation only by an emotional commitment to celebration and communion. But the ending of the poem graphically presents, in unresolved form, a conflict between "yes" and "no"—two interpretations of what has been accomplished. One, which Rukeyser overtly holds, reaffirms that individual change on a dense enough scale has naturally brought about social change through the power of communion with others. The second interpretation cannot but see a defeat or impasse in these attempts, yet the defeat is not discussed. It appears alongside statements of transcendence.

Another political poem of recent years, Levertov's "Staying Alive," is similarly problematic.[16] The poem is full of longing for the revolutionary "life that / wants to live" (p. 29) opposed to the death-giving "unlived life." And one way social change begins—as in Rukeyser—is by the example of individual witnesses to the new life who testify in the present to the values and relationships the new society would bring. Levertov cites several young people as the "harbingers" of just such change. Yet by the end of the poem, we see that the revolutionary longing for life has exacted a price of its own —in fact, death. Among its other functions, the poem is an elegy for those who have killed themselves, living within the pressure for change but finding no outlet. So while to choose revolution over death is at first an apparently easy, clear-cut decision, it is immediately complicated because the threads of energy, commitment, and possibility cannot be woven together. What has stopped the revolution? is the despairing question that underlies the poem.

In a Protestant tradition of meditative self-examination, Levertov embarks on a course of self- and social criticism. Perhaps she has failed to make a diagnosis of what she opposes, or so I interpret a charge to the poet in the words of a friend: "Tell Denise to write about the devil" (p. 53). This may also challenge the poet to understand evil and the capacity for evil. In her section answering his request, she concentrates almost exclusively on whether people are in touch or out of touch with themselves and their world. The "devil" in the banal urban landscape lies in "the toneless ignorance all that I saw / had of itself" (p. 55). The devil also is in her personal loss of connection with the authenticity of the struggle. In both cases she focuses on issues of selfhood and consciousness: the incomplete life is, in her terms, "unconscious."

Beyond the shared religious resonance of these political poems, with sacramental vision in one case and despair in the other, Rukeyser and Levertov share one response to the question of changing society. They go deeper in themselves, not as an act of rejection or a declaration of autonomy, but because they consider inwardness one of the necessary paths to social transformation. So their lyric documents about politics and the war return dramatically to a concern for consciousness and changes in the self. In "Breaking Open" Rukeyser works to combat the feelings of fright, isolation, and powerlessness by acts of "introversion"—the meditative absorption and comprehension of the outer world by the inner (p. 117). In "Staying Alive" Levertov accepts for herself the advice given to someone who has nightmares of being stuck in a terrible tunnel: " 'it's your own well, / Go down / into its depth' " (pp. 71–72; 76). These examples of inwardness show the degree to which the poets emphasize changes of individual consciousness as a solution to the political issues that confront them.

The interpenetration of psyche and history is also a major situation in Adrienne Rich's recent poems. She makes her analysis of individual consciousness and history by uniting the issues of sexuality and war in a way neither of the other poets does. The most intimate relations of love and marriage are traced out in her poems until they are revealed as a terrifying war, and war itself is seen as a fact originating in the patriarchal oppression of women. Domination, depersonalization, and dehumanization are the vectors of the patriarchal soul; multiplied and extended on a national scale, these male traits are, in Rich's view, an ur-political explanation for the Vietnam War and its atrocities.[17] Social dislocation and war stem from an estrangement, at some original moment, between "male" and "female" components of the human psyche. Rich pursues this split, investigating its origins and its costs. In effect she is conducting a historical examination of the psychic life.

"The Phenomenology of Anger" is a poem about this war zone in the half-destroyed human psyche.[18] The poet names an enemy. He is a monster or devil in his actions, and the poet fantasizes first about murdering, then about changing him with the white heat of a pure anger. The man is suddenly particularized. He is her lover, whose actions are, in metaphysical tropes, compared to atrocities in Vietnam. His lack of feeling, his lack of empathy for pain, struggle, and change, his lack of rebellion against the status quo, his lack of growth are all interpreted as acts of war against her and her vision.

> Last night, in this room, weeping
> I asked you: *what are you feeling?*
> *do you feel anything?*
>
> Now in the torsion of your body
> as you defoliate the fields we lived from
> I have your answer.
>
> (p. 201)

In these poems, Rich asserts that the particular history of the psyche explains history as a total category. The history of what happened to male and female has become the primary explanation for the nature of society. Further, the social life at this moment is composed, as the haunting end of "Phenomenology of Anger" tells us, of many atomized people hurtling on the underground path of the subway, united only by making the same kind of search.

These poems record an impasse: the near impossibility of creating social change simply through a change in consciousness, although the poets write as if continuing to know and feel more—rage in Rich, communion in Rukeyser, participation in Levertov—could create social change by the explosive needs of consciousness itself. Yet these poems about the interaction of history and the individual also reveal that nothing—not the deepest aspects of the psychic life—exists apart from the pressures of a historical era. This realization will involve a critical revaluation of the nature of myth.

The new myths entail critical perceptions because they recast long-sanctified plots, especially quest patterns, and reenvision such familiar figures as the hero, the lady, and the reborn god. The poems of the critique of myth are so strongly reevaluative that they may even appear antimythological, for they record the realization that old myths are invalid and crippling for women: "a book of myths / in which / our names do not appear," in Rich's words, or they celebrate an apparent rejection of myth: "No more masks! No more mythologies!"—Rukeyser's statement. Further, incorporating critical perceptions about the immersion of the individual in history, the poems are resolutely nonarchetypal. They do not investigate moments of eternal recurrence but rather present historically specific formative events in opposition to cyclic patterns. With the exception of Levertov, whose ambivalence I will discuss, the poets want to create prototypes—original, model forms on which to base the self and its action—forms which are open to transformation in time rather than being static and unhistorical. Yet these poems are at the same time reimaginations of myth, appropriating and rediscovering the essential human experiences: journey, rebirth, transformation, and centering.

One of the most curious of these poems is Rukeyser's "The Poem as Mask."[19] Explicitly antimythological, the poem is also an act of self-criticism, for it was written in direct opposition to an earlier mythic poem by Rukeyser called "Orpheus."[20] The older poem, constructed like a court masque of English tradition, uses an organizing symbol of the power of music, centers on a static drama of transformation, and ends with a final song of unity. This is one of the few of her own poems which Rukeyser discusses in her critical work *The Life of Poetry*. Her section about the writing of "Orpheus" is the climax of that book. For the singer as sacred, the fragments of the human reunited as the divine, the transcendent experience of healing and power combined in the figure of Orpheus are motifs with great resonance for Rukeyser. But the poem, read now, is sluggish, wordy, held back from fullness. "The Poem as Mask" brings this earlier poem into question in a deliberate act of self-examination and self-criticism.

> There is no mountain, there is no god, there is memory
> of my torn life
>
> > (p. 3)

Rukeyser asks why she had censored her feelings, writing *him, god, myth* when she meant *me, human, my life*. She answers that as a woman, she was unable to affirm the concreteness and actuality of her life: a real loss of love, a real birth with actual dangers, the rescue of her newborn child and of herself. Thus her old use of the myth blunted her access to herself; the myth of Orpheus was a "mask" which now must be removed, not a "masque" of unity and joy. The old myth gave her feelings a shape, but it tampered with their authenticity. So she makes a vow at the end of the poem: "No more masks! No more mythologies!" But, while the vow is specifically and understandably antimythological, that refusal is an enabling act, and "for the first time" the myth is alive.

Now, for the first time, the god lifts his hand,
the fragments join in me with their own music.

(p. 3)

The new myth comes from the poet's orphic experiences of suffering, inspiration, and birth. In these final lines the "fragments" of the broken self are allowed to bring or to retain "their own music"; a polyphonic, multifaced composition contrasts with the linear, hierarchic melody sung out in the earlier "Orpheus," in which she stated:

His life is simpler than the sum of its parts
The arrangement is the life. It is the song.

(p. 107)

Rukeyser finds the sources of real sacredness in the commonplace, in the biographical, and in the act of self-criticism itself, incorporating a changed attitude to her life and her work. "The Poem as Mask" is a myth of self-healing based on the process of critique.

Adrienne Rich's poem "Diving into the Wreck" is similar to Rukeyser's in its statements critical of the existing cultural "book of myths," in its focus on the act of criticism, and in its centering on reality.[21] In "Diving into the Wreck" detection and exploration are metaphors for the acts of critique of consciousness and myth. The poet, as an undersea diver, takes a journey down to the individual and collective past, a past where some mysterious, challenging "wreck" occurred that no prior research or instruction can clarify. The poet's intellectual and emotional isolation on this quest is pointedly recalled in the first four stanzas; "the book of myths," other people, science have all failed to elucidate the wreck. Her exploration moves to the unembellished truth:

the thing I came for:
the wreck and not the story of the wreck
the thing itself and not the myth

(p. 197)

As in Rukeyser, but in a darker tone, Rich places her emphasis beyond the culturally validated frames of story and myth on the absolute and concrete perception of the seeker.

In her analysis of the wreck, the poet discovers that she has herself become the object of the search:

I am she: I am he

whose drowned face sleeps with open eyes....

(p. 198)

This discovery of androgynous, unifying identities is part of the truth of the wreck. The "one" who is revealed under water is constructed of opposites prior to their split: I and we, she and he, dead and living, individual and collective, cargo and instruments, seeker and sought.

In this poem of journey and transformation Rich is tapping the energies and plots of myth, while re-envisioning the content. While there is a hero, a quest, and a buried treasure, the hero is a woman; the quest is a critique of old myths; the treasure is knowledge: the whole buried knowledge of the personal and cultural foundering of the relations between the sexes, and a self-knowledge that can be won only through the act of criticism.

In order to understand the significance of these changes, we can turn to Erich Neumann's *The Origins and History of Consciousness*, whose chapter on the "transformation myth" involving hero, captive, and treasure is the model Rich purposely violates. In a traditional myth, a male hero (like Perseus) engages in a struggle or quest to liberate a captive woman and possibly a treasure from a female monster. At the successful end of the struggle, the hero marries the captive, having extricated her from the "terrible mother," a snake or dragon who represents the captive's own dangerous and despised matriarchal past. The captive woman is the necessary contributor to the hero's development, representing a fruitfulness and creativity which he appropriates and which transforms him. The hero severs (or rescues) the creative, supportive, enriching aspects of the female from the baleful, destructive, devouring aspects, becoming the custodian of the "good" and the repressor of the "wicked" aspects of female power. "With the freeing of the captive and the founding of a new kingdom, the patriarchal age comes into force."[22]

The ultimate intention of "Diving into the Wreck" is to call this whole patriarchal myth into question. Rich does so by dramatizing the process of critique and self-exploration in a new myth that constructs her own version of the origin and history of consciousness. Nor is Rich's myth a simple reversal of Neumann's model. For, unlike the fecund captive-treasure of the patriarchal myth, here the captive is dead, arrested in the strained posture of unfulfilled searching. Nothing can be won from this figure except the fact of death. The new "fruitful center" in Rich's myth has become the creative antagonism of the woman–hero to traditional consciousness and old patterns of myth—an antagonism motivated because that book of stories and explanations excludes her. So in the course of the journey an androgynous woman has been invented, one appropriating her own fruitfulness and power, and brought into being by her own creative momentum—that is, from the process of critique.

Setting Denise Levertov into this context of critique reveals something about her major mythopoetic work, "Relearning the Alphabet," which chronicles the journey of the self and the rediscovery of the roots of vision.[23] "Re-learning the Alphabet," while also a poem making a new myth, is ambivalent to the critique of myth, and therefore is not antimythological in the way that the other two poems are. In this poem the problem is the loss of contact with her deepest sources; the solution is finding them again through a pilgrimage in which each letter of the alphabet marks the route. By this distinctive (even unprecedented) formal arrangement, the poet sensitizes the reader to the sound of each letter and the emotional value of each word on her route. The form is thus a primer of meaning for the reader, teaching the reader to attend to the concrete experience of each thing and each emotion, which bears its special resonance or pitch.

At the beginning of the poem, the poet is estranged from self and world and suffers a loss of authenticity. Levertov hints that the missing "L" words (love, and also, from the name Levertov, self-identity) as well as love distorted by jealousy are jointly responsible for all her losses. So, although the opening sections of the poem contain the seeds of the later cyclic renewal, the poet is blind to them. In the poem's central sections—"I" moving through the mid-alphabet to "O," the low point in the quest—there are sets of tensions, to cite significant words, between love and limbo, moon and man, never and presence, jealousy and karitas. In the "O," or zero, section former certainties and core concepts (such as "home," "other," "order") are reduced to solitary harsh words without syntax and strained phrases without context.

To the loss of both self and love, Levertov first proposes a false solution: the will, imagistically related to the cold moon. The "cinder" to which she is reduced by the moon contrasts throughout the poem with the fire's warm embers of potentiality, which are always ready to flare up again in true renewal. In the poem Levertov records her experiment with how far the bad faith of the moon can carry her; she tries to feign or trick the experiences of loss into gain by will and by words, but inner avatars, who take the form of men, compel her to stop. Only by retracing the steps of her journey, moving backwards to a point where the wrong path was taken, can the true path be found. Levertov exposes the limitations of the linear, evolutionary journey and accepts the revolutionary—transformative and cyclic—journey.

A reading of this poem in conjunction with the earlier "Hypocrite Women" reveals Levertov's continued ambivalence toward the moon-inspired state of egotistical coldness. The moon is both necessary, as are the "caves of the Moon" in the earlier poem, and feared for causing the isolating self-absorption of the women—and the woman artist. In "Relearning the Alphabet" this tension is resolved in a distinctive fashion. In section W, the moon, so tempting and destructive a presence in the poem, is tamed.

> Wisdom's a stone
> dwells in forgotten pockets—
> lost, refound, exiled—
> revealed again
> in the palm of
> mind's hand, moonstone
> of wax and wane, stone pulse.
>
> (p. 120)

She can accept the moon's cycles while rejecting its otherness, for the moonstone is satisfyingly refound in a pocket or palm. Thus Levertov miniaturizes the moon to partake of its necessary light in a containable form.

For Levertov the linear, the cold, the desire to wound and be wounded, and judgment, rather than charity, are all part of one harsh cluster which distorts the poet's vision. Only a surrender to the already established axes of the self, and a genuine, unfeigned submission to the tides of experience, allow the poet to find authentic self and authentic time. The cycle of discovery, loss, and rediscovery is endless and redemptive; equally redemptive is the intimate, endless contact with the real. So this whole quest myth is an example of the balance between active striving ("doing") and passive attention ("looking") which Levertov characteristically shows.

> Relearn the alphabet,
> relearn the world, the world
> understood anew only in doing, under-
> stood only as
> looked-up-into out of earth
>
> (p. 119)

states the "U" section. The focus on *under-stood* is a call for a return to basic detail, to the event entirely rooted in concrete, daily life. For this understanding, the poet forges the syntactically entangled set of prepositions ("up-into out of") to situate herself in the real, at that moment, always decisive in Levertov, when its inner energy is known.

In two ways Levertov's poem is similar to the poems of the critique of myth I have already discussed, yet Levertov's use of myth, while suggesting a critique, shears off from a complete commitment to it. First, in "Relearning the Alphabet," as in the poems by Rukeyser and Rich, the hero is a woman, and she is also her own prize or treasure, for she rediscovers the authentic self. In section "P, Q," she says:

> In childhood dream-play I was always
> the knight or squire, not
> the lady:
> quester, petitioner, win or lose, not
> she who was sought.
> The initial of quest or question
> branded itself long since on the flank
> of my Pegasus.
>
> (p. 116)

Here the woman is quester, not heroine, and the passivity of the lady is rejected. To do this, the girl had simply imagined herself as a man ("knight or squire"), but the grown person struggles (as the moon imagery tells us) with the feminizing of the quest so that a woman can be the hero and remain womanly.

The formal use of the alphabet is also a measure of how far Levertov goes into critique and the point at which she stops. The poem's significant action is the "relearning" of the most ordinary things in order to comprehend the world anew. And, as an image of that quest, what is more basic than the alphabet, what more ubiquitous or more taken for granted? So the alphabet form of the poem focuses incredibly subtle attention on building-blocks of being, deconstructing, and reperceiving the poet's key words: here the form works critically. However, the alphabet is a self-limited area for critique to take shape, for finally the letters must be put back in the familiar order. The material of reality is "relearned," not reimagined, and the alphabet is the sign of that familiar order, newly invested with wonder, re-entered, but not called into question. As a corollary, Levertov remains engaged with cyclic and archetypal patterns, unlike the other two poets.

The fact that the poets write as women is deeply involved with their critiques of myth. Each poet invents myths from the conviction that the production and maintenance of traditional myths about her is simply untrue to her experience and that the readily available cultural forms that women may be tempted to use are an evasion, a form of self-censorship, and not the *truth*— to note a recurrent word. Therefore, all three poets reimagine quest patterns from a woman's perspective—an act of cultural displacement. In all, though they handle this differently, the woman is the hero, and she investigates material of consciousness and culture once felt to have been satisfactorily solved or fixed. In Levertov's case her sometime critique of consciousness and the political poems about the role of the individual in history do not lead her fully to reenvision the nature of myth, which remains a cycle of loss and rebirth, with a blurred shadow of critique. In the cases of Rich and Rukeyser their critiques of consciousness and of society have led them to reformulate the basis of myth itself. This can be marked in three key words: Levertov's "relearn," Rich's "re-vision," Rukeyser's "re-imagine."

For besides being based on a critique of quest patterns and incorporating the act of criticism into the heart of the myth, the myths of Rich and Rukeyser are also noncyclic and nonarchetypal. The myths entail perceptions of a changing self in a historical context, reinterpreting elements of the quest or motifs of rebirth by a reevaluation of who the poets are, the time and place they have entered, and the cultural stances their lives were normatively expected to embody.

This is because the myths replace archetypes by prototypes. They do not investigate moments of eternal recurrence, but rather break with the idea of an essentially unchanging reality. I would define prototypes as original, model forms on which to base the self and its action—forms open to transformation, and forms, unlike archetypes, which offer similar patterns of experience *to* others, rather than imposing these patterns *on* others. A dictionary definition reveals the significant distinction between the words.[24] While both archetype and prototype "denote original models," an archetype "is usually construed as an ideal form that establishes an unchanging pattern for all things of its kind." However, "what develops from a prototype may represent significant modification from the original." A prototype is not a binding, timeless pattern, but one critically open to the possibility, even the necessity, of its own transformation. Thinking in terms of prototypes historicizes myth.

Two related aspects of postmodern mythopoetic writing are seen in these three poets: the concentration on the immanent moment unites them, but while Levertov rests in the reapprehension of archetypal, cyclic patterns, both Rukeyser and Rich have passed to historical critique of mythopoesis, replacing archetype by prototype. In contrast to the classic modernists—Yeats and Eliot are examples—who use myth as a framework by which a total culture can be organized, postmodern use of myth is distinguished by attention to inwardness, to the energies of process, to learning to inhabit a world, not creating one.[25] In Levertov, for instance, the immanent apprehension of reality is the source for the sacred, which is refelt and reexperienced in a highly charged "Here and Now."[26] This idea may be contrasted with T. S. Eliot's "mythical method": which "is simply a way of controlling, of ordering, of giving a shape and a significance to the immense panorama of futility and anarchy which is contemporary history."[27] Eliot's opposition between myth and history, and his use of the eternal pattern to control the transient—and the chaotic—is precisely different from the procedures of postmodern poets. In these methods, myth and the lived moment in the present are mutually involved. But then the question becomes whether the immanent moment in time is seen in itself as an absolute, repetitive experience entailing wonder, or seen instead as something which one's own consciousness—evolutionary, relative, and historical—can respond to and judge. To this question the three poets give different answers. Further, Levertov, Rich, and Rukeyser are quite committed to creating a new world, as their political poems testify, and their immanent poetics should not be interpreted as sanctioning the status quo.

The historical and prototypical character of these myths owes much to the fact that the writers are women. For a woman must often take a critical stance toward her social, historical, and cultural position in order to experience her own quest, transformation, centering, or rebirth. She must often undergo a change of consciousness that challenges her traditional roles or that evokes the conflicts and images she feels as important truths, not as material to be repressed. Poems of the self's growth, or of self-knowledge, may often include, or be preceded by, a questioning of major cultural prescriptions about the shape women's experience should take. Criticizing the nature of myth is one of the reimaginations of culture that women writers consciously undertake, for their own lives allow them to see the culturally repressive function of archetypes, and their own experiences of personal and social change, recorded in poems of consciousness and politics, belie the illusion of a timeless, unhistorical pattern controlling reality.

Selected Bibliography

Theoretical Feminist Criticism

Auerbach, Nina. *Communities of Women: An Idea in Fiction.* Cambridge, Mass.: Harvard University Press, 1978.

Bernikow, Louise. "Introduction," *The World Split Open: Four Centuries of Women Poets in England and America, 1552–1950.* New York: Random House, 1974.

Bowles, Gloria. "Criticism of Women's Poetry," *Signs,* vol. 3, no. 3 (Spring 1978), 712–18.

Daly, Mary. *Beyond God the Father: Toward a Philosophy of Women's Liberation.* Boston: Beacon Press, 1973.

de Beauvoir, Simone. *The Second Sex,* trans. H. M. Parshely. New York: Bantam Books, 1961.

Diamond, Arlyn and Lee R. Edwards, eds. *The Authority of Experience: Essays in Feminist Criticism.* Amherst: University of Massachusetts Press, 1977.

Dinnerstein, Dorothy. *The Mermaid and the Minotaur: Sexual Arrangements and Human Malaise.* New York: Harper Colophon Books, 1977.

Donovan, Josephine, ed. *Feminist Literary Criticism: Explorations in Theory.* Lexington: The University Press of Kentucky, 1975.

Ellmann, Mary. *Thinking About Women.* New York: Harcourt Brace Jovanovich, 1968.

Feit-Diehl, Joan. " 'Come Slowly——Eden': An Exploration of Women Poets and Their Muse." *Signs,* vol. 3, no. 3, pp. 572–87.

Gilbert, Sandra and Susan Gubar. *The Madwoman in the Attic: Re-Visions of Nineteenth-Century Women Writers.* New Haven: Yale University Press, 1979.

Gilbert, Sandra and Susan Gubar. *The Madwoman in the Attic: The Woman Writer and the Nineteenth-Century Literary Imagination.* New Haven: Yale University Press, 1979.

Hardwick, Elizabeth. *Seduction and Betrayal: Women and Literature*. New York: Random House, 1970.

Heilbrun, Carolyn G. *Toward a Recognition of Androgyny*. New York: Harper Colophon Books, 1973.

Howe, Florence and Ellen Bass, eds. "Introduction," *No More Masks!* Garden City, N.Y.: Doubleday, 1973.

Juhasz, Suzanne. *Naked and Fiery Forms: Modern American Poetry by Women, A New Tradition*. New York: Harper Colophon Books, 1976.

Martin, Wendy. "Seduced and Abandoned in the New World," in *Woman in a Sexist Society,* ed. Vivian Gornick and Barbara Moran. New York: New American Library, 1971.

Millett, Kate. *Sexual Politics*. New York: Avon, 1973.

Moers, Ellen. *Literary Women*. Garden City, N.Y.: Doubleday, 1976.

Olsen, Tillie. *Silences*. New York: Delacorte Press, 1978.

Rich, Adrienne. "When We Dead Awaken: Writing as Re-Vision." *Adrienne Rich's Poetry*, ed. Barbara Charlesworth Gelpi and Albert Gelpi. New York: Norton, 1975.

_____. *Of Woman Born: Motherhood as Experience and Institution*. New York: Bantam, 1977.

Robinson, Lillian. *Sex, Class, and Culture*. Bloomington: Indiana University Press, 1978.

Rogers, Katharine. *The Troublesome Helpmate: A History of Misogyny in Literature*. Seattle: University of Washington Press, 1966.

Showalter, Elaine. *A Literature of Their Own*. Princeton, N.J.: Princeton University Press, 1977.

Spacks, Patricia Meyer. *The Female Imagination*. New York: Knopf, 1975.

Watts, Emily Stipes. *The Poetry of American Women from 1632 to 1945*. Austin: University of Texas Press, 1977.

Woolf, Virginia. *A Room of One's Own*. New York: Harcourt Brace & World, 1929.

_____. *Three Guineas*. New York: Harcourt Brace & World, 1938.

_____. *The Common Reader*. New York: Harcourt Brace & World, 1925.

Editions of Poetry and Relevant Criticism Arranged Alphabetically

MARGARET ATWOOD

Atwood, Margaret. *The Animals in That Country*. Boston: Little, Brown, 1968.

_____. *The Circle Game*. Toronto: House of Anansi, 1968.

_____. *The Edible Woman* (novel). Boston: Little, Brown, 1969.

_____. *The Journals of Susanna Moodie*. Toronto: Oxford University Press, 1970.

_____. *Lady Oracle* (novel). New York: Simon & Schuster, 1976.

_____. *Power Politics*. New York: Harper & Row, 1973.

_____. *Procedures for Underground*. Toronto: Oxford University Press, 1970.

_____. *Selected Poems*. Toronto: Oxford University Press, 1976.

_____. *Surfacing* (novel). New York: Simon & Schuster, 1973.

————. *Survival: A Thematic Guide to Canadian Literature.* Toronto: Anansi Press, 1972.

————. *You are Happy.* New York: Harper & Row, 1975.

GWENDOLYN BENNETT. See entries under Dunbar-Nelson.

ANNE BRADSTREET

Ellis, John Harvard, ed. *The Works of Anne Bradstreet.* New York: Peter Smith, 1932.

Hensley, Jeannine, ed. *The Works of Anne Bradstreet,* Foreword by Adrienne Rich. Cambridge, Mass.: Harvard University Press, 1967.

Piercy, Josephine K. *Anne Bradstreet.* New York: Twayne Publishers, 1965.

————, ed. *The Tenth Muse* (1650) *and from the Manuscripts, Meditations Divine and Moral together with Letters and Occasional Pieces.* Scholars Facsimiles and Reprints: Gainesville, Florida, 1965.

Stanford, Ann. "Anne Bradstreet: Dogmatist and Rebel." *New England Quarterly* 39, 1966, 373–89.

————. *Anne Bradstreet: The Worldly Puritan.* New York: Burt Franklin, 1977.

White, Elizabeth Wade. *Anne Bradstreet: "The Tenth Muse."* New York: Oxford University Press, 1971.

EMILY BRONTË

Drew, David P. "Emily Brontë and Emily Dickinson as Mystic Poets." *Brontë Society Transactions,* 15 (1968), 227–32.

Gérin, Winifred. *Emily Brontë: A Biography.* Oxford and New York: Oxford University Press, 1971.

Grove, Robin. " 'It Would Not Do': Emily Brontë as Poet." *The Art of Emily Brontë,* ed. Anne Smith. New York: Barnes & Noble, 1976, 33–67.

Hardy, Barbara. "The Lyricism of Emily Brontë." *The Art of Emily Brontë* 94–118.

Hatfield, C. W., ed. *The Complete Poems of Emily Jane Brontë.* New York: Columbia University Press, 1941.

Miles, Rosalind. "A Baby God: The Creative Dynamism of Emily Brontë's Poetry." *The Art of Emily Brontë,* 68–93.

Ohmann, Carol. "Emily Brontë in the Hands of Male Critics." *College English,* 32 (1971), 906–913. [On *Wuthering Heights* but defines key issues in Brontë criticism and feminism.]

Ratchford, Fannie E. *The Brontës' Web of Childhood.* 1941; rpt. New York: Russell & Russell, 1964.

————, ed. *Gondal's Queen: A Novel in Verse.* 1955; rpt. Austin: University of Texas Press, 1977.

Roarke, Jesse. "The Poems of Emily Brontë: A Reflection." *Visvabharati Quarterly,* 38 (1972–73), 108–119.

Schmidt, Emily T. "From Highland to Lowland: Charlotte Brontë's Editorial Changes in Emily's Poems." *Brontë Society Transactions,* 15 (1968), 221–26.

Starzyk, Lawrence J. "Emily Brontë: Poetry in a Mingled Tone." *Criticism*, 14 (1972), 119–36.

————. "The Faith of Emily Brontë's Immortality Creed." *Victorian Poetry*, 11 (1973), 295–305.

GWENDOLYN BROOKS

Baker, Houston, Jr. "The Achievement of Gwendolyn Brooks." *Singers of Daybreak: Studies in Black American Literature*. Washington, D.C.: Howard University Press, pp. 43–53.

Barrow, W. "Five Fabulous Females." *Negro Digest*, 12 (July 1963), 78–83.

Brooks, Gwendolyn. *Annie Allen*. New York: Harper & Row, 1949.

————. *The Bean Eaters*. New York: Harper & Row, 1960.

————. "Black Wedding Song: On the Occasion of the Marriage of Safisha N. Laini to Haki R. Madhubuti." *Black World*, 23 (September 1974), 36.

————. "Boys, Black." *Ebony*, 27 (August 1972), 45.

————. "Boy Died in My Alley." *Black Scholar*, 6 (June 1975), 8.

————. *A Broadside Treasury*. Detroit: Broadside Press, 1971.

————. *In the Mecca*. New York: Harper & Row, 1968.

————. "In Montgomery." *Ebony*, 26 (August 1971), 42–48.

————. *Jump Bad: A New Chicago Anthology*. Detroit: Broadside Press, 1971.

————. *Maud Martha*. New York: Harper & Row, 1953.

————. "Paul Robeson." *Freedomways*, 11 (1971).

————, et al. *A Portion of that Field: The Centennial of the Burial of Lincoln*. Urbana: University of Illinois Press, 1967.

————. *Report from Part One*. Prefaces by Don L. Lee (Haki R. Madhubuti) and George Kent. Detroit: Broadside Press, 1972.

————. *Riot*. Detroit: Broadside Press, 1969.

————. *Selected Poems*. New York: Harper & Row, 1963.

————. *A Street in Bronzeville*. New York: Harper & Row, 1945.

————. "Thank You." *Black World*, 21 (November 1971), 42.

————. "To a Proper Black Man." *Black Scholar*, 6 (June 1975), 8.

Brown, F. L. "Chicago's Great Lady of Poetry." *Negro Digest*, 11 (December 1961), 53–57.

Clark, E. "Studying and Teaching Afro-American Literature." *College Language Association Journal*, 16 (September 1972), 96–115.

Davis, A. P. "Black and Tan Motif in the Poetry of Gwendolyn Brooks." *College Language Association Journal*, 6 (December 1962), 90–97.

————. "Gwendolyn Brooks: Poet of the Unheroic." *College Language Association Journal*, 7 (December 1963), 114–25.

Hull, Gloria T. "Notes on the Poetic Technique of Gwendolyn Brooks." *College Language Association Journal*, 19 (December 1975), 280–85.

Kent, George. "The Poetry of Gwendolyn Brooks." *Blackness and the Adventure of Western Culture*. Chicago: Third World Press, 1972, 104–139.

Walker, Margaret. "New Poets." *Black Expression*, ed. Addison Gayle, Jr. New York: Weybright and Talley, 1969, 89–100.

Winslow, Henry F. "Maud Martha" (book review). *Crisis*, 61 (February 1954), 114.

ELIZABETH BARRETT BROWNING

Adams, Ruth M., introd. *The Poetical Works of Elizabeth Barrett Browning*. Cambridge Edition. Boston: Houghton Mifflin, 1974.

Boas, Frederick S. *From Richardson to Pinero*, Chapter 7. New York: Columbia University Press, 1936; rpt. New York: Books for Libraries Press, 1969.

Clarke, Isabel C. *Elizabeth Barrett Browning*. New York and London: Kennikat Press, 1929; rpt. 1970.

Hayter, Alethea. *Mrs. Browning*. London: Faber and Faber, 1962.

Hewlett, Dorothy. *Elizabeth Barrett Browning*. New York: Knopf, 1952.

Heydon, Peter N. and Philip Kelley, eds. *Elizabeth Barrett Browning's Letters to Mrs. David Ogilvy*. New York: Quadrangle/The New York Times Book Co. and The Browning Institute, 1973.

Kelley, Philip and Ronald Hudson, eds. *Diary by E.B.B.* Athens, Ohio: Ohio University Press, 1969.

Kenyon, Frederick G., ed. *The Letters of Elizabeth Barrett Browning*. 2 vols. in 1. New York: Macmillan, 1897.

Kintner, Elvan, ed. *The Letters of Robert Browning and Elizabeth Barrett Barrett 1845-1846*. 2 vols. Cambridge: The Belknap Press of Harvard University Press, 1969.

Landis, Paul, ed. *Letters of the Brownings to George Barrett*. Urbana: University of Illinois Press, 1958.

Lupton, Mary Jane. *Elizabeth Barrett Browning*. Old Westbury, N.Y.: The Feminist Press, 1972.

McCarthy, Barbara P., ed. *Elizabeth Barrett to Mr. Boyd*. New Haven: Yale University Press, 1955.

Miller, Betty, ed. *Elizabeth Barrett to Miss Mitford*. London: John Murray, 1954.

Pope, William Bissell, ed. *Invisible Friends: The Correspondence of Elizabeth Barrett Barrett and Benjamin Robert Haydon 1842-1845*. Cambridge: Harvard University Press, 1972.

Taplin, Gardner B. *The Life of Elizabeth Barrett Browning*. New Haven: Yale University Press, 1957.

Twenty-Two Browning Letters: *E.B.B. and R.B. to Henrietta and Arabella*. New York: The United Feature Syndicate, 1935.

Woolf, Virginia. "Aurora Leigh." *The Second Common Reader*. New York: Harcourt Brace and World, 1932.

LUCILLE CLIFTON

Clifton, Lucille. *Good News about the Earth*. New York: Random House, 1972.
_____. *Good Times: Poems*. New York: Random House, 1969.
_____. *An Ordinary Woman*. New York: Random House, 1974.

EMILY DICKINSON

Anderson, Charles R. *Emily Dickinson's Poetry*. New York: Holt, Rinehart and Winston, 1960.

Bennett, Paula. "The Language of Love: Emily Dickinson's Homoerotic Poetry."
   Gai Saber, 1 (Spring 1977), 13–17.
Chase, Richard. *Emily Dickinson*. n.p.: William Sloane Associates, 1951.
Cody, John. *After Great Pain: The Inner Life of Emily Dickinson*. Cambridge,
   Mass.: Harvard University Press, 1971.
Dickinson, Emily. *The Letters of Emily Dickinson*, ed. Thomas H. Johnson and
   Theodora Ward (3 vols.). Cambridge, Mass.: The Belknap Press of Harvard
   University Press, 1958.
————. *The Poems of Emily Dickinson*, ed. Thomas H. Johnson (3 vols., with
   variant readings). Cambridge, Mass.: The Belknap Press of Harvard University
   Press, 1955.
————. *The Complete Poems of Emily Dickinson*, ed. Thomas H. Johnson (1
   vol., without variant readings). Boston: Little, Brown, 1960.
Faderman, Lillian. "Emily Dickinson's Letters to Sue Gilbert." *Massachusetts
   Review,* 18 (Summer 1977), 197–225.
Gelpi, Albert J. *Emily Dickinson: The Mind of the Poet*. Cambridge, Mass.: Har-
   vard University Press, 1966.
————. *The Tenth Muse: The Psyche of the American Poet* (Cambridge,
   Mass.: Harvard University Press, 1975.
Greene, Elsa. "Emily Dickinson Was a Poetess." *College English*, 34 (October
   1972), 63–70.
Jennings, Elizabeth. "Emily Dickinson and the Poetry of the Inner Life." *A Re-
   view of English Literature*, 3 (April 1962), 78–87.
Jong, Erica. "Visionary Anger." *Ms.* (July 1973), 30–31.
Juhasz, Suzanne. " 'A Privilege So Awful': Emily Dickinson as Woman Poet."
   San José Studies, II, 2 (1976), 94–107.
Leyda, Jan. *The Years and Hours of Emily Dickinson*. 2 vols. New Haven: Yale
   University Press, 1960.
Mudge, Jean McClure. *Emily Dickinson and the Image of Home*. Amherst, Mass.:
   University of Massachusetts Press, 1975.
Sewall, Richard B., ed. *Emily Dickinson: A Collection of Critical Essays*. Twen-
   tieth Century Views. Englewood Cliffs, N.J.: Prentice-Hall, 1963. [See espe-
   cially Donald E. Thackrey on the theme of silence.]
————. *The Life of Emily Dickinson*. 2 vols. New York: Farrar, Straus and
   Giroux, 1974.
Weisbuch, Robert. *Emily Dickinson's Poetry*. Chicago: University of Chicago
   Press, 1975.

ALICE DUNBAR-NELSON

Bernikow, Louise, ed. *The World Split Open: Four Centuries of Women Poets
   in England and America, 1552–1950*. New York: Random House, 1974.
Cullen, Countee, ed. *Caroling Dusk: An Anthology of Verse by Negro Poets*.
   New York: Harper and Brothers, 1927.
Hughes, Langston and Arna Bontemps, eds. *The Poetry of the Negro, 1746–1970*.
   Garden City, N.Y.: Doubleday, 1970.
Hull, Gloria T. "Alice Dunbar-Nelson: Delaware Writer and Woman of Affairs."
   Delaware History (Fall-Winter 1976), 87–103.

Johnson, James Weldon, ed. *The Book of American Negro Poetry*, rev. ed. New
York: Harcourt Brace, 1931.
Kerlin, Robert T., ed. *Negro Poets and Their Poems*, 2nd ed. Washington: Asso-
ciated Publishers, 1938.
Sherman, Joan. *Invisible Poets: Afro-Americans of the Nineteenth Century*. Ur-
bana: University of Illinois Press, 1974.

JESSIE FAUSET. See entries under Dunbar-Nelson.

ANNE FINCH

Finch, Anne. *The Poems of Anne Countess of Winchilsea*, ed. Myra Reynolds.
Chicago: University of Chicago Press, 1903.
_____. *Selected Poems of Anne Finch, Countess of Winchilsea*, ed. Katharine
M. Rogers. New York: Frederick Ungar, forthcoming.
Rogers, Katharine M., ed. *Six Eighteenth-Century Women Authors*. New York:
Frederick Ungar, forthcoming.

SUSAN GRIFFIN

Griffin, Susan. *Like the Iris of an Eye*. New York: Harper & Row, 1977.
_____. *Voices*. New York: The Feminist Press, 1976.

ANGELINA GRIMKÉ. See entries under Dunbar-Nelson.

FRANCES HARPER

Robinson, William H., Jr. *Early Black American Poets*. Dubuque, Iowa: Wm. C.
Brown, 1971.
Sherman, Joan. *Invisible Poets: Afro-Americans of the Nineteenth Century*.
Urbana: University of Illinois Press, 1974.

H. D. (HILDA DOOLITTLE)

Friedman, Susan. "Who Buried H. D.? A Poet, Her Critics, and Her Place in
the Literary Tradition." *College English*, 36, 7 (March 1975), 801–814.
H. D. *Bid Me to Live*. New York: Grove Press, 1960.
_____. *Collected Poems*. New York: Liveright Publishing Corporation, 1925.
_____. *Helen in Egypt*. New York: New Directions, 1974.
_____. *Hermetic Definitions*. New York: New Directions, 1972.
_____. *Hippolytus Temporizes*. Boston: Houghton Mifflin, 1927.
_____. *Palimpsest*, ed. Harry T. Moore. Carbondale: Southern Illinois Univer-
sity Press, 1968.
_____. *Red Roses for Bronze*. New York: AMS Press, 1970.
_____. *Selected Poems*. New York: Grove Press, 1957.
_____. *Tribute to Freud*. New York: Pantheon Books, 1956.
_____. *Trilogy: The Walls Do Not Fall; The Flowering of the Rod; Tribute
to the Angels*. New York: New Directions, 1973.

Holland, Norman. *Poems in Persons: An Introduction to Psychoanalysis and Literature.* New York: Norton, 1973.

Levertov, Denise. "H. D.: An Appreciation." *Poetry,* (June 1962), 182–86.

Quinn, Vincent. *Hilda Doolittle.* New York: Twayne Publishers, Inc., 1967.

Special Issue on H. D., *Contemporary Literature* (Autumn 1969) contains essential essays by Joseph N. Riddel, Norman N. Holland, Norman Holmes Pearson, Linda Wagner, and others.

Swann, Thomas. *The Classical World of H. D.* Lincoln: University of Nebraska Press, 1962.

GEORGIA DOUGLAS JOHNSON. See entries under Dunbar-Nelson.

Dover, Cedric. "The Importance of Georgia Douglas Johnson." *Crisis* (1952).

HELENE JOHNSON. See entries under Dunbar-Nelson.

JANE LEAD

Lead, Jane. *The Heavenly Cloud now breaking. The Lord Christ's Ascension-Ladder sent down* ... (London, 1681).

_____. *The Revelation of Revelations Particularly as an Essay Towards the Unsealing, Opening, and Discovering the Seven Seals, the Seven Thunders, and the New Jerusalem State* ... (London: A. Sowle, 1683).

_____. Introduction to John Pordage, *Theologica Mystica* (1683).

_____. *The Enochian Walks with God, found out by a Spiritual Traveller, whose Face towards Mount Sion above was set. With an Experimental Account of what was known, seen, and met withal there* ... (London, 1694).

_____. *The Laws of Paradise given forth by Wisdom to a Translated Spirit* ... (1695).

_____. *The Wonders of God's Creation manifested in the variety of Eight Worlds, as they were made known experimentally unto the Author* ... (London, 1695).

_____. *A Message to the Philadelphian Society whithersoever dispersed over the whole Earth* ... (London, 1696).

_____. *The Tree of Faith, or the Tree of Life springing up in the Paradise of God, from which all the Wonders of the New Creation must proceed* ... (1696).

_____. *The Ark of Faith, a supplement to the Tree of Faith* ... (1696).

_____. *A Fountain of Gardens watered by the Rivers of Divine Pleasure, and springing up in all the variety of Spiritual Plants, sending forth their Sweet Savours and Strong Odours, for Soul Refreshing* ... 4 vols. (London, 1697–1701).

_____. *A Revelation of the Everlasting Gospel Message* ... (1697).

_____. *The Ascent to the Mount of Vision* ... (1698).

_____. *The Signs of the Times: forerunning the Kingdom of Christ, and evidencing when it is to come* ... (1699).

_____. *The Wars of David and the Peaceable Reign of Solomon* ... *containing:*

1. *An Alarm to the Holy Warriors to Fight the Battles of the Lamb.*
2. *The Glory of Sharon in the Renovation of Nature, introducing the Kingdom of Christ,* [with a preface containing autobiographical remarks] (1700).
————. *A Second and Third Message to the Philadelphian Society* . . . (1698).
————. *A Living Funeral Testimony, or Death overcome and drowned in the Life of Christ* . . . (1702).
————. *The First Resurrection in Christ* [dictated shortly before her death and published almost immediately in Amsterdam; intended title: *The Royal Stamp*].

DENISE LEVERTOV

Levertov, Denise. *The Double Image.* London: The Cresset Press, 1946.
————. *Footprints.* New York: New Directions, 1972.
————. *The Freeing of the Dust.* New York: New Directions, 1975.
————. *Here and Now.* San Francisco: City Lights Pocket Bookshop, 1957; rpt. Kraus, 1973.
————. *The Jacob's Ladder.* New York: New Directions, 1961.
————. *O Taste and See.* New York: New Directions, 1964.
————. *Overland to the Islands.* Highland, N.C.: Jonathan Williams, 1958.
————. *The Poet in the World.* New York: New Directions, 1973 (essays).
————. *Relearning the Alphabet.* New York: New Directions, 1970.
————. *The Sorrow Dance.* New York: New Directions, 1967.
————. *To Stay Alive.* New York: New Directions, 1971.
————. *With Eyes at the Back of Our Heads.* New York: New Directions, 1959.
Wagner, Linda. *Denise Levertov.* New York: Twayne, 1967.

AUDRE LORDE

Cornwell, Anita. " 'So Who's Giving Guarantees?': An Interview with Audre Lorde." *Sinister Wisdom* (Fall 1977), 15–21.
Gilbert, Sandra. "On the Edge of the Estate." *Poetry,* CXXIX, 5, 296–301.
Lorde, Audre. *Between Our Selves.* Pt. Reyes, California: Eidolon Editions, 1976.
————. *The Black Unicorn.* New York: Norton, 1978.
————. *Coal.* New York: Norton, 1976.
————. *From a Land Where Other People Live.* Detroit: Broadside Press, 1973.
————. *The New York Head Shop and Museum.* Detroit: Broadside Press, 1974.

EDNA ST. VINCENT MILLAY

Atkins, Elizabeth. *Edna St. Vincent Millay and Her Times.* 1936; rpt. New York: Russell & Russell, 1964.
Brittin, Norman A. *Edna St. Vincent Millay.* New York: Twayne, 1967.
Cheney, Anne. *Millay in Greenwich Village.* University, Ala.: University of Alabama Press, 1975.
Cowley, Malcolm. "Two Poets: Jeffers and Millay." *After the Genteel Tradition.* Carbondale: Southern Illinois University Press, 1965.

Dabbs, James McBride. "Edna St. Vincent Millay: Not Resigned." *South Atlantic Quarterly*, 37 (January 1938), 54–66.

Dash, Joan. *A Life of One's Own: Three Gifted Women and the Men They Married*. New York: Harper & Row, 1973.

Gassman, J. "Edna St. Vincent Millay: 'Nobody's Own.'" *Colby Library Quarterly*, 9 (1971), 297–310.

Gould, Jean. *The Poet and Her Book*. New York: Dodd, Mead, 1969.

Gray, James. *Edna St. Vincent Millay*. University of Minnesota Pamphlets on American Writers, No. 64. Minneapolis: University of Minnesota Press, 1967.

Gurko, Miriam. *Restless Spirit: The Life of Edna St. Vincent Millay*. New York: Crowell, 1962.

Haight, Elizabeth Hazelton. "Vincent at Vassar." *Vassar Miscellany* (May 1951), 14–20.

Millay, Edna St. Vincent. *Collected Lyrics*, cl. ed. New York: Harper & Row, 1943.

————. *Collected Lyrics*, pa. ed. New York: Harper & Row, 1969.

————. *Collected Poems*, cl. ed. New York: Harper & Row, 1956.

————. *Collected Poems*, pa. ed. New York: Harper & Row, 1975.

————. *Collected Sonnets*, cl. ed. New York: Harper & Row, 1941.

————. *Collected Sonnets*, pa. ed. New York: Harper & Row, 1970.

————. *Flowers of Evil: From the French of Charles Baudelaire*. New York: Harper & Row, 1936.

————. *Letters of Edna St. Vincent Millay*, ed. Allan Ross Macdougall. New York and London: Harper and Brothers, 1952.

————. *Poems Selected for Young People*. New York: Harper & Row, 1929.

————. *Renascence & Other Poems*. New York: Arno Press; rpt. of 1917 edition.

Monroe, Harriet. "Edna St. Vincent Millay." *Poetry*, 24 (August 1924), 260–66.

Patton, John J. "A Comprehensive Bibliography of Criticism of Edna St. Vincent Millay." *Serif*, 5, iii (1968), 10–32.

Preston, John Hyde. "Edna St. Vincent Millay." *Virginia Quarterly Review*, 3 (July 1927), 342–55.

Ransom, John Crowe. *The World's Body*. 1938; rpt. Port Washington, N. Y.: Kennikat Press, 1964.

Sheean, Vincent. *The Indigo Bunting*. New York: Harper & Brothers, 1951.

Wilson, Edmund. "Epilogue, 1952: Edna St. Vincent Millay." *The Shores of Light: A Literary Chronicle of the Twenties and Thirties*. New York: Farrar, Straus and Young, 1952.

Yost, Karl. *A Bibliography of the Works of Edna St. Vincent Millay*. New York: Harper and Brothers, 1937.

MARIANNE MOORE

Hall, Donald. *Marianne Moore: The Cage and the Animal*. New York: Pegasus, 1970.

Hayes, Ann L. "Marianne Moore." *A Modern Miscellany*. Pittsburgh: Carnegie Series in English #11, 1970.

Kenner, Hugh. "The Experience of the Eye: Marianne Moore's Tradition." *The Southern Review*, NS I, 4 (October 1965), 754–69.

Moore, Marianne. *Complete Poems*. New York: Viking Press, 1967.

—————. *A Marianne Moore Reader*. New York: Viking Press, 1961.

—————. *Predilections*. New York: Viking Press, 1955.

EFFIE LEE NEWSOME. See entries under Dunbar-Nelson.

SYLVIA PLATH

Aird, Eileen. *Sylvia Plath: Her Life and Work*. New York: Harper & Row, 1975.

Alvarez, A. *The Savage God: A Study of Suicide*. New York: Random House, 1972.

Brinnin, John Malcolm. Review of Sylvia Plath, *Ariel*. *The Partisan Review*, 34 (Winter 1967), 156–57.

Butscher, Edward. *Sylvia Plath: Method and Madness*. New York: Seabury, 1976. (Hostile but nevertheless sometimes useful.)

Chesler, Phyllis. *Women and Madness*. New York: Avon, 1972.

Corrigan, Sylvia Robinson. "Sylvia Plath: A New Feminist Approach." *Aphra* 1 (Spring 1970), 16–23.

Donovan, Josephine. "Sexual Politics in Sylvia Plath's Short Stories." *Minnesota Review*, 4 (1973), 150–57.

Evans, Nancy Burr. "The Value and Peril for Women of Reading Women Writers." *Images of Women in Fiction*, ed. Susan Koppelman Cornillon. Bowling Green, Ohio: Bowling Green Popular Press, 1972.

Hoffman, Nancy Jo. "Reading Women's Poetry: The Meaning and Our Lives." *College English*, 34 (October 1972), 48–62.

Holbrook, David. *Sylvia Plath: Poetry and Existence*. London: The Athlone Press, 1976. (Hostile but full of significant readings and misreadings.)

Kroll, Judith. *Chapters in a Mythology: The Poetry of Sylvia Plath*. New York: Harper, 1976.

Newman, Charles, ed. *The Art of Sylvia Plath: A Symposium*. Bloomington, Ind.: Indiana University Press, 1970. See especially " 'Candor Is the Only Wile': The Art of Sylvia Plath."

Plath, Sylvia. *Ariel*. New York: Harper & Row, 1966.

—————. *The Bell Jar*. New York: Harper & Row, 1971.

—————. *The Colossus and Other Poems*. 1962; rpt. New York: Knopf, 1971.

—————. *Crossing the Water*. New York: Harper & Row, 1971.

—————. *Letters Home: Correspondence 1950–1963*, ed. Aurelia Schober Plath. New York: Harper & Row, 1975.

—————. *Winter Trees*. New York: Harper & Row, 1972.

Ries, Lawrence. *Wolf Masks: Violence in Contemporary Poetry* (chapter on Plath). Port Washington, N.Y.: Kennikat, 1977.

Rosenstein, Harriet. "Reconsidering Sylvia Plath." *Ms.*, 1 (September 1972), 44–51.

Stein, Karen F. "Reflections in a Jagged Mirror: Some Metaphors of Madness." *Aphra*, 6 (Spring 1975), 2–11.

Steinbrink, Jeffrey. "Emily Dickinson and Sylvia Plath: The Values of Mortality." *Women and Literature*, 4, 1 (1976), 45–58.

Zatlin, Linda G. " 'This Holocaust I Walk In': The Poetic Vision of Sylvia Plath." *Papers on Women's Studies*, 1 (October 1974), 158–73.

ADRIENNE RICH

Gelpi, Barbara C. and Albert Gelpi, eds. *Adrienne Rich's Poetry* (texts of the poems, the poet on her work, reviews, and criticism). New York: Norton, 1975.

Rich, Adrienne. *A Change of World*, Foreword by W. H. Auden. New Haven: Yale University Press, 1951; rpt. New York: AMS Press, 1971.

_____. *The Diamond Cutters, and other poems*. New York: Harper, 1955.

_____. *Diving into the Wreck; Poems, 1971–1972*. New York: Norton, 1973.

_____. *The Dream of a Common Language*. New York: Norton, 1978.

_____. *Leaflets; Poems, 1965–1968*. New York: Norton, 1969.

_____. *Necessities of Life; Poems, 1962–1965*. New York: Norton, 1966.

_____. *Of Woman Born: Motherhood as Experience and Institution*. New York: Norton, 1976.

_____. *Poems: Selected and New, 1950–1974*. New York: Norton, 1974.

_____. *Snapshots of a Daughter-in-Law; Poems, 1954–1962*. New York: Harper & Row, 1963.

_____. *Twenty-One Love Poems*. Emeryville, Ca.: Effie's Press, 1976.

_____. *The Will to Change; Poems, 1968–1970*. New York: Norton, 1971.

CHRISTINA ROSSETTI

Crump, Rebecca W. *Christina Rossetti: A Reference Guide*. Boston: Hall, 1976.

Fass, Barbara. "Christina Rossetti and St. Agnes' Eve." *Victorian Poetry*, 14 (Spring 1976), 33–46.

Greer, Germaine. Introduction to *Goblin Market*. New York: Stonehill Publishing, 1975.

Rossetti, Christina. *The Poetical Works*, ed. William Michael Rossetti. London: Macmillan, 1904. A three-volume variorum edition, *The Complete Poems of Christina Rossetti*, ed. Rebecca W. Crump, is forthcoming from Louisiana State University Press. An edition is also planned by Hans B. de Groot of the University of Toronto.

Weathers, Winston. "Christina Rossetti: The Sisterhood of Self." *Victorian Poetry*, III (Spring 1965), 81–89.

MURIEL RUKEYSER

Rukeyser, Muriel. *Beast in View*. Garden City, N.Y.: Doubleday, Doran and Co., 1944.

_____. *Body of Waking*. New York: Harper, 1958.

_____. *Breaking Open*. New York: Random House, 1973.

_____. *The Gates*. New York: McGraw-Hill, 1976.

_____. *The Green Wave*. Garden City, N.Y.: Doubleday, 1948.

_____. *The Life of Poetry*. New York: Current Books, 1949; rpt. Kraus, 1968; Morrow, 1974 (prose).

_____. *Selected Poems*. New York: New Directions, 1951.

_____. *The Speed of Darkness*. New York: Random House, 1968.

_____. *Theory of Flight*, Foreword by Stephen Vincent Benet. New Haven: Yale University Press, 1935; rpt. New York: AMS Press, 1971.

————. *A Turning Wind.* New York: Viking Press, 1939.

————. *U.S. 1.* New York: Covici, Friede, 1938.

————. *Waterlily Fire; Poems, 1935–1962.* New York: Macmillan, 1962.

SONIA SANCHEZ

Sanchez, Sonia. *A Blues Book for Blue Black Magical Women.* Detroit: Broadside Press, 1974.

————. *Homecoming.* Detroit: Broadside Press, 1969.

————. *It's a New Day: Poems for Young Brothas and Sistuhs.* Detroit: Broadside Press, 1971.

————. *We a BaddDDD People.* Detroit: Broadside Press, 1970.

ANNE SEXTON

McClatchy, J.D., ed. *Anne Sexton: The Artist and Her Critics.* Bloomington, Ind.: Indiana University Press, 1978.

Sexton, Anne. *All My Pretty Ones.* Boston: Houghton Mifflin, 1962.

————. *The Awful Rowing Toward God.* Boston: Houghton Mifflin, 1974.

————. *To Bedlam and Part Way Back.* Boston: Houghton Mifflin, 1960.

————. *The Book of Folly.* Boston: Houghton Mifflin, 1972.

————. *The Death Notebooks.* Boston: Houghton Mifflin, 1974.

————. *Live or Die.* Boston: Houghton Mifflin, 1966.

————. *Love Poems.* Boston: Houghton Mifflin, 1969.

————. *Transformations.* Boston: Houghton Mifflin, 1971.

————. *45 Mercy Street,* ed. Linda Gray Sexton. Boston: Houghton Mifflin, 1976.

Sexton, Linda Gray and Lois Ames, eds. *Anne Sexton: A Self-Portrait in Letters.* Boston: Houghton Mifflin, 1977.

ANNE SPENCER. See entries under Dunbar-Nelson.

MAY SWENSON

"Craft Interview with May Swenson," in *The New York Quarterly,* 19, with photographs by Lael Silbert (1977).

Howard, Richard. "Turned Back to the Wild by Love." *Alone with America.* New York: Atheneum, 1969.

Stanford, Anne. "Poet of Perception." *The Southern Review* (Spring 1969).

Swenson, May. *A Cage of Spines.* New York: Rinehart, 1958.

————. *Half Sun Half Sleep.* New York: Scribner's, 1967.

————. *Iconographs.* New York: Scribner's, 1970.

————. *New & Selected Things Taking Place.* Boston: Atlantic/Little, Brown, 1978.

————. *To Mix with Time, New & Selected Poems.* New York: Scribner's, 1963.

MARGARET WALKER

Walker, Margaret. *For My People*. New Haven: Yale University Press, 1942.
————. *October Journey*. Detroit: Broadside Press, 1973.
————. *Prophets for a New Day*. Detroit: Broadside Press, 1970.

PHILLIS WHEATLEY

Robinson, William H., Jr. *Early Black American Poets*. Dubuque, Iowa: Wm. C. Brown, 1971.
Wheatley, Phillis. *The Poems of Phillis Wheatley*, ed. Julian Mason. Chapel Hill: University of North Carolina Press, 1966.

Notes

Introduction

1. Anne Finch, "The Introduction," in *The Poems of Anne Countess of Winchilsea*, ed. Myra Reynolds (Chicago: University of Chicago Press, 1903), pp. 4–5.

2. Virginia Woolf, *A Room of One's Own* (New York: Harcourt Brace and World, 1929), pp. 48–52.

3. Letter to Charlotte Brontë, March 1837, quoted in Winifred Gérin, *Charlotte Brontë* (Oxford, London, and New York: Oxford University Press, 1967), p. 110.

4. See, for instance, Elaine Showalter, *A Literature of Their Own* (Princeton: Princeton University Press, 1977), Ellen Moers, *Literary Women* (Garden City, N.Y.: Doubleday, 1975), Patricia Meyer Spacks, *The Female Imagination* (New York: Knopf, 1974), and Arlyn Diamond and Lee Edwards, eds., *The Authority of Experience* (Amherst: University of Massachusetts Press, 1977).

5. Showalter, p. 73.

6. *The Letters of Elizabeth Barrett Browning*, ed. Frederick G. Kenyon (2 vols. in 1, New York: Macmillan, 1899), I, 230–32. Compare Woolf's "For we think back through our mothers if we are women. It is useless to go to the great men writers for help, however much one may go to them for pleasure" (*A Room*, p. 79).

7. Thomas Johnson, ed., *The Complete Poems of Emily Dickinson* (Boston: Little, Brown, 1960), #613.

8. See especially "Aurora Leigh" and "I am Christina Rossetti" in *The Second Common Reader* (New York: Harcourt Brace, 1932), pp. 182–92 and 214–21.

9. Reprinted in Richard B. Sewall, ed., *Emily Dickinson: A Collection of Critical Essays* (Englewood Cliffs, N.J.: Prentice-Hall, 1963), p. 120. In fairness to Reeves, we should note that he quotes this statement in order to dispute it.

10. Theodore Roethke, "The Poetry of Louise Bogan," *Selected Prose of Theodore Roethke*, ed. Ralph J. Mills, Jr. (Seattle: University of Washington Press, 1965), pp. 133–34.

11. "Emily Dickinson: A Poet Restored," in Sewall, p. 92.

12. Ibid., p. 89.

13. Quoted in Reeves, p. 119.

14. John Cody, *After Great Pain: The Inner Life of Emily Dickinson* (Cambridge, Mass.: The Belknap Press of Harvard University Press, 1971), p. 495.

15. Gardner B. Taplin, *The Life of Elizabeth Barrett Browning* (New Haven: Yale University Press, 1957), p. 417.

16. *The Edinburgh Review,* vol. 189 (1899), 420–39.

17. Samuel B. Holcombe, "Death of Mrs. Browning," *The Southern Literary Messenger,* 33 (1861), 412–17.

18. *The Christian Examiner,* vol. 72 (1862), 55–88.

19. "Poetic Aberrations," *Blackwood's,* vol. 87 (1860), 490–94.

20. *A Room,* p. 65.

21. See Pater, "Conclusion" to *The Renaissance,* and, for a general discussion of the poet as priest, M.H. Abrams, *Natural Supernaturalism* (New York: Norton, 1971).

22. See Pope, "An Essay on Criticism," Part I, ll. 135–40.

23. Suzanne Juhasz, *Naked and Fiery Forms: Modern American Poetry by Women, A New Tradition* (New York: Harper & Row, 1976), "The Double Bind of the Woman Poet," pp. 1–6.

24. Ransom, ibid.; Sewall, pp. 99–100.

25. See T. S. Eliot, "Tradition and the Individual Talent," and Emily Dickinson, letter to T. W. Higginson, July 1892, in *The Letters of Emily Dickinson,* Thomas Johnson, ed. (Cambridge, Mass.: The Belknap Press of Harvard University Press, 1958), vol. II, p. 412.

26. Letter to John Wheelock, July 1, 1935, in *What the Woman Lived: Selected Letters of Louise Bogan, 1920–1970,* ed. Ruth Limmer (New York: Harcourt Brace Jovanovich, 1973), p. 86. For more detailed commentary, see Gloria Bowles, "Louise Bogan," forthcoming in *Women's Studies.*

27. Plath, "Stings," in *Ariel* (New York: Harper & Row, 1966), p. 62.

28. *A Room,* p. 118.

1. Jane Lead: Mysticism and the Woman Cloathed with the Sun

1. Jane Lead, *A Fountain of Gardens Watered by the River of Divine Pleasure, and Springing Up in all Variety of Spiritual Plants . . .* (London, 1697–1701), I, pp. 18–21.

2. Ibid., p. 27; IV, pp. 106–107; II, p. 126; I, pp. 470, 77. Since the image of Sophia is almost formulaic in Lead and develops cumulatively, and since the chronology of that development is not the point here, I have freely combined sections of it from throughout her journal.

3. Sylvia Plath, "Fever 103°," *Ariel* (New York: Harper & Row, 1966), p. 54, and Diane Wakoski, "Sun Gods Have Sun Spots," *Dancing on the Grave of a Son of a Bitch* (Los Angeles: Black Sparrow Press, 1973), p. 38.

4. My primary sources are principally Lead's journal *A Fountain of Gardens*; "The Publisher's Address to his Readers" in Lead's *Wars of David,* 2nd ed. (1700); Francis Lee, "Letters to Henry Dodwell" in Christopher Walton's *Notes and Materials for an Adequate Biography of William Law* (London, 1856), pp.

181ff.; *The Last Hours of Jane Lead by an Eye and Ear-Witness* (Dr. Williams's Library, London, MS. Walton 186.18 c. 5. 30); and *Three Epistles, addressed by Francis Lee to . . . Peter Poiret in Holland* . . . (ibid.). For secondary sources I have used Nils Thune, *The Behmenists and the Philadelphians: A Contribution to the Study of English Mysticism in the Seventeenth and Eighteenth Centuries* (Uppsala, 1948) and Désirée Hirst, *Hidden Riches: Traditional Symbolism from the Renaissance to Blake* (New York: Barnes and Noble, 1964). Uncertainties in Lead's biography include the year of her birth and the spelling and pronunciation of her last name. The *Dictionary of National Biography* and other sources give 1623 as the birth date; internal dating in her writing indicates 1624. Spelling of her name varies between "Leade" and "Lead"; signed prefaces and title pages of her work give "Lead." Occasional punning on her name, and lack of other information, leave unclear whether she pronounced it "leed" or "led."

5. Paul Delaney, *British Autobiography in the Seventeenth Century* (London: Routledge & Kegan Paul, 1969) and Joan Webber, *The Eloquent "I": Style and Self in Seventeenth-Century Prose* (Madison: University of Wisconsin Press, 1968).

6. Thune, pp. 68–69.

7. Ibid., p. 69. This vision, similar to one of John Bunyan's, is among formulaic elements discussed in Delaney, *British Autobiography*.

8. Hirst, *Hidden Riches*, pp. 107–108, and "The Riddle of John Pordage," *The Jacob Boehme Society Quarterly*, 1, no. 6, Winter 1953–54, pp. 6, 12.

9. Thune, pp. 60–61.

10. The quotation is from Francis Lee, "Advertisement," *Fountain of Gardens*, IV.

11. Thune, p. 85.

12. Hirst, *Hidden Riches*, p. 103.

13. Jacob Boehme, *The Clavis* in 'William Law,' *The Works of Jacob Behmen, The Teutonic Theosopher (1764–81)*, ed. George Ward and Thomas Langcake, II, p. 8.

14. Tr. H. M. Parshley (New York: Knopf, 1953). For historical and critical considerations of androgyny, see *Women's Studies, An Interdisciplinary Journal*, II, 2 (1974).

15. Roach, *The Great Crisis; or The Mystery of the Times and Seasons Unfolded* . . . (London, 1727), p. 96. Lee, "Preface," *Fountain of Gardens*, III, p. 271.

16. Virginia Woolf, *Three Guineas, A Room of One's Own*, and elsewhere in the fiction, criticism, and letters. Adrienne Rich, "When We Dead Awaken: Writing as Re-Vision," Barbara Charlesworth Gelpi and Albert Gelpi, eds., *Adrienne Rich's Poetry* (New York: Norton, 1975), pp. 90–98, and "Toward a Woman-Centered University," Florence Howe, ed., *Women and the Power to Change* (New York: McGraw-Hill, 1975), pp. 15–46, and elsewhere in the poetry and criticism.

17. Roach, *Great Crisis*, p. 99.

18. Lead, *A Fountain of Gardens*, I, p. 334; II, p. 231; *Revelation of Revelations*, p. 53; Francis Lee and Richard Roach, "A Serious Proposal to the Ladies..." in *Theosophical Transactions by the Philadelphian Society...* , I, pp. 59–60.

19. Blake, Letter to Flaxman, 1800, in David V. Erdman and Harold Bloom, eds., *The Poetry and Prose of William Blake* (Garden City, N.Y.: Doubleday, 1965), p. 680; Coleridge, Pencil notes to flyleaf and margins of vol. 1, *Works of Behmen*, British Museum copy, L. 126, k. 1; Yeats, *A Vision* (1938 New York: Macmillan, 1961), pp. 23–24.

20. Bodleian mss. Rawlinson D. 1262, p. 130; D. 1338, January 24, 1693 (unpaginated).

21. In the introduction to *British Autobiography*, Delaney points out the need for special consideration of work by women in that period. His chapter "Female Autobiographers" treats six aristocratic women, without extensive comment on sectarian "lives."

22. " 'I am in Danger—Sir—,' " *Poetry*, p. 31.

23. Rich, ibid., pp. 24–25. Robin Morgan, in *Lady of the Beasts* (New York: Random House, 1976), p. 39. Wakoski, *Dancing on the Grave of a Son of a Bitch*, p. 38. Plath, *Ariel*, pp. 54, 62–63.

24. Special thanks to Jane Lilienfeld, Assumption College, for naming this form of female selfhood.

25. " 'My Name is Darkness': The Poetry of Self-Definition," Dana V. Hiller and Robin Ann Sheets, eds., *Women and Men: The Consequences of Power* (Selected Papers from the National Bicentennial Conference Pioneers for Century III, published by the Office of Women's Studies, University of Cincinnati, 1977), pp. 372–85.

26. Catherine F. Smith, "Mysticism and Feminism: Jacob Boehme and Jane Lead," ibid., pp. 398–408, and "Jane Lead: The Feminist Mind and Art of a Seventeenth Century Protestant Mystic," forthcoming in Rosemary Ruether and Eleanor McLaughlin, eds., *Women of Spirit* (Simon and Schuster).

27. Rich, "Women's Studies: Renaissance or Revolution?" in *Women's Studies, An Interdisciplinary Journal*, III, 2, p. 124. Cynthia Secor, conversation, Philadelphia, Pa., November 1974.

28. See especially Alice Rossi, ed., *The Feminist Papers: From Adams to Beauvoir* (New York: Bantam, 1974).

29. Caroline F.S. Spurgeon, *Mysticism in English Literature* (Cambridge, England: 1927), p. 1.

30. Written before I had read Adrienne Rich's study of women's related biological and cultural being, *Of Woman Born: Motherhood as Experience and Institution* (New York: Norton, 1976), this is compatible with much of her thesis, especially concerning the transformative power inherent in the association of woman and vessel, pp. 93–101.

31. 1970; rev. ed. (London: Barrie and Jenkins, 1973). For the psychoanalytic argument, see Norman Cohn, *The Pursuit of the Millennium* (Fairlawn, N.J.: Essential Books, 1957; rev. ed. London: Oxford University Press, 1970).

2. Anne Bradstreet's Poetry: A Study of Subversive Piety

1. Anne Bradstreet, "Letter to My Dear Children," in *The Works of Anne Bradstreet in Prose and Verse*, ed. John Harvard Ellis (Charlestown: Abram E. Cutter, 1867), p. 361. All future citations of this text will be by page number only.

2. For biographical background, see Elizabeth Wade White, *Anne Bradstreet, The Tenth Muse* (New York: Oxford University Press, 1971); Josephine K. Piercy, *Anne Bradstreet* (New York: Twayne Publishers, 1965), p. 22; Ann Stanford, *Anne Bradstreet: The Worldly Puritan* (New York: Burt Franklin, 1975).

3. John Berryman, "Homage to Mistress Bradstreet" (New York: Farrar, Straus and Cudahy, 1956), p. 6.

4. See Perry Miller, *Errand Into the Wilderness* (Cambridge, Mass.: Harvard University Press, 1956), for the classic study of the Puritan mission in the new world. For a more recent analysis of this theme, see Sacvan Bercovitch, *The Puritan Origins of the American Self* (New Haven: Yale University Press, 1975).

5. Norman Petit, *The Heart Prepared: Grace and Conversion in Spiritual Life* (New Haven: Yale University Press), p. 19.

6. *New England Primer*, ed. Paul Leicester Ford (New York: Dodd, Mead, 1897), p. 101.

7. White, *Anne Bradstreet*, p. 67.

8. Cotton Mather, *Diary in Massachusetts Historical Society*, VII (Boston, 1878–1882), pp. 437–38. Quoted in Kenneth Murdock, *Literature and Theology*, p. 110.

9. John Winthrop, *Winthrop Papers* (Boston) III, 338–44. Quoted in Edmund Morgan, *The Visible Saints* (Ithaca, N.Y.: Cornell University Press), p. 72.

10. See Herbert Schneider, *The Puritan Mind* (Ann Arbor: University of Michigan Press, 1958), pp. 60–67, for a discussion of Hutchinson's trial and banishment.

11. John Cotton, *A Practical Commentary, or An Exposition with Observations, Reasons and Uses Upon the First Epistle Generall of John* (London, 1656), p. 193. Quoted in Morgan, *The Puritan Family, Essays on Religion and Domestic Matters in Seventeenth-Century New England* (Boston, 1944), p. 15.

12. Cotton Mather, *A Family Well-Ordered* (Boston, 1669), p. 3. Quoted in Morgan, *Puritan Family*, p. 88.

13. John Cotton, *A Meet Help. Or, A Wedding Sermon* (Boston, 1699), p. 21. Quoted in Morgan, *Puritan Family*, p. 107.

14. Although Puritan codes regarding women's participation in church organization were repressive, there were women who participated in public life by running their own businesses or in partnership with their husbands or by representing their husbands in court. For an extensive bibliography of the economic activities of colonial women, see Eugenie Andruss Leonard, Sophie Hutchinson Drinker, and Miriam Young Holden, *The American Women in Colonial and Revolutionary Times* (Philadelphia: University of Pennsylvania Press, 1962). It is important to understand that during this period of economic development, all able people, including children, were expected to work. Puritan women were excluded from positions of power and influence in the church much more than they were from the marketplace.

15. John Winthrop, *The History of New England from 1630 to 1649*, ed. James Savage (Boston, 1826), II, p. 216.

16. Ibid.

17. Thomas Parker, *The Coppy of a Letter Written . . . to His Sister* (London, 1650), p. 13.

18. White, *Anne Bradstreet*, pp. 42–70.

19. Piercy, *Anne Bradstreet*, p. 22.

20. Berryman, "Homage to Mistress Bradstreet," p. 12.

21. Elizabeth Wade White observes that Anne Bradstreet "could be possessed by a sort of mental rage that might, if once allowed to break out from the intellectual discipline under which she kept it, have caused irreparable damage," *Anne Bradstreet*, p. 177. In "Anne Bradstreet—Dogmatist or Rebel" (*New England Quarterly*, XXXIX, no. 3, September 1966), p. 388, Ann Stanford asserts that "it is this clash of feeling and dogma that keeps her poetry alive. . . . [she] went as far as her place in a society which condemned Ann Hutchinson and Anne Hopkins would allow."

22. A transcript of the trial is in Charles Francis Adams, *Antinomianism in the Massachusetts Bay Colony, 1636–1638* (Boston: Prince Society, 1894). It has been reprinted in David D. Hall, *The Antinomian Controversy, 1636–1638* (Middletown, Ct.: Wesleyan University Press, 1968), and in Wendy Martin, *The American Sisterhood* (New York: Harper & Row, 1972), pp. 17–32. For further background see Edmund S. Morgan, *The Puritan Dilemma: The Story of John Winthrop* (Boston: Little, Brown, 1958), pp. 134–54.

23. Piercy, *Anne Bradstreet*, pp. 99 and 101.

24. Ibid. Piercy observes that this poem is Bradstreet's "farewell to the world," p. 353.

25. *Essex County Court Papers*, vol. XLIII, p. 66. Quoted in Piercy, p. 358.

3. Anne Finch, Countess of Winchilsea: An Augustan Woman Poet

1. See, for example, "Song. Upon a Punch Bowl" and "La Passion Vaincue." All Winchilsea's poems will be quoted from *The Poems of Anne Countess of Winchilsea*, ed. Myra Reynolds (Chicago: University of Chicago Press, 1903).

2. Sedley's otherwise touching tribute to Celia says the whole female sex "can but afford / The Handsome and the Kind." Sir Charles Sedley, *The Poetical and Dramatic Works*, ed. V. De Sola Pinto (London: Constable and Co., 1928), I, 7.

3. William Wycherley, *The Complete Works*, ed. Montague Summers (New York: Russell & Russell, 1964), IV, 8.

4. See Sedley, I, 17–19; Wycherley, IV, 39–40.

5. See Wycherley, IV, 249, and John Wilmot, Earl of Rochester, *The Complete Poems*, ed. David M. Vieth (New Haven: Yale University Press, 1968), pp. 37–40.

6. Rochester, pp. 10–11, 81, 87–88. Compare Wycherley, III, 100; and Matthew Prior, *The Literary Works*, ed. H. Bunker Wright and Monroe K. Spears (Oxford: Clarendon Press, 1959), I, 705.

7. Prior, *Literary Works*, I, 441, 444–45, 707–708. Prior was decidedly unkind to Chloe in real life as well.

8. Her fondness for pastoral names for her husband, herself (Ardelia), and her friends is the most obvious concession to convention in her work.

9. The feminine point of view appears more seriously in her song "The Nymph, in vain, bestows her pains," which counteracts the usual picture of joyous drinking by soberly describing what it is like to be married to an alcoholic. Some of Winchilsea's lyrics are, it is true, conventional for her period: for example, a complimentary poem to Prior (*Poems*, p. 102), "The Bargain," "A

Song. Melinda to Alcander," "Timely Advice to Dorinda," "A Pastoral Dialogue: Between Two Shepherdesses." But, despite the emphasis on female beauty in these songs, her more consistent attitude is represented by "Clarinda's Indifference at Parting with Her Beauty," which puts in their place the joys of love as celebrated by male poets. What did beauty ever get her, Clarinda asks—certainly not "a pleasing rule," meaning a satisfying influence over a man.

10. Interestingly, Rochester expressed values similar to Winchilsea's in his "A Letter from Artemisia in the Town to Chloe in the Country," where he chose a woman for his mouthpiece.

11. See Reynolds' note to this poem, p. 420. Winchilsea added four lines on Wycherley to her poem, including specific mention of his satire on women.

12. Winchilsea's "The Circuit of Apollo" likewise shows her distinctive adaptation of a popular Restoration form, in which a clear-sighted judge reviews contemporary poets. Her version differs from the usual both because the roster of poets is female and because—remarkably in a genre that consisted of wholesale detraction relieved only by a little grudging praise—she indulges in no acrimony against her contemporaries. She commends even Aphra Behn, though admitting that she wrote "a little too loosly." The only satire in the poem is directed against the conceited posturing of the male judge, Apollo, and his complacent assumption that he can easily cajole women. Contrast Rochester's "An Allusion to Horace, the Tenth Satyr of the First Book," which finds nothing but faults in most contemporary poets, including Dryden.

13. In "The Equipage," a translation from l'Abbé Reigner, she wishes for the qualities that will help her get through the vicissitudes of life; they are exactly what a virtuous man would wish for: justice, charity, independence, truth, health, and gaiety.

14. Compare John Stuart Mill's analysis of women's lack of time as an impediment to creative endeavor, in *The Subjection of Women, Essays on Sex Equality*, ed. Alice S. Rossi (Chicago: University of Chicago Press, 1970), pp. 209–211.

15. Prior, pp. 437–38. It used to be thought that Phoebe Clinket, the female author in *Three Hours*, was a satire on Winchilsea; but it is now agreed that their numerous disparities refute this theory. The identification does show the popular tendency to lump together all women authors, as if no distinctions among them could counterbalance the one anomaly they shared: being female and writers.

16. In the "Preface" that follows her "Introduction," Winchilsea declares that she cannot help writing and showing her works to friends, thus implying that a poet's talent cannot (and should not) be suppressed. But she goes on to suggest that her poems represent lapses from rational conduct and that she withholds them from publication not only to avoid abuse as a woman author, but because they are not worthy of publication.

17. *Literary Criticism of William Wordsworth*, ed. Paul Zall (Lincoln: University of Nebraska Press, 1966), p. 173.

18. Contrast Winchilsea's "The Tree," where she appreciates the tree for itself—its beauty and shade—not for its utility as lumber.

19. See, for example, "The Losse" (a lament for a woman friend who has died), "Friendship Between Ephelia and Ardelia" (an Augustan version of "How do I love thee"), "Some Reflections. In a Dialogue Between Teresa and Ardelia" (Teresa's wise correction of Ardelia for a lapse in faith), and "The Petition for

an Absolute Retreat" (a section on how Arminda's love has helped her). She frequently compared the love between herself and a woman friend to that of David and Jonathan, there being no biblical or literary precedents for friendship between women. In "An Epistle, From Ardelia to Mrs. Randolph" she even applies the biblical phrase that their love surpassed the love of women (meaning, of course, as in the Bible, that their love surpassed sexual love).

4. This Changeful Life—Emily Brontë's Anti-Romance

1. In *The Complete Poems of Emily Jane Brontë*, ed. C. W. Hatfield (New York: Columbia University Press, 1941), p. 14. Future references to Brontë's poems in the text will be to the headings, numbers, and lines in Hatfield's edition.

2. See Keith Sagar, "The Originality of *Wuthering Heights*," in *The Art of Emily Brontë*, ed. Anne Smith (New York: Barnes & Noble, 1976), p. 159: "Emily Brontë was a great romantic rebel and a great religious mystic, and at the same time an unsparing critic of romantic rebellion and religious mysticism. Her stage spans, like a cosmic rack, the space between the necessary and the possible."

3. *The Poetry and Prose of William Blake*, ed. David V. Erdman (New York: Doubleday, 1965), p. 16. Future references to this edition will appear in the text.

4. Emily Brontë, *Wuthering Heights* (1846; rpt. New York: Norton, 1963), p. 72.

5. Robert Browning, *The Ring and the Book* (1868–69; rpt. New York: Norton, 1961), p. 31.

6. See Fannie E. Ratchford, *The Brontës' Web of Childhood* (1941; rpt. New York: Russell & Russell, 1964), p. 102.

7. I should like to thank Stuart Curran for his patient readings of successive versions of this essay and for our invaluable discussions of Blake and Byron. His ideas were an important illumination to me as I wrote, though all prejudices and misconceptions remain my own. I should also like to thank the Gyral Foundation for its most generous support during the writing of the essay.

5. Working into Light: Elizabeth Barrett Browning

1. Christened Elizabeth Barrett Moulton Barrett, the poet shortened her maiden name to Elizabeth Barrett Barrett—E.B.B. These initials remained unchanged when she took her husband's name in 1846. Half her work was published under the name Elizabeth Barrett Barrett, half under Elizabeth Barrett Browning. I have decided to use the latter name throughout this discussion of her work, as it is the one she herself adopted.

2. *The Letters of Elizabeth Barrett Browning*, ed. Frederic G. Kenyon. (New York: Macmillan, 1897), I, 231–32.

3. Sir Arthur Quiller-Couch, *The Art of Writing*. Quoted in Virginia Woolf, *A Room of One's Own* (New York: Harcourt, Brace and World, 1929), pp. 111–12.

4. *The Letters of Robert Browning and Elizabeth Barrett Barrett*, 1845–1846, ed. Elvan Kintner (Cambridge, Mass.: Harvard University Press, 1969), I, 113–14.

5. *Letters of EBB*, I, 260–61.

6. Ibid., II, 254.

7. Quoted in *Poetical Works of Letitia Elizabeth Landon* (London: Longman, Brown, Green, and Longmans, 1850), I, xiv.

8. *Letters of EBB*, I, 232.

9. *Poems by Felicia Hemans*, ed. Rufus Griswold (Philadelphia: John Ball, 1850), p. x.

10. *Diary by E.B.B.*, ed. Philip Kelley and Ronald Hudson (Athens, Ohio: Ohio University Press, 1969), p. 88.

11. Gardner B. Taplin, *The Life of Elizabeth Barrett Browning* (New Haven: Yale University Press, 1957), p. 21.

12. *Letters of EBB*, I, 180. Editor's note.

13. *Elizabeth Barrett to Miss Mitford*, ed. Betty Miller (London: John Murray, 1954), p. 102.

14. *Aurora Leigh*, Fifth Book, 202.

15. *Letters of EBB*, I, 153–56.

16. Ibid., I, 187.

17. Ibid., II, 110–11.

18. Ibid., 189.

19. Ibid., 213.

20. Henry F. Chorley, *Memorials of Mrs. Hemans* (Philadelphia: Carey, Lea & Blanchard, 1836), p. 56.

21. *Letters of EBB*, II, 444.

22. Ibid., 445.

23. Taplin, p. 194.

24. Ibid., p. 397.

25. *Letters of RB and EBB*, I, 469.

6. Christina Rossetti: The Inward Pose

1. Christina Rossetti, *The Poetical Works of Christina Georgina Rossetti*, ed. William Michael Rossetti (London, 1904; rpt. London: Macmillan, 1911), p. 304. Subsequent quotations from the poems are from this edition.

2. Christina Rossetti, *Time Flies: A Reading Diary* (London: Society for Promoting Christian Knowledge, 1885), pp. 121–22.

3. See Mackenzie Bell, *Christina Rossetti: A Biographical and Critical Study* (London: Thomas Burleigh, 1898), p. 55 (although Bell stresses the passage's parabolic intent), and Lona Mosk Packer, *Christina Rossetti* (Berkeley: University of California Press, 1963), p. 175.

4. Simone de Beauvoir, *The Second Sex*, trans. H. M. Parshley (New York: Knopf, 1952), p. 335.

5. Bell, p. 53.

6. Ibid., p. 8.

7. Annette Kolodny has commented tellingly on the significance of the heroine's profession in Joan Didion's *Play It As It Lays*: the heroine is a "model" who cannot "act." Kolodny sees this situation as representative of woman's "fear of being fixed in false images or trapped in inauthentic roles." "Feminist Literary Criticism," *Critical Inquiry*, II (Autumn 1975), 82–83.

8. *Time Flies*, p. 169.

9. This is a frequent tag in Rossetti's poems, derived from Isaiah 50:7. See "The Lowest Room," "From House to Home," "Whither the Tribes go up . . . ," and "If thou be dead. . . ."

10. Packer, p. 222.

11. For evidence that Rossetti consciously contrived a mask see the coy 1857 poem, "Winter: My Secret," in which she claims that "I wear my mask for warmth," and that "my secret's mine, and I won't tell. / Or, after all, perhaps there's none."

12. In his notes to the poem William Michael Rossetti states that if written by someone else these verses could describe Christina, but he denies the possibility that Christina would have indulged in this kind of self-reference (*Works*, p. 483). Quite likely, but hardly to the point, William Michael's comment only indicates that Rossetti's impulse to hide behind a mask was reinforced by the hedging that went on around her.

13. See Packer, p. 99, and Marya Zaturenska, *Christina Rossetti* (New York, 1949), pp. 81–83.

14. Packer, pp. 86–87.

15. The latter assumption is supported by Dante Gabriel's denunciation of the poem. In his notes to the poem William Michael provides this excerpt from a letter from Dante Gabriel to Christina: "A real taint, to some extent, of modern vicious style, derived from that same source [Mrs. Browning]—what might be called falsetto muscularity—always seemed to me much too prominent in the long piece called *The Lowest Room*. . . . Everything in which this tone appears is utterly foreign to your primary impulses. . . . If I were you, I would *rigidly keep guard on this matter* if you write in the future; and ultimately exclude from your writings everything (or almost everything) so tainted" (my italics; *Works*, p. 461).

16. Christina Rossetti, *Goblin Market*, introduction by Germaine Greer (New York: Stonehill, 1975), p. xxxvi.

17. Ellen Moers, *Literary Women: The Great Writers* (Garden City, N.Y.: Doubleday, 1976), pp. 102–106.

18. Greer, pp. xxxii–xxxvi.

19. Winston Weathers, "Christina Rossetti: The Sisterhood of Self," *Victorian Poetry*, III (Spring 1965), 81–89. The "larger integrity of sisterhood itself" is a compelling phrase, but one wishes it could be made to accommodate unmarried sisters as well.

20. See the ninth sonnet in Rebecca Crump's "Eighteen Moments' Monuments: Christina Rossetti's *Bout-Rimés* Sonnets in the Troxell Collection," *The Princeton University Library Chronicle*, 33:3 (Spring 1972), 221–22.

7. Vesuvius at Home: The Power of Emily Dickinson

1. Carroll Smith-Rosenberg, "The Female World of Love and Ritual: Relations Between Women in 19th Century America." *Signs: Journals of Women in Culture and Society*, I, 1 (1975).

2. *A Choice of Emily Dickinson's Verse,* ed. Ted Hughes (London: Faber & Faber, 1969), p. 11.

8. Emily Dickinson and the Deerslayer:
The Dilemma of the Woman Poet in America

1. *The Poems of Emily Dickinson*, ed. Thomas H. Johnson (Cambridge, Mass.: Harvard University Press, 1955).

2. Albert Gelpi, *The Tenth Muse: The Psyche of the American Poet* (Cambridge, Mass.: Harvard University Press, 1975), pp. 247ff.; see also Albert Gelpi, *Emily Dickinson: The Mind of the Poet* (Cambridge, Mass.: Harvard University Press, 1965), pp. 109–115.

3. *Prose Works 1892*, ed. Floyd Stovall (New York: New York University Press, 1963), I, 250.

4. *The Letters of Emily Dickinson*, ed. Thomas H. Johnson and Theodora Ward (Cambridge, Mass.: Harvard University Press, 1958), II, 474. For volcano poems, see *Poems*, III, 1141, 1153, and 1174.

9. Armored Women, Naked Men:
Dickinson, Whitman, and Their Successors

1. Walt Whitman, *Leaves of Grass*, ed. Harold W. Blodgett and Sculley Bradley (1965; rpt. New York: Norton, 1968), p. 276; hereafter cited in the text as *LG* followed by page number.

2. Poem 165 in *The Complete Poems of Emily Dickinson*, ed. Thomas H. Johnson (Boston: Little, Brown, 1960); hereafter poems are referred to in the text by their number as they appear in this edition.

3. *The Letters of Emily Dickinson*, ed. Thomas H. Johnson (Cambridge, Mass.: Harvard University Press, 1958), III, 847.

4. For Dickinson's use of the house image, see Jean McClure Mudge, *Emily Dickinson and the Image of Home* (Amherst, Mass.: University of Massachusetts Press, 1975). For the theme of silence, see Donald E. Thackrey, "The Communication of the Word," in Richard B. Sewall, ed., *Emily Dickinson: A Collection of Critical Essays* (Englewood Cliffs, N.J.: Prentice-Hall, 1963), pp. 60ff.

5. Originally quoted in an article by Ellen E. Dickinson in the Boston *Evening Transcript*, 12 October 1895, excerpted in Jay Leyda, *The Years and Hours of Emily Dickinson* (New Haven: Yale University Press, 1960), II, 482.

6. *The Poetry of Robert Frost*, ed. Edward Connery Lathem (New York: Holt, Rinehart and Winston, 1969), p. 224; all references to Frost's poetry are to this edition.

7. Frank Lentricchia, *Robert Frost: Modern Poetics and the Landscapes of Self* (Durham, N.C.: Duke University Press, 1975), p. 64.

8. Ibid., p. 66.

9. Mudge, p. 142.

10. Sylvia Plath, *The Colossus and Other Poems* (1962; rpt. New York: Knopf, 1971), pp. 24–25, 31.

11. Plath, *Crossing the Water* (New York: Harper & Row, 1971), p. 21.

12. Ibid., p. 16.

13. Kenneth Clark, *The Nude: A Study in Ideal Form* (New York: Pantheon, 1956), pp. 158, 219.

14. Plath, *Ariel* (New York: Harper & Row, 1966), p. 6; all references to poems from *Ariel* are to this edition.

15. For some suggestive comparisons between the two and the argument that the "confessional" label distorts both, see Charles Newman, " 'Candor Is the Only Wile': The Art of Sylvia Plath," in Charles Newman, ed., *The Art of Sylvia Plath* (Bloomington, Ind.: Indiana University Press, 1970), pp. 21–55.

10. The Art of Silence and the Forms of Women's Poetry

1. I am referring here to what still stands as the most influential work of these poets: for Dickinson, the poems were written in the early 1860s; for H.D. and Marianne Moore, the volumes produced before 1940. In these periods, by which they are best known, all three wrote in an intensely "hermetic" style (to borrow H.D.'s term) which has shaped, to greater or lesser degree, the work of their successors.

2. Eleanor Wilner, "The Poetics of Emily Dickinson," *JELH*, XXXVIII (1970), 145.

3. "More Than a Bolus of Idiosyncracies," *New York Times Book Review* (July 17, 1977), 14.

4. The term is Francis Manley's, in "An Explication of Dickinson's 'After Great Pain,' " *MLN*, LXXIII (April 1958), 263.

5. "The Experience of the Eye: Marianne Moore's Tradition," *The Southern Review*, NS I, 4 (October 1965), 763.

6. "Some Notes on Organic Form," in *The Poet and the World* (New York: New Directions, 1973), p. 13.

7. I am indebted to James L. Machor of the University of Illinois, whose paper on "Emily Dickinson and the Feminine Rhetoric" sent me to Wheelwright's book (Bloomington, Ind.: Indiana University Press, 1962) and gave me more precise terms for the type of metaphorical activity I wanted to describe in these poets. The paper was delivered at the annual MMLA meeting, November 1976.

8. "The Experience of the Eye," 760.

9. Ibid., 769.

10. (Berkeley: University of California Press, 1969), p. 31.

11. Ibid., p. 15.

12. Ibid.

13. "More Than a Bolus of Idiosyncracies," 14.

14. *Art and Visual Perception*, p. 106.

15. Ibid., 108.

11. Afro-American Women Poets: A Bio-Critical Survey

1. *A Room of One's Own* (New York: Harcourt, Brace and World, 1929), p. 52.

2. Phillis Wheatley, *Poems on Various Subjects, Religious and Moral* (London: Bell, 1773). Quotations from her poems are from this first edition.

3. Arthur P. Davis, "Personal Elements in the Poetry of Phillis Wheatley," *Phylon*, XIV (1953), p. 192.

4. *The Negro Caravan*, ed. Sterling A. Brown, Arthur P. Davis, and Ulysses Lee (New York: Arno Press and *The New York Times*, 1969), p. 293.

5. Quoted from *Early Black American Poets*, ed. William H. Robinson, Jr. (Dubuque, Iowa: Wm. C. Brown, 1971), p. 27. Quotations from Harper's poetry are also taken from this collection.

6. Gwendolyn Brooks, *Report from Part One* (Detroit: Broadside Press, 1972), p. 56.

7. Robert T. Kerlin, ed., *Negro Poets and Their Poems*, 2nd ed. (Washington: Associated Pub., 1938), p. 146.

8. James Weldon Johnson, ed., *The Book of American Negro Poetry*, rev. ed. (New York: Harcourt, Brace and World, 1931), p. 181. All quotations of her poems are from this work except "The Suppliant," which is taken from *The Poetry of the Negro, 1746–1970*, ed. Langston Hughes and Arna Bontemps (Garden City, N.Y.: Doubleday, 1970), p. 76.

9. *Caroling Dusk: An Anthology of Verse by Negro Poets*, ed. Countee Cullen (New York: Harper, 1927), p. 47.

10. *The Book of American Negro Poetry*, p. 214. All other quotations of her work come from *The Poetry of the Negro*.

11. Johnson, p. 279.

12. *The Book of American Negro Poetry*, p. 280. "Magalu" is quoted from *The Poetry of the Negro*, p. 263.

13. Langston Hughes, *The Big Sea*. Taken from *The Langston Hughes Reader* (New York: George Braziller, 1958), p. 388.

14. Margaret Walker, *For My People* (New Haven: Yale University Press, 1942), p. 13. This is the source for all citations of her poetry.

15. From "liberation / poem" in *We A BaddDDD People* (Detroit: Broadside Press, 1970), p. 54.

16. *Home Coming* (Detroit: Broadside Press, 1969), p. 32.

17. "Update on Part I: An Interview with Gwendolyn Brooks," by Gloria T. Hull and Posey Gallagher, *CLA Journal* (September 1977).

18. *A Blues Book for Blue Black Magical Women* (Detroit: Broadside Press, 1974), p. 41.

19. Sonia Sanchez, "Notes from a Journal: A Column," *The American Poetry Review* (May/June 1977), 17.

20. *Coal* (New York: Norton, 1976), p. 19.

21. *From a Land Where Other People Live* (Detroit: Broadside Press, 1973), p. 39.

22. *The New York Head Shop and Museum* (Detroit: Broadside Press, 1974), p. 24.

23. See my review of her *Between Our Selves* in *Conditions, I* (Spring 1977), where I more fully discuss some of the points that follow.

24. *Between Our Selves* (Point Reyes, Calif.: Eidolon Editions, 1976).

25. *Chrysalis: A Magazine of Woman's Culture*, no. 3, 7–9.

26. Ellen Moers, *Literary Women* (Garden City, N.Y.: Doubleday, 1976), p. 9.

27. *American Poetry Review* (May/June 1977), 16.

12. Edna St. Vincent Millay and the Language of Vulnerability

1. Edna St. Vincent Millay, *Collected Poems*, ed. Norma Millay (New York: Harper & Row, 1956), p. 138. All poetry citations are from this edition, and page numbers are indicated in the text following the quotations.

2. Allan Ross Macdougall, ed., *Letters of Edna St. Vincent Millay* (1952; rpt. Westport, Ct.: Greenwood Press, 1971), p. 77.

3. Critical treatment abounds which fails to perceive either the scope of her subject matter or the real intentions of her work and which denies her the serious critical perspective so vital to art. See, for example, James M. Dabbs, "Edna St. Vincent Millay: Not Resigned" (*South Atlantic Quarterly,* 37, January 1938), who finds her quarrelsome; John Crowe Ransom, "The Poet as Woman" (*The World's Body,* 1938; rpt., Port Washington, N.Y.: Kennikat Press, 1964), who faults her for failure to write more like a man; Louis Untermeyer (cited in Dabbs), who associates the pangs of love in her poetry with pettiness; Edmund Wilson, "Epilogue, 1952: Edna St. Vincent Millay" (*The Shores of Light: A Literary Chronicle of the Twenties and Thirties,* New York: Farrar, Straus and Young, 1952), p. 778, who regrets that she had "no children to occupy her, to compel her to outgrow her girlhood."

4. Virginia Woolf, *A Room of One's Own* (New York and Burlingame: Harcourt, Brace and World, 1957), p. 51.

13. The Echoing Spell of H. D.'s Trilogy

1. H. D., *The Hedgehog* (England: Bredin Publishing, 1936), pp. 1 and 13. Subsequent references will appear parenthetically in the text.

2. H. D., *Tribute to Freud: Writing on the Wall: Advent* (Boston: Godine, 1976), p. 19.

3. Ibid., p. 25.

4. Norman N. Holland, *Poems in Persons: An Introduction to the Psychoanalysis of Literature* (New York: Norton, 1975), p. 32.

5. A very fine discussion of the limits of male-dominated criticism of H. D. appears in Susan Friedman, "Who Buried *H. D.*? A Poet, Her Critics, and Her Place in Literary Tradition," *College English,* XXXVII (March 1975), 801–814, although she seems to ignore some of the exceptionally sensitive insights of Joseph N. Riddel in "H. D. and the Poetics of 'Spiritual Realism,'" *Contemporary Literature,* X (Autumn 1969), 447–73. For earlier criticism of the *Trilogy,* see Vincent Quinn, *Hilda Doolittle* (Boston: Twayne Publishers, 1967), pp. 116–26, and Thomas Burnett Swann, *The Classical World of H. D.* (Lincoln: University of Nebraska Press, 1962), pp. 163–73.

6. *Tribute to Freud,* p. 51.

7. H. D., *Tribute to the Angels in Trilogy* (New York: New Directions, 1973), 1, p. 63. Subsequent references to poems in the *Trilogy* will be parenthetically marked in the text by the capitalized initials of the volume and the number of the poem.

8. H. D. would seem to agree with the secret gnostic gospels that celebrate God in masculine and feminine terms. These gospels and their social implications for religious women are examined by Elaine H. Pagels in "What Became of God the Mother? Conflicting Images of God in Early Christianity," *Signs,* II (Winter 1976), 293–303.

9. See Suzanne Juhasz, *Naked and Fiery Forms: Modern American Poetry by Women, A New Tradition* (New York: Harper, 1976), pp. 33–56, on Moore.

"Snail" appears in *Relearning the Alphabet* (New York: New Directions, 1970), p. 77.

10. *The Poetics of Space,* trans. Maria Jolas (Boston: Beacon Press, 1969), p. 134.

11. In his Introduction to H.D.'s *Trilogy,* her friend Norman Holmes Pearson quotes a letter she wrote in 1943 about *The Walls Do Not Fall,* p. viii.

12. H.D., "The Poet," *The Poet and the Dancer* (1935; rpt. San Francisco: Five Trees Press, 1975), no. 3.

13. Bachelard discusses the conch of Venus that represents a woman's vulva, as well as representations in the shell museum of the toothed vagina in *The Poetics of Space,* p. 114; in *The Second Sex,* trans. H.M. Parshley (New York: Bantam, 1961), Simone de Beauvoir describes how "feminine sex desire is the soft throbbing of a mollusk," p. 362.

14. Bachelard, p. 117; Benjamin Boyce, "Sounding Shells and Little Prattlers in the Mid-Eighteenth-Century English Ode," *Eighteenth - Century Studies,* III (Spring 1975), 245–64.

15. Denise Levertov, "H.D.: An Appreciation," in *The Poet in the World* (New York: New Directions, 1973), p. 246.

16. See "Stepping Westward," "The Earth Worm," and "The Postcards: A Triptych," in *The Sorrow Dance* (New York: New Directions, 1967), pp. 15, 16, and 69.

17. De Beauvoir, p. 285. Significantly, one of the new women's journals is entitled *Chrysalis.*

18. Emily Dickinson, #1099, *Final Harvest: Emily Dickinson's Poems,* ed. Thomas H. Johnson (Boston: Little, Brown, 1961), p. 245.

19. Lecture delivered at Indiana University on October 24, 1975. Judy Chicago also discussed flower imagery as a representation of women's sexuality in *Through the Flower: My Struggle as a Woman Artist* (New York: Doubleday, 1975).

20. Lewis Carroll, *Through the Looking Glass,* Chapter VI.

21. I am referring here to the sequence of poems from 40 to 43 that concludes *The Walls Do Not Fall.* The significance of the Isis–Osiris myth to H.D. is at least partially explained by Arthur Weigall, *The Paganism in Our Christianity* (New York: Putnam, 1928), pp. 124–34, a book that Pearson describes as "a favorite" of H.D.'s in his Introduction to the *Trilogy,* p. vii.

22. See the discussion of shamanism in *Myths, Rites, Symbols: A Mircea Eliade Reader,* ed. Wendell C. Beane and William G. Doty (New York: Harper, 1975), vol. II, pp. 262–82. The magical identification achieved by the shaman with dead ancestors, his trance as he is carried away to learn the secrets of the gods, his healing role in the community, and his ability to speak in secret languages make him a model of the kind of artist H.D. saw herself becoming.

23. Weigall, p. 129.

24. *Tribute to Freud,* p. 90.

25. H.D., "Sagesse," *Hermetic Definition* (New York: New Directions, 1972), no. 18, p. 75.

26. To understand how this places H.D. in a romantic tradition encompassing Tieck, Fichte, Novalis, Coleridge, and Goethe, see Georges Poulet, *The Metamorphoses of the Circle,* trans. Darley Dawson and Elliott Coleman (Maryland: The John Hopkins Press, 1966), pp. 91–118.

27. In *Tribute to Freud* H.D. associates a magnifying glass stolen by her Promethean brother with "a circle and the stem of the circle, the stalk or support of this flower, is the handle of the glass ... This is the sacred *Ankh*, the symbol of life in Egypt ...," p. 25. In *The Flowering of the Rod*, Kaspar sees the prehistoric city as if it were "enlarged under a sun-glass," no. 32, p. 155.

28. Marge Piercy, *To Be of Use* (New York: Doubleday, 1973), pp. 56 and 72, where Piercy echoes H.D. in her insistence that "What we use we must remake"; Monique Wittig, *Les Guérillères*, trans. David Le Vay (London: Peter Owen, 1971); in *You Are Happy* (New York: Harper & Row, 1974), Margaret Atwood's "Circle/Mud Poems" are each presented with the sign of a circle and conclude with an image of another island on which Circe would not be limited by Odysseus' story; Adrienne Rich, *Diving Into The Wreck* (New York: Norton, 1976).

29. Levertov, "H.D.: An Appreciation," p. 247.

14. May Swenson and the Shapes of Speculation

1. Elizabeth Bishop, Letter to May Swenson, Nov. 13, 1962.

2. "Forest," in *To Mix with Time: New and Selected Poems* (New York: Scribner, 1963), p. 129.

3. *To Mix with Time*, p. 138.

4. Anthony Hecht in *New York Review of Books*, I, 2 (Spring 1963), 33.

5. X.J. Kennedy in *Poetry* 103, 5 (February 1964), 330.

6. "The Beam," in *Iconographs* (New York: Scribner, 1970), p. 50.

7. *Iconographs*, p. 23.

8. *To Mix with Time*, p. 9.

9. *Iconographs*, p 19.

10. *To Mix with Time*, p. 85.

11. "Order of Diet," in *To Mix with Time*, p. 100.

12. *Iconographs*, p. 31.

13. "Question," in *To Mix with Time,* p. 154.

14. "Organs," in *To Mix with Time*, p. 149.

15. *Iconographs*, p. 86.

16. Ibid., p. 13.

17. Ibid., p. 34.

18. Ibid., p. 80.

19. Ibid., p. 71.

15. Gwendolyn the Terrible: Propositions on Eleven Poems

1. Gwendolyn Brooks, *Report from Part One: An Autobiography*, introd. Don L. Lee and George Kent (Detroit: Broadside Press, 1972), p. 183.

2. Gwendolyn Brooks, *The World of Gwendolyn Brooks* (New York: Harper & Row, 1971), p. 315. (All quotations from Brooks's poetry come from this edition, hereafter designated *WGB*, with pagination noted in the text.)

3. Brooks's reading of "We Real Cool" is somewhat different from my own. *Report from Part One*, p. 185.

4. Ibid., p. 158.

5. Northrop Frye, "Emily Dickinson," *Fables of Identity: Studies in Poetic Mythology* (New York: Harcourt Brace Jovanovich, 1963), p. 202.

6. Kenneth Burke, "On Words and the Word," *The Rhetoric of Religion: Studies in Logology* (Berkeley and Los Angeles: University of California Press, 1970), pp. 14ff.

16. A Fine, White Flying Myth: The Life/Work of Sylvia Plath

1. *Seventeen* (May, 1951), 127, 144–45.

2. Foreword, *Ariel* (New York: Harper & Row, 1966), p. ix.

3. See Ellen Moers, *Literary Women* (New York: Doubleday, 1976), pp. 90–110.

4. Mrs. Sara Ellis, *The Family Monitor* (New York, 1844), p. 9.

5. See Ellis, p. 15.

6. See G. H. Lewes, "The Lady Novelists," *Westminster Review*, n.s. II (July 1852), 129–41.

7. Newman, "Candor Is the Only Wile," in Charles Newman, ed., *The Art of Sylvia Plath* (Bloomington: Indiana University Press, 1971), p. 48.

8. Ted Hughes, "Notes on the Chronological Order of Sylvia Plath's Poems," in Newman, *Art*, p. 188.

9. George Stade, Introduction to Nancy Hunter Steiner, *A Closer Look at Ariel* (Harper's Magazine Press, 1972), p. 9.

10. *Jane Eyre*, Ch. 2.

11. "Ocean 1212–W," in Newman, *Art*, p. 272.

12. Emily Dickinson, "It was not Death, for I stood up," #510, and "The Soul has Bandaged moments—," #512, *The Complete Poems of Emily Dickinson*, ed. Thomas H. Johnson (Boston: Little, Brown, 1960).

13. "The Fifty-Ninth Bear," *London Magazine* (February, 1961), 20.

14. Simone de Beauvoir, *The Second Sex* (New York: Bantam, 1961), p. 467.

15. *Frankenstein*, Ch. 24.

16. Anne Sexton, "Third Psalm," *The Death Notebooks* (Boston: Houghton Mifflin, 1974), pp. 83–84.

17. De Beauvoir, p. 468.

18. Ibid., p. 469.

19. Otto Plath, *Bumblebees and Their Ways* (New York: Macmillan, 1934).

20. Quoted in Douglas Cleverdon, "On Three Women," Newman, *Art*, p. 228.

21. D. H. Lawrence, "The Song of a Man Who Has Come Through," *The Complete Poems of D.H. Lawrence*, ed. Vivian DeSola Pinto and F. Warren Roberts (New York: Viking, 1964), vol. 1, p. 250.

22. Hughes, p. 192.

23. Quoted in A. Alvarez, "Sylvia Plath," Newman, *Art*, p. 59.

24. See Robert Bly, *Sleepers Joining Hands* (New York: Harper & Row, 1973), pp. 39–43.

25. "Context," *London Magazine* (February, 1962), 45–46.

17. Seeking the Exit or the Home: Poetry and Salvation in the Career of Anne Sexton

1. "Rowing," *The Awful Rowing Toward God* (Boston: Houghton Mifflin, 1975), p. 2.
2. Linda Gray Sexton and Lois Ames, eds., *Anne Sexton: A Self-Portrait in Letters* (Boston: Houghton Mifflin, 1977), pp. 266–67.
3. *Letters*, p. 144.
4. "Rats Live on No Evil Star," *The Death Notebooks* (Boston: Houghton Mifflin, 1974), p. 19.
5. "Rats Live on No Evil Star," p. 19.
6. " 'The Excitable Gift': The Poetry of Anne Sexton," *Naked and Fiery Forms: Modern American Poetry by Women, A New Tradition* (New York: Harper and Row, 1976), pp. 117–43.
7. *To Bedlam and Part Way Back* (Boston: Houghton Mifflin, 1960), pp. 51–52.
8. *Letters*, p. 105.
9. *Letters*, p. 110.
10. P. 6.
11. *The Death Notebooks* (Boston: Houghton Mifflin, 1974), p. 97.
12. *Letters*, p. 267.
13. *45 Mercy Street*, Linda Gray Sexton, ed. (Boston: Houghton Mifflin, 1967), p. 106.
14. "The Big Boots of Pain," *45 Mercy Street*, p. 103.
15. *45 Mercy Street*, p. 89.
16. *Letters*, pp. 270, 271.

18. A Common Language: The American Woman Poet

1. Margaret Atwood, *Survival: A Thematic Guide to Canadian Literature* (Toronto: Anansi, 1972), and Arnold Rampersad, "The Ethnic Voice in American Poetry," *San José Studies*, II, 3 (November 1976), 26–36.
2. Another analysis similar to Atwood's and Rampersad's is that used by Kate Ellis at the December 1975 meeting of the MLA to discuss the work of modern women novelists. In her talk, entitled "Women, Culture and Revolution," Ellis identified women's growth in consciousness with that of Third World colonials and described four stages based on the three-stage model used by Frantz Fanon in *The Wretched of the Earth*. His stages in colonial writing are: 1) a direct imitation of writing in the mother country, 2) an attempt to recover the past that the writer's people share outside the disfiguring experience of colonialism, and 3) a revolutionary national literature arousing the people to new awareness of themselves. To these Ellis adds a fourth classification in which writers, having experienced all the previous stages, incorporate them into their art. The parallels, especially in positions 3 and 4, with the Atwood and Rampersad analyses are clear, although each critic, of course, was thinking and working independently.
3. Adrienne Rich, "I am in Danger—Sir—," *Poems: Selected and New, 1950–1974* (New York: Norton, 1975), p. 85.

4. Quoted in the Introduction to *Adrienne Rich's Poetry*, ed. Barbara C. Gelpi and Albert Gelpi (New York: Norton, 1975).

5. H.D., *Tribute to Freud: Writing on the Wall: Advent* (Boston: Godine, [ca. 1974]), p. xxxvi. The dream is described on pp. 180–81. "Ezra" is Ezra Pound.

19. The Critique of Consciousness and Myth in Levertov, Rich, and Rukeyser

1. Adrienne Rich, *Diving into the Wreck, Poems 1971–1972* (New York: Norton, 1973).

2. Prior to these fifteen years' work (1958-73), none of the poets was unaware of the relations of consciousness and society. On this one issue Rukeyser merits a separate study. Yet the Vietnam War had a particular role in focusing these concerns.

3. I will discuss the precise nature of Levertov's myths, which do not fully conform to this model.

4. Denise Levertov, "Stepping Westward," *The Sorrow Dance* (New York: New Directions, 1967).

5. For the myth of Psyche and for an interpretation of its significance to women, see Erich Neumann, *Amor and Psyche: The Psychic Development of the Feminine. A Commentary on the Tale by Apuleius* (New York: Pantheon Books, 1956).

6. Denise Levertov, *O Taste and See* (New York: New Directions, 1964).

7. Muriel Rukeyser, *Breaking Open* (New York: Random House, 1973).

8. Virginia Woolf, *Collected Essays*, vol. II (New York: Harcourt, Brace and World, 1967).

9. Adrienne Rich, "When We Dead Awaken: Writing as Re-Vision," *College English* 34, 1 (October 1972), 24. The essay is reprinted in the Norton Critical Edition of *Adrienne Rich's Poetry*. In this essay, from which I have taken the term "re-vision," Rich speaks of women's "drive to self-knowledge," which is necessarily accompanied by a "radical critique of literature" and of cultural ideologies.

10. Adrienne Rich, *Poems, Selected and New, 1950-1974* (New York: Norton, 1975). "Snapshots of a Daughter-in-Law," pp. 47–51.

11. For this ending, Rich has borrowed from the peroration of Simone de Beauvoir's *The Second Sex*, but in her use of the helicopter image, Rich has reversed de Beauvoir's intention, which was to argue against the expensive, costly charm of women.

12. Rich, "When We Dead Awaken," 19.

13. Muriel Rukeyser, *The Speed of Darkness* (New York: Random House, 1968).

14. Rukeyser, *Breaking Open*.

15. By "rational man," Rukeyser means "human"; the problem is not exclusive to the male sex, as several images in the poem indicate.

16. Denise Levertov, *To Stay Alive* (New York: New Directions, 1971).

17. Rich has written, "The bombings, for example, if they have anything to

teach us, must be understood in the light of something closer to home, both more private and painful, and more general and endemic, than the institutions, class, racial oppression, the hubris of the Pentagon or the ruthlessness of a right wing administration: the bombings are so wholly sadistic, gratuitous and demonic that they can finally be seen, if we care to see them, for what they are: acts of concrete sexual violence, an expression of the congruence of violence and sex in the masculine psyche." *American Poetry Review* II, 3 (May/June 1973), 10.

18. Rich, *Poems, Selected and New.*

19. Rukeyser, *The Speed of Darkness.*

20. Muriel Rukeyser, *Selected Poems* (New York: New Directions, 1951).

21. Rich, *Poems, Selected and New.*

22. Erich Neumann, *The Origins and History of Consciousness* (Bollingen Series XLII, Princeton, N.J.: Princeton University Press), p. 199. For Neumann in general, "consciousness" is always masculine, and a higher form, while the unconscious life is feminine and lower. In his interpretation, male heroes engage in acts of self-creation, while female figures simply exist, in creative unawareness. Except for his discussion of the Psyche myth, Neumann views human development as male development.

23. Denise Levertov, *Relearning the Alphabet* (New York: New Directions, 1970). The poem is dated 1968-1969.

24. *The American Heritage Dictionary* at the word "ideal" was the source.

25. Charles Altieri, "From Symbolist Thought to Immanence: The Ground of Postmodern American Poetics," *Boundary 2*, I, 3 (Spring 1973), especially pp. 632–37.

26. Denise Levertov, "The Sense of Pilgrimage," *The Poet in the World* (New York: New Directions, 1973), 69. The essay is dated 1967.

27. T.S. Eliot, "*Ulysses*, Order and Myth," in Richard Ellmann and Charles Feidelson, Jr., eds., *The Modern Tradition* (New York: Oxford University Press, 1965), p. 681. The essay was originally published in 1923.

About the Authors

NINA AUERBACH is Associate Professor of English at the University of Pennsylvania. She is the author of *Communities of Women: An Idea in Fiction* (Cambridge, Mass.: Harvard University Press, 1978) and of numerous articles on Victorian literature and women's fiction.

HELEN COOPER teaches at Rutgers University, where she is engaged in research on Elizabeth Barrett Browning. She has published poetry and reviews in *Ms.*, *13th Moon*, *The Common Woman*, and other magazines.

TERENCE DIGGORY is currently Assistant Professor of English at Skidmore College. He is working on a book that explores the relationship between W.B. Yeats and a number of American poets.

RACHEL BLAU DUPLESSIS teaches English at Temple University and serves on the editorial board of *Feminist Studies*. She is writing a critical study of the reimagination of women, culture, and society in the work of twentieth-century women writers. She has published poetry in a number of feminist and postmodern journals.

ALBERT GELPI is Coe Professor of American Literature at Stanford University. He has written *Emily Dickinson: The Mind of the Poet* (1971) and *The Tenth Muse: The Psyche of the American Poet* (1975). He edited *The Poet in America: 1650 to the Present* (1973) and, with Barbara Charlesworth Gelpi, *Adrienne Rich's Poetry* (1975). He received a Guggenheim Fellowship in 1977-78 to work on a companion volume to *The Tenth Muse* to be called *The American Poetic Renaissance 1910-1930*.

BARBARA CHARLESWORTH GELPI teaches at Stanford University. She has written *Dark Passages: The Decadent Consciousness in Victorian Literature* (Madison,

Wis.: University of Wisconsin Press, 1975) and has published essays on nineteenth-century British literature, Jungian psychology, and feminist theory. She is now working on a study of Percy Bysshe Shelley and the feminine.

SANDRA M. GILBERT is Associate Professor of English at the University of California, Davis. *Acts of Attention*, her study of the poems of D.H. Lawrence, was published by Cornell University Press in 1972, and *In the Fourth World*, a collection of poems, appeared in 1978. With Susan Gubar, she has coauthored *The Madwoman in the Attic: The Woman Writer and the Nineteenth-Century Literary Imagination* (New Haven: Yale University Press, forthcoming). Her poetry, fiction, and criticism have been published in many periodicals and anthologies.

SUSAN GUBAR teaches at Indiana University, where she is an Associate Professor of English and a Poynter Fellow. She has written essays on women and fiction and collaborated with Sandra M. Gilbert on *The Madwoman in the Attic: The Woman Writer and the Nineteenth-Century Literary Imagination* (New Haven: Yale University Press, forthcoming).

GLORIA T. HULL is Associate Professor of English at the University of Delaware. Her articles on black American literature and especially black women writers have appeared in numerous journals. She is also a poet and a co-editor of *Black Women's Studies*, Vol. XI of The Feminist Press Female Studies series. She edited *The Diaries of Alice Dunbar-Nelson* for Burt Franklin Publishers.

SUZANNE JUHASZ teaches at the University of Colorado, Boulder. Her books of criticism are *Naked and Fiery Forms: Modern American Poetry by Women, A New Tradition* (New York: Harper and Row, 1976) and *Metaphor and the Poetry of Williams, Pound, and Stevens* (Lewisburg, Pa.: Bucknell University Press, 1974). Her poetry appears in journals and anthologies; a chapbook, *Benita to Reginald: A Romance,* is forthcoming from Out of Sight Press.

JEANNE KAMMER is Assistant Dean for Academic Affairs and an ACE Fellow in Academic Administration at Wheeling College, West Virginia. In 1975 she received a Woodrow Wilson Dissertation Fellowship in Women's Studies for a thesis on women poets from which the article in this collection is derived. She is a published poet and short-story writer. Her first volume of poetry, *Bone Music,* is currently looking for a publisher.

WENDY MARTIN teaches at Queens College of the City University of New York. She founded and edits *Women's Studies: An Interdisciplinary Journal,* and she edited *The American Sisterhood: Writings of the Feminist Movement from the Colonial Times to the Present* (New York: Harper & Row, 1972). She has published articles on the early American novel and on American women writers. A book on American women writers is in progress.

ALICIA OSTRIKER, Professor of English at Rutgers University, is the author of *Vision and Verse in William Blake* (Madison, Wis.: University of Wisconsin

Press, 1965) and editor of the annotated *William Blake: The Complete Poems* (New York: Penguin, 1978). She has written on contemporary American women's poetry for several journals. As a poet, Ostriker is author of *Songs* (New York: Holt, Rinehart & Winston, 1969), *Once More Out of Darkness* (Berkeley, Ca.: Berkeley Poets' Press, 1974), and *A Dream of Springtime* (New York: Smith/Horizon Press, 1978).

ADRIENNE RICH has published ten volumes of poetry, of which the most recent is *The Dream of A Common Language* (1978). She is author of *Of Woman Born: Motherhood as Experience and Institution* (1976). A volume of her essays and criticism, *On Lies, Secrets and Silence*, will be published in 1979.

KATHARINE ROGERS, Professor of English at Brooklyn College and the City University Graduate School, has published *The Troublesome Helpmate: A History of Misogyny in Literature* (1966), as well as a critical biography of William Wycherley and numerous articles. She is writing a book on feminism in eighteenth-century England, and is editing a collection of Anne Finch's poems, forthcoming from Frederick Ungar.

DOLORES ROSENBLUM is working on a book-length critical study of Christina Rossetti's poetry. She is Assistant Professor of English at the State University of New York at Albany. In the year 1977-78 she held an Andrew Mellon Post-Doctoral Fellowship at the City University of New York Graduate Center.

CATHERINE F. SMITH is Assistant Professor of English at Bucknell University. She is author of essays in feminist literary criticism appearing in collections published by the University of Cincinnati Office of Women's Studies, Bucknell University Press, and Simon and Schuster.

HORTENSE J. SPILLERS teaches literature and writing at Wellesley College. Her articles and stories have appeared widely in journals. For one of her short stories she was the recipient of the National Magazine Award for excellence in Fiction and Belles Lettres in 1976.

JANE STANBROUGH is Associate Professor and Chairperson of the Department of English at the University of Colorado, Colorado Springs. A regular reviewer for the *University of Denver Quarterly*, she is currently editing a book of letters by Elizabeth Manning Hawthorne, Nathaniel Hawthorne's older sister.